THE STUDY OF INTERNAT

The Study of International Relations

The State of the Art

Edited by
Hugh C. Dyer
and
Leon Mangasarian

Foreword by Philip Windsor

MACMILLAN

in association with
Millennium: Journal of International Studies

First published 1989

Published by
THE MACMILLAN PRESS LTD
Houndmills, Basingstoke, Hampshire RG21 2XS
and London
Companies and representatives
throughout the world

Printed in the People's Republic of China

British Library Cataloguing in Publication Data
The Study of international relations: the
state of the art.
1. Foreign relations. Research
I. Dyer, Hugh C., *1957*– II. Mangasarian,
Leon, *1960*–
III. Millennium
327′.072
ISBN 0–333–46527–X (hardcover)
ISBN 0–333–46528–8 (paperback)

Contents

PART II   COUNTRY AND REGIONAL APPROACHES

Foreword

Perhaps the best place in which to undertake the study of International Relations is the park surrounding Blenheim Palace. The magnificent trees there were planted in the opposing lines of the battle after which the palace is named, so that the lineaments of battle now surround a peaceful seat and the memorial has become a grove. Such is the aspiration represented by the undertaking: the transformation of old, unhappy far-off things and battles long ago into groves. The only trouble is that the unhappy things International Relations studies are not far off: the battles are still raging, and the groves are hardly those of academe.

As this volume makes clear, those who teach and study International Relations are rightly convinced of the importance of their subject, and equally rightly unconvinced that it amounts to an intellectual discipline. Its importance lies in the fact that it literally considers the fate of the world – and in this sense it might be said to supersede earlier preoccupations of History and Political Philosophy. Kant, whose noble essay on *The Perpetual Peace* might be said to have been one of the first modern works in the field, was nonetheless writing within a set of assumptions about the indefinite future of Man. Hegel would have been astonished to hear that the *Geist* was, after all, capable of committing suicide. Marx aspired to Species Being as the criterion for the future of humanity; but, if he had been around today, would probably have had a great deal to say about International Relations. In spite of all the nonsense that has been talked about the global village, the very existence of the subject implies that in the twentieth century, mankind has been moving further and further away from the comprehensive approach towards a unitary goal which Marx attempted to create. And this indicates the central difficulty in the study of the non-discipline itself. It is bound to be comprehensive by virtue of its preoccupation, but it can not be unitary because of its preoccupations.

Those range from the question of how 'best' to avoid a third world war to whether it is possible to achieve some kind of justice in the relations between North and South, and whether if it is not achieved the human race is heading for an all-out conflict, or else for an ecological disaster comparable to a third world war itself. Within the field of International Relations, therefore, it is perfectly legitimate for a teacher to present a course, or a student to write a thesis, on the hermeneutic problems of thinking about nuclear deterrence or for either to conduct a much more specific enquiry into the question of whether the revision of the Antarctic Treaty is likely to have a benign or maleficent effect on the global ecology – and whether the benign effect can be achieved within the framework of the present international 'system'.

In other words, the preoccupation of International Relations, concerned as it is with the fate of Man, rapidly splinters into a series of very different kinds of subject-matter which it is extremely difficult to hold together – and most of the 'classic' works in the field (probably beginning with E.H. Carr's *The Twenty Years' Crisis*) have dwelt at length on the fissiparous nature of what is involved. So, while there is a unifying theme, born out of the experience of the First World War and given added urgency today by all the questions concerning human survival, there is neither a unifying method nor an agreed philosophy by which these questions can be tackled simultaneously.

Is the whole undertaking then an exercise in fatuity? If the subject lacks an agreed intellectual base, and if the problems of the world are still growing, is there any point in it? This volume makes clear that there is indeed a purpose in the undertaking. It is not a purpose harnessed to any one set of goals: few would contend (though *some* do) that the understanding of International Relations can of itself ensure that peace breaks out or that Man can be saved overnight from his own shortsightedness. But what can be achieved is the gradual creation of criteria by which it might be possible to harmonise positive analysis with normative aims, the principles of order with those of justice, and the interests of states with those of humanity. The point here is not that the subject attempts to create a strategy for accomplishing millennarian objectives but that it attempts to create criteria by which imperfections and injustices can be recognised, and dangerous risks avoided. In this sense its very diversity can become a source of strength.

In the past (to some extent this is still true even today), far too much scholarly time has been wasted in disputes about what actually *is* the field of International Relations. Was it a social science in search of a method? Was it a minor branch of moral or political philosophy? Today, there is a growing mutual understanding between those whose study is primarily hermeneutic and those who analyse the behaviour of states, organisations and economies. The endless, and endlessly tiresome, paradigm debates seem to be pretty well over. Perhaps one reason for this is that the utility of the idea of the paradigm is being increasingly recognised as rather limited. In the sense in which it was made popular through the work of Thomas Kuhn, the paradigm in science came almost to resemble a kind of secular theodicy – a way of justifying Man's thinking to himself – and a paradigm shift was something of cataclysmic importance. Such an approach is obviously of central concern to the philosophy of science, but it has little to offer to that of International Relations (though one unfortunate American lady of my acquaintance was told that her book would not be accepted for publication unless it offered the promise of a major paradigm shift in the subject). Most scholars are, however, less pretentious. They are not casting around either for paradigm shifts or paradigmatic unity; they are engaged in a discourse.

Until recently, this discourse was dominated by the United States. Much of the debate about the nature of the subject and about its proper preoccupations was conducted between Americans. The study of International Relations elsewhere was regarded by many such Americans (and, indeed, by European non-specialists) as a kind of history without dates or an eccentric form of jurisprudence without laws. The difficulty with such a situation was that while the intra-American debates were ostensibly concerned with the nature of the subject, their real focus was the definition of the American role in the world – Hans Morgenthau's work being a classic case in point. But now that the study of International Relations has expanded to many countries, some of which are discussed in this volume, a more fruitful interchange is possible both about the development of the field, and about 'national styles' in dealing with it. That is not to say that different countries have ceased, or should cease, to be concerned with their own particular roles, but it is to say that much of the semi-conscious ethnocentrism of earlier years has disappeared.

But the discourse goes further than that between nations and styles. It is also concerned with the agenda (as opposed to the nature) of the subject itself. That involves questions of priorities but it also involves an understanding of the origins of particular ways of thought. Certain traditions of International Relations, for example, exclude the discussion of human rights: to others, it is central. The ventilation of such disagreements helps to illuminate the sources of particular modes of thought but also to define what can (and cannot) be done in this and other areas. Perhaps of particular importance, in recent years, has been the the growth of structuralist analysis, especially of international economic relations. Its practitioners are conscious of its Marxist ancestry, but it is very much part of the mainstream. And this development indicates that those who are concerned with the subject in general can never get very far away from its philosophical headwaters. I suggested earlier that, in some ways, International Relations has superseded previous endeavours in political philosophy because it is concerned with the survival of humanity as they were not. But to supersede is not to transcend; and one of the striking features of the teaching and study of the subject in recent years has been a growing consciousness of the need to scrutinise the philosophical background of its assumptions and tasks. This has certainly expanded the agenda. It has also made the discourse more fruitful and led to greater mutual comprehension.

The discourse, then, is between nations, among scholars and about an agenda. It takes place in areas where other disciplines meet, and clash on occasion. But can one describe it further? Two of the chapters in this volume suggest that one can. One of them (Chapter 4) is concerned with the application to International Relations of Critical Theory, particularly as it was developed by Horkheimer. But the other (Chapter 5), discussing the subject from an historian's point of view, makes an implicit case that International Relations is indeed itself an exercise in Critical Theory. That is perhaps a useful way of looking at it. This exercise is concerned with the relationship between knowledge and social relations. It does recognise that it might itself have a social function. And, finally, if it is engaged in the search for survival, it must also be engaged in the articulation of values. Not a bad vineyard to toil in, after all, even though never likely to be a grove.

PHILIP WINDSOR

Acknowledgements

This volume is based on a special issue of *Millennium: Journal of International Studies* (Volume 16, No. 2, Summer 1987), produced under our editorship. The debt we owe to those involved with the journal is consequently very great: J. Kurt Barling and Spyros Economides (editors of Volume 15), Edwin Fountain, Rebecca Grant and David Long (editors of Volume 17), Priya Mukherjee, Dirk Rumberg and Mark E. Schaffer were all members of the management board through the production of Volume 16, and shared with us the burdensome tasks associated with producing an academic journal, along with vigilant members of the editorial board. Many others assisted us in different ways, not least the Department of International Relations at the London School of Economics and Political Science, whose members are generous with their advice and support. Hilary Parker and Susan Trubshaw deserve special mention for providing secretarial and administrative assistance with cheerful efficiency.

HUGH C. DYER
LEON MANGASARIAN

Notes on the Contributors

Ulrich Albrecht is Professor in the Fachbereich Politische Wissenschaft, Institut für Internationale Politik und Regionalstudien at the Freie Universität Berlin, West Berlin.

Olajide Aluko is Professor of International Relations at the University of Ife, Nigeria.

Fulvio Attina is Professor of International Relations in the Department of Political Studies at the University of Catania, Italy.

Michael Banks is Reader in the Department of International Relations at the London School of Economics, United Kingdom.

Ingrid Detter de Lupis is Professor of International Law, Stockholm, Sweden, and a visiting teacher in the Department of International Relations at the London School of Economics, United Kingdom.

Hugh C. Dyer is a PhD candidate in the Department of International Relations at the London School of Economics, United Kingdom.

Gelson Fonseca, Jr. is a diplomat and Professor at the Rio Branco Institute, Brazil.

B.K. Gills is a research student in the Department of International Relations at the London School of Economics, United Kingdom.

Fred Halliday is Professor in the Department of International Relations at the London School of Economics, United Kingdom.

Christopher Hill is Lecturer in the Department of International Relations at the London School of Economics, United Kingdom.

Mark Hoffman is Lecturer in the Department of International Relations at the London School of Economics, United Kingdom.

xiii

Takashi Inoguchi is Professor of Political Science in the Institute of Oriental Culture at the University of Tokyo, Japan.

Aharon Klieman is Professor of International Relations in the Department of Political Science at Tel Aviv University, Israel.

Ekkehart Krippendorff is Professor in the John F. Kennedy-Institut für Nordamerikastudien at the Freie Universität Berlin, West Berlin.

Margot Light is Lecturer in the Department of International Relations at the London School of Economics, United Kingdom.

Hugh Macdonald is Lecturer in the Department of International Relations at the London School of Economics, United Kingdom.

Leon Mangasarian is a PhD candidate in the Department of International Relations at the London School of Economics, United Kingdom.

Ali A. Mazrui is Professor of Political Science and Professor of Afroamerican and African Studies at the University of Michigan. He is also Andrew D. White Professor-at-Large at Cornell University, USA.

Neil R. Richardson is Associate Professor in the Department of Political Science at the University of Wisconsin-Madison, USA.

Mark S.C. Simpson is Research Associate at the Centre for Afro–Asian studies Rio de Janeiro, Brazil and a PhD candidate in the Department of International Relations at the London School of Economics, United Kingdom.

Alan Sked is Senior Lecturer in the Department of International History at the London School of Economics, United Kingdom.

Steve Smith is Lecturer in the Department of Economics and Social Studies and Director of the Centre for Public Choice Studies at the University of East Anglia, United Kingdom.

Marie-Claude Smouts is Directeur de Recherche at CNRS and CERI, and teaches International Relations theory in the political science DEA programme at the Fondation Nationale des Sciences Politiques, France.

Roger Tooze is Principal Lecturer in International Relations at North Staffordshire Polytechnic, United Kingdom.

Peter Vale is Research Professor and Director of the Institute of Social and Economic Research at Rhodes University, South Africa.

Philip Windsor is Reader in the Department of International Relations at the London School of Economics, United Kingdom.

Paulo Wrobel is Research Associate at the Institute of International Relations of the Pontifical Catholic University, Rio de Janeiro, Brazil, and a research student in the Department of War Studies at King's College, London, United Kingdom.

Michael B. Yahuda is Reader in the Department of International Relations at the London School of Economics, United Kingdom.

Editors' Introduction

International Relations (IR) encompasses a sweeping area of study, and a number of authors and editors have attempted to pull together some of the divergent strands in recent years.[1] This volume attempts to survey the present state of IR as an academic field, and to locate and assess recent developments – in short, to find out what is being done where, by whom, and why. We have approached the subject along three avenues, represented by the three groups of chapters – those addressing broad issues and theoretical debates; those commenting on various approaches to the field in different countries; and those focusing on principal sub-fields.

A concern of the editors, and a partial motivation for this volume, is that the study of IR in the United States and Great Britain remains frustratingly parochial in its approach. One manifestation of this parochialism can be seen in contemporary IR literature from Britain and the United States: Anglo-Saxon sources are the most frequently quoted modern works, and there are few references to works not published in English.[2] This is perhaps not surprising since the development of IR as an academic field took place in, and remains dominated by, the United States and Great Britain. Yet the implications of this dominance are quite profound, and in this volume, Steve Smith and Ekkehart Krippendorff investigate the consequences of post-1945 US dominance in the field. Writing in 1977, Stanley Hoffmann captured the phenomenon in the title of his seminal paper on the subject: 'An American Social Science: International Relations'.[3] Clearly, a wealth of IR literature originates in the Anglo-Saxon world and academics in that community must be cognisant of their Anglophone colleagues' work. Indeed, the flow of IR publishing in English alone is likely to swamp the average scholar. One argument for ignoring foreign sources may thus simply be that the English language literature leads the field, both in volume and innovation. Yet this results in an unfortunate deficiency in the study of international relations in Britain and the United States. Neil Richardson notes in chapter 17 that the IR discourse in the US 'is almost autarchically insulated from scholarship in other countries'. Even as between British and American scholarship, as Chris Hill notes in chapter 15, 'many excellent

[British] books get swamped in the sheer tide of material (some of it ethnocentric) which distracts American students from outside work'. The deficiency is thus perpetuated. Behaviouralists and quantifiers have accused those who reject their approaches of not making sufficient effort to learn the methodology – perhaps the same can be said with respect to the utilisation of non-English sources. Foreign languages are simply not taken seriously as an academic tool by many IR practitioners, though of course there are notable exceptions. But what is at one level a problem of language and culture, is at another level a problem of knowledge. It is not simply a matter of translation: working in different languages allows access not only to different cultural and historical experience, but also to different modes of thought. Whether there is a general malaise in IR scholarship, and to what extent it is being addressed by emerging critiques, is a central theme of this volume. The problem of parochialism may have rather deeper roots in the theoretical and philosophical foundations of IR.

Writing in 1969, Charles A. McClelland discussed the differences between what he termed the 'wisdom' and the 'scientific' approach to the study of IR.[4] The wisdom approach requires intensive grounding in the histories of many countries, mastery of several languages and direct experience in living and working abroad, and even then, 'secure knowledge can be obtained only in a few circumscribed areas'. McClelland wrote that those with faith in the development of IR as a science do not believe it is necessary for everyone to go through the process the wisdom approach requires: 'No extended apprenticeship in histories and languages is required as a prerequisite'. He goes on to observe that the scientific approach has failed to produce enough material to support a general survey of international relations: 'The accomplishment to date amounts to little "islands" of research floating in a "sea" of wisdom'.

Nearly 20 years later the islands remain small, and the ebbing tide of wisdom has left something of a vacuum into which critical perspectives are now being drawn. In the post-Behaviouralist revitalisation of Realism can be seen the tendencies of the scientific approach blended with the classical concerns of Realism. To the extent that these theoretical inclinations are seen to be inadequate, a number of emerging critiques have been articulated, often drawing on IR's growing range of cognate disciplines. These critiques may be viewed, collectively, as an effort to give substance to the sea of wisdom, and provide context for the islands of research whose foundations are ultimately at issue. In this sense it may be reasonable to accept claims to epistemological anarchy (cf. Feyerabend)[5] without entirely abandoning the pursuit of systematic knowledge. It is possible, after all, to point to some progress despite continuing philosophical debates.

Part I addresses some key theoretical issues in IR. There has, of course, always been criticism and some degree of introspection, particularly at points of transition between key periods in the development of these studies (and corresponding practice): legal, historical and philosophical traditionalism; the Idealism of the inter-war period; the reaction of post-war Realism; the Behavioural revolution of the 1950s and 1960s; post-Behaviouralism; and more recently, Neorealism. What is to follow is a matter of academic debate, of which this volume partakes.

In considering the practical matters of teaching and study, it may be useful to suggest what could, and should, be retrieved from the wisdom approach. The following excerpt from an Anglo–German report on revising the standard curriculum of IR indicates a possible approach to the study of history:

(i) *Modern world history*, covering the period from roughly the fifteenth century to the present day, emphasising *not* diplomatic events as such but *structural* themes. These might include the rise and development of the state and of the inter-state system; industrialisation, trade and the spread economic activity; welfare and nationalism; the role of warfare; imperialism and subsequent decolonisation; ideology and communication systems.

(ii) *The history of thought* about international relations, including both the pre-twentieth century work in the fields of philosophy, law and historiography, and also the twentieth century development of academic IR studies.[6]

As for living and studying abroad, desirable as it may be, such experience is sadly often beyond the financial means of the average student. The market approach to education in North America and the United Kingdom, which often leaves students heavily indebted at the close of their studies, hardly stimulates individuals to undertake activities which will add to the financial burden or prolong the required period of study for a degree. The spiralling tuition fees of these countries serve as a deterrent to foreign students, either because they have institutions at home which charge negligible tuition fees or because of fluctuating rates of foreign exchange. These conditions apply to all academic disciplines, but are perhaps especially relevant for IR.

Attitudes toward foreign education vary among academics and politicians. Regarding the United Kingdom, one recent study concluded: 'it is legitimate to suggest that the dominant attitude of British higher education to study abroad has been one of cultural imperialism: it is still widely believed that foreigners may have something to gain from studying in high quality British institutions but British students will derive little academic benefit from study abroad'.[7] In some other Western countries, however, academics and politicians are calling for expanded programmes of foreign study. The European Community's ERASMUS programme for foreign study may remain underfunded but its importance has increasingly come to be recognised.[8]

Languages, as suggested above, should once again be regarded as an important tool for the study of IR. Yet language study remains the exception rather than the rule.[9] How, then, will new generations of IR academics in Anglophone countries ever be able to evaluate the growing volume of work produced by their colleagues elsewhere? English may indeed be the *lingua franca* for the academic world, and works in other languages may eventually be translated, especially if they fit the dominant approaches followed in the Anglophone world. The same holds for important memoirs and to a lesser extent official documents. However, to ignore the proliferating volume of untranslated works would seem to be intellectually reckless.

IR is also, though by no means exclusively, concerned with the present. Sources addressing contemporary events are always in short supply, for despite the wealth of material that is published, there is a considerable time-lag in the publication of academic papers, let alone books. The IR practitioner may well be concerned with deeper or more esoteric matters, but as Aharon Klieman points out in Chapter 19, he/she will nevertheless also be called upon to interpret current trends in international politics. There are sound arguments against tailoring academic work to policy relevance, yet when it comes to analysing or merely discussing current events in the international scene, if it is not IR academics who are reading and interpreting foreign sources, who then? Access to foreign works, including much-maligned journalistic sources, is thus essential. It is not of the least concern that novel ideas and important critiques are more likely than not to originate outside the traditional locus of IR scholarship.

Because this volume was partly conceived in response to the growth of an introspective critique, it seemed important to examine the structures and priorities of academic approaches to international relations in a number of different countries. Part II of this volume incorporates thirteen country studies and one regional study (Hispanic America), providing an indication of how and why particular concerns or traditions have influenced developments in the field.

Part III investigates developments in various sub-fields, whose influence may be felt in determining new directions for the discipline as a whole (notwithstanding the question of whether IR is a discipline proper, or merely a 'subject area'). The existence and proliferation of sub-fields is itself an indication of academic pressures and trends: specialisation has become a necessity in modern academic practice, as the demand for specific expertise has overtaken the traditional expectation of broad knowledge. Though it is difficult to manage without general skills in a field as diverse as IR, specialisation may (for example) diminish the inclination, if not the ability, to attempt grand theory.

Restrictions of space require that this collection be selective, and strict word limits have been imposed on the authors. No doubt we have omitted significant issues and debates (such as environmental politics), some areas of endeavour (such as development studies), and some countries and areas (such as India and the Nordic countries) which deserve attention. Attempts to acquire views from Eastern Europe met with failure, for reasons which remain unclear. What appears here is thus a somewhat eclectic series of studies and is in no way exhaustive.

However, we hope that this volume will contribute, in some small way, to furthering the discussion about the nature of this inherently diverse field, and the various ways in which it is studied and taught. For, in as much as the future is implicated, these are not small matters.

H.C.D. *London*
L.M. *Berlin*

NOTES AND REFERENCES

We are grateful to João Cravinho and Mark Hoffman for comments on this introduction.

1.   See, for example, K.J. Holsti, *The Dividing Discipline: Hegemony and Diversity in International Theory* (London: Allen & Unwin, 1985)

and also Margot Light and A.J.R. Groom, *International Relations, A Handbook of Current Theory* (London: Francis Pinter, 1985). Holsti's book presents among other things a study of the literature used in the teaching of IR in various countries, while Light and Groom's collection serves as a useful guide to recent theoretical and conceptual trends in the study of IR.

2. Of course well-known authors such as Raymond Aron and Fernand Braudel may be quoted in their native language, but as they *are* well-known their works are also translated.

3. Stanley Hoffmann, 'An American Social Science: International Relations', *Daedalus*, Proceedings of the American Academy of Sciences (Vol. 1 issued as Vol. 106, No. 3, 1977), pp. 41–60.

4. Charles A. McClelland, 'International Relations: Wisdom or Science?', in James N. Rosenau (ed.), *International Politics and Foreign Policy: A Reader in Research and Theory*, revised edn (New York: The Free Press/Macmillan, 1969), pp. 3–5.

5. Paul Feyerabend, *Against Method* (London: Verso Books, 1975).

6. *Revising the Standard Curriculum of International Relations: An Anglo–German Initiative*, Report on a series of inaugural meetings held on 21 and 22 November 1985 at the London School of Economics.

7. Gareth Williams, 'The International Market for Overseas Students in the English-speaking World', *European Journal of Education* (Vol. 22, No. 1, 1987), p. 15.

8. ERASMUS (European Community Action Scheme for the Mobility of University Students). The first three year period of the Erasmus programme is designed to provide the Community with a pool of some 25000 students who have benefited from studying for a part of their degree in another Community country. At a cost of 80 million ECU (56 million pounds sterling) the programme will provide maximum grants of 5000 ECU (3500 pounds sterling) per year to students to cover the 'mobility costs', i.e., travel, language tuition and cost of living differential. (*Source*: Commission of the European Communities, 'Policies for Young People in the European Community' (London: 17 March 1988, p. 4).

    The president of the West German Conference of Rectors, Hinrich Seidel, has called for the expansion of the ERASMUS programme so as to allow university students from all subjects the chance to spend at least one semester at a foreign institution. Rainer Nahrendorf, 'Die Studenten aller Fachrichtungen sollten ein Auslandssemester absolvieren', *Handelsblatt*, 9 February 1988.

    In a recent interview, François Mitterrand argued that in the twenty-first century knowledge of three languages will be a minimum and that with this goal in mind, the ERAMUS programme 'necessary and useful though it is, is still but a timid experiment': François Mitterrand, interviewed by Peter Ruge and Juergen Liminiski, 'Sprache ist die Mörtel für Steine Europas', *Die Welt*, 20 January 1988, Nr. 16.

9. The University of London, for example, grants the PhD in International Relations with no foreign language proficiency requirement

and the Department of International Relations at the London School of Economics has not yet imposed a foreign language requirement on its graduate students. Although North American universities tend to have foreign language requirements for nearly all degrees, the standards required are often not high.

Part I
Theoretical Issues and Debates

Part I
Theoretical Issues and Debates

1 Paradigm Dominance in International Relations: The Development of International Relations as a Social Science*

Steve Smith

The concern of this study is admittedly narrow; it is focused on the issue of how International Relations has developed as a social science. Within that general focus it is concerned specifically with the dominance of a US view of the subject as a social science. Of course, such a definition of International Relations theory is partial, and certainly many would resent the very suggestion that the subject is, or should become, a social science. However, my interest is with the reasons why US views of the subject have dominated the broad development of paradigms within the discipline. This issue has crucial relevance for any understanding of the evolution of the discipline, and for any possibility of inter-paradigm debate. My broad argument will be two-fold: on the one hand, the US view of International Relations as a social science has led to the subject strongly reflecting US policy concerns; on the other, this US concern with policy relevance has made it very difficult for the subject to evolve on a cross-national, cumulative basis. Both of these factors make the task of paradigm confrontation even more complex than is implied by those philosophers of social science who have taken the concept of 'paradigm' to imply an essentially relativistic epistemology. After outlining the development of the subject as a social science, this study will discuss the existence of a US dominance of the discipline, then conclude with an examination of the implications for the inter-paradigm debate.

We should start our survey of the development of paradigms in International Relations by noting that although it is unquestionable that the subject has developed as a social science in ways that,

3

broadly speaking, parallel (albeit with a lag) the development of
other social sciences, it is by no means as clear that International
Relations as social science dominates the ways in which the subject
is studied. This is probably the case even in the United States, but
it is certainly so in Britain, where even a cursory glance at the
journals reveals a powerful, perhaps even dominant, concern with
International Relations as something other than a social science.
Not only is there a strong body of opinion that concentrates on
analysing current events solely from a policy dimension, but there is
also a distinctive 'English School' of studying International Relations,
usually identified with the work of Martin Wight and Hedley Bull.[1]
Even more importantly, there is a very vocal body of opinion,
centred around the work of Charles Reynolds,[2] which fundamentally
takes issue with the notion that International Relations can ever be
a social science at all. According to Reynolds, there is no way
in which International Relations can appropriate the canons of
scientific enquiry that he sees as applying in the natural sciences. His
alternative is for an International Relations that seeks to understand
the thoughts of key decision-makers, and he thus sees International
Relations as essentially a branch of a certain form of history. There
is no need to rehearse the standard arguments on each side of this
debate, but it is important to note that this view has many adherents
in Britain;[3] it was, after all, Hedley Bull who fired the first shot in the
(misnamed) 'Great Debate' about methodology in the mid-1960s.[4] The
point here is really only to state that defining International Relations
as a social science automatically skews our purview so as to define
the field in a way that stresses US dominance of the discipline.[5]

However, before we can examine the implications of this US
dominance of International Relations it is necessary to offer a brief
overview of how the subject has developed. There are many extant
accounts of this, so only the main landmarks of the discipline's growth
will be noted,[6] and our discussion will proceed chronologically rather
than thematically; we will return to discuss other paradigamatic
classifications later in the study. The starting date that is usually
given for the development of the discipline of International Relations
is the period immediately following the First World War; yet this
is rather misleading since it implies that there was no study of the
subject before then. Of course, this is not the case, although it is
only in the post-First World War period that a distinct approach to
the subject emerges. Before then the subject matter of International
Relations was studied within a variety of perspectives, most centrally

law, history and philosophy. These approaches predisposed scholars
to think about International Relations in essentially contradicatory
ways: on the one hand, international society was evidently very
different from domestic society, with diplomacy representing almost
a small 'club' of nationals from different states. As such, International
Relations was not a subject for major political dispute at home, and
what was needed to understand it was primarily a comprehension of
the precise historical circumstances involved. Yet there was another
implication of the way international relations were studied: this was
that the subject could be discussed using the same kinds of intellectual
tools as applied to politics within the state, hence the close connections with law, history and philosophy. But, above all, International
Relations was not seen as a separate discipline, merely one that was
basically self-contained in its empirical dimension. Not surprisingly,
the dominant world power in the late nineteenth and early twentieth
centuries, Great Britain, dominated the thinking in this area; and,
again not surprisingly, the values stressed in the subject reflected
the problems that the country faced given the structural influences
of a multipolar world order. To understand what was going on
meant understanding the nuances of great-power rivalry, the history
of conflict between their interests, and the attempts of international
law and skillful diplomacy to mediate any conflicts that resulted.

The impact of the First World War on this mode of thought was
enormous; the carnage of that war, combined with a view that it had
been a war that no one had wanted, conditioned post-war thinking
about the subject. It is critical to note the interplay between these
two factors. War had always been bloody and costly, but the sight
of mass armies battling over a few yards of territory in Flanders
seemed literally senseless if it was all for a war that no one had
actually wanted. The school of thought that emerged from this
process of revulsion and reflection, usually termed Idealism, had
as its overriding goal the prevention of such wars in the future. For
the Idealists it was accepted that international relations could, and
should, be managed in a more peaceful manner. As Hedley Bull
has commented, the most distinctive characterisic of Idealism was:

> the belief, in particular that the system of international relations
> that had given rise to the First World War was capable of being
> transformed into a fundamentally more peaceful and just world
> order; that under the impact of the awakening of democracy, the
> growth of 'the international mind', the development of the League

of Nations, the good works of men of peace or the enlightenment
spread by their own teachings, it was in fact being transformed; and
that their responsibility as students of international relations was to
assist this march of progress to overcome the ignorance, the prejudices, the ill-will, and the sinister interests that stood in its way.[7]

Accordingly, this first phase of a distinctive subject of International
Relations was directed towards preventing the occurrence of a
war like the First World War, and most attention was paid to
reforming the international system in such a way as to ensure that
change came about peacefully. Thinking was not directed towards
empirical investigation but towards the technical issues of how to
establish the best procedures for ensuring peaceful change. Thus,
academics working on international relations tended to be primarily
concerned with international law and International Organisations.

Such a focus was not accidental, since it accompanied the establishment of a political consensus over why war had broken out in 1914; a
consensus most explicitly represented in Woodrow Wilson's Fourteen
Points. Underpinning this was (1) a liberal world-view that stressed
both the inherent rationality of decision-makers and (2) the fact
that the two countries (the United States and the United Kingdom)
in which the subject developed were basically satisfied, status-quo
powers. The first of these factors implied that since the First World
War had been so plainly dysfunctional for all parties involved,
decision-makers would prefer to use peaceful means for managing
change; the task of International Relations scholars was to refine
and perfect these peaceful means. The second factor was critical in
determining the orientation of the discipline in that it predisposed
scholars to assume that war had ceased to be a rational instrument of
policy for all decision-makers; their world-view reflected the fact that
their countries were not seeking large-scale change in International
Relations. In such a situation, with Idealism intimately connected
with the interests of those who had defined the terms of the peace
settlements, the tendency was to assume that the benefits of peaceful change channelled through international law and organisations
applied universally. This first phase of the development of International Relations therefore saw war as something that could occur only
by accident or by the presence of 'sinister interests', so international
law and international organisations should be refined so as to prevent
the first, and democratisation encouraged to prevent the second.
Crucially, this view was based on an epistemology that was rather

different to that which applied in the other infant social sciences. Whereas these were beginning a search for general laws of behaviour, International Relations was still firmly located within an essentially historical epistemology, in which the major focus for explanations of war was the decision-makers involved. As Richard Little has noted:

the new specialists in International Relations felt under no compunction to search for general laws which could describe and explain the action of states. In line with the diplomatic historian it was assumed that the future course of events was neither predetermined nor beyond the control of decision-makers; instead it was accepted that the course of history would unfold on the basis of deliberate actions taken by the key decision-makers.[8].

As such, International Relations started life in a way that was very different from the other social sciences: it was prescriptive, normative and based on a conception of scholarly activity that stressed the immediate policy-relevance of work. This led to the discipline being concerned above all with devising procedures and techniques to assist rational decision-makers to avoid war. In all of this the lesson of the way the First World War had started loomed large. International Relations developed as a response to events in the real world and defined its purpose as preventing their repetition.

The problems inherent in the Idealist view of international relations are well-documented, with E. H. Carr's *The Twenty Years Crisis* being the most widely-cited critique of their thought.[9] The problems were, however, made only too apparent by events in the 1930s, when a series of international conflicts revealed that the assumptions of Idealist thought were far removed from the views held by decision-makers in a number of states. The mechanisms preferred by Idealists proved incapable of preventing war, and the outbreak of the Second World War shattered the Idealist world view. Specifically, mediation did not work, and more saliently, assumptions about the dysfunctional nature of war proved to be illusory. The explanation of this is not so much that the Idealists were utopian as that their view of International Relations was axiomatically bound up with the interests of the two states in which the subject first took root. In this sense, there is a powerful strand of continuity running through the history of the development of International Relations. This study started by pointing to an American dominance of the subject as it is now practised, but it says something about the nature of the subject that there is a linkage between the dominance of certain states in the international system and the subject as studied in those countries. It is all too easy to accept this point as obvious or trivial without following through its implications for the study of the subject in countries that are non-hegemonic, and we will return to this theme later.

The response to the failure of Idealism to explain the dominant events of the 1930s was the emergence, in good Kuhnian fashion, of an alternative paradigm, Realism. In many ways Realism has been *the* dominant paradigm in International Relations, despite the obituaries that were written in the 1960s and 1970s. Were this study to have been written ten years ago it would, I must admit, have concluded that we had moved beyond Realism, but this, although a consensual view in International Relations circles, was a mistaken view. There are two main aspects of this argument: first, as John Vasquez has so admirably indicated,[10] the main assumptions of Realism pervade approaches that were presented as alternatives to it. Specifically, he argues that Realism had three central assumptions: that nation states are the most important actors; that there is a sharp distinction between domestic and international politics; and that the focus of International Relations is the study of power and peace. In an earlier version of this analysis, an unpublished paper by Handelman, Vasquez, O'Leary and Coplin, the authors argued that:

> Reviewing the literature of the 1960s, we find a number of schools which appear to challenge the Morgenthau paradigm because they use different concepts. However . . . all . . . must be considered elaborations of the initial paradigm. . . In effect the international relations literature on [*sic*] the 1960s was a set of variations on the Morgenthau paradigm.[11]

Second, there has been a revival of Realism, usually termed Neorealism, in the last decade; a revival found in the works of structuralists such as Waltz,[12] as well as regime theorists such as Keohane and Krasner.[13] This revival is closely related to a set of international events that the United States had to deal with in the late 1970s, and leads one to the conclusion that the 1970s may well have been abnormal in the development of International Relations theory in so far as this was a time when Realism was pronounced dead. These two factors indicate that Realism never really went away, even though many working in the field thought that it had, and even proclaimed that their own work was not Realist. We shall return to discuss the 'rise' of Neorealism in order to link it to the foreign policy dilemmas facing the United States, the country in which it first took root.[14]

But to resume the historical overview, Realism was associated with two founding works, E.H. Carr's critique of Idealism, *The Twenty Years' Crisis*, mentioned above, and Hans Morgenthau's *Politics Among Nations*.[15] Of these two, it was Morgenthau who attempted the most explicit reformulation of how International Relations should be studied; Carr's book being primarily a critique of Idealism (although it was Carr who called for a 'realist' interpretation of world events). Morgenthau openly spoke of laws and regularities in international events, with his 'Six Principles of Realism', added in the second edition, offering the clearest statement at that time of the assumptions of the approach. The essence of Realism, of course, was that human behaviour was rooted ultimately in immutable laws of human nature, a nature that Morgenthau saw variously as merely selfish or downright evil. To comprehend International Relations, Morgenthau argued that a theory was needed 'to bring order and meaning to a mass of phenomena which without it would remain disconnected and unintelligible'.[16] Although he wished to argue against the role of morality in explaining the actions of states, Morgenthau's main claim was that states were power-maximisers, and that an explanation of international relations arose from that premise, informed by a certainty about human nature. For Morgenthau, what was needed was an empirical science of International Relations, as opposed to utopian or normative thought. Not that Morgenthau wished to avoid normative statements, rather he wanted these to emerge from the realities of how politics actually operated. In all this, his reliance on a specific view of human nature was crucial.[17] That there were numerous problems with Morgenthau's formulation is in an important sense irrelevant for our purposes.[18] What is more salient is the impact of his argument about the need for theory on the development of the discipline, and the linkage between his proposals and the situation of the United States at the time the book was published.

With regard to the development of the discipline, Morgenthau's work, precisely because it called for the development of a theory, was central in that it pushed the subject towards the creation of an identifiable theoretical framework. This had not been logically implied by the work of the Idealists. For Morgenthau, international relations was to be thought of as an autonomous sphere of action, with an understanding of this action dependent on the creation of a theoretical framework that was specific to the international political world. This was aided by Morgenthau's assertion that the basic characteristics of international politics were essentially unchanging.

Yet, as Stanley Hoffmann has argued, Morgenthau's impact has to be understood within the context of the academic community at the time.[19] Specifically, Hoffmann notes three aspects of the intellectual predispositions of the period: First, a belief in the role of a value-free science in resolving problems which was supported by the US national experience of economic development, social integration and external success.[20] Second, the spillover effect from the prestige of the natural sciences and the then-dominant faith in the 'science' of economics. Third, the impact of the scholars who had moved to the US in the 1930s and 1940s; a group of scholars who were concerned with large-scale questions, who brought with them a powerful sense of history and who 'wanted to find out the meaning and the causes of the catastrophe that had uprooted them, and perhaps the key to a better world'.[21] The key point is that Morgenthau's approach appeared at a time when this set of factors was combined with another, political, set of occurrences, namely those resulting from the emergence of the United States as a superpower. Whilst the intellectual climate was ripe for following the road to understanding proposed by Morgenthau, the political climate gave Realism a much more immediate credibility.

The role of the United States in the post-Second World War period was not only central, but in many respects novel. As the Cold War unfolded, all aspects of world politics seemed to involve the United States–Soviet relationship. Given the pre-war isolationist tendency in US foreign policy, this involvement was undertaken with little of the traditional European framework of an experienced and elite band of foreign policy specialists. In such a situation, national leaders were receptive to ideas to help guide them, and this is exactly what Realism offered. As Robert Rothstein has noted, Realism was popular because it 'encapsulated what they [the politicians] took for granted, especially after the failures of the 1930s and during the height of the cold war'.[22] Accordingly, he argues that Realism became 'the doctrine which provided the intellectual frame of reference for the foreign policy establishment for something like twenty years . . . it did determine the categories by which they assessed the external world and the state of mind with which they approached prevailing problems'.[23] Indeed, as Hoffmann has noted, it was the very ambiguity of Realism, specifically in its view of the relationship between the maximisation of power and the operation of the balance of power so as to avoid conflict, that made it so popular; it could be used to stress the need for accommodation or the need to build up power. It was 'nothing but a rationalization of cold war policies'.[24]

Realism, therefore, hàd a massive impact on the emerging discipline of International Relations because it encouraged the development of a separate field of study, and because it fitted well with the
foreign policy of the country in which that subject was undergoing
the most analysis. The combination of these two influences was
vital to the way the subject developed. What Realism did was to
focus attention on the general issues of International Relations in
a country that was itself having to deal, for the first time in its
history, with exactly these general issues in its day-to-day foreign
policy. No other country in the Western world had this combination
of an intellectual community receptive to social science theory and
a foreign policy agenda that so closely mirrored the theoretical
agenda of Realism. In other countries there was either a tradition
of historical research that stressed piecemeal empirical investigation
of 'unique' events, and thereby an aversion to the development of
a scientific theory, or a foreign policy setting in which leaders
did not have the global agenda and the power to do anything
other than focus more parochially, or both. This specific US
position was reinforced by a set of unique institutional patterns: the
considerable movement back and forth between the academic and
the political worlds, the role of grant-awarding foundations to spur
research, and a large buoyant university system. The combination of
these institutional patterns encouraged exactly the kind of research
that Realism called for and which the politicians wanted. There
was really no similar set of circumstances in any other country.

Yet if Realism encouraged the growth of a separate discipline
of International Relations, aimed at the creation of an identifiable
theoretical framework, the subject was soon caught up in a very
different set of intellectual developments. For just at the time that
Morgenthau was urging the establishment of a distinct approach to
studying international relations, the movement in other social sciences was toward the breaking down of the boundaries imposed by, it
was argued, artificial subject divisions. According to this perspective,
what was needed was a concentration on explaining behaviour, using
a variety of tools developed in specific subject areas, but using them
so as to cross subject boundaries. This movement became known as
Behaviouralism, and was committed to using the methods of natural
science to resolve disputes. This positivistic orientation was in one
important sense very much at odds with the Realist notion of social
science, since Morgenthau was explicit in his desire to make normative statements. Furthermore, Morgenthau's acount of International

Relations relied on unobservable laws of human nature: all of this was· unacceptable to positivists, whose definition of theory started with a desire to explain that which was observable. The dominance of Realism meant that Behaviouralism's impact on International Relations occurred some time after its impact on the other social sciences, with the two most significant early examples being Snyder's work on decision-making[25] and Kaplan's work on international systems.[26] Each of these indicates the influence of other social sciences (Snyder's use of psychology, Kaplan's development of systems theory)and each undermined the assumptions of Realism in a critical way: Snyder indicated that Morgenthau's reliance on rationality in decision-making was mistaken given the role of decision-makers' subjective perceptions of the situation; Kaplan's alternative models of the international system were based not on history, as was Morgenthau's concept of the system, but on hypothetical structures – they also indicated that the structure of the system could change, thereby producing different characteristic modes of behaviour.

By the late 1950s Behaviouralism had become widely accepted in the subject area, and it was common to see Behaviouralism portrayed as an alternative to Realism. The history of the subject until the 1970s is really one of a self-conscious rejection of Realism, with scholars seeing themselves as engaged in an enterprise that was altogether different from the traditionalism of Morgenthau. Yet, as has been noted above, Vasquez has indicated most plausibly that this was all rather misleading. Behaviouralism was essentially concerned with method, and when it comes to looking at the assumptions of the approaches the link with Realism is obvious. Even the post-Behaviouralist attack on the methodological assumptions of Behaviouralism did little to alter the subject's reliance on a Realist view of international relations. Up until the mid-1970s, then, Realism, in a variety of guises and disguises dominated the discipline. What happened in the mid-1970s was the emergence of approaches to studying International Relations that did question the assumptions of Realism. Of these, the ones that had the most impact were world systems theory (as represented in the work of, for example, Wallerstein[27] and Burton's cobweb theory[28]), and above all, the transnationalist approach.[29] In all of these cases the attack was on the assumptions of Realism, specifically the three central tenets of it noted above (dominance by states, separation between domestic and international politics, and the primacy of issues of power and peace). In many ways the 1970s witnessed the most sustained challenge to date against the prevailing nature of the discipline, so much so that one may argue that the major dispute in the history of the subject has been between state-centric and transnationalist accounts. To reiterate a point made earlier, had this study been written a decade ago it would have concluded that this debate represented a sea-change in the study of the subject, with the assumptions of Realism finally being exposed for the over-simplification that they are. Indeed, for Maghroori and Ramberg the challenge of transnationalism and interdependence constituted the 'third debate' in the discipline's history, paralleling the earlier ones between Idealism and Realism and between Realism and Behaviouralism.[30]

Yet the transnationalist onslaught was overtaken by events, as the late 1970s and early 1980s witnessed a series of developments in world politics that allowed Realism to return to dominance under a new guise, Neorealism. The events, of course, were the rise of a Second Cold War and the re-evaluation of the definition of Realism so as to include an explanation of the economic dimension of US hegemony. While there are a variety of approaches to studying International Relations in the mid-1980s it is evident that, in the United States at least, Realism in one form or another is dominant in content, if not in name. There are competing paradigms, but even this brief review of the history of the subject must conclude that if we were forced to say which paradigm dominates, it is Realism.

Many will argue that the picture I have painted of the discipline's development is incomplete (which it certainly is) and misleading as to the variety of approaches contained within the subject area. Specifically, we should note that there are other ways of classifying the status of paradigms in the discipline, the most common alternative to the chronological method used here being the approach of Banks[31] and Smith *et al.*,[32] who distinguish between three accounts: Realism, Pluralism and Structuralism. This distinction is one that attempts to simplify the confusion over the state of the discipline since the decline of Realism's dominance of the subject. Each of these three paradigms focuses on a rather different aspect of international relations: respectively, states, all relevant actors and class formation. My concern, though, is not to argue that this alternative classification is insufficient, but only to make the point that if our focus is on the dominance of one approach to studying international relations, then that focus must be on Realism. The division of the subject into Realist, Pluralist and Structuralist paradigms is a relatively recent departure, and one that follows the breakdown of methodological consensus in the 1960s and 1970s. We will return to discuss the extent to which it is possible for debate to occur between paradigms, but for now we need simply to reassert the central argument thus far, namely that Realism has dominated the discipline precisely because the discipline itself has mainly been developed in a specific country, with a specific set of foreign policy problems. My main assertion is therefore that, to paraphrase the words of Hoffmann, International Relations is a US social science. Not only is this evident in the way in which Realism dominated the subject in the post-Second World War period, but it is also indicated by the impact of 'Behaviouralism on the discipline. In both cases, it was the combination of US foreign policy concerns and the specific intellectual climate in the United States that was crucial. Just as the earlier manifestations of the discipline in Britain reflected sociology of knowledge factors and the types of problems faced by that country in its foreign relations, so the development of International Relations was dependent on the unique situation of the United States and its academic community. Since 1945 the subject has been overwhelmingly dominated by US literature, and this literature reflects the dilemmas facing the United States during this period.

The dominance of US policy concerns in the literature of the subject has two aspects. First, there is the very strong commitment to a policy-relevant approach to the subject of International Relations in the United States. To any audience outside the United States, this concern seems at best quirkish and at worst corrupt. Of course, it is realised that this orientation is intimately related to the pattern of financing research in the United States, and more insidiously to the fortunes of academic departments and individual scholars; but, certainly in Britain, it never ceases to amaze academics just how large looms policy-relevance in US research. This is not, hopefully, merely smugness or a holier-than-thou attitude, but reflects the entirely different system of tenure and research financing in Britain. Similarly, in Britain there is a nearly total absence of a movement from the academic world to the political world. Nor is there anything like the support for social science among academics working in the discipline that one finds in the United States. Finally, in Britain the whole system of graduate training is different, with work for a PhD being exclusively concentrated on a thesis, with no course work and little support in the form of methodology or data-management classes. It goes without saying that the situation in Britain leads to a certain way of analysing International Relations, especially given the dominance of a handful of universities in graduate training, and there are considerable limitations of the British academic situation. The point is not to say that one is better than the other, but rather to point out that the subject in the United States is far more explicitly connected to the policy community than is the case in Britain, where scholarly activity is still basically an individual enterprise, unconnected to the policy community (even shunned by it) and where policy-relevance has been, until very recently, rather a dirty word. It is not surprising, then, that the social dimension of international relations knowledge in the United States has encouraged a far greater concern with the situation of the state in the international system than has occurred elsewhere.

This leads to a second aspect of the dominance of US policy concerns in the literature. Not only is there the obvious influence of US issues in the success (and timing) of Realism and Neorealism, but an examination of the major theoretical developments in the subject reveals US policy concerns. This is evident in the way in which work on nuclear strategy and arms control has unfolded both in terms of the analytical work on deterrence theory and in empirical areas of concern, for example nuclear proliferation. Even in the more rarified areas of International Relations theory the linkage is enormous; to cite just the most immediate examples, consider why, and when, the following approaches developed – post-Behaviouralism, tripolarity, interdependence, transnationalism and regime theory. More generally, even the transnationalist alternative to state-centric approaches was a product of a specific set of developments facing the United States. Even in areas as arcane as comparative foreign policy analysis the history of the sub-field's development is critically related to wider concerns as to what was happening to US foreign policy. None of this is surprising, nor is it necessarily something to be criticised *per se*; what is important, though, is that because International Relations has developed as a US social science, these parochial concerns have distorted the development of the subject globally. Again, it is the particular concern with policy-relevance pervading the US academic community (with a number of notable exceptions) that has made the subject twist and turn as the concerns of US policy shift. The situation is particularly problematic when other countries do not share the same policy agenda as the United States; in this light, Fred Northedge characterised transnationalism as an 'American Illusion'.[33] His argument was that the whole transnationalist account was a product of US experience in the early 1970s and reflected an American predisposition to measure transactions combined with a notion that the state was declining in importance. As he writes: 'American "analysts", one cannot but sometimes think, simply do not know what Europe was like . . . before 1914 – or even before 1939. They write as though transnationalism was a new phenomenon, and as though it was increasing; but it is an old phenomenon, and it is decreasing.'[34] Much the same argument would go for regime theory or tripolarity: in each case the subject in the United States has gone off on a quest to understand these concerns, and the rest of the International Relations community has, in due course, had to follow this direction in the literature. Of course, this is not to deny that the subject has had to deal with new developments in world politics, but these developments have been overwhelmingly those that have been salient for the United States. In this process the guiding question for the profession has been what the United States should do. In a situation in which other academic communities are not so receptive to social science methods, this United States-domination of the subject's development has been compounded by an absence of large research communities able to propose alternative strands of development of the subject. Even when they have attempted to do so, their work has all-too-often been largely ignored in the United States; after all, the route to publication (and tenure) does place an emphasis on being in an identifiable research tradition.

However, if US International Relations has dominated the development of the subject, the impact of Realism has had a lasting impact on the way the subject has conceptualised the issues involved. Precisely because US International Relations is so closely identified with the foreign policy concerns of the country, it is not surprising that the assumptions of Realism have proved to be so difficult to overcome. This is because the focus of Realism – namely how to maximise power so as to manage international events – fits extraordinarily well with the needs of a hegemonic power. The three key elements of Realism's account of world politics – the national interest, power maximisation and the balance of power – are particularly well-suited to the requirements of a foreign policy for the United States. The American fascination with controlling events, with managing the process of change, and with seeking technical solutions for what are political and economic dilemmas, can easily be accommodated within the Realist world-view. Realism, in this sense, is the approach of those satisfied with the existing world order, in much the same way as Idealism was in its time.

This situation has led to a noticeable gap emerging between International Relations and Political Science, as well as the other social sciences. To an extent, this is because of the rather different environments in which international and domestic politics take place; but this must not be overemphasised. Rather, the notion that domestic and international politics are separate activities is encouraged by Realism. This is not to deny the impact of structural features of the international system on the behaviour of states and the persons who act as their agents, but it is to propose the view that Realism has grossly exaggerated the division between the two environments. One might add that, until recently, major areas of Political Science did the same; after all, for the bulk of Political Science the state is the ceiling of the political system and the steps up to that ceiling seem to go only one way.[35] Similarly, in much political theory (certainly pluralist liberal-democratic thought), the impact of the international system on the possibility of democratic control over certain defence and foreign policy arenas is ignored.[36] So, although it would be absurd to argue that there is no impact of the international system on states and on the persons occupying leadership roles, this is not the same as accepting the Realist definition of this linkage. In short, it does not seem to me that the subject matter of International Relations requires us to treat the subject as wholly separate from Political Science and the other social sciences; rather the way that the subject has developed has over-stressed the differences and prevented the formation of linkages between the subject and other social sciences – most notably in the Realist treatment of domestic politics and of economics. There are very powerful reasons for arguing that the kind of linkage between international and domestic politics that Peter Gourevitch postulated[37] should lead us in a direction directly opposed to that advocated by Realism. That is to say that International Relations does not seem to be in a position that is different in kind to that of the other social sciences; for example in Sociology, Anthropology, Economics and Psychology, analysts are concerned with tracing the interrelationship between actors, perceptions and structures. In all social sciences there are issues of the impact of the system on the unit, of the sources of perceptions and the linkages between individuals, groups and environments. Yet the Realist account carries with it a set of mental baggage that accords primacy *by definition* to the (unchanging) structure of the system, thus obstructing inputs from other social sciences. Added to this is the problem of accepting notions of a monolithic state aiming to maximise something objective called 'power', with its own hierarchy of values. The division of International Relations from other social sciences seems more a logical consequence of the pervasiveness of Realist asumptions than a reflection of some specific features of its subject matter. If anything, there seems to be a convergence between International Relations and Political Science over issues such as the control of technology and the influence of systemic characteristics (albeit different systems) on political processes. Yet, Realism has encouraged us to see International Relations as a distinct enterprise in the political firmament, as if it was only in International Relations that persons were constrained or enabled by the structures that surround them.

What effect, then, does the dominance of the US International Relations community have for the study of the subject in other countries? With regard to US dominance in the literature, scholars in other countries in the Western world evidently do rely on the US literature in their teaching and research, and therefore tend to be in a situation of having to respond to US initiatives in the subject. This is well illustrated by the findings of Kal Holsti's recent excellent survey of the sources used in the discipline in eight countries[38] (the United States, Britain, Korea, India, France, Canada, Australia and Japan). He argues that US literature dominates the field to such an extent that the evidence suggests 'that international theory barely exists outside the anglophone countries'.[39] And this finding comes from a survey of international *theory*. This, of course, makes it difficult for an international intellectual community to develop, and he comments that, if anything, academics in other countries are increasingly writing for their own academic communities. This is certainly the case in Britain where the social science oriented community is generally in a position of following the US community's lead (many, of course, reject a social science approach altogether and restrict themselves to decrying the latest US 'fads' and 'fashions'). It may be a sad reflection on the state of the subject in other countries, but the scholars there are simply overwhelmed by the sheer size of the US community and find it difficult to be at the leading edge of the discipline. The point does not need labouring; suffice it to say that today's developments in the subject in the United States define tommorow's work in other countries. There notable exceptions, but they are the exceptions that prove the rule. Paradigm formation is a process fundamentally determined by what happens in the US academic community.

The major problem this causes is that the paradigms that are formed in the United States are, because of the desire there for policy-relevance, focused on a US view of the international agenda. If we follow the division of work in the subject suggested by Alker and Biersteker[40] (although I have reservations over their claimed distinction between Traditional and Behavioural approaches; following Vasquez, I see them as more closely related than they suggest) then their finding that the bulk of work is undertaken within the Behavioural tradition – about 70 per cent of reading list citations, with only about 20 per cent of citations being material in the Traditional paradigm and 10 per cent from the Dialectical tradition[41] – indicates the danger very clearly. Indeed, given that they define about 72 per cent of Behavioural citations as Neorealist,[42] the impact of the Realist or Neorealist world view on the subject in the United States is considerable, accounting for over two-thirds of these citations. The point of citing this evidence is to support my argument that the US study of International Relations is within traditions whose core assumptions are most appropriate to the policies of a hegemon. Certainly, the low ranking of Dialectical works indicates the dominance of what Alker and Biersteker call a parochial approach to the subject. As they state: 'our brief discussion of the historical and national context of alternative approaches to international relations theorizing suggests the deep connections between the social and political contexts of particular theoretical enterprises and the kind of work actually done'.[43] Given the dominance of the US academic community in Behavioural International Relations work, this situation not only creates parochialism in the United States but also makes it very difficult for Behaviouralists in other, non-hegemonic, countries to challenge the ruling (US-determined) paradigms. To reiterate the point at issue here: if the United States dominates International Relations, and if US work on the subject is parochial, then how can International Relations scholars in other countries use this work when their own countries face different policy agendas? After all, if you are not a great power, in Morgenthau's use of the term, what foreign policy options do you have?

The reaction to this problem has been that International Relations in other countries has either tried to keep up with the discipline as it develops in the United States or tended to concentrate on more immediate 'empirical' problems which face their particular country. And, for any academic community in which either historical or dialectical thought has strong adherents, the tendency is for the US academic study of the subject to be seen as remote, or even irrelevant. The danger of this is that the study of the subject in the United States becomes increasingly divorced from what is happening elsewhere.

What, then, is the state of discipline in the late 1980s? Although we can characterise the subject as progressing chronologically through

periods in which Idealist, Realist and Behavioural approaches dominated, it is nonetheless evident that as a social science the discipline
has been dominated by Realism, and by a US version of Realism at
that. Behaviouralism was not so much an attack on the assumptions
of Realism as a dispute about the most appropriate methodology;
after all, for Kaplan, Bull, Snyder and Singer, whatever their disputes
over method, the actor was still the state, and the hierarchy of
values was a given. The brave new world of quantitative techniques
may have bestowed academic status and 'scientific' precision on the
'Young Turks' but it did not fundamentally question the definition
of who acted over what issues with which resultant patterns. It is
for this reason that the 'debate' between the Traditionalists and
the Behaviouralists was really a phoney war; there was not a real
battle to fight as they were within the same paradigm. The calm
was broken in the 1970s by those who argued for Structuralist or
Pluralist accounts of International Relations: for the first time,
these accounts actually saw different actors at work and different
issues involved, the crucial result of which was to break down
the monolithic conception of the state and the very notion of
the state as dominant actor. In its initial phase, Pluralism (in
its Transnationalist and Interdependence guises) was led from
the United States, reflecting that country's policy agenda, whereas
Structuralism was very much an input into the US academic debate.

In the United States it is still correct to say that Realist assumptions
dominate, whether in a more sophisticated Waltzian form or (more
commonly) as the implicit mental baggage of the quantitative
researchers. This has a critical effect on the subject precisely
because of the dominance of the United States in the academic study
of International Relations. The crucial issue, therefore, is whether
paradigms can compete, for if they cannot, it will be very difficult
either to challenge the US definition of any of them or to resist the
dominance of the paradigm that dominates the US community. The
extent to which paradigms can compete is, as is well established in
the philosophy of science literature, very questionable; this is simply
because the proponents of each paradigm literally do not see the
same world, or the same issues as dominant. For a Structuralist
the central questions concern the ways in which the processes of
International Relations result in the structural dominance of some
groups (or, more accurately, classes) over others; this is just not the
same world as that of the Realist. Nor is there any neutral body of
facts against which competing paradigms can be assessed. This is

not a problem confined to the social sciences, as recent debates in physics over the wave and particle theories of light or the nature of sub-atomic particles attest, but this only serves to confirm the view that inter-paradigm debate is essentially problematic. Having said that, it is not at all obvious that an inter-paradigm debate is the same as the resolution of conflict between paradigms. That is to say, it is very mistaken to think of the issue of competing paradigms as if it was a question of one being 'right' and the others 'wrong'. To propose this would be to mistake the nature of theory, and to confuse the link between evidence and data. In this light, the inter-paradigm debate is not something that can be resolved by an appeal to evidence since there is not, nor can there be, any theory-independent set of evidence; evidence is evidence precisely, and only, because it fits within a theoretical framework. Paradigms therefore define the central questions in accordance with their different assumptions and what is relevant data comes from this *a priori* definition.

How, then, can paradigms compete? They compete by virtue of the accounts they provide in explaining what we as scholars or practitioners define as central to our purpose, enquiry or ideology. Just as it has been argued previously that the US policy agenda dominated the study of international relations by dominating Realism within the United States, so we should expect different paradigms to appeal to persons in different settings. For this reason, it is difficult to see how we could expect one paradigm to dominate another completely in a world of such diverse definitions of what is involved in international relations. Realism dominated partly because it dominated the largest and most well-financed academic community, partly because the world it spoke of was then dominating policy agendas throughout the globe, and partly because there was little in the way of alternatives, save for residual appeals to Idealism. Behaviouralism's contribution was to continue this dominance by bringing the semblance of scientific rigour to Realism.

In the late 1980s, it looks as if the prospects for inter-paradigm debate are improving. There are two reasons for this: first is the existence of work outside the US that engages in debate with the subject as defined in that country, as a look through recent volumes of journals such as *International Studies Quarterly* and *International Organization* will show. The other is the concern of a (small) group of scholars in the United States to open up the discipline both to material from other discourses, often based outside the United States, and to a greater self-awareness as to why the subject has developed as it has in the United States. One thinks here particularly of the work of Alker and Biersteker cited above, as well as that of Richard Ashley, and in Canada, Robert Cox and Robert Walker. The task facing these scholars is, however, an enormous one, for the reasons discussed above. It is also a task made more difficult because of the nature of the literature that is involved; the works of Habermas and Foucault are unlikely to prove popular reading for academics steeped in a Traditional or Behavioural literature. These works, and the arguments of the US scholars who work within this discourse, simply do not fit the prevailing US paradigm. One hopes that it is possible for such dialectical International Relations scholars to present their ideas in a way that indicates the salience of their arguments to the US International Relations community, lest the force of their position be lost in claims that the articles are irrelevant to the 'real' study of the subject. They will face a formidable hurdle in presenting an argument about the relativistic nature of discourses to a community committed to 'scientific' investigation.

In summary, this paper has argued that International Relations has indeed developed as a US social science. Only in the United States has there been the combination of an intellectual predisposition towards social science, a system of policy communities that takes people back and forth from the academic and political worlds, and a political climate that was looking for guidelines for managing international events. This combination was crucial for the success of Realism, and since 1945 the policy concerns of the United States have determined the direction of the discipline. In other countries, because policy agendas are not the same as in the United States (in either political, military or economic dimensions), the US dominance of the literature, and of the formation of its paradigms, commonly leads either to following the US lead or to a rejection of its methods and assumptions, turning instead towards historical or Idealist forms of analysis. Yet this situation is not inherent in the nature of the subject, rather it is a reflection of the size of the US International Relations community and the dominant paradigm found in that country. Specifically, adherence in the United States to variants of the Realist paradigm, utilising Behavioural methods, places academics in other countries in a position where it is difficult for them to challenge the orthodoxy. When they do, their work may be seen as outside the dominant paradigm in the United States, and therefore dismissed. The central problem is that the Realist definition of the subject stresses focal points - notably order and control, that are irrelevant to the foreign policy concerns (whether political or economic) of non-hegemonic states. As such, Realism performs an essentially ideological role in the United States.

International Relations remains dominated by the ruling paradigm, but the current situation is different in two rather important ways from the period until the late 1970s. First, the end of the predominance (if not the dominance) of Realism and Behavourialism has not been accompanied by the widespread acceptance of another US paradigm. As Alker and Biersteker have shown there is a dominance of Behavioural literature, but their work does. not make it clear quite what this category contains of our threefold division of Realism, Pluralism and Structuralism. Nevertheless, it is evident that there are strong lobbies for Pluralism and Structuralism in the United States, so that there is now more than at any time in the history of the discipline a *set* of distinct paradigms in the US academic community. Secondly, the assumptions of Pluralism and Structuralism actually encourage a definition of the key issues of International Relations that is more applicable to the policy agendas of many more states than was ever the case with Realism. It is certainly the case with Structuralism that there is a truly international academic community developing, simply because adopting a structural perspective actually predisposes an analyst to consider the effect of patterns of dominance on those dominated; it is, of course, also liberally sprinkled with a Marxian conception of real interests.

Outside the United States, it is not enough simply to bemoan the United States's dominance of the subject: rather it is important to engage in US discourses so as to bring in non-US concerns and agendas, thereby shifting the empirical focus of the discipline. In addition it is important to point out the ways in which US policy concerns dominate the United States academic community's definition of the subject. For these reasons, the current state of paradigm crisis (in the Kuhnian sense) is actually rather healthy for the discipline, since it opens up the possibility of genuine debate and confrontation between alternative paradigms. The current post-Behavioural division of the subject into the three paradigms of Realism, Pluralism and Structuralism results in a discipline that is more open than at any time in its history to cross-national debate. This will not lead to a genuinely international theory applicable to all, because there is not one world to explain but many. However, the emergence of Structuralist and Pluralist alternatives to positivistic accounts of Realism may allow the discipline to become more applicable to the concerns of scholars working in other countries, and there may be room for the development of international communities of adherents to the alternative paradigms. In this way, International Relations may become a non-hegemonic discipline that, by developing cross-national research communities, can engage in a meaningful debate between competing paradigms.

NOTES AND REFERENCES

*   This study is an expanded version of a paper presented at a conference on Paradigm Hegemony and International Relations Theory at Carleton University, Ottawa, in October 1986. The original study has been published in G. Legare and A. Dorsch (eds), *Paradigm Hegemony and International Relations Theory* (Ottawa: Carleton University Press, 1987).

1.   See Martin Wight, 'Why is there no International Theory?' in H. Butterfield and M. Wight (eds), *Diplomatic Investigations* (London: Allen and Unwin, 1966), pp. 17–34; Hedley Bull *The Anarchical Society* (London: Macmillan, 1977); Hedley Bull and Adam Watson (eds) *The Expansion of International Society* (Oxford: Clarendon Press, 1984). For a review of the 'English' school see Hidemi Suganami, 'The Structure of Institutionalism: An Anatomy of British Mainstream International Relations', *International Relations* (Vol. 7, No.5, 1983), pp. 2363–81. A critical review of the approach can be found in Roy Jones 'The English School of International Relations: A Case for Closure', *Review of International Studies* (Vol. 7, No. 1, 1981), pp. 1–14.

2.   See especially Charles Reynolds, *Theory and Explanation in International Relations* (Oxford: Martin Robertson, 1973). For a debate over this interpretation see Geoff Berridge 'International Relations', *Teaching Politics* (Vol. 10, No. 1, 1981), pp. 78–84; and Steve Smith 'Berridge on International Relations', *Teaching Politics* (Vol. 11, No. 1, 1982), pp. 23–9, followed by Berridge's reply, pp. 30–32.

3.   For a recent survey of the differences between the British and American international relations communities see Gene Lyons, 'The Study of International Relations in Great Britain: Further Connections', *World Politics* (Vol. 38, No. 4, 1986), pp. 626–45. The same concern formed the theme for the essays in Steve Smith (ed), *International Relations: British and American Perspectives* (Oxford: Basil Blackwell, 1985). For a discussion of the situation of the subject in France, see Gene Lyons 'Expanding the Study of International Relations: The French Connection', *World Politics* (Vol. 35, No. 1, 1982), pp. 135–149.

4.   Hedley Bull, 'International Theory: The Case for a Classical Approach', *World Politics* (Vol. 18, No. 3, 1966), pp. 361–77. This essay along with a number of rejoinders, is reprinted in Klaus Knorr

and James Rosenau (eds), *Contending Approaches to International Politics* (Princeton, N.J.: Princeton University Press, 1969).

5. For an excellent analysis of US dominance of international relations see Stanley Hoffmann 'An American Social Science: International Relations', *Daedalus* (Vol. 106, No. 3, 1977), pp. 41-60. This has been invaluable in writing this paper.

6. For a good overview of the history of the subject see William Olson and Nicholas Onuf 'The Growth of the Discipline: Reviewed' in Steve Smith (ed), *International Relations*, pp. 1–28. See also Richard Little, 'Teaching International Relations: Working with Paradigms', *Interstate: A Journal of International Relations* (1984, No. 1), pp. 3–10; Richard Little 'The Evolution of International Relations as a Social Science' in Randolph Kent and Gunnar Neilsson (eds), *The Study and Teaching of International Relations* (London: Francis Pinter, 1980), pp. 1–27; Steve Smith 'The Development of International Relations Theory', *Teaching Politics* (Vol. 14, No. 1, 1985), pp. 103–23; Michael Banks 'The Evolution of International Relations Theory', in Michael Banks (ed), *Conflict in World Society* (Brighton: Wheatsheaf Books, 1984), pp. 3–21.

7. Hedley Bull 'The Theory of International Politics 1919–1969', in Brian Porter (ed) *The Aberystwyth Papers: International Politics 1919–1969* (Oxford: Oxford University Press, 1972), p. 34.

8. Little, 'The Evolution of International Relations', p. 90.

9. E. H. Carr, *The Twenty Years Crisis* (London: Macmillan, 1939).

10. John Vasquez, *The Power of Power Politics* (London: Frances Pinter, 1983). A summary of the argument of this book can be found in John Vasquez 'Colouring it Morgenthau: New Evidence for an Old Thesis on Quantitative International Politics', *British Journal of International Studies* (Vol. 5, No. 3, 1979), pp. 210–28.

11. J. Handelman, J. Vasquez, M. O'Leary and W. Coplin, 'Color it Morgenthau: A Data-Based Assessment of Quantitative International Relations Research', unpublished paper, Prince Research Studies, Syracuse University, 1973, p. 31.

12. Most clearly expressed in K. Waltz, *Theory of International Politics* (Reading, Mass.: Addison-Wesley, 1979).

13. See, for example, Robert Keohane, 'The Theory of Hegemonic Stability and Changes in International Regimes, 1967–1977', in Ole Holsti, Randolph Siverson, and Alexander George (eds), *Change in the International System* (Boulder, Col.: Westview Press, 1980), pp. 131–62; Robert Keohane and Joseph Nye, *Power and Interdependence* (Boston: Little Brown, 1977); Stephen Krasner, *Defending the National Interest: Raw Materials Investments and U.S. Foreign Policy* (Princeton, N.J.: Princeton University Press, 1978).

14. For a review of Neorealism see the powerful attack on it in Richard Ashley, 'The Poverty of Neorealism', *International Organization* (Vol. 38, No. 2, 1984), pp. 225–86, and comments by Gilpin, Kratochwil and Andrews that follow (pp. 287–304, 305–20, 321–7). See also the collection of essays on the topic in Robert Keohane (ed), *Neorealism and its Critics* (New York: Columbia University Press, 1986).

15.   Carr, *The Twenty Years Crisis.*; Hans Morgenthau, *Politics Among Nations* (New York: Knopf, first published 1948, 5th edn 1973). Quotations from the 5th edn.
16.   Morgenthau, *Politics Among Nations*, p. 3.
17.   For a discussion of the role of Morgenthau's assumptions about human nature see Steve Smith, 'War and Human Nature' in Ian Forbes and Steve Smith (eds), *Politics and Human Nature* (London: Frances Pinter, 1983), pp. 164–179.
18.   For an early, and still most helpful, critique of Morgenthau's Realism see Stanley Hoffmann (ed), *Contemporary Theory in International Relations* (Englewood Cliffs, N.J.: Prentice-Hall, 1960), pp. 30–9.
19.   Hoffmann 'An American Social Science', pp. 45–70.
20.   Hoffman, 'An American Social Science', p. 45.
21.   Hoffman, 'An American Social Science', p. 47.
22.   Robert Rothstein, 'On the Costs of Realism', *Political Science Quarterly* (Vol. 87, No. 3, 1972), p. 348.
23.   Rothstein, 'Oh the Costs of Realism', p. 348.
24.   Hoffmann 'An American Social Science', p. 48.
25.   Richard Snyder, H.W. Bruck and Burton Sapin, 'Decision-Making as an Approach to the Study of International Politics' in Richard Snyder, H.W. Bruck and Burton Sapin (eds), *Foreign Policy Decision Making* (New York: Free Press, 1962), pp. 14-185.
26.   Morton Kaplan, *System and Process in International Politics* (New York: John Wiley, 1957).
27.   See Immanuel Wallerstein, *The Modern World System: Capitalist Agriculture and the Origins of the European World-Economy in the Sixteenth Century* (New York: Academic Press, 1974); and Immanuel Wallerstein, *The Modern World System II* (New York: Academic Press, 1980).
28.   John Burton, *International Relations: A General Theory* (Cambridge: Cambridge University Press, 1965); John Burton, *Systems, States, Diplomacy and Rules* (Cambridge: Cambridge University Press, 1968); and John Burton, *World Society* (Cambridge: Cambridge University Press, 1972).
29.   See, for example, Robert Keohane and Joseph Nye (eds), *Transnational Relations and World Politics* (Cambridge, Mass.: Harvard University Press, 1972); Richard Mansbach, Yale Ferguson and Dale Lampert, *The Web of World Politics* (Englewood Cliffs, N.J.: Prentice-Hall, 1976).
30.   Ray Maghroori and Bennett Ramberg (eds), *Globalism Versus Realism: International Relations' Third Debate* (Boulder, Col.: Westview Press, 1982).
31.   Michael Banks, 'The Evolution of International Relations Theory'.
32.   Michael Smith, Richard Little and Michael Shackleton (eds), *Perspectives on World Politics* (London: Croom Helm, 1981).
33.   Fred Northedge, 'Transnationalism: The American Illusion' *Millennium: Journal of International Studies* (Vol. 5, No. 1, 1976), pp. 21–7.
34.   Northedge, 'Transnationalism', p. 23.
35.   For a stimulating article that challenges this division see Peter Gourevitch, 'The Second Image Reversed: The International Sources

of Domestic Politics', *International Organization* (Vol. 32, No. 4, 1978), pp. 881-912.

36. I have discussed this assumption in democratic theory in Steve Smith, 'Reasons of State' in David Held and Christopher Pollit (eds), *New Forms of Democracy* (London: Sage, 1986), pp. 192–217.
37. Gourevitch, 'The Second Image Reversed'.
38. K. J. Holsti, *The Dividing Discipline: Hegemony and Diversity in International Theory* (London: Allen & Unwin, 1985).
39. Holsti, *The Dividing Discipline*, p. 127.
40. Hayward Alker and Thomas Biersteker, 'The Dialectics of World Order: Notes for a Future Archeologist of International Savoir Faire', *International Studies Quarterly* (Vol. 28, No. 2, 1984), pp. 121–142.
41. Alker and Biersteker, 'The Dialectics of World Order', p. 129.
42. Alker and Biersteker, 'The Dialectics of World Order'.
43. Alker and Biersteker, 'The Dialectics of World Order', pp. 138–9.

2 The Dominance of American Approaches in International Relations

Ekkehart Krippendorff

'A Big Power Such as the United States. . .'

There is none like it. Here, in a nutshell, we have the whole problem. There is hardly any scholarly text or general treatise on International Relations, trying to be as objective, sober, unbiased and clear-mindedly neutral as possible towards its subject (the relations between by now more than 150 nation-states and the so-called international system formed by them) where we would not find that innocuous little phrase 'a big power such as the United States'. It implies normality, a rational approach, equidistance, a neutral assessment of the general laws and rules of politics, and yet we all know that there is no other such power. Everybody knows that the second so-called superpower, the USSR, is a superpower remotely comparable to the United States only in terms of its military capacity and, upon closer examination, not even here. And there is certainly, for the forseeable future at least, no 'third superpower' emerging anywhere, let alone in existence. Neither Western Europe nor China, India or Japan, each 'big' in a certain way, can qualify let alone aspire to such rank and status. At first sight the innocent sounding modesty and self-belittlement of the 'such as' qualification, to be found, as I said, in scholarly textbooks as well as in high-level, policy-orientated analyses of the foreign affairs offices (but certainly also in journalistic columns) contains the very problem and challenge we are trying to deal with. What are the consequences and the implications of this terminology? It follows from it that the rules, the generalisations, the political laws deduced from, or associated with, this one nation and its political behaviour appear as universal, as scientifically sound and proven, as natural and normal, and yet, they describe or apply to this one country only; they are its laws and its rules of legitimate behaviour. It is the uniqueness of the United States, the

28

unprecedented and, above all, unrivalled concentration of economic, military and, not least, ideological power in one country which characterises the enormous disequilibrium of international politics. The term 'unprecedented', however, needs an historical qualification: Spain in the sixteenth, the Netherlands in the seventeenth and, most of all, Great Britain in the eighteenth and nineteenth centuries were equally without any serious rivals on the international stage, at least with regard to their will and designs to hegemonise world politics (which only one other great power during the large part of these centuries, Imperial China, did not have). However, in terms of capacities at least, considering the present very real threat of bringing the whole game of power-play to a final and suicidal end, these former 'leading powers' were inferior to the present hegemon.

In discussing the state of the discipline of International Relations, rather than world politics itself, we are obviously dealing only with a minor, probably even only a marginal aspect of the overall problem and phenomenon of the hegemony of one 'actor' on the world stage. On the other hand, if we think this one problem through, we might gain more general insights and a better, more differentiated view of the complexity of the issue of hegemony than from a global, politicoeconomic assessment of US power and predominance.

What then is 'the problem' when reflecting on the academic discipline of International Relations? In the last analysis we would have to rethink the nature of scholarship in general and the function and purpose of the social sciences in particular: who are we scholars, what are we doing, why are we doing it, whom do we serve? Obviously, these are questions that cannot be dealt with in a brief and simple way, yet we cannot avoid them. It should not be an intellectual luxury to reflect upon the nature and function of scholarship which has become, in modern times, such an enormous enterprise, absorbing so much energy, employing so many tens of thousands of people (intellectuals) organised in large institutions and international networks, demanding that society at large provide it with funds and resources at the expense of other possible investments. How can we justify that? What is the purpose of our work? If we look back into the history of the social sciences, it is both obvious, as well as complex in the details, that the systematic efforts at knowledge acquisition made by societies are always the reaction to given serious problems that need to be understood in order to be solved. Institutionally, it was once priests, wise men or philosophers who were given privileges in order to analyse, to explain and to suggest solutions that arose within or between societies. The quest for explanations of social phenomena arose from a desire for the maintenance or the reconstruction of social order. Today it is largely universities which have become entrusted with the performance of this seemingly necessary function. Let us, in brief, call it 'problem solving' or, to use the term more familiar to international relationists, 'conflict resolution'.

At the same time priests, wise men, philosophers – and consequently, the academic intelligentsia as well – have a further commitment to something as ambitious and vital as the search for truth. In order not to get lost in the epistemological labyrinth of defining 'truth', let me quickly replace this with another, less evocative yet sufficiently multidimensional conception of the undertaking: scholarship is committed to enlightenment, to emancipation, to the search and presentation of knowledge that might enable society at large to become the master of its destiny. What does this mean? It means that knowledge about society and its conflicts enables man, 'the people', to learn about the causes and effects of public actions, about the purposes and mechanisms of power wielded by those who rule and govern, about ways and means of solving social conflicts in the least damaging and harmful manner. By its very nature, the search for conflict resolution through the systematic discovery of truth is essentially dialectic: its aims at the maintenance or reconstruction of social stability and order, and it is driven beyond that narrow scope by its critical commitments when seeking root causes of conflicts. Socrates was condemned to death when his critical, questioning approach was seen (quite rightly) as undermining the privileged position of Athens's ruling classes although he aimed to be 'the teacher of man', and to achieve man's emancipation through reason. The history of (Western) social thought has produced and reproduced time and again this dialectic of truth as conflict resolution and truth as subversion of the powers that be: it has had its great martyrs (from Thomas More to Rosa Luxemburg), it has its great success stories (Enlightenment, with the American and French Revolutions as historic achievements), but also the permanent struggle of thousands of unknown academics torn between an expected commitment to serve those who play the tune and a commitment to the moral imperatives of telling undesired truths as they see it. We have to live with this, and we would be well advised to suspect that public success of academic work might have been achieved at the expense of the critical dimensions of the search for truth which, by definition, is subversive and transcends existing paradigms of order and stability.

These all too brief and synthetic remarks are necessary in order to give a proper perspective to the more modest task of discussing the state of International Relations and the problem of an alleged American intellectual hegemony over it. I think the problem lies somewhat deeper than in seeing this empirically relatively easily demonstrated dominance as yet another manifestation of 'American imperialism', as a corollary to US economic and military power in the world arena. There is more to it than that. The problem of International Relations being torn between big-power rationalisation and the raising of critical, transcending questions has to be recognised in the discipline since it is being institutionalised and practised through research and teaching wherever we are. Let me start with what is, to my mind, a correct observation by Fred Halliday who, when reviewing two recent books on our discipline (one British and one American) talked about the 'apparently weak impact of the discipline upon contemporary academic and intellectual culture. . . Few cognate disciplines seem to take note of what occurs in International Relations. . . In the wider intellectual culture, the names and controversies of International Relations have far less diffusion and recognition than the debates and personalities of economics or sociology, philosophy or psychology'. Why is this so? Halliday sees a basic fault in the fact that the discipline, because of something that one might call an 'inferiority complex' about the 'hard sciences' and the natural sciences in particular, had given in to becoming more and more empirical, quantitative, ahistorical, even mathematical; a tendency that is certainly strong, maybe even prevalent in the social sciences in general. 'The sooner International Relations can emancipate itself from the myths of empiricism, and the feckless taxonomies thrown up by its enthusiasts, the quicker it will be able to realise its own theoretical potential'. I will return to this point later.

The real explanation of why International Relations, even though strong and growing in quantitative terms, unsurpassed in the size and international participation of its conferences, overwhelming in the papers, books and magazines it produces, is nevertheless so weak and stale, so barren and intellectually boring seems to lie in a different direction which Halliday indicates by saying: 'Practitioners of International Relations acquire wider intellectual reputations only when they cross the portals of state power. . .'. It is what one might call 'the Kissinger syndrome': the secret, never or only rarely openly admitted ambition of the members of this particular branch of the academic community to be accepted by or adopted into the real world of policy making, to gain access to the inner halls of power. Here we touch upon something that is specifically American in the sense of an American tradition and understanding of Political Science, and upon something that is more academic to the discipline of International Relations at large.

From its very beginning, even as far back as the foundation of the American republic, a science of politics was seen as a necessary and integral part in the education of a democratic public. Quite differently from Western Europe, and for very obvious or at least well-known reasons, American democracy could evolve without the obstacles of *ancien régimes*, of feudal institutions, of aristocratic classes and structures to be overcome by force or slowly transformed and dissolved as was the case in Europe. If there was anything like 'political education' as a programme in European societies, it developed and was practiced as an 'oppositional project' on the margins or 'from the bottom' of society by radical political groups and parties, notably by and within the socialist parties. Not so in the United States, where 'civic education' was a major concern of the 'centre', of the establishment, of the enlightened elites who wanted and needed an educated public able to vote and participate on the basis of sound, balanced judgements and not on the basis of emotions or narrow class interests; not the least concern was the integration of people with a large variety of national and ethnic backgrounds. Thus there was a vested interest in the creation of a 'political science' (even though not yet under this name, of course) that served the function of political or civic education. The later emergence of a Political Science discipline had, therefore, always a practical, educational, institutional orientation. Its purpose was not, as tended to be the case in Europe, to educate the masses to fight for their rights and for 'more democracy' or even for a 'new (socialist) society', but quite the contrary: to make people accept the results of the American revolution, to teach them the value of the constitution given to them by the Founding Fathers, to make them identify with and 'love' their country and its institutions. Consequently (and these are obviously very broad and crude generalisations), to be a Political Science teacher or even professor and also to shoulder the responsibilities of political power was not seen as a contradiction. On the contrary, it would be the fulfilment of one's academic and intellectual profession. In Woodrow Wilson the United States had, in fact, a renowned Political Science professor in the highest office. And, in reverse, it is to this day not at all unusual for former government officials to finish their public lives as teachers of 'government' in colleges or as prominent researchers in renowned academic or quasi-academic institutions. What I called the 'Kissinger syndrome' is therefore not at all new. It is rather a mainstream phenomenon in American political culture. This is a relatively unique phenomenon (relatively, because there are similarities in Italy, for example, where quite a few members of the governing elite come from academic professions and keep these ties even while in office). The 'critical dimension' of the social sciences, its subversive, status-quo-transcending commitment to social change, to radical innovations and/or to underprivileged classes of society is, crudely put, rather underdeveloped in the US. This is even more true of the later offspring of Political Science, International Relations.

International Relations as a new discipline came into being in the United States as a government initiative, an effort not only to enhance research on the origins of international conflicts and their solutions for the benefit of those in charge of international politics, but also to train qualified diplomatic and analytically knowledgeable personnel at the higher and middle level of government departments concerned with the outside world. The view that the conduct of foreign policy was something too complex and remote for the ordinary citizen to have a balanced and knowledgeable opinion on, has a long tradition in the practice of governments and dating back certainly to long before the revolutions of the eighteenth and nineteenth centuries. Here was, and is, a realm that should and must be protected from 'democracy', from 'the people', the *arcanum imperii*', the occasional rhetoric of 'open covenants openly arrived at' notwithstanding. Certainly the centrepiece of foreign policy, military and security matters, should not be made subject to the whims and the emotions of a fluctuating and narrowly provincial 'public opinion', presumably more interested in bread-and-butter issues than in expensive grand designs or the complex and sophisticated games of international diplomacy. There is thus a built-in logic for international relationists, whether in the United States or elsewhere, leading them to be government- and power-oriented, to do research that is policy-oriented and to train young people for future government positions, rather than to be critical and committed to questioning the existing order or the 'national interests' of their respective states. With such a 'negative' attitude and orientation they would not even get a job, to say the least.

I indicated that the discipline of International Relations came into existence on the initiative of interested governments who followed the US example. The history of this discipline tells us something about its character and function, to be sure a function that can be – and, I think, should be – changed, but which must be understood particularly for the purposes of the topic of 'The Dominance of the American Approaches'. Roughly speaking, the discipline as a systematic and purposeful scholarly enterprise was born as a side product of the Versailles Peace Conference in 1919. In its immediate aftermath the American Council on Foreign Relations, the British Royal Institute of International Affairs and others were founded, by-passing the more rigid, conservative university institutions and aiming specifically at analysing the causes of the breakdown of the pre-war order for the explicit purpose of learning from it for the future. In fact, however, the solution was believed to have been found already with the creation of the League of Nations: that is, it was international law and an embryonic organisation of the sovereign nation states in the form of a 'states' parliament' which was seen as the guarantee for international peace. We know now that it was not, and the lesson was heeded after the next world war in institutionalising the hegemony of the so-called major powers within a universal assembly of nation states. This meant, in effect, the institutionalisation of US hegemony, with a secondary and regionally limited role conceded to the Soviet Union and its smaller 'empire'. During these important formative years we observe the second and now serious foundation of International Relations as an academic discipline, where the United States, with an infinitely more flexible system of higher education, took the lead in that direction. The American initiatives were propelled by the dramatic need for qualified diplomatic and other politico-economic personnel for the post-war tasks awaiting the newly born 'superpower': the creation and consolidation of an international order in its own image, the 'free world'.

This is the political background, the framework for the emergence of the discipline, for teaching and writing about International Relations: it meant, in effect, teaching and writing about US foreign policy or at least about the reconstruction of a United States-led world order. This bias was its birthmark – or, more pointedly, it was the very reason for its creation. The critique, the denunciation of American dominance in this particular field is, therefore, immanent: it states nothing but the obvious. It was and remained an American discipline not only because of the aforementioned flexibility of the American university system which allowed it to adopt this newcomer and give it a proper place next to the older faculties and departments (one need only look at the often successful resistance of European academic institutions to accept even the much less controversial and much older field of Political Science as a legitimate discipline); its success was also a function of the resources made available to it. If (West) Germany is typical of Western Europe, then it took until the mid-1960s for the first chairs in International Relations to be created (a country like Italy has still hardly more than three or four of them). By that time International Relations was, as we all know, already an academic community in its own right with dozens of specialised journals, hundreds of chairs, dozens of departments, regular large conferences and professional organisations in the United States, with marginal appendices of non-American participants as the poor relations on the backbenches. Not until the 1970s did European academic planners realise that they would have to make an effort as well if they did not want to remain hopelessly behind. The European initiatives were motivated largely by the realisation that they, too, needed qualified personnel to make their voices heard in world politics. This need was felt particularly in the increasingly important area of 'security', of arms control negotiations and strategic thinking, the language and terminology of which had to be learned. The language was English, of course, or rather American English. What could be more natural and obvious than to send students to the United States to learn from the Big Brother, to study and translate American books. Not the least advantage was (and is) that they were infinitely richer in terms of empirical data, often based on first-hand experience in extra-European (and extra-American of course) regions of the world.

To repeat, this was by definition and intent policy-oriented research and scholarship. But did it contain that other crucial dimension of the commitment to truth, the transcending critical faculty? Was it aiming at the transcendence of the government-service function toward the higher, the only ultimately dignifying orientation of emancipation? This would have meant, concretely speaking, the emancipation from a US or Free World national interest perspective. It is not by chance that the scholars involved in the protest movement of those years came from so many disciplines and fields of study, but rarely from Political Science and hardly at all from International Relations. It would be wrong to interpret the abstinence of the International Relation community from getting involved (concerning Vietnam) as a sign of its greater intellectual maturity and its commitment to a more rational, *realpolitik* understanding as opposed to the emotional idealism of poorly informed and poorly qualified non-experts. It shows, rather, that International Relations had never really been a strictly academic, independent, critical scholarly enterprise. And it still is not. It should give us something to think about, how little if at all this discipline has been affected by the Vietnam experience; how little if at all the enormous losses of lives and the destruction of the social and ecological fabric of a small and distant culture by American power have made an impact on the orientation and the self-conscience of the large community of international relationists. Hardly anybody has seen the need for a critical reassessment of the categories, the paradigms and the socio-political functions of this particular field of scholarship. Just as in public political consciousness at large, 'Vietnam' has been forgotten. It has been reduced, at best, to another case study for empirical analysis. The search for theory has not been disturbed by it. We, and they go on as academically aloof as ever.

This aloofness should be interpreted within the framework of the historical educational function of American Political Science as indicated earlier: to provide a rationale for, and legitimacy to, the working and the work of government and governments, to make people understand and accept, rather than criticise and reject. The seemingly sterile, formalised, rigidly sober and dispassionate debates about concepts and approaches, about patterns and variables, systems and hypotheses, levels and frameworks of analysis, are all implicitly designed to be variations of one theme: 'a big power such as the United States'. One might disapprove of a particular policy, a particular decision, but basically American foreign policy is to appear as normal, reasonable, legitimate by the objective standards of the international behaviour of any state. 'Since Morgenthau', writes K.J. Holsti (i.e., since the 1950s), 'the essential questions to be explored, the emphasis on recurrence and generalisation, the assumption of all-encompassing theory, and the underlying model of a world of independent nation-states have remained, for the most part, unaltered'.[1] This is still true today: a world of independent nation states of which the US is just one out of more than 150.

This, then, is the Great Lie of American International Relations: the seductive search for a theory that can qualify as 'scientific' by positivistic standards, a theory above and aloof from history and political economy, a theory valid for the relations between state actors at any time and any place, irrespective of the size, dimension, ideological profile and overall position of given states in the international system. It has led to the production of a set of categories, paradigms and parameters which make the United States as *the* world power disappear behind the smokescreen of a seemingly scholarly and objective academic language. I call this search for a general theory 'seductive' because it plays upon the hidden dream of discovering, eventually, some law equivalent to the law of gravity, some formula similar to Einstein's theory of relativity. It is the dream, of a value-free discipline, modelled after the natural sciences and not forced to come to terms, critically, with the unique and frightening accumulation of power in conjunction with the world mission of the United States of America. That central problem and concern of most non-American scholars and observers is relegated to the realm of opinion, but is not part of the work of scholars in the field of International Relations theory. In K.J. Holsti's words: 'Contemporary theory. . . guides research into specific phenomena, problems, or processes, and avoids explanations at a high level of generality.' It avoids not only explanations: it avoids, paradoxically, dealing with and facing American international politics. There are more books written on American foreign policy than can be counted, let alone read, including solid ones, critical ones but also, of course, poor and superficial ones. Yet these do not spring from explicit theoretical foundations, and they are not being produced by those engaged in the formulation, testing and reformulation of hypotheses aiming at a better, more scholarly and thus a critical understanding of the United States in the second half of the twentieth century. US International Relations theoreticians have contributed very little indeed to foreign policy analysis in general and to the analysis of the United States in particular. They have left this important and crucial task to the political generalists, to journalists or to men with political ambitions. The products of the latter should not be judged by the standards of scholarship or academic–intellectual achievements; they are written for the day and will be forgotten as soon as they have been discussed by their peers and the restricted circle of foreign policy intellectuals. I agree with the recent assessment on 'Progress in the Study of International Conflict' by Simowitz and Price who state that in fact the theoreticians themselves often confuse hypothesis-building and classifications with theory: 'most hypotheses tested in international relations research are not logical consequences of some theory', and consequently they 'have not yielded much progress over the past thirty years' yet there 'continues to be a proliferation of studies seeking to uncover additional empirical generalizations'[2]. The more this search continues, as a sort of self-propelling and self-generating activity, the more elusive are the results: 'we appear to have more "facts" than we can account for' and 'we lack any sense of direction regarding the road in which our search should be heading'. In short, judging by standards of scholarship and the purpose of scientific knowledge as a problem-solving social activity, International Relations as practised in the United States is largely a misdirected failure. It is certainly not directly responsible for the 'clear and present danger' the United States presents today in the international arena, but it shares a good deal of the responsibility by not contributing to a critical perspective, transcending the present in the emancipatory tradition and through the truth-seeking function of academia.

What is largely absent in American International Relations theory is the realisation that such theory has to be historical: not in the sense of, again, hypothesis testing based on historical data, but in the sense of a historical understanding and conceptualisation of the international system and of the emergence of the United States as a hegemonic power, as *the* hegemonic power today. There is no neat formula for this and the search for it is bound to fail. But a theory based upon history, working with historical categories (not historical data), interpreting the structures of the present in the light of the past requires also a creative incorporation and learning from the thinking about politics on the part of the great political philosophers of the past as our contemporaries. By acting as if nobody has ever seriously and systematically thought about the great problems of conflict and co-operation, of war and peace, of wealth and deprivation, of order and justice in the relations between societies and states, the theory of International Relations is impoverished and becomes reduced to research techniques void of content and perspective. It becomes blind to the rich intellectual and analytical heritage not only of our Western past but of other cultures as well. The result is a tendency to identify International Relations theory with the rationalisation and legitimation of US power and interests. It contributes to the destruction of this discipline as an intellectually stimulating enterprise, undermines its problem-solving function and its role as a critical instrument of change for a better world.

NOTES AND REFERENCES

1. K.J. Holsti, *International Politics: A Framework for Analysis*, 2nd ed. (Englewood Cliffs, N.J.: Prentice-Hall, 1971).
2. Roslyn L. Simowitz and Barry L. Price, 'Progress in the Study of International Conflict: A Methodological Critique', *Journal of Peace Research* (Vol. 23, No. 1, 1986)

3 State and Society in International Relations: A Second Agenda

Fred Halliday

For the last two decades much of the theoretical debate within International Relations has focused on the question of the state. Some discussion has been around the analytic primacy of the state as the constitutive actor in international relations, while some has focussed on normative questions, of the degree to which the state can be regarded as the primary guarantor of what is good, within and between states. 'State-centric' realism has reasserted traditional positions on the state and has, through the emergence of Neorealism, asserted new ones, especially in the field of international economic relations. Other paradigms have challenged the primacy of the state, either by asserting the role of non-state actors, as in theories of interdependence and transnationalism, or by asserting the primacy of global systems and structures over specific actors, state or non-state. All three of these approaches have been influenced by broader trends within political science: Realism by orthodox political theory; Transnationalism by the Pluralist and Behavioural rejection of the state in favour of studying actions; Structuralism by theories of socioeconomic determination.

In the late 1980s it would seem that this debate within International Relations has reached an impasse. The three paradigms, with their many variations and reformulations, remain vigorous, and the numbers of their adherents have waxed and waned with professional development and intellectual fashion. However, there is no sign that any one of them can or will prevail over the others. The challengers to Realism are still seeking to refute it and displace it, while proponents of Realism repeat the reasons why the challengers are inadequate. The search for a single paradigm, for a 'normality' defined in Kuhnian terms, has produced a situation of, for many, unsatisfactory pluralism.[1]

It can, however, be argued that a pluralism of paradigms is, in fact, more of an indication of a healthy discipline than a mono-paradigmatic normalcy in which other perspectives, the research programmes they suggest, the very concepts and indeed facts they point us to, are precluded. The exclusive and chloroforming world of the 1950s in many social sciences, where one paradigm reigned in an institutionalised self-confidence, is one to which few friends of International Relations or social science more generally would want to return. It can, moreover, be argued that the very pursuit of paradigm refutation, on narrowly intel-lectual grounds, is a misplaced venture, since the reasons for the attractiveness and tenacity of a specific approach are multiple: not only intellectual coherence, but also institutional support, the influence of trends and conventional wisdoms within social science as a whole and the broader climate of the times.

International Relations has, in general, been too defensive about the degree to which its own history and development have been the product of influences from outside the discipline itself, whether from other university departments or from the real world. It is striking the degree to which it lacks historical self-awareness (beyond that of intellectual evolution) or a sociology of its own growth, something all disciplines need for proportion and self-criticism. Such a self-awareness, historical and sociological, is not a form of self-negation: the fact that intellectual fashion or the preferences of funding agencies – not least governments – influence the development of an academic subject is unavoidable. What can result from such a broader awareness and acknowledgement of what all practitioners know, without saying so, to be the case is that the survival of paradigms, and their eventual demise, owe much to factors that mere intellectual assault or criticism cannot reach: old paradigms go marching on, until the non-academic as well as the academic worlds no longer have use for them. This will remain true of realism however many times it is refuted. Similarly, as long as there are people who wish to change the world on moral grounds, and there are lawyers who believe in the, albeit limited, effectiveness of their trade, then forms of Idealism will remain with us.[2]

To accept the legitimacy and inevitability of paradigmatic pluralism is not, however, to suggest that the reasons for theoretical diversity are not of interest, nor that all paradigms can be treated as equally valid: in the case of the debate on the state, it is worth posing the question as to why the debate of the last three decades has made so little progress. There has been no resolution, and relatively little conceding of ground. One reason, inscribed in Kuhn's own work and in that of his followers, is that paradigms are incommensurable, i.e., because they deploy different concepts and conceptual systems, and ask different questions and select different facts, their arguments cannot be matched one against the other.[3] Any cogent paradigm can provide a plausible explanation of 'anomalies', or trends in the real world, that others might see as threatening its validity: thus Realists can incorporate multinational corporations (MNCs), Interdependence theorists the continued role of security issues, and Structuralists the rise of the newly industrialised countries (NICs). As Kuhn has written: 'All historically significant theories have agreed with the facts, but only more or less'. The impasse on the state is, therefore, in part a product of a deeper theoretical impasse that itself determines a non-encounter on the state. A second reason, identified in, amongst other places, much recent literature on international political economy, is that the development of perspectives of the state's place in International Relations has itself been a contradictory process confirming neither simple Realist nor non-Realist analyses. The identifying and accumulating of ways in which the state has lost its previous dominance can be countered by another list of ways in which it has maintained or even enhanced it: the state has both strengthened *and* weakened its position. No simple empirical resolution of these competitive listings is possible, any more than one is in theory. If the Realists do appear to be unduly complacent in the assertion that little or nothing has really changed, the challengers often overstate the degree to which states are no longer central actors, both in their analysis of the recent course of international relations and in the recurrent tendency to extrapolate current trends into an apparently proximate and desirable stateless future. The theoretical comprehension of the contradictory process (state-enhancement/state-displacement) is one that can take us beyond the present polarisation.

There is, however, a third reason for the impasse, one that goes to the heart of International Relations – to the concepts it bases itself upon, to the research programmes it stimulates, and to its relation with other disciplines within the social sciences. This is the question of the definition of the state which is used. If it can be said that many politicians are working with the theories of long-dead economists, it sometimes appears as if theorists of International Relations are working with the concepts of long-dead political theorists (and, in a dogged pursuit of 'science', long-dead philosophers of science). For parallel to, but largely unacknowledged within, the International Relations debate on the state over the past twenty years there has been another debate on the state, within sociology, on how exactly the state operates. Most significantly perhaps, at the very time when the innovators and proponents of new paradigms within International Relations have been seeking to reject or reduce the salience of the state, the comparable trend within sociology has been to re-examine the state and to reassert its centrality in historical and contemporary contexts. A major exchange in favour of the state has been taking place. The title of a collection of essays on this issue, *Bringing the State Back In*, which resumes this debate and contains articles by many of its leading practitioners, suggests a contrary but crucially relevant development in a cognate discipline to International Relations which has considerable implications for our own, often unwarrantedly solipsistic, discussion on this issue.[4] What this development suggests is that one way to reassess the debate on the state within International Relations is to study this parallel discussion, and in so doing to question the exclusive definition of the state around which much of the International Relations debate has implicitly revolved. The argument is not about whether we are or are not 'state-centric', but what we mean by the state.

It is not at first obvious that there is a problem about the definition of the state in International Relations, for the simple reason that the operative distinction is implicit and not conventionally subject to extended theoretical or empirical analysis. It is indeed paradoxical that a concept so central to the whole discipline should escape explication as this one has. One can find many discussions of war, sovereignty, institutions and so forth, but one can search in vain in the textbooks for comparable discussion of the state. International Relations theorists assume we know what it is: Bull that it is a political community, Waltz that it is in practice coextensive with the nation.[5] The reason is that International Relations as a whole takes as given one specific definition: what one may term the national-territorial totality. Thus the 'state' (e.g., Britain, Russia, America, etc.) comprises in conceptual form what is denoted visually on a map – the country as a whole and all that is within it: territory, government, people, society. There could be no better summary of this view than that of Northedge in the introductory chapter to his *The International Political System*: 'A state, in the sense used in this book, is a territorial association of people recognized for purposes of law and diplomacy as a legally equal member of the system of states. It is in reality a means of organizing people for the purpose of their participation in the international system'.[6] It is not argued by those who use this concept favourably, especially Realists, that such a state exists empirically, but only that an abstraction of this kind, derived from political theory and international law, is heuristically the most appropriate for International Relations. In other words, theory based on this concept explains more about international relations and should, therefore, be maintained. This is a valid reason for maintaining an abstraction: the question is not whether it provides a basis for explanation, but rather how adequate the explanation it provides is. It should be evident, of course, that once this concept is accepted then, by definition, the question of non-state actors is largely prejudged.

The alternative concept of the state, as it is used in much recent sociological writing, is of a more limited kind. It denotes not the social–territorial totality, but a specific set of coercive and administrative institutions, distinct from the broader political, social and national context in which it finds itself. Influenced by the German tradition of Max Weber and Otto Hintze, Skocpol defines the state 'a set of administrative, policing and military organizations headed, and more or less well coordinated, by an executive authority'.[7] Many alternative definitions of the state can be provided within this sociological approach. However, this concept of coercive and administrative institutions serves to distinguish a quite separate concept of the state, and to suggest an alternative way in which the concept can be incorporated within discussion of international relations.

Within the sociological discussion of the state that has emerged over the past decades many problems remain unresolved. One is the question of delimiting the extent of the state: if the state is seen as the mechanism for dominating, regulating and reproducing a society under given social relations then the question arises of where to locate institutions that are formally independent but which are influenced by the state and parallel its regulatory and reproductive functions: schools, universities, churches, and, in some of its roles, the family. The debate on Althusser's conception of educational establishments as Ideological State Apparatuses was an example of this.[8] A second debate, well represented in *Bringing the State Back In*, concerns the 'autonomy' of the state: once the state is seen as institutionally distinct from society, the question arises of the degree to which it can act autonomously, and represent values separate from that society, even if it is ultimately constrained by it. The institutional concept of the state is, in part a means of resisting those Marxist theories that see the state as simply an expression of class or economic interest. The degree to which those in power can pursue policies against the apparent wishes of much of society (by imposing reforms or pursuing wars that are unpopular and destructive) poses this issue of autonomy quite clearly. For some, such as Skocpol, there is a distinct area of autonomy which is greatly enhanced by the state's international role; for others, such as Robert Brenner, a division of labour between societal administration and private appropriation should not be confused with any real autonomy,[9] and the Marxist theory of the state as a class instrument remains valid. A third debate, one located more specifically within the Marxist sociological tradition, has concerned the precise relation of the state to capitalism in the contemporary world. Going beyond the initial Marxist-Leninist view of the state as a mere instrument of class rule, this debate has generated a variety of alternative theses from the capital logic approach, to that which stresses the management of intra-elite conflicts, to the approach influenced by one reading of Gramsci according to which the function of the state is to maintain class hegemony, in all its dimensions – coercive, administrative, regulative, and ideological.[10]

The difference between these two conceptions of the state is reflected, in everyday language. In discussing land, we distinguish between the territory of the state, in its total sense, and the areas of land owned by the state, in its institutional sense. Similarly we distinguish between the population or working population of a state, and the percentage of that population who are directly employed it. In revolutions the institutional state is overthrown, but the total state remains. Yet much of the International Relations debate does seem to involve a confusion of these two meanings. Thus when critics of Marxism say it is a form of Realism because it is 'state-centric', this mixes up the two concepts of the state: Marxists use the term 'state' quite differently from Realists. The result is a prevailing dominance of the totality concept that, because of the very definition involved, precludes other areas of theoretical investigation. This is what a paradigm should do: Realists can and do argue that the issues, and the data, identified as relevant by other paradigms, are relatively insignificant.

Whether or not the sociological concept has greater analytic and explicatory potential than the national–territorial totality concept is a matter of debate. Yet whatever the final judgement on this score two broad contrasts are immediately evident. The first is that, for a discipline concerned with the interpretation of reality, the sociological concept is far less of an ideological abstraction than is the national-territorial totality one. The concept normally used in International Relations is not merely an analytic abstraction, but also one replete with legal and value assumptions (i.e., that states are equal, that they control their territory, that they represent their peoples). There could indeed be few concepts less 'realistic' than that of the sovereign state in its conventional International Relations guise. A second immediately relevant contrast is that the sociological approach enables us to pose much more clearly the question of the effectivity of the international dimension; i.e., why and how participation in the international realm enhances and strengthens states – and, in particular, why it enables them to act more independently of the societies they rule. This most central feature of the modern world – that states can be less responsive to, and representative of, their societies precisely because of their international role – is submerged, *ab initio*, by the assumptions of the totality concept.

The least that can be said, therefore, is that an alternative conceptualisation of the state permits analytic questions and avenues of research markedly different from those permitted within the totality approach. In the first place this alternative definition of the state opens up a set of conceptual distinctions that are often confused and conflated in literature on international relations, but which need to be separated out if the state–society relationship is to be more clearly identified. The very concept 'international' has, as many critics have pointed out, confused the issue by denoting as between nations what are usually relations between states. Morgenthau's classic, *Politics Among Nations*, is symptomatically mistitled. One distinction is that between the state, in this delimited sociological sense, and society, i.e., the range of institutions, individuals and practices lying beyond the direct control and financing of this central entity. Society itself may well not be homogeneous, comprising as it does different social classes and interest groups, and the access of these to the state may be different, depending upon the power, wealth and political skill of these groups.[11] The state–society relation is therefore variable. A second distinction is between state and government, i.e., between the ensemble of administrative apparatuses and the executive personnel formally in positions of supreme control. Conventional political discourse assumes that these are identical, just as the state–government pair are assumed to represent society as a whole. In orthodox usage, the indications 'prime minister' or 'president' of a country are thus readily replaced with the name of the country itself: 'Britain's position on INF is', etc. However, the state–government distinction may, in some situations, become of considerable relevance as elements within the state resist or actively oppose the policies of government. This may take relatively innocuous forms (press leaks, dragging of feet, arrangements of an agenda) but it can take much more acute forms, culminating in that most extreme of state–government contradictions, the military *coup d'état*. A third central distinction, is that between state and nation. The term 'nation–state', based as it is on an assumption of ethnic homogeneity and political representativity, is, in empirical terms, inappropriate to the modern world. Coercive states may well not represent the nation (i.e., the society they rule) at all, and where there is ethnic diversity, as there is in most states of the world, the state may represent the interests of one national group more than those of another. The question is therefore open as to how far the state represents the nation. While some International Relations theory, notably foreign policy analysis, has challenged the Realist conflation of these terms no alternative conceptualisation of the state has so far been counterposed to it.[12]

The sociological approach suggests, secondly, an alternative and less benign view of the origins of states. Its emphasis is on the state as intitially an instrument of coercion and extraction, both against the populations subjected to states and against rivals. As Tilly has shown, on the basis of detailed historical investigations, European states began as instruments of subjugation[13]; as protection rackets.[13] It may be that over the centuries these protection rackets have developed a more representational function, but this is contingent, something that varies in degree from country to country and may not be a completed process. It is worth remembering that the principle of one person one vote is something introduced into major Western states only since the Second World War.[14] The fact that in its origins the main function of the state is the seizure of land and goods, the subjugation of populations, and the waging of war against rivals is rather understated in conventional accounts of the rise of the modern system, which imply that states have been representative ever since 1648.

A third central theme is that states, and their internal organisation, have developed in a world-historical context, i.e., in interaction with, and imitation of, other states. Far from the internal constitution of states and societies being immune, at least until recently, to international phenomena it can be asserted that the international dimension provided the context and formative influence for these states, not only for the majority of the world states that are post-colonial and so shaped by the colonial experience, but equally for European states. The world economy, the breakup of mediaeval Christianity, the values of legitimacy – and above all, the pressures of economic and military competition – ensured this.[15] Important as this is in the critique of Marxism (as in Giddens and Mann) it is equally relevant as an alternative international theory to that of Realism, which derives the system from states.

A fourth constitutive theme is that states are formative of societies; of national consciousness; of the national ideologies that turn the arbitrary assemblages of people into nations; of national economies. States have always played a role in forming economies, not just through planning, taxation, and the promotion of sectors tied to the national, (specifically military) interest, but also through the regulation of economies through legislation specifying what is and is not legitimate and through the financial mechanisms of central banks. However international capital may or may not be in the 1980s, it cannot escape the regulatory powers of states. This was nowhere clearer than in the fluctuations of that most international of money markets, the City of London, at varying prospects for the 1987 UK General Election and in the face of the new powers of the Securities and Investments Board (SIB), as well as in the nervous response of the New York Stock Exchange to the appointment of a new US Federal Reserve Board chairman in June 1987. If the policies of the British and US states did not affect the money market, they would have ignored the polls and the advent of the SIB. The fallacy of much current writing on the state's role in the economy, in identifying state control only with formal state ownership of productive and financial services, ignores the much broader powers that states have historically maintained and still maintain *vis-à-vis* their economies.

Finally, there is an important set of questions pertaining to the state's own internal composition and relation to society that are raised by the development of historical sociology. As Michael Mann has shown, the question of state capacities, of how states administer populations and territories, and the manifold mechanisms for imposing and extending control, is one that richly repays comparative and historical investigation.[16] This approach frees the study of the state from the concept of sovereignty, the assumption that the state *does* have a monopoly of power and legitimacy within a delimited territory, and instead asks *how*, and how far, and with what changes, such control has developed. The premise of much

International Relations writing is that the state *is* sovereign, in controlling effectively the territory and population over which it rules. This is, however, an empirical simplification, even for the most effective of states. It precludes analysis of just how control is exercised and developed and how other factors, including international ones, may modify and affect a state's capacities to control.

These broad themes, recurrent in much of the recent sociological and historical–sociological literature, suggest many areas in which the alternative concept of the state can affect the study of International Relations. What follows are a few suggestions as to how, given this alternative paradigm, the study of international relations may be developed.

3.1 THE STATE AS DOMESTIC AND INTERNATIONAL ACTOR

The first, and for International Relations most significant, theme pervading this literature is that the state is seen as acting in two dimensions, the domestic and the international. In its simplest form, the state seeks both to compete with other states by mobilising resources internally, and to use its international role to consolidate its position domestically. For example, a state may appropriate territory, go to war, or pursue an arms control agreement to gain domestic advantage, while it may promote industrialisation, raise taxes, or treat an ethnic minority better, in order to achieve international goals. Conducted successfully, this two-front policy may work to the benefit of the state, and it is evident that those holding state power have many advantages in pursuing this approach. This two-dimensionality does, however, involve major risks: a state that places undue pressure on its own society in order to mobilise resources for international competition may provoke such an intense reaction that it is overthrown.[17] Alternatively, the pursuit of a domestically advantageous policy may lead the state into destructive conflicts with other states. Successful or not, however, this two-dimensional perspective on state policy indicates that for all actors within a specific society the international dimension is important for the conducting of policy and the waging of conflicts. Those in state power, and those associated with the state, will deploy international resources to contain domestic threats. These resources may be military, up to and including allied troops; economic, whether from other branches of an MNC or from international economic institutions as aid to embattled holders of state power; or political, in the form of moral support, treaties, or alliances proferred by friendly states. Much of international relations can be seen therefore as an internationalisation of domestic conflicts, of relations between state and society. Those opposed to states also seek such international contacts, and have, throughout modern history, made much of this dimension. There is certainly room for an International Relations of Anti-Systemic Forces, a substantial study of how those opposed to established states have, and can, internationalise their support. However, the reality would seem to be that here, as in purely domestic conflicts, the state and its associates have a distinct advantage and can mobilise resources within and beyond state boundaries far in excess of those who challenge them. The latter often lack resources and access to mechanisms for appropriate, and sufficiently powerful, international integration of anti-systemic activity.[18]

The sociological perspective on the state indicates the need to study, in a comparative and historical context, just how the international functioning of the state has affected the internal workings of the state apparatus itself. This theme in Hintze's studies of state formation involves examining how the international activities of states (war, territorial appropriation, diplomacy) have affected the social origin of personnel in the state, the predominance of some administrative branches within it, the values of state personnel, and the overall size and financing of the state. The role of military elements (the army as a whole, or individual commanders) within states and societies is the most eloquent example of this international determination of state formation. The longevity of aristocratic influence within European states, persisting long after the displacement of aristocratic landed power in the societies concerned, is an index of how the diplomatic function has affected the state as a whole. The influence on the United States state of its post-1945 adoption of a global role has been much commented upon and has led some liberal critics to talk of a 'national security state' in the United States. The enhanced power of the President, the ebb and flow of Congressional controls, the rise of new bureaucracies with international functions (CIA, NSC), and the changed character of the State Department are all instances of this impact of the international realm on the state apparatus. Nor is it necessarily the case that the ideologies and personnel of state apparatuses reflect only current changes in the outside world: the enduring influence of a colonial and great power past upon the post-1945 British state and its senior personnel is evident enough. In embattled revolutionary states, where the survival of the state is uncertain from month to month, the practicalities of ensuring security against invasion and subversion take an enormous toll on the allocation of resources, and on the time, nerves, and concentration of those in power, as well as affecting the conception of what is licit dissent.[19]

3.2 STATE INTERESTS AND SOCIAL FORCES

Equally, the relation of state to society is constantly affected by the international function. This is clear in all four of the dimensions that Michael Mann has seen as constitutive of state power: the ideological, the military, the administrative and the political. The economic benefits of imperialism to the British state have been much debated, but few can doubt the ideological benefits that did, and still do, accrue to the state because of its assertion of British power in far-flung places. The need to sustain armed forces, in peace as well as in war, has given the state a fundamental interest in intervention in the economy and in establishing close relations with those in society most relevant to this issue. This was as true in early modern Europe as it is today. The supportive role of the military lobbies in the United States, and the mechanisms (personal, institutional, financial) of interaction between the military firms, Congress, and the Pentagon have been well documented, as has the link (*e.g.*, in the Irangate affair) between covert operations abroad and private interests at home in the implementation of state policies.

The state recruits sections of domestic society for its international activities. At the same time both the state and society seek to gain support for their internal conflicts from international sources. Earlier, it was pointed out that the institutional concept of the state makes it possible to distinguish between the terms state, society, government and nation. Much of the relationship between these is constituted within specific societies, but there are many ways in which these relations acquire an international dimension: states seek to regulate their own position by obtaining international support; governments, social groups and ethnic groups try to enhance their position, *vis-à-vis* their own states, by obtaining international backing such as economic or military aid; and external actors seek to advance themselves against competitor states by establishing direct relations with elements within the latter's societies. One obvious case of such an interaction is the sponsoring of military coups in independent states: the promotion of government–state conflicts in rival countries. Another is the promotion of social unrest or ethnic upheaval in rival countries through money, arms, radio broadcasts, and diplomatic backing. Overall, the existence of the state–society relation permits alternative means of conducting international relations, in as much as it encourages states and social forces to pursue international policies that will enhance their positions with respect to each other.

3.3   SOCIETIES AND STATE SYSTEMS

The reciprocal interaction of international society and specific societies is not, however, effected solely through the mediation of the state or with the purpose of eventually influencing the state. There are other processes within society that are influenced by, and which can themselves influence, the relationship of a particular state to the international system, but which reflect processes quite separate from that of state activity on the international level. There are, on the one hand, long-term changes within a specific society that, at a moment of increasing impact on the state and on the politics of the government or executive, have major impact on the international activities of that state. Short of revolutionary upheavals, these can be changes of balance between different social groups, changes in ideology and attitude, and geographical shifts reflecting economic change. The rise of a merchant bourgeoisie in western Europe in the early modern period, with its resultant impact on state policy and religious–ideological orientation, was one of the constituent influences upon the emergence of the international system. The shifts in the United States polity, with the decline of the north-east hegemonic bloc in favour of the sunbelt, do much to explain the sharp changes in US policy between the 1970s and the 1980s. At the same time, the international may have a major impact on the social composition of a society such that it may also shape and influence the state. The most extreme instances of this are conquest and colonial rule, when new state systems may simply be imposed on subjugated societies. Short of such dramatic impositions of the international upon the individual society, there are many other means through which international economic and social changes can affect a particular society, enhancing the position of some social groups, and reducing the influence of others. Incorporation into the world system affects not only the international balance of (military) power, but also the balance of social power within societies.

3.4 DOMESTIC INTERESTS AND STATE POWER

This focus on the state-society relation may also help in re-examining, and re-theorising, the manner in which interests in a society that also have an international interest relate to state power. Some of this is encapsulated in empirical work on lobbies: campaigns to keep out foreign goods, to back associated enterprises abroad, to put pressure on foreign states to make concessions. Yet much of the debate on the relative influence of states and non-state actors has assumed a polarity in this regard, as if the MNC operating abroad wishes to act independently of states. This touches upon the unresolved question of the autonomy of the state, but the least that can be said is that in many areas the state is acting in harness with, and at the behest of, influential interests within society. Here again, a traditional 'black box' approach makes it difficult to answer the question of the MNC–state relationship, since it permits us only to examine the relationship internationally. Once it becomes possible, however, to examine the relation within a society, and to identify the degree of collaboration in the relative symbiosis of state and some sectors of society, then the nature of the international collaboration and apparent division of labour becomes clearer. There are cases where MNCs defy states by trading with countries, such as Nicaragua, Angola, South Africa or Russia, upon which the state wishes to impose economic pressure. In many other cases the state acts to promote and defend the MNC. When International Telephone and Telegraph (IT&T) ran into trouble in Chile, Geneen (head of the firm) called the White House. Congress has imposed conditions on US aid to countries that nationalise US firms without adequate compensation arrangements. If the relationship of state and (some parts of) society is seen as constituted domestically, and the international activities of each are seen in this light, then it may become easier to resolve the vexed question of how far states or non-state actors act independently of each other in world affairs.

3.5   REVOLUTIONS

The state–society relationship is central to another dimension of international relations, namely that of social upheaval and revolutions, and in particular the question of why revolutions have international effects. International Relations literature, in general, has relegated revolutions to a marginal position, while most of the sociological literature on revolutions tends to neglect the international implications.[20] It is the great merit of Skocpol's work that it seeks to interrelate the two, by showing the degree to which revolutions are to a considerable extent a product of inter-state and international factors, and by suggesting how the post-revolutionary consolidation of states and the extension of state power are influenced by international pressures. There could be no clearer demonstration of the interlinking of internal and international politics than the ways in which revolutions can be brought on by international factors, whether the mobilisation of dominated groups, or the weakening of previously secure dominators. Equally, however, the international consequences of revolutions suggest further consequences of the state–society relation: the compulsion of revolutionaries to promote, if not 'export', revolution abroad, and the anxiety and counter-revolutionary response which revolutions, even in the weakest of states, may provoke in hegemonic powers. The answer to both questions may lie to a considerable extent in the state–society relationship. Revolutionary states see an internationalisation of their struggle as part of domestic consolidation: militarily, in the gaining of like-minded allies: economically, in the winning of collaborative relationships with such allies; and ideologically, in the promotion at the international level of similar ideals to those which legitimate their own regime. On the side of those opposed to revolution, similar concerns may operate: the loss of a comparable society to a rival system weakens a state internationally, but also domestically; it serves to weaken its domestic legitimacy. As Raymond Aron has indicated, it is the preference for homogeneity in political arrangements for international legitimacy and stability that shows up both the crucial, if often understated, dependence of domestic power arrangements upon international factors, and the degree to which domestic factors, including the state–society relationship itself, influence the foreign policy of states.[21] The historical record of the past two centuries suggests that both projects (the promotion of revolution in other states and the overthrow of revolutionary regimes) usually fail in their declared goals. However, as with economic sanctions, the purposes of such ventures may be multiple, and may reflect broader ideological and domestically-orientated goals as much as the specifically declared goal of the operation. The study of the international dimensions of revolutions may, therefore, provide insight both into the considerable area of international relations that is affected by such upheavals and into the broader transnational causes of, and influences upon, domestic change.[22]

3.6 THE INTERNATIONAL SYSTEM

A distinctive theorisation of the state–society relationship has implications for the comprehensive question concerning the nature of the international system. Within current theory the term 'system' is used in a variety of ways, from the Realist conception of a system of states, in which the term is used in the loosest sense, to the applications of systems theory to International Relations (with rather modest results) and assertions of an international capitalist system by writers of Marxist or Marxist-influenced persuasion. The problem with the Realist theorists is that they avoid the question of the relationship of socioeconomic factors within states and internationally to the functioning of the system, the latter being seen in narrowly political terms. The problem with much Marxist writing is that it understates the role and distinct efficacy of states. This latter paradigm begs the question of why, if there is a world economy in which class interests operate transnationally, there is a need for states at all. What, in other words, is the specificity and effectivity of distinct states within a single economic totality? These dilemmas (the determinancy of the socioeconomic, the specificity of the political) cannot be answered within either a uniquely domestic or international context, but they suggest the need to identify how far each level does determine the system, and of how states function not only as independent actors in the system, but also as mediators and regulators of a broader set of interactions that, taken as a totality, constitute international society (however this 'society' is conceived).

Beyond an alternative grounding of the concept of system at the international level, and as it affects analysis of the contemporary world, such an alternative theorisation of the state also suggests another variant of conventional International Relations approaches,

namely an alternative *history* of the international system. Hitherto
we have been offered a predominant Realist view, through which
the international system, constituted by states, develops, grows, and
'expands' through the multiplication of states and the acceptance
by states of what Bull has termed the 'institutions' of inter-state
relations. That such a view has an implicitly evolutionist and
diffusionist foundation does not need underlining. For all the
pessimism of the Realist view, it tends to suggest an international
history that is rather too benign, and at variance with the sanguinary
process of imposition, resistance and reassertion of control that is
characteristic of International Relations in the colonial or third world
over the past four centuries. The alternative, and to date minority,
view of the system is that outlined by writers such as Wallerstein and
Wolf, whose surveys of the expansion of capitalism since 1450 have
offered a quite distinct international history depicting a system based
on capitalist market relations.[23] The theoretical presupposition of
Wallerstein's approach, that the development of international society
is constituted by the spread of a social system at the international
level, as distinct from the Realist stress upon a growth of relations
between separate and analytically primary states, is cognate with that
of historical sociology with its stress upon the world-historical context
of international developments and the multiple conflicts, intra- and
inter-national, that have marked it. However, where this history of
world society may be questioned, as already indicated, is in its neglect
of the political instance, the state, and in its market-based assumption
about the capitalist homogeneity of the contemporary world.

To stress the broader, capitalist, character of the international
system is not to argue that social relations are in any simple sense
transnational. Marx in the nineteenth century and much apparently
contemporary sociological thinking make the same mistake in assuming that the state was simply being swamped by transnational
processes. This view, rather, takes the state seriously, but questions
more precisely its role within this broader socioeconomic context.
In other words, it examines the function of distinct states within a
broader socioeconomic context; whether it is to represent different
ruling groups, or to represent distinct and autonomous state interests,
or to regulate and maintain a system of international hierarchy. There
is the further question concerning the implications of a world composed of two socioeconomic systems: in broad terms, one capitalist
and one centrally planned. The functions of states – and, not least, of
their military aspects – in administering, prosecuting and controlling

this rivalry between competitive and contrasting social systems, invite further investigation. Many is the writer on International Relations who has told us, on the basis of exhaustive comparative data, that there is little or no correlation between foreign policy output and socioeconomic system: at the risk of profanity, students of post-1945 history may be forgiven for questioning this assumption.

The implications for International Relations of this alternative conceptualisation of the state will take time to work out, and will involve greater recognition of trends in other social sciences, sociology, and the more sociologically literate branches of history, that have hitherto received little recognition. There is no doubt that any such evolution will involve uncertainties and disappointments: a world in which the state is no longer conveniently taken to represent the totality, and in which 'nation state', 'sovereignty', and 'national interest' are no longer secure landmarks, will be harder to chart. On the other hand, there are substantial areas of International Relations, notably foreign policy analysis and international political economy, where significant work along these lines has already taken place. Ultimately, the validity and relevance of any conceptual approach lies in the relevance of its conclusions and the degree of explanatory power they display. It may therefore be that one way to overcome the current immobility on the state will be to redefine the state itself.

NOTES AND REFERENCES

1. The argument for a diversity of paradigms is energetically made in Paul Feyerabend, *Against Method* (London: Verso Books, 1975). Feyerabend's anarchist theory that any paradigm 'goes' is implausible, but his demonstration of the benefits of paradigm competition, and of the many 'non-scientific' factors that go into scientific development, and into the acceptance of paradigms, is convincing.
2. One notable exception is Stanley Hoffmann's 'An American Social Science: International Relations', *Daedalus* (Vol. 106, No. 3, October 1977). Hoffman avoids the tendency of some others who have criticised the manner in which a certain North American orthodoxy has dominated International Relations, namely to pose the question in national terms as that of an 'American' or 'non-American' approach. What both the orthodox exponents of International Relations, and their nationalist critics, obscure is that there is immense diversity within the US literature, and that it is the denial of this diversity that constitutes the real problem with the orthodox US presentation.
3. On incommensurability, see T.S. Kuhn, *The Structure of Scientific Revolutions* (Chicago: University of Chicago, 1970), pp. 148ff.

4. Peter Evans, Dietrich Rueschemeyer and Theda Skocpol (eds), *Bringing the State Back In* (Cambridge: Cambridge University Press, 1985). Among other contributions see John Hall, *Powers and Liberties* (Harmondsworth: Penguin, 1986), John Hall (ed.), *States in History* (Oxford: Basil Blackwell, 1986), and Anthony Giddens, *The Nation State and Violence* (Cambridge: Cambridge University Press, 1985). Giddens, p. 17, distinguishes the two meanings of the state but does not see this as posing a major problem. A recent discussion of some implications of Giddens's work for International Relations is found in Andrew Linklater, 'Realism, Marxism and Critical International Theory', *Review of International Studies* (Vol. 12, No. 4, October 1986).

5. Hedley Bull, *The Anarchical Society* (London: Macmillan, 1977), p. 8; Kenneth Waltz, *Man, The State and War* (New York: Columbia University Press, 1954), pp. 172–8.

6. F.S. Northedge, *The International Political System* (London: Faber & Faber, 1976), p. 15. A more recent statement of this classical position can be found in Alan James, *Sovereign Statehood* (London: Allen & Unwin, 1986). James presents the concept of the state as straightforward, using it to comprise 'territory, people and a government' (p. 13).

7. Theda Skocpol, *States and Social Revolutions* (Cambridge: Cambridge University Press, 1979), p. 29.

8. Louis Althusser, 'Ideology and Idological State Apparatuses', in *Lenin and Philosophy* (London: New Left Books, 1971).

9. Robert Brenner, 'The "Autonomy" of the State', Isaac Deutscher Memorial Lecture, London School of Economics, 21 November 1986.

10. For a detailed overview see Bob Jessup, *The Capitalist State* (Oxford: Martin Robertson, 1982).

11. Any concept of 'international society' presupposes a concept of domestic society. The concept of 'society' implicit in the English Realist concept of 'international society' is as selective as the concept of 'state'. If we take Bull's definition, of international society as 'a group of states, conscious of certain common interests and common values', it can thus be asked how pertinent such a definition of society is to many specific societies existing in the world today.

12. The long-run implications of foreign policy analysis are such as to challenge the prevailing totality concept of the state: but much of the literature has been within a behavioural framework that ignores the relevance of sociological writing on the state, or has become restricted by a fetishism of decision-making as an end in itself.

13. Charles Tilly, 'War Making and State Making as Organised Crime' in Evans, Rueschemeyer and Skocpol, *Bringing the State Back In*, and Charles Tilly (ed.), *The Formation of National States in Europe* (Princeton, N.J.: Princeton University Press, 1975). For a masterful exposition of the role of violence in constituting modern states see J.B. Barrington Moore, *The Social Origins of Dictatorship and Democracy* (London: Allen Lane, 1966).

14. Goran Therborn, *What Does the Ruling Class do When it Rules?* (London: New Left Books, 1978) provides an illuminating survey

of the relationship of external factors to the functioning of state apparatuses.

15. Felix Gilbert (ed.), *The Historical Essays of Otto Hintze* (New York: Oxford University Press, 1975), Chapters 4–8, provides detailed historical analysis of the relationship between individual state formation and the international competition between states in modern European history. For an illuminating study of the impact of international political factors on state economic policies see Gautam Sen, *The Military Origins of Industrialisation and International Trade Rivalry* (London: Frances Pinter, 1984).

16. See Michael Mann, *The Sources of Social Power*, Vol. 1 (Cambridge: Cambridge University Press, 1976), and his essay in John Hall (ed), *States in History*, and his 'The Autonomous Power of the State: Its Origins, Mechanisms and Results', *Archives Européenes Sociologiques* (Vol. 25, 1984).

17. See Skocpol, *States and Social Revolutions*, Chapter 1.

18. A pioneering survey of the relative international accesses of hegemonic and dominated classes is that of Carolyn Vogler, *The Nation State* (Aldershot: Gower, 1985).

19. Goran Therborn, 'The Rule of Capital and the Rise of Democracy', *New Left Review* (No. 103, May–June 1977). As Therborn points out, the principle of 'one person – one vote' was not effective in either the United States or the United Kingdom until the 1960s.

20. The briefest glance at standard International Relations textbooks can show how little the implications, theoretical and empirical, of these events have been taken into account, with the partial exceptions of discussion of intervention and 'subversion'. For a comparable neglect of the international dimension within most conventional sociological literature on revolution see Stan Taylor, *Social Science and Revolutions* (London: Macmillan, 1984).

21. Raymond Aron, *Peace and War* (London: Weidenfeld & Nicolson, 1966), pp. 373–81.

22. See Martin Wight, *Power Politics* (Harmondsworth: Pelican, 1979), p. 92. In an illuminating footnote, Wight suggests that for the majority of the years between 1492 and 1960 international relations have been 'revolutionary' rather than 'normal'. The implications of this have not, however, been conventionally recognised.

23. Immanuel Wallerstein, *The Modern World System* (New York: Academic Press, 1974) and Eric Wolf, *Europe and the People Without History* (Berkeley, CA: University of California Press, 1984).

4 Critical Theory and the Inter-paradigm Debate*

Mark Hoffman

4.1 INTRODUCTION

International Relations as an academic discipline is at a major crossroads. Since it was first constituted as an academic discipline in the immediate aftermath of the First World War, International Relations has moved through a series of 'debates' with the result that in the course of its development, and as a consequence of these debates, International Relations theory has been undergoing constant change and modification. After moving through the debate between Idealism and Realism in the inter-war period, between Realism and Behaviouralism in the Great Debate of the 1960s, through to the complementary impact of Kuhn's development of the idea of 'paradigms' and the post-Behavioural revolution of the early 1970s and on to the rise of International Political Economy and neo-Marxist, Structuralist dependency theory in the late 1970s and early 1980s, International Relations has arrived at a point that Banks has termed the 'inter-paradigm debate'.[1] The effect of this evolutionary process is contradictory. On the one hand, it makes the discipline exciting and alive because of the diversity of approaches, issues and questions within it, creating opportunities for research which would previously have been deemed to be outside the boundaries of the discipline. On the other hand, the lack of an agreed core to the subject has lead to confusion and a degree of intellectual insecurity. The problem the discipline faces is that, unlike the 1950s and 1960s when Realism reigned supreme, there is no longer any clear sense of what the discipline is about, what its core concepts are, what its methodology should be, what central issues and questions it should be addressing. In many ways, it is now easier to say what International Relations is *not* than what it *is*.[2]

It is important to highlight two important aspects of the breakdown of the Realist consensus that has dominated International Relations. The first is that it has undermined the legitimacy of claims that International Relations is a discrete area of action and discourse,

60

separate from social and political theory. The second is a similarity to the pattern of development which Bernstein pointed to in *The Restructuring of Social and Political Theory*.[3] Bernstein characterised this restructuring as a 'dialectical movement' of thought from the positivistic, empirically-based social sciences which sought to develop knowledge in a fashion analogous to the natural sciences, through to the tradition of phenomenology and hermeneutics and the recognition of the necessity to seek an interpretative understanding of the inter-subjective values which underlie and constitute the social world. The problem with Positivism and Empiricism is that they have the capacity to describe but not to understand or explain. The problem with interpretative social sciences is that they have the capacity to understand but not to critique the boundaries of understanding. It is this dialectical movement which gives rise to the need for critical theory to shift the bases of both empirical and interpretative knowledge. Critical theory, through the process of self-understanding and self-reflection, is able to provide a critique of the existing social order and point to its immanent capacity for change and for the realisation of human potential. The movement that Bernstein describes as taking place in social and political theory has developed to the point that it is now possible to talk about the beginnings of a critical theory of international relations, both in terms of individuals working in and developing this area and in terms of a body of literature.

4.2   THE DEVELOPMENT OF CRITICAL THEORY

Critical theory is most closely associated with the 'Frankfurt School' which was developed at the Frankfurt Institute of Social Research.[4] The Frankfurt Institute was set up in 1923 during the Weimar Republic, moved to the United States when the Nazis came to power and returned to Frankfurt in the early post-war years (though some of its members stayed on in the United States). Critical theory was a view of society and social theory that was developed by a group of individuals, spanning two generations, who were closely associated with the Institute. The most important figures in the development of these ideas were Max Horkheimer, Theodor Adorno, Herbert Marcuse, Erich Fromm and, in the present day, Jürgen Habermas.

Critical theory, as associated with the Frankfurt School, was first articulated by Max Horkheimer in his 1937 essay, 'Traditional and Critical Theory'.[5] There were three driving forces behind

Horkheimer's efforts to develop a critical theory of society: first, the belief that society was in need of radical transformation and not simply reform: second, that theory should be dependent of existing forms of social consciousness: and third, that the ideal of the objective, disinterested, independent theorist, which might hold true for the natural sciences, did not hold true for the social sciences. Building on these premises, Horkheimer's essay identifies two enduring features of critical theory: its view of the nature and purpose of theory and its relationship to Marxism.

The central characteristic of critical theory is the recognition of the connection between knowledge and interests. Horkheimer saw that this connection, in traditional theory, took either of two forms. It was either the inductive formulation of concepts, theorems, rules and laws that were amenable to empirical quantification and testing, or it was the phenomenological discerning of the essential core laws of society independent of empirical testing. Both these approaches held in common the separation of the object under observation from our knowledge of it, in the same way that the natural sciences maintain a subject–object relationship. They also operated on the premise that the development and growth of knowledge was governed by its own internal logic. But, Horkheimer argued, the reality is that social changes are the most powerful forces for change in theory. Knowledge is therefore not independent of our existence, but is integral to social relations and has a social function. In traditional theory, knowledge was seen to derive from the activity of describing the world. However, this did not mean that there was a development of any understanding of the world, of why it is as it is, because traditional theory had a narrowly proscribed view of rationality and lacked a self-reflective application of reason. Nor did traditional theory critique the bases of society it described, as this entailed value judgements which could not be scientifically substantiated. Traditional theory thus saw the world as a set of ready-made facts awaiting discovery through the application of scientific methodology, with the perception of these 'facts' being quite independent of the social framework in which perception takes place.

Horkheimer argued that traditional theory in the social sciences was the mirror image of positivism in the natural sciences, and as such offered no basis for choosing between competing human values. Not only was traditional theory not concerned with the realisation of human potential, but it was actually enhancing the capacity for manipulation and control which impeded the realisation of human potential. It is for this reason that Horkheimer associated Empiricism and Positivism with the rise of technocratic tendencies in modern society, and with the rise of the modern bureaucratic state which he saw as indifferent to human values. The problem which Horkheimer addressed was how to create the conditions for the realisation of human potential. It was through critical theory that these conditions could be identified and developed.

Critical theory was, for Horkheimer, an intellectual and practical effort. It did not see 'facts' in the same way as traditional theory. For critical theory, facts cannot be separated from their social genesis; they are social and historical products, partly determined by the collective action of human beings in society. The world we study is the product of ideas and human action, which traditional theory seeks to identify as ahistorical and transcendental in quality rather than as the product of history and social action. Critical theory does not accept prevailing ideas, actions and social conditions as unchanging or immutable. It refuses to accept the existing rules of society, the boundaries of action and knowledge, as natural and inevitable. Instead it seeks to understand society by taking a position outside of society while at the same time recognising that it is itself the product of society. Its central problematic is the development of reason and rationality that is directly concerned with the quality of human life and opposed to the elevation of scientific reasoning as the sole basis for knowledge. To this extent, it involves a change in the criteria of theory, the function of theory and its relationship to society. It entails the view that humanity has potentialities other than those manifested in current society. Critical theory, therefore, seeks not simply to reproduce society via description, but to understand society and change it. It is both descriptive and constructive in its theoretical intent: it is both an intellectual *and* a social act. It is not merely an expression of the concrete realities of the historical situation, but also a force for change within those conditions.

The second important characteristic of critical theory that can be derived from Horkheimer's essay is its view of its relationship to Marxism.[6] Although it recognised that it was a derivative of Marxism, critical theory also entailed a critique of Marxism. It did not see Marxism as a body of thought to which strict fidelity was necessary. Rather than seeing Marxism as the culmination of social and political theory, critical theory regarded it as a starting point, as a necessary step in the development of a critical social theory. Critical theory saw itself as a movement away from the (largely incorrect) view of Marxism as being mechanistic and deterministic, with a passive view of human consciousness. As a result of changes in historical conditions and circumstances, it argued that there was a need to rethink Marx's ideas. Critical theory was considered to be the development of a post-Marxist social and political theory that built upon the tradition of Marx and his spirit, but not upon the detail of his descriptive analysis.[7] Critical theory departed from classical Marxism in two important respects: it moved away from the idea of the proletariat as the embodiment of class-consciousness and the focus of revolutionary change, and it moved away from Marx's embracing of technology as having a positive effect on the development of society. What it did retain from Marxism was Marx's concept of critique, his concept of 'reification' (via Lukács) and his view that emancipation from the system of beliefs sustaining capitalism was the necessary precondition to radical change.

The most widely recognised of the modern proponents of critical theory is Jürgen Habermas.[8] Habermas sought to build upon the central features of Horkheimer's argument – the basic dichotomy between traditional and critical theory and the recognition of the connection between knowledge and interests – through an epistemological critique of Positivism designed to show that no theory can be properly based on the criteria it puts forward. Integral to this critique is Habermas's view that in modern society we have lost the classical notion of politics.[9] This was an understanding of politics as being part of the realm of ethics, and relating to practical philosophy which in turn provides an understanding of society, of the possibilities for change inherent in it, and of the constraints and limitations on these possibilities. Most importantly for Habermas, the classical notion of politics was open-ended; there were no assumptions about the final state of affairs. Habermas contrasts this with the view of politics which dominates modern society. This modern view, derived from eighteenth century political thought, attempts to ground social theory in the scientific aim of establishing and constructing the conditions under which human beings will behave in a calculable manner.

The result is the transformation of politics from being concerned with the nature of social order to being concerned with making possible a life of well-being within a preordained order. Reason, Habermas argues, has lost its emancipatory function and has been incorporated into scientific rationality.[10] The elevation of this scientific rationality to the core of politics results in the state being seen as a purely technical and functional institution and civil society as rooted in the idea of an order external to the individual. Politics is reduced to management within the confines of that order: the order itself becomes reified and no longer open to question.[11] Political problems become technical problems and politics is about who gets what, when and how but not *why*. Science and technology take on an 'ideological' function reinforcing the image of society based upon a technical model. Technocratic ideologies come to dominate, depriving the individual of political consciousness. The result is that ideology and social reality become entwined and can no longer be contrasted as they are in classical Marxism. It is for this reason that Habermas focuses on the critique of ideology rather than on the classical Marxist critique of capitalism.

Habermas argues that in order to move away from this technocratic view of politics we must undermine the belief that scientific reasoning and rationality are the sole foundations of genuine knowledge. Central to this argument is Habermas's concept of 'knowledge-constitutive interests'.[12] These are *a priori* interests by which human beings organise their life experience. They are the basis on which the constitution of knowledge is guided: they provide a guide as to what does and does not constitute genuine knowledge and they provide a guide as to how that knowledge is to be used. Habermas points to three knowledge-constitutive interests, each of which is related to a dimension of social existence: technical interests, which are related to work; practical interests, which are related to interaction; and emancipatory interests, which are related to power.

Technical cognitive interests, are interests in knowledge as the basis for extending control over objects in our environment (in which 'objects' may also be fellow human beings).[13] They guide knowledge to gain information that expands the powers of technical control. The technical cognitive interest is the knowledge-constitutive interest of the empirical, analytic sciences with its foremost expression in scientific Positivism. It seeks to provide the basis for instrumental action governed by technical rules based on empirical knowledge. This type of knowledge necessitates the isolation of objects and events into dependent and independent variables which allows investigation of the patterns of regularity of interaction amongst them. Humanity has an interest in the creation of technical knowledge because we must produce from nature what is needed materially for our existence. This can be done only through the manipulation of objects in the form of work or labour.

Practical cognitive interests are interests in knowledge as the basis for furthering mutual, inter-subjective understanding.[14] They provide the basis for the understanding of action within a common tradition. This practical cognitive interest is the knowledge-constitutive interest of the historical, hermeneutic and cultural sciences. Knowledge in this form is constitutive of the norms which underlie society and provides the basis for the mutual understanding of intentions and actions. The central element of this form of knowledge is the understanding of meaning in language and action and not simply of observation. Humanity has a practical cognitive interest, an interest in maintaining and expanding communication, because we must communicate with each other through the use of inter-subjectively understood symbols within the context of rule-governed institutions. It is practical in the sense that it clarifies the conditions for communication and interaction.

It is important to note that both technical and practical knowledge are ideal types which are in reality closely linked, and indeed require one another as constitutive parts of knowledge.[15] In other words, technical knowledge, or empirical observation, presupposes a level of inter-subjective interaction in the form of categories that provide the means of description. In order for technical knowledge to be intelligible and meaningful it has to be communicated to others, and that requires practical interests. In the same manner, what is open to inter-subjective understanding and interpretation is defined by what is deemed to fall within the bounds of the observable. The result is that these two forms of knowledge are mutually reinforcing in defining what is to count as knowledge and what is to be the focus of study. Knowledge within this dialectical relationship is internally unlimited but is categorically bounded. Because they are mutually reinforcing there is little scope for an internal dynamic that will lead to a change in the nature of what is to count as genuine knowledge. The impetus for change must therefore be external to both technical and practical interests, and it is this which leads Habermas to identify his third category of knowledge constitutive interests: emancipatory interests.

Emancipatory cognitive interest is the interest in securing freedom from static social conditions and from conditions of distorted communication which result from the mutual reinforcement of technical and practical interests.[16] It is rooted in the human capacity to engage in reflective reason in light of human needs. Emancipatory interests are a guide to knowledge about previously unapprehended constraints on the realisation of human potential. They are the knowledge-guiding interests of all critically-oriented sciences. They are at once derivative and basic forms of knowledge. Humanity has a stake in emancipatory interest because of the need for unrestrained communication and reflective reason: the means by which we can become aware of unacknowledged or unapprehended influences that constrain self-realisation. It provides the basis for insight into the past, so that through the process of self-reflection we become aware of the historical compulsions of the past. The task of the critical sciences is to identify the possibilities for higher levels of human freedom within a particular historical period. It identifies these possibilities as inherent in the very structure of society that technical and practical interests take as given. The goal of critical theory becomes the construction of a politics oriented towards the development of a rational consensus between human beings – a return to the classical understanding of politics, to the development of an emancipatory politics in which the individual is subject and not object and in which constraints on human autonomy are removed. The purpose of critical theory is to isolate and critique those rationalisations of society which are advanced as self-evident truths, but which may be ideological mystifications.

It is important to recognise that this third category of interests, though related to the other two, is also a distinct form of knowledge. It has its own epistemological integrity and as such critical theory cannot be seen merely as methodology. At the same time, it is important to recognise that the other forms of knowledge are not denigrated: each is an important dimension of human existence. Habermas's intention in separating out these three interrelated cognitive interests is to attack the claim that knowledge based on technical interests – empirically derived knowledge – is the only type of legitimate knowledge. It is also important to note that there is a substantial normative component in Habermas's view of critical theory.[17] There is, as a result of his view of politics, an underlying conception of the nature and purpose of society. There is a substantive background normative theory which is unarticulated but which is grounded in the discovery, through an understanding of historically determined forms of society, of the realisation of human potential. These norms are not external to what humans do, but are immanent to the historically determined forms of action by which men shape themselves. The normative foundation of critical theory is implicit in the structure of social action and discourse that it seeks to analyse.

The development of critical theory within International Relations has had two sources – one internal, the other external – and revolves around a central core of authors, notably Robert Cox,[18] John Maclean,[19] Richard Ashley,[20] Kubálková and Cruikshank,[21] Sylviu Brucan,[22] Ekkehart Krippendorff[23] and Andrew Linklater.[24] Internally, the development of critical theory was driven by a reaction to the rearticulation of Realism in Kenneth Waltz's *Theory of International Politics*,[25] with Ashley[26] being the best example. Externally, there was the development of critical theory perspectives independent of the theoretical developments within International Relations that was then used to critique Neorealism from a 'point already arrived at', with Cox[27] being the best example. Both drew from the development of critical theory and saw this as providing the basis for an attack on the epistemological foundations of the discipline.[28]

Perhaps the most important effort in this direction was the article published by Robert Cox in *Millennium* six years ago and recently reprinted in Robert Keohane's volume on Neorealism.[29] In it, Cox argues that International Relations is premised on a set of categories derived from an understanding of the world in which states are the 'principle aggregation of political power' and where there is a clear separation between the state and civil society, with foreign policy as the 'pure expression of state interests'. Cox argues that this separation is no longer tenable: state and civil society are intrinsically related. The degree of interpenetration is such that International Relations must now account for the 'plurality of forms of state expressing different configurations of state/society complexes' as well as a broader understanding of domestic 'social forces' and their relationship to the development of state structures and world orders.

Cox draws implicitly on the links between interests and knowledge that are central to the Frankfurt School.[30] As Cox puts it, theory is always for someone and for something. Theory always serves some purpose and never exists in a vacuum. It is inevitably the product of a certain historical period and circumstances, a reflection of a certain point in time, of a particular social and political order. But in addition to this, theory must reflect on the nature and circumstances of its origins and be able to identify and be aware of its limitations. It must also be aware of the possibilities within it for the transformation of a particular order. Theory must not only describe, explain and understand, but must also be capable of recognising and eliminating the distortions within it which serve to reproduce and reinforce a particular order as universalised and ahistorical. Therefore, in addition to theory being for someone and something, theory must also be able to give an account of itself.

Cox also discusses the nature of theory, which has important similarities with the work of the Frankfurt School. He distinguishes between theoretical perspectives on the basis of the purpose of theory: it can either be a guide to solving problems *within* the terms of a particular perspective, or it can reflect on the process of theorising itself, which raises the possibility of choosing a different perspective – in which case the problematic becomes one of creating an alternative world order. The former perspective gives rise to problem-solving theory, the latter to critical theory. What is interesting is that Cox collapses Habermas's distinction between technical and practical interests into the idea of problem-solving and reverts back to Horkheimer's basic dichotomy between traditional theory and critical theory. It is also important to note that while Cox does draw on the ideas of the Frankfurt School, he also makes use of the writings of Vico and particularly of Gramsci. Indeed, his ideas may owe more to the latter two than to the former.[31]

Critical theory, as set out by Cox, entails a series of basic elements:[32]

1. It stands apart from the prevailing order of the world and asks how that order came about; it is a reflective appraisal of the framework that problem solving takes as given.
2. It contemplates the social and political complex as a whole and seeks to understand the process of change within both the whole and its parts.
3. It entails a theory of history, understanding history as a process of continuous change and transformation.
4. It questions the origins and legitimacy of social and political institutions and how and whether they are changing; it seeks to determine what elements are universal to world order and what elements are historically contingent.
5. It contains problem-solving theory and has a concern with both technical and practical cognitive knowledge interests and constantly adjusts its concepts in light of the changing subject it seeks to understand.
6. It contains a normative, utopian element in favour of a social and political order different from the prevailing order but also recognising the constraints placed on possible alternative world order by historical process: the potential for transformation exists within the prevailing order but it is also constrained by the historical forces that created that order.

7.   It is a guide for strategic action, for bringing about an alternative order.

It can be seen that the development of a critical theory of International Relations has drawn substantially from the development of critical theory within social and political theory, as outlined by Bernstein, as we as from other sources. It offers a perspective that entails an historical component, a normative component, a self-reflective critical component and that is related to the real world as a practical guide for action. The question arises, however, of how it relates to what has preceded it in International Relations theory. How does critical theory relate to Banks's three paradigms? Does either Realism, Pluralism or Structuralism measure up to the standards set out by Cox for a critical theory of International Relations?

4.3   CRITICAL THEORY AND REALISM

Within the Realist paradigm it is possible to identify a number of distinct and divergent strands. Although they share a set of basic assumptions, they are also characterised by a number of important distinctions in terms of the theory they put forward, the concepts they use and the factors they emphasise. Ashley makes use of Habermas's three cognitive knowledge interests to highlight some of these differences.[33]

Technical cognitive interests manifest themselves in what Ashley terms 'techical Realism'[34] which he identifies with structural Realism and Neorealism. The prime examplar of this approach is Waltz's *Theory of International Politics*. This form of realism is epistemologically based upon Empiricism and Positivism. Waltz argues that there is a remarkable similarity in the political behaviour of states. He takes this to indicate an international system in which there is a structure of constraints and conditions to which no state is immune. The structure of the system is such that it has the capacity to frustrate virtually all anti-systemic forces. This results in a uniformity in the nature of state behaviour. The diversity of state forms is of no consequence for Waltz's theory: a state is a state is a state. The only thing that distinguishes one state from another is its military and political power. The important aspect of International Relations thus becomes the distribution of power within the system at any one time. Waltz's theory can therefore account for change *within* the system but not a change *of* the system. But Waltz would argue that the latter is a near impossibility in any case. The anarchic nature of the state system, and the fact that states are reliant on themselves for their security, means that a self-help system constantly reproduces itself. As a consequence the best we can hope for is an understanding of the structure which will provide the basis for the development of rational policies in the pursuit of stable balances of power.

To be fair to Waltz, he does not accept the possibility of a critical theory of International Relations.[35] Waltz could argue that a fundamental premise of critical theory is that the social, economic and political structure it is dealing with has to have the potential for change within it. But Waltz's argument is that when we come to the realm of the inter-state system, such a potential does not exist precisely because of the nature of the system. In 'A Response to My Critics', Waltz accepts that he has engaged in problem-solving theory (on Cox's criteria) but more or less says that, given the nature of the state system, nothing else can be done.[36]

Practical cognitive interests manifest themselves in what Ashley terms 'practical realism'.[37] Ashley identifies this form of realism with the work of Morgenthau. This is accurate up to a point, but it is also possible to read Morgenthau in a manner which would place him in the realm of technical Realism.[38] An example of practical realism that more clearly exemplifies this category is the 'English School' and in particular Hedley Bull's *Anarchical Society*.[39] For the English School, the central starting point is the uniqueness of the system of states in displaying both order and elemental society in the absence of an overarching sovereign. It seeks to describe, explain and understand the nature of the consensus that provides the basis for stability and order in international society. Through the ideas of a 'diplomatic culture' and an 'international political culture' it outlines the norms, rules, values and language of discourse and action that are essential to the cohesion of the society of a state and the maintenance of order within it. International order is not premised on a distribution of power, as it is for Waltz, but on the strength of the diplomatic and international political cultures. The reproduction of this order depends on the willing consent of the member-states and adherence to its basic norms regarding diplomacy, sovereignty and international law. Through an historical understanding of the nature of these norms, the approach provides the basis not only for their preservation but also their expansion: it provides an understanding of the society of states' origins, development, evolution and potential transformation (though Bull sees the possibilities of devolving into an international system as more likely than its evolution to a higher plane). Practical Realism is an advance on technical Realism in its incorporation of both an historical and normative dimension. However, it fails the test of critical theory by virtue of its failure to understand the ideological component of the approach, particularly the content of the norms, rules and values that underpin the society of states.

This problem is compounded by its relationship to technical Realism. Technical Realism constrains the potential for transformation within practical Realism by identifying what Ashley terms the 'true tradition'.[40] This defines what is worthy of interpretation and understanding by practical Realism, but it cannot call into question the nature of Realism itself. Realism, defined in terms of this relationship between technical and practical Realism, thus takes the world as given; it reifies a world order and as a consequence can engage only in problem-solving. It performs an ideological function in legitimising an order in which only certain interests are realised – the technical and practical interests of states and the state system. This leaves it void of emancipatory interests, of the humanist element that is central to critical theory.

The most notable effort at developing a critical Realist theory of International Relations is that of Ashley.[41] Ashley's 'Dialectical Competence Model' argues for the need to preserve classical Realism's rich insights into international political practice, while at the same time exposing the conditions and limits on the potential for change in this tradition. The difficulty with Ashley's alternative model, as Waltz argues,[42] is that it does not look very different from Waltz's approach, except that it is wrapped up in a capitalist world economy blanket. Ashley, like Waltz, starts by asserting a structurally determined system in which his balance of power regime produces sovereign states. It is not clear, however, how this structural dominance is to be overcome. Ashley seems to be pointing to the dynamics of the capitalist world economy, but, as Waltz asks, does this change lead away from the balance of power regime?[43] If not, then Ashley has substituted one form of a structural system that is immune to anti-systemic forces for Waltz's, and the differences between the two become of little consequence in terms of their overall effect. Thus, while it is possible to point to a dialectical component in Ashley's model, it is open to question whether there is a critical or emancipatory component. Ashley's model is critical only if the criteria for critical theory are narrowed to mean simply a dialectical relationship: that within the existing order there exists the seed of its own destruction. But Ashley's model lacks Cox's criteria of critical theory being able to stand outside itself. It does not offer a different set of ordering principles, nor is there any component of self-realisation or emancipation of human potential. What we are offered is a determining principle, the balance of power, and an argument that the state system produced by this ordering principle is historically and economically contingent. But what Ashley does not indicate is whether it is this ordering principle that is open to transformation or merely the historically contingent form of social, political and economic organisation that arises from it. If it is only the latter, then we are left with a structural determinism that is in many ways anathema to critical theory.

The difficulty with trying to develop a critical Realist theory of International Relations is that there is an inherent contradiction in this effort. Critical theory, which has as a central concern the enhancement of the self-realisation of human potential, runs up against the core assumptions, concepts and concerns of political Realism. The central elements of Realism necessarily limit the potential for critical theory in that tradition.[44] The limitations are so great as to make it almost impossible to conceive of the nature and content of a critical Realist theory of international relations. If a theory of international relations moved in the direction that critical theory suggests, it would have moved so drastically from the core assumptions of political Realism that it would be a misnomer to speak of it as a critical Realist theory.

This is not to imply that there is not much of value in Ashley's work. Ashley has done a great deal of work in laying down the foundations for a critical theory of international relations. It is particularly valuable in pointing to the limitations that exist within political Realism and its emphasis on technical cognitive interests. However, what Ashley doesn't seem to recognise is that the nature of his critiques of Realism are so devastating as to leave little left to build on. Gilpin,[45] Waltz[46] and Herz[47] all point in this direction in their replies: Gilpin by arguing that Ashley misunderstands the nature of political Realism; Waltz by accepting that he has engaged in problem-solving; Herz by moving away from Ashley's characterisation of his Realism as 'emancipatory'. The process of breaking down the cognitive reinforcement of technical and practical Realism means that there will be little left of the central assumption of Realism on which to build a critical theory of international relations.[48]

4.4   CRITICAL THEORY AND PLURALISM

There has been little contact between critical theory and what Banks describes as the Pluralist paradigm. What contact there has been has been for the most part disparaging of Puralist approaches. Cox, for example, lumps Pluralist approaches into the category of problem-solving theory.[49] This is odd given that the Pluralist approaches developed in reaction to the very reification of an international order founded on Realism, which Cox himself critiques. Rather than taking the world as given, pluralism was concerned with describing and developing an alternative conception of world order.

Nevertheless, within the diversity of Pluralist approaches it is possible to identify some approaches which correspond to technical cognitive interests and which we may term, after Ashley, 'technical Pluralism'. The study of issue–regime politics by Vasquez and Mansbach,[50] of interdependence by Keohane and Nye,[51] and the development of regime theory,[52] are all examples of this form of Pluralism. They manifest a technical cognitive interest in that they seek an understanding of these new phenomena in the international system in order to enhance the capability to cope with, control and manipulate them in the pursuit of the national interest. Others, such as transnationalism[53] (and some work on interdependence), are epistemologically tied to technical cognitive interests via empiricism. However, the nature of the links between technical and practical interests also provides the empirical basis for the development of forms of pluralism which seek to go beyond the enhancement of state capabilities. In defining a new set of phenomena, largely related to the action of individuals, it expands the set of social relations which are open to understanding. Two efforts along these lines are worth mentioning: the World Order Models Project (WOMP) and Burton's world society approach.

WOMP[54] starts with a rejection of political Realism as the empirical basis for a theory of International Relations. It attacks the Hobbesian notion of politics contained in Realism (which, as mentioned above, Habermas attacked as undermining the classical notion of politics) and Realism's historical understanding of an unchanging and transcendent structure of International Relations. WOMP's analysis builds upon four central components: the belief that a fundamental transformation is occurring at the global level due to the actions of individuals and changes in technology; that a wide range of problems has been created by these transformations resulting in the internationalisation of social, economic and political issues; that the state is an inappropriate agency for dealing with these problems; and that there is a need to develop alternative future worlds, fundamentally concerned with values relating to the solution of these problems and the development of human beings.[55] The problems it points to are not tied necessarily to the capitalist world economy but point to problems with the system of states itself. WOMP therefore does not point to change and radical restructuring of the system. It details a set of norms which provide the inter-subjective basis for the development of a new global culture and community. Importantly, this new global community will not be arrived at or develop organically but will be necessitated by external factors relating to the four major problems identified by WOMP, requiring a fundamental change in human values. It seeks to illustrate paths to alternative future worlds and to provide a guide to action. What is interesting to note is that WOMP starts with emancipatory cognitive interests and then develops alternative world orders incorporating technical and practical cognitive interests. In relation to Cox's outline of critical theory, WOMP lacks an historical understanding and may fall foul of Cox's point that a critical theory, in addition to having a normative content, must also be able to clarify the range of possible alternatives, and that its utopianism is constrained by an understanding of historical processes which limit the choice of alternative orders to those which are feasible transformations of the existing world.[56]

Burton offers an eclectic approach to International Relations. He starts with a fundamentally different conception of the world, seeing it as a world society – a cobweb of relationships between a diverse range of actors. This approach moves beyond the analysis of relationships between similar units and focuses on relationships that criss-cross and transcend levels of analysis.[57] Burton's world society approach manifests practical and emancipatory cognitive interests. Though there is a large element of description in Burton's approach it is almost completely lacking in technical cognitive interests relating to manipulation and control. Two components of Burton's very rich and varied tapestry are worth focusing on: his approach to conflict resolution and his ideas relating to human needs.

A large element of Burton's work has been concerned with the development of what Burton terms 'problem-solving techniques' for third-party mediation of conflicts.[58] The first thing to note is that it is wrong to equate Burton's use of the term 'problem-solving' with Cox's. Burton's use of the idea of 'puzzle-solving' is more or less the same as Cox's notion of problem-solving theory. What Burton has attempted to do is develop a set of techniques that facilitate the process of understanding and reflection, by parties to a conflict, about the nature of conflict itself, the nature of their particular conflict and the possibilities of developing a shared consensus about the problem which allows for a self-sustaining resolution of the conflict. Though it does spell out a series of techniques for the mediators, these are not techniques for manipulation or control, but ones that provide a means of assisting the processes of self-realisation by the parties to the conflict. The mediators do not impose or even suggest a solution. To do so would run counter to everything Burton has tried to do in developing mediation techniques: it would result in settlement, not resolution; it would be an exercise in power or control. The premises of Burton's approach coincide very closely with Habermas's ideas about self-understanding and self-realisation and conform to the idea that the transformation of a situation has to be immanent. Burton is not seeking outcomes on a grandly utopian scale, but the development of universalised principles that provide a guide to action.

The second major feature of Burton's approach is the centrality he accords to the fulfilment of human needs,[59] which can be seen as a manifestation of emancipatory cognitive interests despite Burton's effort to present them as scientifically and objectively knowable. For example, Burton points to a naturalistic, ontological craving for identity and security within a community or group, but he does not accept the idea of the state as the legitimate or natural embodiment of this need for identification. It is on the basis of the fulfilment of needs such as this that the legitimacy of relationships and institutions is based: the failure to meet human needs on the part of institutions, through the development of a gulf between human needs and institutional needs, is a primary source of conflict that can be avoided. There is, then, a strong affinity with critical theory in Burton's emphasis on human needs, on the notion of legitimacy and on the need for autonomy from the exercise of coercive power.

The component of Cox's critical theory that is lacking from Burton's approach is, as with WOMP, an understanding of historical contexts. This is particularly important in relation to the satisfaction of human needs.[60] The understanding of the deprivation of human needs cannot take place without an analysis and understanding of the historical, social, economic and political contexts that give rise to them. It is also important in recognising that human needs and their content cannot be ahistorically defined or determined. In particular, their content may be historically contingent. Furthermore, since outcomes are a central concern in Burton's approach, it needs to develop an understanding of what types of institutions facilitate the fulfilment of human needs, other than those very broad defined as 'legitimate' institutions. Despite these problems, Burton's world society approach and WOMP may have stronger claims to critical theory credentials than might at first appear likely.

4.5 CRITICAL THEORY AND STRUCTURALISM

The approaches that are incorporated within the Structuralist paradigm have, in some senses, the closest affinity to critical theory. This is partly because they share common roots as developments of the Marxist tradition in social and political theory, and partly because they have a similar relationship to International Relations in that they developed outside of the discipline and there have only recently been attempts to incorporate them into the subject. Most of the approaches developed as a reaction to positivism and modernisation theories which took an historically contingent understanding of development and attempted to universalise it both in theory and in practice. One of the most widely known of these efforts at developing an alternative explanation of the development problem is the world system analysis approach.[61]

Unlike Realism, which posits a pattern of recurrence and repetition and sees the international system as a set of relations among relatively separate entities with the state as the basic unit of analysis, the world systems approach argues that there is a single integrated world system with a logic and structure of its own. The logic of the system is the logic of a world capitalist economy.[62] It argues that the barriers to development are not internal but external, relating to the structural characteristics of the global economy which defines a core, semi-periphery and periphery. There is no real prospect for meaningful change in the status or position of the periphery without a system-wide transformation. Most importantly for International Relations, the state system is seen as the historically contingent political organisation of the capitalist world economy.

Some authors, such as Anderson,[63] take the analysis a step further in combining an analysis of domestic society, state structures and the organisation of societies within an international economic and military order. The effect of such an approach is a complete breakdown of the boundaries between domestic and international politics and the centrality of political economy in the study of the world system.

The strengths of such an approach are its conceptual categories and its method of concrete analysis drawing on the tradition of historical materialism.[64] It provides the potential for a unified theory of domestic and international politics which Waltz[65] argues is the prerequisite for a critical theory of International Relations. It provides an understanding of the complex arrangements of various social formations within the world system and an unprecedented level of sophistication in the analysis of the fundamental constraints on the possibilities for transformation of the system. This theoretical and descriptive knowledge of the system of states provides the basis for the development of practical knowledge geared towards change by distinguishing those elements which are central to world order, and those which are historically contingent.

Structuralist approaches, on the whole, tend to coincide with the first four elements of Cox's criteria for critical theory which point to the need to explain our position within historical processes as a basis for system transformation. As such they provide the theoretical and empirical foundation for a critical theory, as well as a mode of analysis. What the Structuralist approaches lack is any substantive development of practical cognitive interests, an explicit normative element other than that which it implicitly draws from Marxism and a guide to action. They therefore constitute an important component of a critical theory of International Relations, but cannot constitute such a theory on their own.

4.6 CONCLUSIONS

Critical theory represents the next stage in the development of International Relations theory. However, as the preceding discussion has shown, critical theory will need to draw on several diverse components of current International Relations theory.[66] In this sense it has the potential for creating a new focus within the discipline of International Relations that is post-Realist and post-Marxist.[67] It provides the basis for the reintegration of International Relations into the broader traditions and concerns of social and political theory,[68] and it allows us to build on the distinctiveness of International Relations as a contribution to the development of critical social theory. This does not mean of course that International Relations as an area of study, or its sub-fields, are to be discarded. It does mean that they will have to be *reformulated* and *restructured*.[69] Paraphrasing Sheldon Wolin,[70] the point of International Relations theory is not simply to alter the way we look at the world, but to alter the world. It must offer more than mere description and an account of current affairs. It must also offer us a significant choice, and a critical analysis of the quality and direction of life.

NOTES AND REFERENCES

*   Some of the material in this article was first presented at Michael Banks's 'Concepts and Methods Seminar' at the LSE in 1984. In addition, I benefitted greatly from discussions on International Relations theory with Hidemi Suganami during my year teaching at Keele University. Finally, a word of thanks to the MSc students at Southampton during recent years who have contributed to this chapter in ways that they may not know or recognise.

1.   See M. Banks, 'The Inter-Paradigm Debate' in M. Light and A.J.R. Groom (eds), *International Relations: A Handbook of Current Theory* (London: Frances Pinter, 1985), pp. 7–26.

2.   Not everyone would agree with these comments regarding the state of the discipline and could, rightly, point to the continued dominance of the realist approach in both teaching and research to support the claim that there *is* an agreed core in the subject. Nevertheless, in the area of International Relations theory, these comments seem to be an accurate assessment of the current state of affairs. See, for example, M. Banks, 'The Evolution of International Relations Theory', in M. Banks (ed), *Conflict in World Society* (Brighton: Wheatsheaf, 1984), pp. 3–21; M. Banks, 'Where are we now', *Review of International Studies* (Vol. 11, No. 3, 1985), pp. 220–37; Fred Halliday, 'A "Crisis" of International Relations', *International Relations* (November 1985), pp. 407–12; W. Olsen and N. Onuf, 'The Growth of the Discipline Reviewed', in S. Smith (ed), *International Relations: British and American Perspectives* (Oxford: Basil Blackwell, 1985), pp. 1–8; H. Alker and N. Biersteker, 'The Dialectics of World Order: Notes for a Future Archaeologist of International Savoir Faire', *International Studies Quarterly* (Vol. 28, No. 2, 1984), pp. 121-42; J. Rosenau, 'Order and Disorder in the Study of World Politics' in R. Maghroori and R. Bennet (eds), *Globalism vs Realism: International Relations' third Debate* (Boulder, CO: Westview Press, 1982); and J.K. Holsti, *The Dividing Discipline* (London: Allen & Paul, 1985).

3.   R. Bernstein, *The Restructuring of Social and Political Theory* (Oxford: Basil Blackwell, 1976).

4. For discussion of the background and development of critical theory and the Frankfurt School, see D. Held, *Introduction to Critical Theory: Horkheimer to Habermas* (Berkeley, CA.: University of California Press, 1980); T. McCarthy, *The Critical Theory of Jürgen Habermas* (Cambridge, MA.: MIT Press, 1978); G. Friedman, *The Political Philosophy of the Frankfurt School* (Ithaca, N.Y.: Syracuse University Press, 1981); R.J. Antonio, 'The Origins, Development and Contemporary Status of Critical Theory', *The Sociological Quarterly* (No. 24, 1983); L. Kolakowski, *Main Currents of Marxïsm, vol. 3: The Breakdown* (Oxford: Oxford University Press, 1983), pp. 341–95; G. Lichtheim, *From Marx to Hegel* (New York: Herder & Herder, 1971); A. Wellmer, *The Critical Theory of Society* (New York: Herder & Herder, 1971); M. Jay, *The Dialectical Imagination: A History of the Frankfurt School and the Institute of Social Research, 1923–1950* (Boston, MA.: Little, Brown, 1973) and P. Anderson, *In the Tracks of Historical Materialism* (London: Verso, 1983).

5. M. Horkheimer, 'Traditional and Critical Theory', in *Critical Theory: Selected Essays* (New York: Seabury Press, 1972).

6. Critical theory's Marxist credentials are not unproblematic and have been a major component of criticisms of critical theory. Kolakowski, for example, describes critical theorists as 'para-Marxists' (*Main Current of Marxism*), while Bernstein notes that Habermas's critical theory may be more of a return to Kant than a moving beyond Marx, (*The Restructuring of Social and Political Theory*, p.224. For a discussion of critical theory and Marxism see, in addition to the works mentioned in Note 4 above, J. Sensat, Jr, *Habermas and Marxism: An Appraisal* (Beverly Hills, CA.: Sage, 1979); G. Therborn, 'Frankfurt Marxism: A Critique', *New Left Review* (No. 63, 1970), pp. 65–96 and T. Flood, 'Habermas's Critique of Marxism', *Science and Society* (No. 41 Winter 1977-78), pp. 448-464.

7. G. Friedman, *The Political Philosophy of the Frankfurt School*.

8. Habermas's published works are numerous and not all are available in English translation. His most important works, in relation to this study, are: *Knowledge and Human Interests* trans. by J.J. Shapiro (Boston, MA.: Beacon Press, 1971); 'A Postscript to *Knowledge and Human Interests*', *Philosophy of the Social Sciences* (Vol. 3 1973), pp. 175–185; *Theory and Practice* trans. by J. Viertel (Boston, MA.: Beacon Press, 1973); *Towards a Rational Society* trans. by J.J. Shapiro (Boston, MA.: Beacon Press, 1970) and *Legitimation Crisis* trans. by T. McCarthy (Boston, MA.: Beacon Press, 1975). For a discussion of Habermas's ideas, see, in addition to the works cited in Notes 4 and 6 above, J.B. Thompson and D. Held (eds), *Habermas: Critical Debates* (London: Macmillan, 1982); G. Kortian, *Metacritique: The Philosophical Argument of Jurgen Habermas* (Cambridge: Cambridge University Press, 1980); R. Guees, *Habermas and Critical Theory* (Oxford: Oxford University Press, 1982), G. Therborn, 'Habermas: A New Eclectic', *New Left Review* (No. 67, 1971), pp. 69–83 and F.R. Dallmayr, 'Critical Theory Criticized: Habermas's *Knowledge and Human Interests* and Its Aftermath', *Philosophy of the Social Sciences* (Vol. 2, 1972), pp. 211–29.

9. Habermas, *Theory and Practice*.
10. Habermas, *Theory and Practice*.
11. Habermas, *Theory and Practice*, and Habermas, *Towards a Rational Society*.
12. Habermas, *Knowledge and Human Interests*.
13. Habermas, *Knowledge and Human Interests*.
14. Habermas, *Theory and Practice* and Habermas, *Knowledge and Human Interest*.
15. For a discussion of this relationship see, Held, *Introduction to Critical Theory;* R.K. Ashley, 'Political Realism and Human Interests', *International Studies Quarterly* (Vol. 25, No. 2, 1981), pp. 221–6 and Habermas, *Legitimation Crisis*.
16. Habermas, *Knowledge and Human Interests*; Held, *Introduction to Critical Theory* and Bernstein, *The Restructuring of Social and Political Theory*, pp. 173–236.
17. For a discussion of the normative aspects of critical theory see Bernstein, *The Restructuring of Social and Political Theory*.
18. See R.W. Cox, 'Ideologies and the NIEO: Some Reflections on Recent Literature', *International Organization* (Vol. 33, No. 2, 1979), pp. 257–302; 'Social Forces, States and World Order: Beyond International Relations Theory', *Millennium: Journal of International Studies* (Vol. 10, No. 2, 1981), pp. 126–55 and 'Gramsci, Hegemony and International Relations: An Essay in Method', *Millennium: Journal of International Studies* (Vol. 12, No. 2, 1983), pp. 162–75.
19. J. Maclean, 'Marxist Epistemology, Explanations of Change and the Study of International Relations' in B. Buzan and R. J. Barry Jones (eds), *Change in the Study of International Relations* (London: Frances Pinter, 1981); 'Political Theory, International Theory and the Problem of Ideology', *Millennium: Journal of International Studies* (Vol. 10, No. 2, 1981), pp. 102–25; and 'An Ideological Intervention' in R.J. Barry Jones and P. Willets (eds), *Interdependence on Trial* (London: Frances Pinter, 1984).
20. R.K. Ashley, 'Political Realism and Human Interests', *International Studies Quarterly* (Vol. 25., No. 2, 1981), pp. 204–36 and 'The Poverty of Neorealism', *International Organization* (Vol. 38, No. 2, 1984), pp. 225–86. An abridged version of the latter is reprinted in R. Keohane (ed), *Neorealism and Its Critics* (New York: Columbia University Press, 1986), pp. 255–300.
21. V. Kubálková and A.A. Cruickshank, *Marxism and International Relations* (London: Routledge & Kegan Paul, 1985).
22. S. Brucan, *The Dialectics of World Politics* (London: Macmillan, 1978).
23. E. Krippendorff, *International Relations as a Social Science* (Brighton: Harvester Press, 1982).
24. A. Linklater, 'Realism, Marxism and Critical International Theory', *Review of International Studies* (Vol. 12, No. 2 1986), pp. 301–12 and *Marxism and the Critical Theory of International Relations* (forthcoming).
25. K. Waltz, *Theory of International Politics* (Reading, MA.: Addison-Wesley, 1979).

26. Ashley, 'Political Realism'.
27. Cox, 'Ideologies and the NIEO'. There is, in addition, a second 'external' source in the form of writers outside of the International Relations discipline who bring a critical theory perspective to bear on issues and problems central to International Relations. See, for example, A. Giddens, *The Nation-State and Violence: Volume Two of a Contemporary Critique of Historical Materialism* (Cambridge: Polity Press, 1985).
28. Kubálková and Cruickshank argue that the 'point of departure for fully fledged "critical studies of International Relations"' came with the publication of and reactions to E.P. Thompson, 'Notes on Exterminism, the Last Stages of Civilization', *New Left Review* (No. 121, 1980). See V. Kubálková and A.A. Cruickshank, 'The "New Cold War" in "critical International Studies"', *Review of International Studies* (Vol. 12, No. 3 1986), pp. 163–85. It is difficult, if not impossible, to point to one single source of the development of critical International Relations theory. What is of greater interest is that it appears to have emerged from a variety of independent sources for a variety of reasons in approximately the same period of 1980–81.
29. The reprinted version also includes a 'Postscript' with a useful discussion of how Cox's ideas developed and how he sees them standing in relation to the study of International Relations in general and to Neorealism in particular. See R.O. Keohane, (ed), *Neorealism*, pp. 204–254.
30. Kubálková and Cruickshank argue that Cox's notion of critical theory is different from that of Horkheimer's or Habermas's. While there are important differences between the three, there are also important points of similarity that allow us to point to an element of continuity between the three. In addition, Kubálková and Cruickshank overstate Cox's views on Habermas. Rather that dismissing Habermas as a 'theorist irrelevant for an understanding of international behaviour', Cox criticises Habermas (and others) for failing to explore the implications of different forms of state/civil society relationships. See Kubálková and A.A. Cruickshank, *Marxism and International Relations*, p.181, n.9.
31. Cox points to the importance of these roots in his 'Postscript' in Keohane, (ed) *Neorealism*, pp. 240–3. Kubálková and Cruickshank make a similar point, *Marxism and International Relations, pp. 181–82, n.15.*
32. This list is distilled from Cox's discussion of critical theory. See Cox, 'Ideologies the NIEO', pp. 129–30.
33. Ashley, 'Political Realism and Human Interests'.
34. Ashley, 'Political Realism and Human Interests', pp. 215–21.
35. See K. Waltz, 'Reflections on *Theory of International Politics*: A Response to My Critics', in Keohane, (ed), *Marxism and International Relations*, pp. 322–46.
36. Waltz, 'Reflections', pp. 338–41.
37. Ashley, 'Political Realism and Human Interests, pp. 210–15.
38. This is something that Ashley is also aware of. *Ibid.*, pp. 209–10.
39. This point is made by Linklater, 'Realism Marxism', p.312, n.57,

though he refers to 'rationalism' which I have equated here with the English School. For a discussion of the ideas of the English School see R. Jones, 'The English School of International Relations: A Case for Closure', *Review of International Studies* (Vol. 7 No. 1, 1981); H. Suganami, 'The Structure of Institutionalism: An Anatomy of Mainstream International Relations', *International Relations* (Vol. 7, No. 5, 1983); S. Grader, 'The English School of International Relations: A Reply to Professor Jones', *Review of International Studies* (forthcoming) and P. Wilson, 'Is There and English School of International Relations?', (MSc Dissertation, University of Southampton, 1987). The exemplar of this approach remains H. Bull, *Anarchical Society* (London: Macmillan, 1977). For discussion of the development of the norms and institutions which underpin international society and their expansion in the international system see M. Wight, 'Western Values and International Society' in M. Wight and H. Butterfield (eds), *Diplomatic Investigations* (Oxford: Oxford University Press, 1966) and H. Bull and A. Watson (eds), *The Expansion of International Society* (Oxford: Clarendon Press, 1985).

40. Ashley, 'Political Realism and Human Interests', pp. 222–5.
41. Ashley 'Political Realism and Human Interests', and 'The Poverty of Neorealism'. In the former article, Ashley points to the potential within Realism, as seen in the writings of John Herz, for 'reflective reason' or critical theory. In the latter article, his outline of a 'Dialectical Competence Model' seems to be in line with his earlier argument that the transformation of Realism, and a return to its classical roots, is possible only if the 'true tradition' espoused by 'technical realism' is undermined It is for these reasons that I have described Ashley's efforts as 'critical realist theory', though it should be noted that there is a fair degree of ambivalence on Ashley's part, particularly in 'Political Realism and Human Interests', as to whether such an enterprise is possible.
42. Waltz, 'Reflections', pp. 337–8.
43. Waltz, 'Reflections'.
44. These are problems that Ashley, himself, points to. See Ashley, 'Political Realism and Human Interests', pp. 232–5.
45. R. Gilpin, 'The Richness of the Tradition of Political Realism', *International Organization* (Vol. 38. No. 2, 1984), pp. 287–304 and reprinted in Keohane (ed), *Marxism and International Relations*, pp. 301–21.
46. Waltz, 'Reflections'.
47. Herz, 'Comment', *International Studies Quarterly* (Vol. 25, No. 2, 1981), pp. 237–41.
48. Despite Realism's inability to provide the basis for a critical theory of international relations, Linklater and others argue that it is the dialogue between Realism and Marxism that provides the necessary starting point for a critical theory of international relations. See, Linklater, 'Realism, Marxism'.
49. Cox, 'Ideologies and the NIEO', p.127.
50. J. Vasquez and R.Mansbach, *In Search of Theory* (New York: Columbia University Press, 1981).

51. R.O. Keohane and J. Nye, *Power and Interdependence* (Boston, MA.: Little, Brown, 1977).

52. S. Krasner (ed), *International Regimes* (New York: Syracuse University Press, 1983).

53   See, for example, R.O. Keohane and J. Nye, *Transnational Relations and World Politics* (Cambridge, MA.: Harvard University Press, 1972) and J. N. Rosenau, *The Study of Global Interdependence* (London: Frances Pinter, 1980). The epistemological tie to technical cognitive interests is also manifested in the effort in the 1960s and early 1970s to develop a 'science' of International Relations modelled on the idea of science found in the natural sciences.

54. The literature produced by WOMP is large and by no means homogeneous. The core volumes detailing the WOMP perspective are R. Falk, *A Study of Future Worlds* (New York: Free Press, 1975); J. Galtung, *The True Worlds* (New York: Free Press, 1980); S. Mendolvitz, *On the Creation of a Just World Order* (Boulder, CO.: Westview Press, 1981); L. Beres, *People, States and World Order* (New York: Peacock Press, 1981) and R. Falk, *et al.*, *Studies on a Just World Order 2 vols.* (Boulder, CO.: Westview Press, 1982, 1983).

55. It is interesting to note that Giddens points to the need to draw on a similar set of values to those espoused by WOMP to provide the teological basis for a critical social theory. See, Giddens, *The Nation–State*, pp. 310-40.

56. For a discussion of the utopian aspects of WOMP see, I Clark, 'World Order Reform and Utopian Thought: A Contemporary Watershed?', *The Review of Politics* (Vol. 41, No. 1, 1979), pp. 96–120; H.D. Laswell, 'The Promise of the World Order Modelling Project', *World Politics* (Vol. 29, No. 2, 1977) and J.J. Farer, 'The Greening of the Globe', *International Organization* (Vol. 31, No. 1, 1977). For a reply to some of these criticisms see, R. Falk, 'WOMP and Its Critics: A Reply', *International Organization* (Vol. 32, No. 2, 1978).

57. The publications of John Burton are numerous and span almost three decades of constant publishing in the form of papers, monographs, articles and books. The core of his views and the manner in which they have developed over time can be found in his major books: *International Relations: A General Theory* (Cambridge: Cambridge University Press, 1967); *Systems, States, Rules and Diplomacy* (Cambridge: Cambridge University Press, 1968); *Conflict and Communication* (London: Macmillan, 1969); *World Society* (Cambridge: Cambridge University Press, 1972); *Deviance, Terrorism and War* (Oxford: Martin Robertson, 1978); *Dear Survivor* (London: Frances Pinter, 1983) and *Global Conflict* (Brighton: Wheatsheaf, 1985). For an informed, sympathetic but not uncritical discussion of Burton's work and ideas see M. Banks (ed), *Conflict in World Society* (Brighton: Wheatsheaf, 1985).

58. Burton, *Conflict and Communication,*.

59. See Burton, *Deviance, Terrorism and War*, and *Global Conflict*.

60. For a more detailed discussion of these problems see R. Coate and C. Murphy, 'A Critical Science of Global Relations', *International Interaction* (Vol. 12, No. 2 1985), pp. 109–32.

61. This approach is most widely associated with the work of Immanuel Wallerstein. See, for example, I. Wallerstien, *The Modern World System*, in two volumes (Beverly Hills, CA.: Sage, 1976); *The Capitalist World Economy* (Cambridge: Cambridge University Press, 1979) and *World Systems Analysis* (Beverly Hills, CA.: Sage, 1982). There have been numerous discussions, commentaries and criticisms of Wallerstein's approach. See, in particular, A. Zolberg, 'Origins of the Modern World System: A Missing Link', *World Politics* (Vol. 33, No. 2, 1981); T. Skocpol, 'Wallerstein's World Capitalist System: A Theoretical Critique', *American Journal of Sociology* (No. 82, 1977); A. Aronowitz, 'A Methodological Critique of Wallerstein's *The Modern World System*', *Theory and Society* (Vol. 10, No. 4 1980); C.H. George, 'The Origins of Capitalism: A Marxist Epitome and a Critique of Immanuel Wallerstein's Modern World System', *Marxist Perspectives* (Summer 1980) and R. Brenner, 'The Origins of Capitalist Development: A Critique of Neo-Smithian Marxists', *New Left Review* (No. 104, 1977).

62. For a discussion of the question of divergent logics within the international system see, C. Chase-Dunn, 'Interstate System and Capitalist World Economy: One Logic or Two', *International Studies Quarterly* (Vol. 25, No. 1, 1981), pp. 19–42.

63. See, P. Anderson, *Lineages of the Absolutist State* (London: New Left Books, 1974) and *In the Tracks of Historical Materialism* (London: Verso Books, 1983).

64. Cox argues that historical materialism is a theoretical corrective in the study of international relations in four ways; (1) its use of the dialectic, (2) its incorporation of a vertical as well as horizontal dimension of power, (3) its emphasis on the relationship between state and civil society and, (4) its focus on productive processes as the central element in the explanation of particular forms of state/civil society. See Cox, 'Ideologies and the NIEO'. See also the discussion of historical materialism in A. Giddens, *op.cit.*; Anderson, *The Nation–State* and by B.K. Gills (Chapter 6 in this volume).

65. Waltz, 'Reflections', p.340

66. Linklater makes the point that a critical theory of International Relations will have to combine 'philosophical, empirical and practical concerns'. At the philosophical level, it will have to provide an alternative world order grounded in concepts of freedom and universality that are historically derived. Empirically, it has to construct a sociology of the constraints upon the realisation of these concepts, and practically, it has to provide us with strategies of transition to bridge the gap between the two. See, Linklater, *Lineages*, p.310.

67. The idea that it will have to be post-Realist is evident in the above discussion; the post-Marxist component is derived from Horkheimer's argument that critical theory, while developing out of the Marxist tradition, needs to build on the spirit and not the letter of Marxism. See, Linklater, *Lineages* and Notes 47 and 6 above.

68. The development of critical social theory is evident in the large volume of literature making use of a critical theory perspective in

other areas of the social sciences. See Kubálková and Cruickshank, *Marxism and International Relations*, p.181, n.11 for a listing of some of this literature.

69.   This point is made by Krippendorff, *International Relations*.

70.   S. Wolin, 'Paradigms and Political Theories' in B.C. Parekh and P. King (eds), *Politics and Experience* (Cambridge: Cambridge University Press, 1968).

5 The Study of International Relations: A Historian's View

Alan Sked

When I was first asked to write this study, I was struck almost immediately by the thought that, in contrast to International Relations specialists, historians are almost never required to write about their own subject as a discipline. International Relations specialists, on the other hand, never seem to cease doing so. Whereas the poor historian, dull fellow that he often is, simply gets on with the task of telling his story (and 'history' and 'story', significantly, are the same word in many languages), the International Relations specialist always seems to feel the need to justify himself. What then explains his apparent lack of self-confidence? Nagging doubts about intellectual respectability? A lack of consensus about what his subject is really about? A growing scepticism, not to say cynicism, regarding its usefulness? My own feeling is that all these factors are indeed involved – yet, given the nature of the subject, they are bound to be, so that it is only proper that from time to time it should be examined in volumes such as this or in Light and Groom's splendid *International Relations: A Handbook of Current Theory*.[1]

To state this is not of course in any way to seek to patronise International Relations. Historians are certainly in no position to do that. After all, theirs is a methodologically much simpler *métier*, made so by the fact that they know what happens next. From this happy hindsight all sorts of blessings flow. For a start, the 'significance' of certain 'facts' as opposed to others is much easier to determine. One can judge by reference to the more recent past, rather than by giving in to prejudice or ideology. That is not to say that historians are ideologically neutral, but merely to assert that attempts on their part to slip ideology into their work tend to look much more blatant and thus in the end prove less successful. International Relations specialists, on the other hand, are subject to far greater temptations

87

in this respect since they are often prejudging the future.

Another factor which makes History a more simple craft to practise is that historians know more of the facts. Archives in several countries now operate a thirty years' rule; private papers and memoirs are often available; so too are many secondary sources. All this means that historians have access to much, much greater detail than their International Relations colleagues. Cabinet minutes and other official documents, after all, provide a much more reliable source for reconstructing government policy-making processes than newspapers or television interviews. The existence of so much research material plus the fact that historians rely on a chronological framework, means that research for the History student is often a relatively straightforward task. In most cases, it means that his time-span is limited, his evidence is plentiful, and his documents relate to one another in particular (chronological) sequence. The International Relations research student, on the other hand, will often find that the relevant sources for his work are unavailable, that those which do exist may bear no obvious relationship to one another, and that the whole subject has to be placed within some philosophical/theoretical/methodological framework – rather than within a simple historical/chronological one.

Historians, it should also be admitted, tend simply to ignore the philosophical and theoretical issues which underlie the so-called 'paradigmatic debate' which so often obsesses their International Relations colleagues. Hindsight has already been cited as one reason for this and the pressure of evidence is yet another. Besides, historians, being sceptical creatures, are rarely theoretically minded. The result is that they tend simply to take it for granted that a number of factors will be involved in their research – economic, political, social, institutional – and they look out for these as they pursue their storyline and try to fit them in. If one factor stands out more than others in the documents they make due allowance for it, although they will also check it against the other evidence available. Mostly, however, they will keep an open mind on the types of factors involved rather than start from a particular theoretical standpoint. The result is that historians who have a particular, often ideological, axe to grind rarely command attention for very long. Others check their sources, their biases get exposed, and their theories are undermined and forgotten.

The International Relations specialist is in a rather different position. He is after all a generalist compared with his historian colleague. His interest may be in the origins of wars in general rather than say the origins of a particular war. Unlike his historian colleague, therefore, he will not want to spend decades of his life researching the causes of any one war, however important, if he has to deal with all the others. In terms of research he will be more likely to go in for model-building, picking and choosing among the historical literature to test his hypotheses; he will not be in a position to spend much of his time doing original work in many archives. His work, moreover, will often concern the present and the future as well as the past. Yet the more he approaches the present the greater vacuum he will be in. As he looks towards the future the more he will become prey to his hopes and prejudices. He may even wish to change the world rather than explain it. He may indeed positively seek to influence government policy or to shape current policy debates. There is nothing inherently wrong with this. To object in principle would be to maintain that universities should become purely ivory towers, cut off from the wider world, with no relevance to contemporary life or thought. On the other hand, one should be aware of the dangers involved and the sacrifices which can too easily be made in pursuit of relevance.

Historians, for their part, have little aspiration to be relevant. Indeed, those who try too hard become embarrassments. History, it is well known, has no lessons to teach, save that those who try to draw any usually get them wrong. People can of course learn from the past, but this never prevents them from making mistakes in the future. That then is perhaps the main lesson to learn from history and from life in general. The historian, therefore, rarely bothers to range over centuries, picking at entrails, divining trends or making predictions. He fills gaps in detail, examines interpretations of past events in the light of new evidence, and tries to construct a better narrative with what little wit and fluency he has at his command. His discipline has long ceased to be thought necessary for 'the education of statesmen', although when well written it might still serve for their entertainment – or for anyone else's for that matter. Indeed, this was really always its function, despite the myth that eighteenth century gentlemen in their country houses used it as a preparation for power. Their real apprenticeships were served running estates and acting as magistrates – even then History was only a pastime for them. Today, participation in a single departmental meeting at a university would surely be enough to convince anyone that historians have no special claims to statesmanship of any kind. The only positive attribute that History can offer, perhaps, is scepticism, born of a professional familiarity with man's past mistakes, crimes, short-sightedness and optimism. It is that scepticism, therefore, which I would now like to employ in taking a closer look at the study of International Relations.

If History is a relatively simple business, International Relations most certainly is not. Its history as an academic discipline proves this. As everyone knows it grew out of the liberal reaction to the First World War. The blame for this catastrophe was assigned by many people to pre-war 'secret diplomacy', arms races, alliance systems and above all else to the lack of any international controls on the ambitions of sovereign states. It seemed obvious, therefore, that after 1918 all men of good will should construct some sort of framework for regulating international differences, preserving peace, and taming what Lowes Dickenson was to term 'the international anarchy'. The result was not merely the establishment of the League of Nations, the holding of disarmament conferences, and the employment of economic sanctions against aggressors, but a great deal of academic research into how a better world might be created based on a growing corpus of international law and the study of international organisation. By the outbreak of the Second World War, however, much of this 'idealism' had been undermined, not merely by German, Italian and Japanese defiance of the League, but also on an intellectual level, particularly in E.H. Carr's study *The Twenty Years Crisis*. The Second World War itself, and the Cold War subsequently, confirmed the dominance of the so-called 'realist school' in the analysis of international politics, an approach to the subject associated with names such as Hans J. Morgenthau, Stanley Hoffmann, Henry Kissinger and others. Morgenthau and his co-author, Kenneth W. Thompson, were to describe the basis of it when they wrote that 'the core of international relations is international politics and . . . the subject matter of international politics is the struggle for power among sovereign states'.[2] If this seemed to mark them off morally from their idealist predecessors, this was far from being the case, since they, too, began from a normative standpoint – the belief that so long as there was no internationally agreed system of morality among nations or individuals, and so long as there was no international organisation capable of enforcing any, statesmen could not be expected to sacrifice national interests for universal principles. They, too, wanted a world in which peace and harmony reigned, but their solution was to seek security in strength rather than in law, and if need be, to manipulate the international state system in the national interest. Indeed, the system derived its coherence by the ways in which states did this.

The 'Realists' in turn were succeeded by the 'Behaviouralists' and the 'Structuralists'. The first believed that the struggle for power between states was insufficient in itself to explain the international system. In the last resort, they argued, clubs might well prove to be trumps, yet states had to co-exist with one another over long periods of time and engage in all sorts of activities – legal, economic, social, intellectual – involving interactions on an assortment of levels and in a variety of ways, none of which could satisfactorily be explained merely by reference to force. Moreover, these interactions need not involve only states but groups and organisations which were distinct from states: classes, special interest groups, public opinion, political parties, the media, universities, companies, religions and even individuals. 'Structuralists', on the other hand, have been more concerned with economic issues and with attempts to explain the (mal)distribution of wealth within the world. Their themes are imperialism, underdevelopment, trade, aid, colonialism and dependency. Like the 'Behaviouralists', therefore, they also place less emphasis on states than 'Realists' and old-fashioned 'Idealists'. Nonetheless the state, or relations between states, remain at the centre of nearly all writings on international relations.

From the above it should have become obvious that the student of International Relations today is under pressure to choose between which of these 'paradigms' he believes most conforms with the workings of the world. Since in practice they all overlap in various ways, this is not an easy task. Nor is it made any easier by the fact that in order to test any of them the student must acquire some knowledge of a whole host of other disciplines – History, Politics, Sociology, Economics, Law, Psychology, Anthropology and Philosophy, to name but a few. Historians occasionally persuade themselves that they are in a similar position, but they rarely feel the need to do anything about it. The documents usually see them through. International Relations is different: the present and future still have to be shaped and the student of International Relations is actually expected to employ these fascinating tools in order to provide the shapes. Yet can this be done? Quincy Wright, a founding father of International Relations, has written: 'It is intriguing to consider whether all this study provides any firmer basis for predicting what the world will be like in the year 2000 than the Book of Revelations provided for the year 1000.'[3] Others, including many historians, have their doubts too. They stem not from intellectual hostility, however, but from a feeling that International Relations too often tries to over-extend itself and may sometimes look foolish as a result. Let us therefore now examine some of the issues which undermine faith in International Relations as an academic discipline.

One criticism is that despite its status as a social science it cannot provide any firm basis for predicting the future. This was the point hinted at by Quincy Wright himself. Other social sciences seem much better at doing this. Economists, after all, are always making predictions – about balance of payments problems, levels of inflation, growth potential, etc.; political scientists can use psephology and other tools to predict election outcomes, public reactions, future developments in political parties and organisations; while sociologists can often make telling predictions regarding social problems after having worked with minorities, prisoners, drug addicts and criminals. International Relations specialists, on the other hand, always seem much more coy about their particular discipline. After all, nobody predicted the Falklands War, the Iran-Iraq War, or even the 1973 oil crisis. Even the fall of the Shah – something which looked a 50–50 per cent chance to the man in the street – came as a surprise to many experts (not least those in the British Foreign Office, if diplomats can be regarded as International Relations specialists). Why then should International Relations have such a poor record in this respect, and can anything be done about it? Should anything be done about it? Historians, of course, are lucky. They are very rarely called upon to make risky judgements in the same way – although occasionally a *cause célèbre* like the Hitler Diaries can ruin a hitherto unbesmirched reputation. They therefore sympathise deeply with their International Relations colleagues when they display due modesty about predictions. Moreover, the past is full to overflowing with examples of those who got it wrong. Nobody, after all, predicted a world war in 1914, and once it broke out everyone expected it to be a short war. Likewise, before 1939, when war seemed almost inevitable, everyone saw aerial bombardment as the key to victory. Yet as things turned out, it was to be developments like radar, sonar, Enigma and other technological advances, including the atom bomb, which were to be of real significance. The historian, therefore, usually expects predictions, those in any case of the sort associated with the study of International Relations, to go awry. Nonetheless, this is not the automatic assumption of all International Relations practitioners.

Take the study of war for example. Thanks to a number of International Relations specialists there is now a huge literature on this particular subject. I am not now referring to the historical literature describing particular wars, their origins, development and consequences. I refer, rather, to those studies of war as a phenomenon associated with human nature, or, in Kantian terminology, as a *Ding an sich*. One example of this genre is Francis A. Beer's *Peace Against War: The Ecology of International Violence*, which has a bibliography more than 60 pages long. On page one of this work we read:

> This book aims to provide an epidemiology of peace and war. It rests on two central assumptions: (1) war is like a disease, for example, cancer or heart disease; and (2) we can develop a scientific knowledge of war, similar to the knowledge we have about disease, that will allow us better to describe, explain, predict and control it.[4]

Both assumptions, in my humble opinion, are absolutely false – for reasons which I need not go into here – but the point to note is the methodology which Beer and others then employ to further their research. A lot of it involves the collection of facts: how many wars there were in each century, how many casualities, how much money the wars cost, how much civil violence accompanied each war. Much of this is written up in a sort of jargon that in the end resembles less an addition to scientific knowledge than a new form of antiquarianism. Moreover, in the welter of statistics produced one tends to forget just how unreliable they are. (For example, we know far too little about ancient and non-European wars to produce the kind of lists of wars and casualties from 3600 BC to 1980 which Beer publishes.) Finally, what do all these statistics tell us? Here is the late Professor Northedge describing the work of Quincy Wright himself:

> Professor Wright examined 126 wars between 1475 and 1940 and found that the 42 which began in the late fifteenth century and the sixteenth centuries averaged 2.4 participating states. The 22 which began in the seventeenth century averaged 3.5 states each; the 19 which began in the eighteenth century averaged 4.8 each; the 32 which began in the nineteenth involved 3.1 states each, and the twentieth century, the era of world wars, had so far, according to Quincy Wright, experienced up to 1942, the date of publication of his *Study*, 11 wars which averaged the greatest number of belligerents each, that is, 5.6.[5]

One is tempted to ask so what? Eighteenth and nineteenth century states, after all, included empires which themselves included the territories of later nation states. Are we then comparing like

with like? Do the figures therefore mean anything? Are they
not in fact of use only to historians who can set them in their
historical context and explain the *unique* nature of developments
in different periods? Professor Beer, however, would dispute this.
He states: 'Our description and explanation of the dynamics of
peace and war provide a basis for predicting the future and a
strategy that might control it'.[6] While admitting that 'projections
of the future are always risky,' he concludes:

> We stated in Chapter 2 that there may be a long-run trend
> towards peace diffusion and war concentration and aggravation.
> Peaceful periods may be longer today while wars may have
> become less frequent and shorter. War casualties may have
> increased both in absolute terms and relative to population.
> The actual existence of such a trend is open to question. If it
> does exist, however, the map of future international relations will
> show longer, lower valleys of peace together with sharper,
> higher peaks of violence.[7]

On this admittedly rather flimsy basis, he then makes a number of
proposals for a better world. Alas, there is no reason to take his trend
very seriously. The Harvard sociologist, P.A. Sorokin, constructed
the following indices of major wars over the centuries: fifteenth,
100; sixteenth, 180; seventeenth, 500; eighteenth, 370; nineteenth,
120; twentieth, 3,080.[8] From these it might be concluded that there
was an upward trend in the fifteenth, sixteenth and seventeenth
centuries, a downward one from the seventeenth till the nineteenth
centuries and an upward one in the present century. Yet it would
be a brave man who would conclude that there was any way of
knowing in any of these centuries which way the trend would go
in the following one. In fact, there is no reason at all why any
series of statistics relating to war in one century should tell us
anything at all about statistics in the next. The body politic is
simply unlike the human body, in that its diseases do not follow
a predictable, pathological course in which stages and outcomes
are predetermined. Professor Beer's work, in other words, is
based on false analogies and premises.

So much for predictability. Historians also have doubts regarding
trends. Here the question is not whether generalisations can be
made. It is whether they can be made on a level higher than the
obvious. Take, once again, the question of war, this time with
respect to origins. A leading International Relations specialist in this

field is Professor John G. Stoessinger, whose book, *Why Nations Go to War*, is now in its fourth edition. Like Professor Beer, Stoessinger believes that war is a disease. He writes: 'I deeply believe that war is a sickness, though it may be human kind's "sickness unto death"'.[9] It is also, he says, 'learned behavior' which can be unlearned and ultimately selected out entirely from human activity. He concludes: 'We must therefore make an effort to look Medusa in the face and to diagnose the sickness. Diagnosis is no cure, of course, but is the first and the most necessary step. I shall attempt this diagnosis by suggesting certain common themes.'[10] Yet his conclusions are either superficial or wrong. For example, on pages 103–4, we read: 'The first general theme that compels attention is that no nation that began a major war this century emerged a winner'.[11] But surely this is untrue? It is not always a simple matter, of course, to say who begins a war. For example, the twentieth century began with the Boer War, at the start of which, technically, the ultimatum was issued by the Boers. But the British had had one of their own ready and it had been Milner in South Africa who had been trying to start a war for the previous eighteen months. The British, of course, won. Stoessinger might object that the matter of the ultimatum is the deciding factor. Yet in that case, his generalisation still fails to compel attention, since in 1939 it was Great Britain that issued the ultimatum to Hitler, which started the Second World War. Once again Great Britain was on the winning side. The Second World War itself, of course, was really a series of wars included in which were Hitler's attacks on a whole string of countries, all of which were successful until the attack on the Soviet Union. It was really only this final war which proved a failure. The case of the Six Day War in 1967 again provides a conundrum. Here there would seem to be a clear-cut example of a preventive war by Israel producing a success. Yet Stoessinger blames Nasser's diplomacy for the war, arguing that the Israelis were pushed into it by Arab pressure. But what then of Pearl Harbor? In 1941, the Japanese believed that they were under just as much pressure from the United States. If Egypt was responsible for 1967, then America was surely responsible for 1941. Yet in the first case the attacker won and in the second it lost. In short, this particular theme of Stoessinger's compels more attention than agreement. His others, by the way, are either very obvious or superficial, such as: 'With regard to the outbreak of war, the case studies indicate the crucial importance of the personalities of leaders'.[12] Many of them have to do with misperceptions of the other side. Yet these so-called misperceptions often amount to little more than hindsight, since people rarely start wars they think they will lose. Victorious powers, on the other hand, are rarely accused of the same mistake. Stoessinger, indeed, at times approaches tautology, for example, when he writes: 'Thus, on the eve of each war, at least one nation misperceives another's power. In that sense, the beginning of each war is a misperception or an accident. The war itself then slowly, and in agony, teaches the lesson of reality'.[13] This is almost as insightful as concluding that in most wars one side loses.

The study of wars and war origins, of course, continues. A recent issue of *Millennium* devoted space to a review article by Darryl Roberts[14] which began: 'The spatial domain and principals [*sic*] of war have changed dramatically in the last three decades'. It informs us, among other things, that 'Cyclical studies of war are longitudinal, but more are ahistorical.'[15] and concludes that 'what emerges from this review is a fundamental belief that there are different forms of war [and that] the explanations and techniques we adopt to examine some wars may be inappropriate for studying all wars'.[16] This latter conclusion would be a welcome one were it not for the fact that it is followed by the sentence: 'The historical formation of the state is plainly less important for explaining international war than for other kinds of war'.[17] Still, historians do little better themselves when it comes to generalisations. For example, Professor Sir Michael Howard in his characteristically elegant 1981 Creighton Lecture on *The Causes of War* discovered that he could little improve on Thucydides: 'What made war inevitable was the growth of Athenian power and the fear this caused in Sparta'.[18] You can vary the names of the actors, according to Howard, but the model still remains valid.

So much then for trends and generalisations. Probably there are areas where more sophistication can reap greater rewards, yet it will be difficult to convince historians that this is so. They will prefer, I think, to avoid generalisations as much as possible, and in this way avoid offering hostages to fortune. Perhaps they may even remember the example of the International Relations specialist, who in 1968 is supposed to have appeared on one television channel explaining that there were six reasons why the Soviets would not invade Czechoslovakia, only to appear the following night on the other explaining that there were six reasons why they had had to.

A third reason why historians have their doubts about International Relations as a discipline is that they all too often see International Relations specialists build up generalisations on faulty historical examples or on the most superficial, and often out-of-date historical research. I have already taken issue with Professor Stoessinger on historical interpretation, but this is a different, although related point. (Even here, however, he is rather remiss, his chapter on the origins of the First World War, for example, being based to a large extent on Barbara Tuchman's *The Guns of August*, with his most recent authority for the chapter listed as 1963.) It is simply infuriating for historians to discover that Professor X concludes Y on the grounds of historical examples A–K, when examples A, B, C and D are wrong and have been known to be wrong for at least 50 years, or when Professor Z cites countries which did not exist at the time, or seems to believe that being a century or two out concerning dates does not really matter. Yet this sort of thing crops up time and time again. For example, Darryl Roberts in the *Millennium* article referred to above talks about Austria–Hungary and Yugoslavia in the First World War,[19] although the Slovenes, Croats and the Serbs from Bosnia–Herzegovina were actually fighting for Franz Joseph and Yugoslavia did not come into existence until the war was over. Naturally, one cannot condemn all International Relations specialists on account of the sloppy standards of only some practitioners, yet there is sufficient sloppiness around to warrant reproof. Fortunately, International Relations, in Britain at least, has at its disposal a large number of specialists whose training in History makes them aware of the pitfalls involved, one of whom indeed, Christopher Hill of the LSE International Relations department, has written an excellent article on the role of history within the discipline in both Britain and the US.[20]

Let me now approach a more specific problem which exercises historians more than their International Relations colleagues – the writing of contemporary history. This is something which International Relations specialists do very often, and often do very well (there are notable exceptions). The objection raised by other International Relations specialists, however, is that it is simply not analytical enough and can sometimes seem like 'one damned thing after another'. This, I think is a valid point, and one which holds not merely for contemporary History. We shall return to it in a moment. The objection from historians, on the other hand – or at least from some historians – is that there is no point in writing contemporary history, since without access to the archives, the end result is merely journalism or propaganda. What attitude therefore should historians and International Relations specialists adopt towards the writing of contemporary history? In my own view, both should seek to practise it on the highest possible level – that is, with due regard to the facts insofar as they are known and with an attempt to give all sides of contemporary arguments without a display of bias. This is not an easy task, but it is certainly a rewarding one. Moreover, from the historian's point of view it is an absolutely essential one. For when a new generation of scholars (International Relations specialists as well as historians) appear in thirty years' time, ready to tackle archival material, they will simply be unable to do their job if they do not have access to already existing secondary works of contemporary History to use as a starting point.

Moreover, my own view is that in many cases – the majority in fact – they will find that the contemporary historian will have already figured out what had been going on even without their access to archives, in which circumstance their job will often be to fill in details and to refine arguments rather than to overturn accepted truths. There is far too much hypocrisy in statements by historians concerning archives. Their condemnation of journalists is equally hypocritical: there are, after all, good as well as bad journalists, many of whom have access to sources denied both to the International Relations specialist and the contemporary historian and whose judgement and accuracy are just as commendable. This in fact has always been the case. As Gavin B. Henderson wrote as far back as 1941:

> In the course of these researches [into the Crimean War] I read many articles in the *Edinburgh Review, Blackwood's, Chambers'*, the *Quarterly*, the *Fortnightly*, and others; and I was amazed by the perspicacity and the balanced judgements of intelligent contemporaries . . . My researches, I felt, were doing no more than cutting away the rank overgrowth of the 'sixties and 'seventies, and bringing things back – with a little additional information – to what the intelligent contemporary had known.[21]

Henderson then made a number of fundamental points in defence of contemporary history, quoting Thucydides and Xenophon, to show that the ancient Greeks themselves had proved conclusively that it 'could be as lively, as impartial, and as authoritative as any other type of history'.[22] Indeed, he is worth quoting once more at some length. He writes:

> The historian has undoubted advantages over the contemporary. He has despatches, cabinet minutes, private letters and memoirs. He has no excuse for not seeing the wood for the trees. But the contemporary has many advantages over the historian. He has the spirit of the age, he can ask questions, and judge from the tone of an answer whether the truth is told or not. He can go at least as far, by intuition and common sense, as the historian with all his sources; and he is just as likely to make an accurate judgement, apart from some matters of detail . . . Certain gaps in our knowledge of contemporary events must certainly be admitted. Yet we know a thousand times more about the collapse of France [he was writing in 1941] than we know about the collapse of Carthage. We know more about the evacuation of Dunkirk than we know about the Battle of Hastings. We can meet and discuss matters, any day we like, with men who were at Dunkirk. Would not any true medievalist give up his whole life's research for the sake of one interview with one Saxon who fought beside Harold at Hastings? Yet historians make their judgements on Carthage and Hastings. They make their judgements on very defective evidence; but it is the only evidence they have, and no-one denies their right to do so. Are historians to be denied the right to make their judgement now, upon Dunkirk and upon France – on a thousand times better evidence – simply because at some future date a little new material will come forward and a rather dubious 'perspective' will be achieved? It seems to occur to no-one that 'perspective' may become worse rather than better, though this has happened more than once in the past.[23]

Henderson's arguments, to my mind, are irrefutable, yet they do not dispose of the problems associated with the study of contemporary History, but merely justify the right to practise it. As we have already noted, these problems, particularly from the point of view of International Relations, involve both style and judgement, so let us now examine them.

With regard to style, the criticism often made by International Relations students that contemporary History is presented merely as a chronology of facts, is often a valid one. It can be true, as has already been admitted, of any period of history. The only answer is for contemporary historians to write in a more lively fashion and to be prepared to ask as original questions as possible. But here the question of sound judgement arises, and in my view it must be connected with the need to give all sides of contemporary arguments. For it is at this point – when the contemporary historian is interpreting facts rather than listing 'one damned thing after another' – that he is most at prey to his hopes, fears and ideological prejudices, much, much more so than when writing of the more distant past. It is at this point, therefore, that he must take every step to beware of propagandising, something I have been personally made aware of in writing my own books on contemporary Britain.[24] For example, in a recent study of *Britain's Decline*[25] I took great care to present a whole spectrum of views, and quite deliberately forbore, despite strong political feelings, to prejudge the ultimate success or failure of Thatcherism.

Other practitioners of the art, however, would no doubt disagree, International Relations specialists prominent among them. My colleague at the LSE, for example, Professor Fred Halliday, has written a history of International Relations since 1945, concentrating on the period since the late 1960s, entitled *The Making of the Second Cold War*.[26] In the preface to it he explains that 'it is an attempt to establish the main parameters of international politics since the late 1960s, and to provide a rival interpretation to that which is conventionally presented, in both east and west'.[27] He also explains that 'part of the impetus to writing this work [came] from the peace movement'[28] and that throughout his writing of it he was 'given sustained and invaluable encouragement by *New Left Review* and the Transnational Institute'.[29] None of this is to be criticised in itself, yet the end result – in my opinion – given its numerous moral judgements and dubious historical interpretations, not to mention its call for an independent, socialist Europe, is as much a political tract as an academic polemic. Such a combination, I fear, is rather disturbing for the historian, although – as I have already conceded – if social scientists are to be allowed to influence policy-making, it is no doubt legitimate for the International Relations specialist. It is just as well that undergraduates are properly trained to weigh up evidence against argument and to reach balanced judgements of their own.

For post-graduate students, of course, the question of balanced judgement is crucial. If theses are to be written on contemporary affairs, then such balanced judgement will alone enable students to make the kind of deductions from secondary sources which are likely to impress examiners. In other words, given their lack of archival materials, their conclusions will have to be argued in such a way as to exclude any possibility of propaganda. This can only be done by marshalling all the available evidence and assessing all the possible points of view, something which, despite the reservations of many of my colleagues, I have no doubt can be done. In short, if there is a place for politics and polemics in the writing of contemporary History, it is not to be found in graduate theses.

There are a few other points which one might raise concerning International Relations. One thinks of the debate over the existence of an international system as opposed to an international society or the question as to whether the international system represents more than the sum of its parts. Yet these are issues which, it seems to me, do not bear on the legitimacy of International Relations as a social science. I shall therefore attempt at this point to sum up my feelings about the discipline in the light of the doubts which I have already discussed.

First, it seems quite obvious to me that International Relations has a legitimate place within university education as a social science devoted to explaining the contemporary world to undergraduates. In doing so, however, it is faced with methodological difficulties and challenges which are greater than those facing historians. Insofar as these concern divining trends and making predictions, I clearly have doubts about how ambitious International Relations specialists can afford to be. Still, using a whole range of disciplines, there should be scope for some progress even here – admittedly more in some fields than in others. In any case, undergraduates should be encouraged to make generalisations, if only to get used to destroying them by testing them against the evidence. That, after all, is the basis of all teaching in the humanities. A great part of International Relations teaching, I am convinced, should also be devoted to contemporary history. This should be taught in an imaginative way and should teach undergraduates to ask questions about the contemporary world. Yet the search for relevance in this context should not be allowed to become the handmaiden to ideology. Finally, on the level of postgraduate research, it seems to me that, in the absence of many verifiable sources, International Relations students must be trained to reach balanced judgements if the wider academic community is to accept their academic credentials. In fact, we are already happy to do so.

NOTES AND REFERENCES

1. Margot Light and A.J.R. Groom (eds), *International Relations: A Handbook of Current Theory* (London: Frances Pinter, 1985).
2. Quoted by William Olson and Nicholas Onuf in 'The Growth of a Discipline Reviewed', in Steve Smith (ed), *International Relations: British and American Perspectives* (Oxford: Basil Blackwell, 1985), p. 5.
3. Olson and Onuf, 'The Growth of a Discipline', p. 28.
4. Francis A. Beer, *Peace Against War: The Ecology of International Violence* (San Francisco: W.H. Freeman, 1981), p. 1.
5. F.S. Northedge, *The International Political System* (London: Faber & Faber, 1976), p. 282.
6. Beer, *Peace Against War*, p. 281.
7. Beer, *Peace Against War*.
8. Northedge, *The International Political System*, p. 281.
9. John S. Stoessinger, *Why Nations Go to War* (London: Macmillan, 1985), pp. 202.
10. Stoessinger, *Why Nations Go to War*, p. 203.
11. Stoessinger, *Why Nations Go to War*, pp. 203–4.
12. Stoessinger, *Why Nations Go to War*, p. 206.
13. Stoessinger, *Why Nations Go to War*, p. 211.
14. Darryl Roberts, 'Logics and Evidences of War: Progress and Contradictions', *Millennium: Journal of International Studies* (Vol. 16, No. 1, Spring 1987), p. 89.
15. Roberts, 'Logics and Evidences', p. 114.
16. Roberts, 'Logics and Evidences'.
17. Roberts, 'Logics and Evidences'.
18. Michael Howard, 'The Causes of Wars', in *The Causes of Wars and Other Essays* (London: Unwin Paperbacks, 1984), p. 16.
19. Roberts, 'Logics and Evidences', p. 114.
20. Christopher Hill, 'History and International Relations', in Steve Smith (ed), *International Relations*, pp. 126–45.
21. Gavin B. Henderson, 'A Plea for the Study of Contemporary History', in *Crimean War Diplomacy and Other Historical Essays* (New York: Russell & Russell for Glasgow University Publications LXVIII, 1975), pp. 242–3.
22. Henderson, 'A Plea', p. 244.
23. Henderson, 'A Plea', pp. 243–5.
24. A Sked and C. Cook, *Post-War Britain: A Political History* (Penguin: Harmondsworth, 1984) and A. Sked, *Britain's Decline: Problems and Perspectives* (Oxford: Basil Blackwell, 1987).
25. A. Sked, *Britain's Decline*.
26. Fred Halliday, *The Making of the Second Cold War* (London: Verso Editions, 1983).
27. Halliday, *The Making of the Second Cold War*, Preface.
28. Halliday, *The Making of the Second Cold War*, Preface.
29. Halliday, *The Making of the Second Cold War*, Preface.

6 International Relations Theory and the Processes of World History: Three Approaches

B.K. Gills

International Relations, as an academic discipline, has the potential to formulate theory concerning general patterns of world historical development. Karl Popper's admonition against the errors of historicism has not prevented a widespread renewal of academic interest in such general theory. However, unlike the claims that were once made on behalf of law-like propositions in Sociology and the Philosophy of History, the International Relations discipline's claims to general theory are more circumspect. The claims of International Relations theorists are less concerned with laws and more interested in discerning patterned processes. Nonetheless, the very holism of world history presents any effort at such theory building with a formidable database. The International Relations discipline has been justifiably cautious in pursuing theoretical generalisations of world historical scope. The subject has been more circumscribed and delimited by the discipline, than in most of the nineteenth century macrotheoretical approaches, to understanding the general behaviour patterns in systems of states. The fact of holism, however, makes abstracting the State as a pure analytical category quite difficult, since real states are embedded in larger and more complex social structures. The problem of setting historical and conceptual parameters thus becomes fundamental at the outset. It follows that the role of historical research becomes of paramount importance to a project designed to generate theoretical generalisations of world historical processes.

In each of the three schools or approaches that will be discussed in this study, a great historian and a great historical research project lay at the core. In the work of Arnold Toynbee, Karl Marx and Fernand Braudel lay the foundations of, respectively, the

Traditional (Historical) International Relations approach, Historical Materialism, and the World-System school of Historical Sociology. The historical scope and the conceptual apparatus employed in each of these three research projects have been widely emulated by successor theorists, thus forming distinct traditions.

The problem of holism in world history can be addressed through two poles of reaction: the 'minimalist' and the 'maximalist'. The minimalist approach sets parameters limited to the subject directly under consideration and excludes all else. In International Relations this has been manifest in the tendency to focus solely on the 'political' aspects of the State, as expressed in diplomacy and war; i.e. upon 'high politics'. The poverty of the minimalist approach, closely associated with the Realist tradition and the concept of Power Politics, has undermined its long-held dominance in the discipline. The decline of Realism has opened the way toward re-evaluation of maximalist approaches to International Relations theory. Maximalism, however, confronts a problem of emcompassing too much data in a tendency toward macro-sociological theory. There is no easy solution to the predicament, but if maximalist approaches are now becoming more common, it is an indication that the discipline has divided into the minimalist tendency and the maximalist tendency, rather than either one being clearly dominant. In this context, the debate concerning the unit of analysis, conceptual framework, and historical scope of International Relations theory will probably become of central importance to the future of the International Relations discipline. It is to these issues that emphasis will be given in the discussion below.

6.1 THE TRADITIONAL (HISTORICAL) INTERNATIONAL RELATIONS SCHOOL

The Traditional (Historical) school of International Relations is most frequently associated with the works of Martin Wight and Hedley Bull.[1] Though often neglected, the legacy of Arnold Toynbee in this school is of considerable importance. It is the special approach to the use of world history that distinguishes this approach from other attempts at International Relations theory such as those of John Burton, Ernst Haas, Morton Kaplan, Robert Keohane and Joseph Nye, Hans Morgenthau, or Kenneth Waltz. Martin Wight collaborated with Toynbee on *A Study of History* through Volume VII. Toynbee's comparative analysis of 'Universal States' in Volume

VI and 'Universal Churches' in Volume VII are perhaps the first great textual contributions of this school to International Relations literature, particularly the volume concerning universal states, which is a comparative analysis of historical hegemonic structures.

The Toynbean concern for 'universal history' and the comparative historical approach employed by Toynbee can be traced in some measure to the work of Frederick J. Teggart, whom Toynbee credited with considerable influence upon his own work.[2] Toynbee's study of universal states is primarily a static comparison of bureaucratic, administrative, military, and other structural features of historical empires, although it forms a part of his overall analysis of the general evolutionary dynamics of civilisation. In a sense, Martin Wight, trained initially as a historian at Oxford, became the interpretor of the Toynbean research project to the field of International Relations. According to Hedley Bull, 'the young Martin Wight was profoundly influenced by Toynbee'. Bull clarifies the distinctiveness of Wight's approach as 'based on the comparative study of state-systems, that have actually existed', but notes that Wight did not seek to present 'a systematic theory of the goals of all states' in the manner of Hans Morgenthau.[3] Wight's approach to theory was not about what the abstract State should or would do, but rather about what configurations of states had *actually* done, in history. The emphasis on states 'that have actually existed' is the key to the Traditional (Historical) school's approach to theory.

Martin Wight replaced Toynbee's amorphous unit of analysis, the 'civilisations', to which Toynbee had attributed both organic and even teleological attributes, but whose actual historical boundaries were extremely indistinct, by a more precise and more elegant unit of analysis, the 'states-system'. In fact, the set of great 'civilisations' that Toynbee had selected in his analysis of world historical processes is practically a set of rubrics for great hegemonic moments in international history. Wight's choice of the states-system as the primary unit of analysis was brilliant in its clarity and simplicity. Wight distinguished between 'primary states-systems', composed of states, and 'secondary states-systems', composed of systems of states. This distinction provided an elegant structural framework that could accommodate the contemporaneous juxtaposition of distinct regional international systems in one coherent world historical process. He embellished this framework with a wealth of erudite historical references. Though Wight's major works were published posthumously in an unfinished form, they represent a major achievement in the attempt to make generalising statements about world historical processes in the International Relations literature.

Wight traced the origins of the concept 'system of states' to Pufendorf's *De Systematibus civitatum*, of 1675. In an essay given the same title, now reprinted in *Systems of States*,[4] Wight poses four questions concerning the comparative analysis of non-European and European states-systems, which bear repeating:

> Do other states-systems show a succession of hegemonies, in which one great power after another tries to transform the states-system, or even to abolish it, by reducing it to unity?

> Do other states-systems embody a system of the balance of power? Does the balance of power system arise only in response to the threat of a hegemony? Has there been any states-system that was innocent of the idea or practice of the balance?

> Do other states-systems colonise or conquer their peripheral regions and afterwards admit these regions to membership?

> Do other states-systems develop sub-systems, and under what conditions?[5]

These four research questions remain even now a superb outline of an historical research project that would lead inexorably to the refinement of general International Relations theory. Wight's question concerning the 'succession of hegemonies' was tentatively answered in the affirmative when Wight commented that '[m]ost states-systems have ended in a universal empire, which has swallowed all the states of the system. It has been particularly clear in the case of primary states-systems, those that are the political expression of a single culture'.[6] Despite Wight's somewhat minimalist phrasing of the research questions, it is clear that the effort to answer them entails latent maximalist research parameters. Wight's question concerning colonisation of 'peripheral regions' and their integration into a pre-existing states-system has in fact been a major concern of numerous theorists in the past two decades, principally in the Development Studies literature. Wight's emphasis on cultural factors was to be amplified by Hedley Bull and lead into new theoretical directions.

Hedley Bull introduced a strong distinction between a system of states and a 'society of states', or 'international society' in pursuit of the cultural variables of the subject. Immediately upon this introduction, however, Bull acknowledged that 'we are, at once involved in difficult problems of tracing the boundaries'.[7] Bull thus implicitly recognises that the significant re-introduction of the enigmatic and often ephemeral cultural variables in a way detracts from the elegant clarity of Wight's formulation of states-systems as the primary unit of analysis. As examples of those 'international systems' – i.e., states-systems – that have also been 'international societies' Bull cites the classical Greek city-state system, the Hellenistic kingdoms, the warring states-system of ancient China, and the states-system of 'ancient India', by which he probably means pre-Mauryan northern India. Bull recognises a prior relationship in which an international society 'pre-supposes an international system', i.e., a states-system. He argues that 'an international system may exist that is not an international society'. This is a different formulation than Wight's structural differentiation between primary states-systems and secondary states-systems. For example, Bull says that 'Persia and Carthage formed part of a single international system with the classical Greek city-states, but were not part of the Greek international society'.[8] In Wight's framework, the Greek states-system could be viewed as part of a secondary states-system including 'Persia' and 'Carthage'. The concept of international society brings Bull's framework closer to Toynbee's, at the cost of similar potential confusion over parameters and historical boundaries. It is most of all the interchangeability of the two terms on the basis of the systemic attributes of 'common rules' that presents difficulty. For instance, whereas in *The Anarchical Society* Bull stresses 'the expansion of the European states system all over the globe, and its transformation into a states system of global dimension', he later characterises that transformation in terms of 'The Expansion of International Society' in the volume of the same title. Bull's formulation based upon cultural criteria, as opposed to purely structural criteria, leads him to a subtle misinterpretation of Wight's question concerning 'successive hegemonies' in states-systems as a recurrent phenomena of historical states systems to the degree that he can say that '[o]ther forms of universal political organisation have existed in the past on a less than global scale; in the broad sweep of human history, indeed, the form of the states-system has been the exception rather than the rule'.[9] But what Bull means here by states-system is actually a multi-state configuration, as opposed to a universal state or unified imperial structure. Unfortunately, Bull seems to miss the point about phase-like or successive development of hegemonies in states-systems as Wight posed it originally. Instead he focuses his research on describing the expansion of the originally

Euro-centred 'international society' to global dimensions.

In the introduction to *The Expansion of International Society*, Hedley Bull and Adam Watson say that:

> When European expansion began in the late fifteenth century the world was not organised into any single international system or society, but comprised of several regional international systems (or what we choose to call international systems with some danger of anachronism), each with its own distinctive rules and institutions, reflecting a dominant regional culture. The global international society of today is in large part the consequence of Europe's impact on the rest of the world over the last five centuries.[10]

This appears to be a factually correct statement which implies, however, that each of the regional states systems constituted a distinct international society in the sense of having a culturally defined set of shared 'common rules and institutions for the conduct of their relations'.[11] The expansion of the European states-system, and its subordination of other states-systems such as those represented by the rubrics of Inca, Aztec, Maya, Ottoman, Mughal and Ch'ing, created one integrated global states-system. Simultaneously, the distinctive international society that each of these other states-systems had previously maintained was undermined in favour of a globalised 'international society', as the corollary of a global states system. However, this indicates that the nature of international society as a cultural nexus is inextricably related to the 'succession of hegemonies' in the sense that what determines the dominant regional culture may in fact be the dominant state(s), in a manner evocative of Galtung's term 'cultural imperialism'.

Bull and Watson maintain that,

> in the three centuries from 1500 to 1800, as European involvement in Asian politics persisted and grew, and with it the armed rivalry of the European powers in Asia, a loose Eurasian system or quasi-system grew up in which European states sought to deal with Asian states on the basis of moral and legal equality, until in the nineteenth century this gave place to notions of European superiority.[12]

This could be interpreted as a way of saying, in Wight's terms, that the secondary states-system was being transformed into a primary states-system, on a global scale. This creation of a global primary states-system was not only unprecedented in world historical terms, but also entailed a rivalry for hegemony on this global scale, so that the 'succession of hegemonies' was no longer confined to distinct, separate, regional systems. Historically, it should be noted that a conjuncture between several regional states-systems of the greatest significance occurred approximately at the beginning of the nineteenth century. In this conjuncture the Ottoman, Mughal, and Ch'ing hegemonic structures were each experiencing an acute phase of entropy, largely precipitated by internal disintegrative social forces, precisely at the historical moment when European powers introduced a qualitative leap in the industrialisation of war. Prior to that conjuncture, European states had annexed technologically inferior regional systems such as those in America, but had made relatively little significant impact on the internal structure of the great imperial powers of the Ottoman, Mughals or Manchus. The bypassing of the Mediterranean trade routes as the key link in the Eurasian trade nexus in favour of the creation of trans-oceanic routes no doubt weakened the former dominant Mediterranean powers, Venice and the Ottoman empire, and encouraged the ascendance in the Eurasian trade nexus of West European maritime powers, but did not in itself determine the eventual subordination of the great continental empires of Asia to the European states.

According to Bull and Watson, what was most distinctive about the European regional international system was that it 'came to repudiate any hegemonial principle and regard itself as a society of states that were sovereign or independent'. Yet in the very same paragraph they note that other historical states-systems had had similar characteristics, including the warring states period of Chinese history, an era marked by incredibly intense rivalry which culminated in the hegemony of Chin, followed by Han, dynasty China and a 'universal state'. They further qualify this repudiation by noting that when Spain conquered and annexed the Aztec and Inca empires in America, the European states had not yet repudiated the hegemonial principle in their relations with one another. They point out that the idea that states – even in the European system – had equality of rights emerged only in the mid-eighteenth century. This idea was to be undermined even in European affairs by the European Concert of the early nineteenth century, in which a self-selected set of great powers assumed superior rights in the states system for themselves. At the global level, the European states established 'a number of empires which, while they were rival and competing, taken together amounted to a European hegemony over the rest of the world, which in the nineteenth century became an immense periphery looking to a European centre'.[13]

The incorporation of concepts such as 'centre' and 'periphery' into Bull and Watson's lexicon is most interesting, since it implies that such concepts as 'great power' and 'sphere of influence' are compatible with 'centre–periphery' analysis. At the same time that Bull and Watson rightly emphasise the 'centre–periphery' relationship in the creation of global European hegemony in its aspect as separate European empires, they nevertheless attribute an overall coherence to the European states system itself within that vast nexus of power relations. The logic of that particular historical phase of the European states-system in which it allegedly repudiated the hegemonial principle in relation to itself while confirming it in relation to each European state's imperial ambitions in the global arena of rivalry is of the utmost theoretical significance. The connection between the two aspects, hegemonial repudiation in the centre and hegemonial affirmation in the periphery is almost certainly not accidental; they are not merely contingent phenomena. The location of this phenomenon in world historical time, in the context of the transformation of a secondary states-system into a global primary states system structurally differentiated into parallel imperial systems each dominated by a European 'centre state' is the key to the logic.

Bull and Watson characterise the historical process in question as one which

> established the domination of one of the several regional international systems that existed in the fifteenth century over the others and over the less developed parts of the world as well – a domination that united the whole world into a single economic, strategic, and political system for the first time.

That the phenomena of successive hegemonies has been carried over into the global system is implied in the statement by Bull and Watson that the 'ebb tide of European dominance' has brought a:

> transition from a universal international system based upon European hegemony to one that is not, even if it may be argued that new hegemonies and new forms of hegemony have replaced old ones.[14]

Since the self-exhaustion of the West European powers in the Second World War, the global rivalry of the Soviet Union and the United States has of course been the principal manifestation of the struggle for succession to hegemony in the international system as a whole, though not the exclusive form of rivalry. The question now becomes whether it is possible to predict that the tendency Wight observed for most states systems to 'end' in a universal hegemony is operative in the modern global states system.

Despite the degree of inconsistency in the use of the units of analysis states system and international society in Bull's works, it is nevertheless his retention of the states-system as the key unit of analysis that gives him continuity with Wight's project. Bull's commitment to actual history becomes manifest in *The Expansion of International Society*, which attempts to describe the world historical processes leading to the first global states-system utilising an approach adapted from Wight. In the process, Bull moved the research project of the Traditional (Historical) school much closer to that of the World-System school of Historical Sociology and to the concerns of Historical Materialism. A common historical discourse is thus accelerating between the three approaches. Bull's initial preoccupation with the minimalist conception of international order gave way to an increasingly maximalist approach to describing the world historical processes which he identified as central to order.

Although there are numerous theorists outside the so-called 'British school' or Classical school whose work could be discussed in relation to the Traditional (Historical) approach, my discussion will focus on two figures, Robert Gilpin and George Modelski. Both of these authors have made significant contributions to the Traditional (Historical) school's theoretical literature which focus on interpreting world historical processes in terms of the overall general dynamics of states systems.

Robert Gilpin's research project in *War and Change in World Politics* was designed to examine the nature of international political change on a world historical scale, though Gilpin disclaims any pretension 'to develop a general theory of International Relations that will provide an overarching explanatory statement'. He does however make the claim that 'it is possible to identify recurrent patterns, common elements, and general tendencies in the major points in international history'.[15] Gilpin defines a general and comprehensive theory of International Relations as one which would 'assess types of international systems (tyrannical–liberal, Christian–Islamic, communist–capitalist, etc.) for their characteristic features and dynamics'.[16]

Gilpin makes direct reference to Toynbee and cites Toynbee's 'universal law': 'the tendency of the locus of power to shift from the center to the periphery of an international system'. Gilpin notes that, 'the tendency for technology and inventiveness to diffuse from dominant power to peripheral states (which in turn become the dominant powers of an enlarged international system) and the occurrence of fundamental shifts in the locus of political and economic power led Arnold Toynbee to formulate in *A Study of History* and elsewhere a set of generalisations regarding the dynamics of international politics'.[17] What Gilpin adds to this is a search for explanation of these shifts in the locus of power as an expression of changes in the production structure and in logistical and infrastructural development.

Gilpin defines the theory of international political change he seeks to develop as resting on the assumption that

'the history of an international system is that of the rise and decline of the empires and dominant states that during their periods of reign over international affairs have given order and stability to the system. We shall argue that the evolution of any system has been characterised by successive rises of powerful states that have governed the system and have determined the patterns of international interaction and established the rules of the system. Thus the essence of systems change involves the replacement of a declining dominant power by a rising dominant power'.[18]

Gilpin maintains that there is a lack of study by International Relations scholars of earlier or non-Western states-systems and suggests the need for a 'comparative study of international systems that concentrates on systemic change in different types of international systems'. This emphasis distinguishes Gilpin's suggested study from the 'regimes' literature of recent years, which concentrates on system change in the modern international system and places his project within Wight's outline.

Gilpin's analysis of the role of the accumulation of social surplus in the ascendance and descendance of hegemonic states has much in common with Historical Materialism. According to Gilpin, the 'territorial, political and economic expansion of a state increases the availability of economic surplus required to exercise dominion over the system. The rise and decline of dominant states and empires are largely functions of the generation and then the eventual dissipation of this economic surplus'. Gilpin ascribes a universality to this pattern in his contention that ancient states and empires of even the earliest civilisations 'sought to expand and extend their dominance over their neighbours in order to increase their share of the economic surplus'.[19]

Once the 'generation and dissipation' of economic surplus has been given centrality in the causal explanation of the expansionary logic of imperialism, the systematic and world historical analysis of production structures and their relationship to the political dynamics of change in states-systems becomes imperative. Gilpin does in fact incorporate the concepts of 'social formation' and 'mode of production' into his discussion. Following Samir Amin, he argues that 'the type of social formation is extremely important because it determines how the economic surplus is generated, its magnitude, and the mechanism of its transfer from one group or society to another'.[20] Thus, says Gilpin, the social formation conditions both the distribution of wealth and power within society as well as between distinct societies. Gilpin views significant differences between social formations as the key feature distinguishing modern from pre-modern international relations. Gilpin concurs with Wight, and Rader, that history reveals a 'cycle of empires' or 'imperial cycle' as a recurrent pattern in which one state eventually unifies the states-system under its imperial domination. However, Gilpin takes exception to Bull's use of international society in relation to these imperial phenomena, commenting that 'the principal ordering mechanisms were territorial control and spheres of influence. These imperial orders constituted merely a system of states, not what Hedley Bull (1977) characterised as an international "society"'.[21] Gilpin accepts the term 'succession of hegemonies' however, and utilises it to demarcate the pre-modern 'cycle of empires' from the 'succession of hegemonies' that he attributes to the modern period, since the nineteenth century. According to Gilpin, beginning first in the European states system and then on a global scale, 'successive political and economic hegemonies have supplanted the pattern of successive empires as the fundamental ordering principle of international relations'.[22] This thesis thus hinges on defining hegemony and empire as separate forms of political hierarchy, and is the corollary to Gilpin's contention that different social formations characterised pre-modern and modern international relations. What Gilpin does not provide is a comprehensive empirical analysis of historical hegemonies and empires based upon their characteristic social formations. Nor does he systematically, empirically, research the historical shifts in the locus of power or the mechanisms of surplus accumulation and its transfer between societies. His work is highly indicative of a research project promising to generate such an analysis, though in the absence of a major historical research project, his hypotheses must be taken as provisional rather than clearly demonstrative.

George Modelski's approach to world historical processes and International Relations theory emphasises 'long cycles' of world leadership and global politics. Modelski views the concept 'long cycles of world leadership' as a 'parsimonious device for describing and analyzing the principal structures and the chief processes of modern world politics' and presents his work as a 'theory of world politics'.[23] Modelski disclaims that long cycles are 'universally valid laws' of political behaviour but maintains confidently that they indicate a 'pattern of regularities characteristic of the modern world system'. His historical research parameters are limited to this 'modern world system' and he demarcates the pre-modern from the modern world system according to the 'degree of structural complexity in inter-regional relations'.[24] The crucial transformation of the inter-regional configuration is identified as the bypassing of the route linking Europe and China via the Middle East, which predominated in the Eurasian trade nexus prior to 1500, to a trans-oceanic nexus based on new logistical capabilities. Modelski's focus on inter-regional structural complexity stands in contrast to Immanual Wallerstein's emphasis on integrated production processes expressed in a specific division of labour as the key criterion distinguishing separate historical world systems. Modelski recognises that the 'thalossocracy' of Venice was the predominant Mediterranean hegemonic model prior to 1500, but chose to defend the model of the Portuguese maritime empire as the prototype of the succession of 'world leaders' to follow.

Modelski identifies a concrete historical set of 'world leaders' and delimits their succession in chronological cycles. He gives five long cycles of world leadership: (1) 1494–1580 (or 1517–1608); (2) 1581–1688 (or 1609–1713); (3) 1689–1791 (or 1714–1815); (4) 1792-1913 (or 1816–1945); and (5) 1914– (or 1946–), in which the 'world leaders' have been Portugal (1), the United Province of the Netherlands (2), Great Britain (3 and 4), and the United States (5), in order of their succession. A new world power emerges from a period of global war and Modelski specifies five periods of global warfare: 1585–1608, 1689–1713, 1793–1815, 1914–1918, 1939–1945, resulting in a high capability concentration at the outset of each new long cycle. In contrast to Fernand Braudel's contention that the European economy since the sixteenth century was characterised by a succession of 'dominant capitalist cities' in a succession list given as: Venice,

Antwerp, Genoa, Amsterdam, and London, Modelski characterises the leading world powers as being nation-states.[25] Modelski
argues that it is 'confusing to regard the '"states-system" as some
sort of external and objective reality within which other developments occur'.[26] *Contra* Hedley Bull, Modelski rejects the idea
that international relations has been 'anarchic' and suggests that
order has been embodied in the 'succession of orders of leadership'
from the Iberian to the Dutch, British and American. Though Bull
certainly acknowledges special perogatives of the great powers in
determining the nature of order, Modelski's formulation is different because of its assumptions about the internal cyclical logic of
the world system considered as an organic totality, not a mere
jumble of actors. In this use of the world system unit of analysis,
Modelski has much in common with the Wallersteinian school of
Historical Sociology. This common ground extends to the search
for conjuncture among different categories of cycles, as evidenced
in Modelski's attention to Kondratieff cycles.[27]

Modelski insists that his concept of world leadership should be kept
clearly distinct from the definition of hegemony as domination. He
regards such dominationist hegemony as a deviant form of regional
or world leadership. He characterises the colonial annexations
conducted by world leaders as aspects of their declining phase and
a deviation from the norms of world leadership. In my own view,
Modelski's emphasis on the role of particular leaders in relation to
order does not really offer any radically new insights different from
those already well-established in traditional International Relations
literature on the function of great powers as discussed by such
authors as E.H. Carr, Raymond Aron, Hedley Bull, or Kenneth
Waltz, except for the fact that Modelski seems to have reified the
world system. He fails to explain the succession of leadership in any
other than a conventional geopolitical manner and omits a detailed
historical analysis of production, though he recognises that there is a
'strong association between the world power and the lead economy'
of each long cycle. His emphasis on the role of sea power in the
world system is clearly indebted to Alfred Mahan and his 'capability
concentration' is quite similar to Kenneth Waltz's emphasis. Aristide
Zolberg has attacked Modelski's reification of the world system, and
particularly challenged Modelski to demonstrate *what* in fact was
the actual entity over which Portugal is said to have first asserted
its world leadership in the 16th century. In Zolberg's mind, 'the
cycles on which the theory is founded are obtained by relating

quite arbitrarily one feature common to widely differing historical configurations for treatment as a formal property'[28]. Modelski offers no empirical description of the economic structure of the global macro-structures over which the world leaders held temporary sway. He thus exaggerates the degree of influence such powers as Portugal or the Netherlands had on the actual historical inter-regional nexus, not only *vis-à-vis* the Asian empires such as the Ottoman, Mughal and Ch'ing but *vis-à-vis* other European powers, such as the Hapsburg Empire, France, and England. It is this confusion caused by his unit of analysis that makes Modelski's rejection of the concept of states-system as 'a concept too general to remain serviceable in analyses of a social science type' untenable. His difficulty in determining precise parameters within his formulation of the unit of analysis is clear in the following passage: 'from 1494 onward, we need to distinguish between a global political system, governed over the next century basically by the Treaty of Tordesillas and comprising principally Portugal and Spain, as well as France, England *et al.*, and partially overlapping with it (European and other) regional systems that would include, *e.g.*, the Ottoman Empire'. He acknowledges that the Ottoman empire was 'pressing upon the Tordesillas regime both in the Mediterranean and in the Indian Ocean' but nevertheless dismisses the Ottoman challenge as a failure to compete effectively for control of the global system. Thus Modelski maintains that, 'the major part of what we know as international politics of the modern period is in fact no more than the regional politics of Europe'[29]. Despite Modelski's commitment to discerning world historical processes as the ground for theory, the conceptual idiosyncracies of his framework distinguish him somewhat from both the mainstream Traditional (Historical) approach and the World-System school of Historical Sociology. His omission of production processes from the scope of his empirical concerns makes any common ground with Historical Materialism extremely difficult, as is the case with the neo-realist analysis of such authors as Kenneth Waltz.

6.2   HISTORICAL MATERIALISM

Karl Marx never fully elaborated a theory of International Relations as such, and this is perhaps the single greatest missing element in the entire corpus of his work. Indeed, it has been noted by Kubalkova

and Cruickshank that not only were 'Marx's ideas on the subject . . .
never explicitly formulated or brought together in one place' but that
even Historical Materialism itself is 'nowhere set out systematically,
but has to be reconstructed from such works as *The Economic and
Philosophical Manuscripts*, *The German Ideology*, *The Preface to a
Contribution to the Critique of Political Economy*, *The Eighteenth
Brumaire* and Engels's *The Origin of the Family, Private Property
and the State*'.[30] The title 'Historical Materialism' owes a great deal
to Bukharin's work *Historical Materialism: A System of Sociology*,
published in 1925. In recent years, there has been an attempt, most
notably by such authors as Robert Cox, to reinvigorate the definition
of Historical Materialism and render it more relevant to the discipline
of International Relations; especially in the critique of neo-realism.[31]

The poverty of international theory in the Marxist tradition
prompted Martin Wight to contend that 'Neither Marx, Lenin, nor
Stalin made any systematic contribution to international theory'.[32]
R.N. Berki concluded that international relations had been accorded
only a 'secondary and derivative' status in Marxism.[33]

Indeed, concerning the theory of the state itself, there is considerable admission among prominent present-day Marxist writers that
Marx failed to contribute a single coherent theory. For instance,
Bob Jessop denies that a 'single, coherent, unitary Marxist theory'
of the state can be distilled from Marx or Engels, and Ralph
Miliband has commented in a similar vein that Marx failed to
elaborate 'a comprehensive and systematic theory of the state';
though Marx had intended to include such a treatment of state
forms in his research project, of which *Capital* was to be only
the first part. Miliband concludes that the only available recourse
is to consult such historical *pièces de circonstance* as *The Class
Struggle in France*, *The 18th Brumaire of Louis Bonaparte*, and *The
Civil War in France* to identify Marx's ideas concerning the state.[34]

What, then, did Marx bequeath to Historical Materialism that
renders the tradition relevant to International Relations? Certainly
it was not a single theory to explain the behaviour of states.
Rather, it was the analytical approach implicit in his historical
research project that constitutes the legacy, and it is particularly
Marx's stress on the dialectical historical development of production
processes and political forms of domination on a world historical
scale that is of the utmost relevance to the International Relations
discipline today. Above all, it is probably Marx's study of 'modes
of production' and 'social formations' that provides the richest

conceptual legacy if adapted to analyse the historical forms of the interaction between states-systems and production structures.

In the opinion of Kubalkova and Cruickshank, international relations may yet 'assume a prestigious Marxist form and status' particularly if the trend set in motion by Althusser's structuralism continues to develop momentum. If so, 'the attempt to establish a general theory of modes of production and their combinations must inevitably give to international relations an important role'.[35] Kubalkova and Cruickshank cite Silviu Brucan and Theda Skocpol as examples of those Marxists who are willing to allocate a more significant, and autonomous, role for the state and states-systems in their analyses, in an effort to jettison the legacy of economic determinism.[36] Brucan has dealt with the category of nation in a manner that does not necessarily subordinate it to class, and Skocpol argues that the overarching context of the states-ststem must be brought into the analysis of classes and production structures even in regard to the internal social configuration in each state, rather than continue with any assumption of the causal primacy of the socio-economic base upon the political superstructure. Her thesis on the logic of revolutions is that they must be comprehended within the context of the rivalries and the configuration of capabilities embodied in the overarching international system.

The most fundamental task for Historical Materialism must be clearly to conceptualise the historical forms of the relationship between modes of production, classes, the State, and states-systems and clarify the nature of the causal relationships embodied in these historical formations. Realism's insights into the behaviour of states-systems remains a truncated vision of reality that only attention to production structures and class stratification can make whole. A plethora of Marxist-influenced approaches to International Political Economy have emerged, particularly in Development Studies, that have sparked widespread debate within the International Relations discipline and challenged the intellectual dominance of the realist and liberal-interdependence interpretations.[37] Indeed, the near ubiquitous discussion of conflicting 'paradigms' within the International Relations discipline is a somewhat euphemistic discourse predicated on the decline of traditional realist state-centric theory, to a considerable extent the result of the challenge posed by the new literature on IPE and imperialism derivative of Historical Materialism.[38] It is impossible to review all of these approaches here, except to repeat an argument made by David Booth; that in the course of the decline of dependency theory, the elaboration of a classical Marxist response by Bill Warren, the critique of Andre Gunder Frank's 'formalism' by Ernesto Laclau, and Robert Brenner's critique of the 'circulationist' interpretation, in the end it has been the 'modes of production debate' which has generated a promising new wave of empirical research.[39] Robert Cox has distinguished Historical Materialism from the 'ahistorical epistemology' of the 'structural Marxism of Althusser and Poulantzas' as 'very largely a study in abstractions'.[40] But this seems to be an unfair characterisation of the empirical research on the articulation of modes of production developing out of the initial Althusserian formulation.

There is indeed a vital role for the concept of the articulation of modes of production in relation to developing a Historical Materialist understanding of the dynamics of states systems as not merely derivative of the economic infrastructure. This potential is particularly evident in the concrete historical analysis of the transition from one socio-economic formation to another, of which Perry Anderson's studies on the transition from the ancient slave mode of production to the feudal mode of production, and on the historical emergence of the Absolutist state in the course of the transition in Europe from feudalism to capitalism is an outstanding example.[41] Though Anderson retains an overall framework of analysis based on the notion of successive 'stages' in world historical development conceived as the transition between discrete modes of production, he nevertheless argues that one of the basic axioms of Historical Materialism is that 'secular struggle between classes is ultimately resolved at the *political* – not at the economic or cultural – level of society. In other words, it is the construction and destruction of States which seal the basic shifts in the relations of production, so long as classes subsist'. In a seminal formulation, Anderson succinctly asserts that:

All modes of production in class societies prior to capitalism extract surplus labour from the immediate producers by means of extra-economic coercion the 'superstructure' of kinship, religion, law or the state necessarily enter into the constitutive structure of the mode of production in pre-capitalist social formations. They intervene *directly* in the 'internal' nexus of surplus extraction . . . In consequence, pre-capitalist modes of production cannot be defined *except* via their political, legal and ideological superstructures, since these are what determine the type of extra-economic coercion that specifies them. The precise forms of juridical dependence, property, and sovereignty that characterize a pre-capitalist social formation, far from being merely accessory or contingent epiphenomena, compose on the contrary the central indices of the determinate mode of production dominant within it.[42]

There can of course be no single 'Marxist' or Historical Materialist interpretation, or theory, of states-systems and social formations, as the methodological and theoretical debates within Historical Materialism will continue to generate divergence of views and considerable controversy.[43] However, the body of existing Historical Materialist literature concerning social formations represents a potentially rich source from which generalisations concerning the International Relations dimensions of world historical development processes could be distilled. These generalisations would encompass both capitalist and pre-capitalist social formations.[44] Marxist Historiography and the corpus of its empirical and theoretical research concerning social formations thus becomes a seed bed of International Relations theory, considered in world historical, and not merely modern, perspective. In this sense, Historical Materialism shares with the Traditional (Historical) International Relations approach a commitment to the direct relationship between empirical research in actual history and formulation of theoretical statements about patterned processes in world historical development.

Marxism has, of course, not neglected the subject matter of International Relations, but the orthodox Marxist approach to war has been dominated by Lenin's epiphenomenalism. It has been unfortunate for the fuller development of Marxist interpretations of International Relations that Lenin's work *Imperialism, the Highest Stage of Capitalism* was elevated to a central theoretical status that was probably beyond the merits of that small and polemical publication. The dogmatisation of Lenin's economistic interpretation of the outbreak of the First World War led to an ossification of international theory in states governed by Marxist-Leninist parties. Lenin's basic approach, the attempt to explain war among capitalist states as a direct consequence of the 'necessity' inherent in the inner logic of the capitalist mode of production itself, was widely emulated even outside the political confines of Stalinist regimes. In this process, the analyses of Bukharin, Hilferding, Hobson, Kautsky, and Luxemburg which were produced in the same period as Lenin's, were too often under-evaluated.[45]

The tendency to subordinate the logic of states and states systems to that of capital has persisted even in recent efforts at addressing the inter-relationship. Claudia von Braunmuhl, working from the context of the German 'derivationist' or 'capital logiç' perspective, argues for a derivation *from* the world market *to* the system of states, transcending the theory of the state as derivative of national capitalist social structures.[46] This position is still indicative of the traditional assumption of the overall causal primacy of the socio-economic base upon the political superstructure, though the unit of analysis has shifted from national parameters to world system parameters, – i.e. to the base as the capitalist mode of production *as a whole*. Martin Shaw, in an excellent critique of 'Orthodox Marxism' on the question of war, imperialism, and the state system, has contrasted the 'economism' of Marxist critiques of Lenin on imperialism to the 'politicism' in the Marxist debate on the state exemplified in the Miliband–Poulantzas debate. Shaw does not view 'preoccupation with the processes of bourgeois rule' as a remedy to the economism of reducing imperialism to mere economic relationships, concluding that 'The Marxist debate about the state, far from developing the connection between capitalist expansion and the militarism of states which even Lenin suggests, or bringing it up to date, has largely remained within a highly one-sided reading of Lenin'.[47] The problem of conceptualising the causal relationship between processes of state formation and processes of class formation must now move to the centre of Marxist concerns in a manner that will render it directly relevant to the development of international relations theory.[48] Martin Shaw's elaboration of basic theses that Marxism should come to terms with seems to me an excellent guideline for future orientation. Though it is too lengthy to be quoted in its entirety, it deserves repeating in excerpts:

1. We need to recognise theoretically the existence of a world system of states, as an analytically separable level within an understanding of world society as a whole. This system of the states pre-exists capitalism, indeed it was in part the framework within which capitalism developed, although it has also been transformed by it. The competition of states, with war as the ultimate means of resolution of conflicts, is integral to this system. This competition also pre-existed, therefore, and is not reducible to, the competition of capitals . . .

2. . . . Insofar as a world economy exists, in the sense of a world market . . . this has never been anything like a pure

market economy . . . It has always been, and remains very much, fragmented by the state-system: a state-segmented world economy . . . international economic relations are always partially relations between states.

3. 'The state' . . . does not exist: what we are concerned with are nation-states within the context of a system of states . . . each state is largely determined by its role within the states-system. At the same time, it is determined by the economy, class relations, political system, culture and ideology of the national society within which it is based.

4. The competition of states within the state-system has always given rise to the tendency of states to dominate other states, or to control people and territory outside the given scope of existing states. The forms of such domination, both in previous historical periods and in the epoch of capitalism, have varied very greatly. The tendency has, however, always been associated with the very existence of states . . . . It makes more sense to define imperialism as a general tendency of states, the particular forms of which are partially determined by the economic relations within which states exist, than to try to restrict the term to particular economically conditioned relations.[49]

However, it is precisely such a perspective which Kubalkova and Cruickshank contend that Karl Marx categorically rejected. They argue that Marx

wholly rejected the idea of a states-system as a form of political structure of the world, and instead clearly favoured what is referred to in the literature of International Relations as *world society* . . . Marx refused categorically to recognize any possibility of a capitalist world economy (characterized by worldwide production and exchange) developing in tandem with the states-system.[50]

Yet what did Engels and Marx mean, when in *The German Ideology*, they said that

The relations of different nations among themselves depend upon the extent to which each has developed its productive forces, the division of labour and internal intercourse. This statement is generally recognised. But not only the relation of one nation to others, but also the whole internal structural of the nation itself depends on the stage of development reached by its production and its internal and external intercourse.[51]

It is of course not proper to claim definitively that Marx categorically rejected a development 'in tandem' between the capitalist states and capitalist production. In the absence of a formal elaboration of International Relations theory by Marx, his productionist bias should not be interpreted too rigidly, nor too vulgarly. In any event, Marx will not have the final word on the subject.

The Marxist interest in war and conflict has recently begun to show new vitality, as exemplified by the work of such authors as E.P. Thompson and Mary Kaldor.[52] Both of these authors tend to· attribute a special logic to the institution of war embedded in the states system and thus differ with the more traditional Marxist explanations of war as an imperative of the capitalist mode of production, such as those by Kidron or Mandel.[53] It is understandable that this discussion of war is often topical and sets its temporal parameters at the most to the past few decades. However, a more fundamental world-historical analysis of the role of force in history should become a research goal in the expansion of the literature of war and conflict studies. Engels's work certainly needs updating. It is precisely such a study of war that must be brought to bear on the existing understanding of the economic and social fabric of modes of production. It is practically obvious that 'imperialism' and the forcible expropriation of surplus have been closely correlated phenomena throughout the entire history of states-systems, and no historical states-system seems to present an exception to this.

States are the products of the continuum of world history. The actually existing states in history have developed characteristic identities that have not been simply derivative of purely economic processes. The phenomena of the ethnic, linguistic, cultural, and geographical identities of states are deeply embedded in real history and must be incorporated into any proper materialist analysis of international relations. This has meant that modern states have not all, or always, developed in strict correlation to·the logic or needs of capital. The 'autonomy' of the states-system is rooted in the nature of states as historical subjects, as entities that embody other values than simply those of capital. The reluctance to recognise the autonomy of the states-system by some Marxists has not been, to my mind, a wilful obfuscation, but rather the result of a preoccupation with class exploitation, due to deeply held normative considerations. Analytically, however, this has proven to be a handicap when it comes to formulating International Relations theory. It is in this sense that the 'economic determinism' of the past must be transcended.

The philosophical basis for the rejection of vulgar economism is extremely important in this process of reformulation. Historiography alone will not suffice to render the tradition more relevant to International Relations theory. The rise of a critical theory of International Relations is perhaps the most powerful stimulus upon the International Relations discipline at present. Critical theory is being advanced within the International Relations discipline by such authors as Richard Ashley, Andrew Linklater, and Robert Cox, all of whom have been involved in the critique of Realism and neo-realism.[54] Mark Hoffman has recently argued that critical theory represents 'the next stage in the development of International Relations theory',[55] and sees such a development as post-Realist and post-Marxist; post-Marxist in the sense of Horkheimer, that it should develop on the spirit and not the letter of Marxism. In my own mind, the acid test of critical theory of International Relations will be whether or not it will successfully combine empirical historical research with epistemological, methodological and normative contributions to International Relations. The work of Robert Cox in the ambitious research project on 'States, Social Orders, and World Production'[56] seems to augur well for the fulfilment of that promise.

6.3 HISTORICAL SOCIOLOGY

In recent years the discipline of sociology has produced a number of significant contributions to the comparative study of world historical processes which have great relevance to International Relations theory. Although many of these contributions, such as those of Immanuel Wallerstein and his school, overlap considerably with Historical Materialism, the distinctly sociological and multi-disciplinary approach of this tradition sets it apart. The following discussion will focus on the 'world-system' school of Wallerstein, *et al.*, and upon the 'LSE school' as exemplified by Michael Mann and John Hall. In the case of the latter, the overlap with Historical Materialism is less apparent, and the Weberian overtones more prominent. Both schools, however, have entered into a direct dialogue with the International Relations discipline.

In treating the world-system approach, it may be appropriate to begin with reference to the project of Fernand Braudel, whose concept of 'total history' was so superbly illustrated in his study of the sixteenth century Mediterranean 'world'.[57] Braudel and the *Annales* school have had a tremendous influence on Wallerstein and the world-system school (e.g. Wallerstein names his research center the Fernand Braudel Center for the Study of Economics, Historical Systems, and Civilizations). Braudel's historical project encompasses not only the critical transitional sixteenth century in which the forces that were to create the modern world-system were set in motion, but traces the economic history of the developing capitalist society of Europe through the eighteenth century.[58]

Braudel not only inspired Wallerstein, but entered into a debate with him as well. In *The Perspective of the World* Braudel makes a rather rare theoretical intervention.[59] He discusses 'world-economies' in which 'a dominant capitalist city always lies at the centre' and indicates a succession of dominant cities in Europe since the fifteenth century. He argues that there is a 'hierarchy of zones' within a world-economy. Though Braudel adopts many such Wallersteinian formulations, he demonstrates a clear difference of opinion with Immanuel Wallerstein on the key issue of the relationship between a world economy and an empire. Braudel contends that although

> Immanuel Wallerstein has argued that wherever there was an empire, the underlying world economy was unable to develop . . . All the same, I am personally inclined to think that even under the constraints of an oppressive empire with little concern for the particular interests of its different possessions, a world-economy could, even if rudely handled and closely watched, still survive and organize itself, extending significantly beyond the imperial frontiers . . . . I grant that Wittfogel is not mistaken when he says that in these political high-pressure areas of the empires of traditional southern and eastern Asia, 'the state was much stronger than society' – stronger than society it may have been, but it was not stronger than the economy.[60]

Braudel's differences with Wallerstein extend beyond the question of causality into that of temporal parameters. Braudel, somewhat paradoxically, claims:

> I do not share Immanuel Wallerstein's fascination with the sixteenth century. Is the problem that perplexes him not in the end the same one that was raised by Marx? Let me quote again

the famous sentence 'The life-history of capital beings in the sixteenth century'. For Wallerstein, the European world-economy was the matrix of capitalism. I do not dispute this point, since to say central zone or capitalism is to talk about the same reality. By the same token however, to argue that the world-economy built in the sixteenth century on its European site was not the first to occupy this small but extraordinary continent, amounts to saying that capitalism did not wait for the sixteenth century to make its first appearance. I am therefore in agreement with the Marx who wrote (though he later went back on this) that European capitalism - indeed he even says capitalist *production* - began in thirteenth-century Italy. This debate is anything but academic.[61]

Braudel's position would seem to imply that Wallerstein's historical parameters for the world-system were chosen somewhat arbitrarily. If capitalism originated in thirteenth century Italy, as Braudel contends, its transformation into world capitalism from the sixteenth century onward seems more contingent upon logistical changes in the Eurasian trade nexus – i.e., the shift from Mediterranean to trans-oceanic routes, than Wallerstein might have it. In this transformation from European to world capitalism, the phenomenon of colonialism became inextricable from that of capitalism.

Wallerstein's historical research project in *The Modern World System* begins with a quote from Marx:

The discovery of gold and silver in America, the extirpation, enslavement and entombment in mines of the aboriginal population, the beginning of the conquest and looting of the East Indies, the turning of Africa into a warren for the commercial hunting of black-skins, signalised the rosy dawn of the era of capitalist production. These idyllic proceedings are the chief momenta of primitive accumulation. On their heels treads the commercial war of the European nations, with the globe for a theatre.[62]

Here, in Marx, the logic of the expansion of capitalism is linked directly with the primitive accumulation of the European powers and their advantages in the historical conjuncture of that period *vis-à-vis* contemporary political systems in America, Africa and Asia, which in turn is related to the logic of inter-state competition in Europe. This raises the issue of the differential structural effects which the penetration of capitalist relations under the auspices of various European powers had upon pre-capitalist modes of production in different historical periods. Braudel, evidently influenced by French structuralism, argues that

> the history of the world is an undivided procession; a cortege of coexisting modes of production which we are too inclined to think of as following one another in successive historical periods. In fact the different modes of production are all attached to each other. The most advanced are dependent on the most backward and vice-versa: development is the reverse side of under-development . . . For several world-economies have succeeded in each other in the geographical entity that is Europe. Or rather the European world-economy has changed shape several times since the thirteenth century, displacing the core, rearranging the peripheries.[63]

Braudel contributes to the identification of historical parameters, designating four successive secular cycles for Europe beginning in the thirteenth century: (1) 1250 (1350) 1507–10; (2) 1507–1510 (1650) 1733–1743; (3) 1733–1743 (1817) 1896; (4) 1896 (1974).[64] The first date in each cycle is the beginning of an upward movement in the mass of prices, the middle date in brackets is the peak, and constitutes the point at which the secular trend begins to go into decline, or what Braudel refers to as 'the moment of crisis'. The final date in each secular cycle is the end of a downward movement. Braudel thus seeks to demonstrate that there were such cycles in pre-industrial economies and that there were 'such things as Kondratieffs before 1791'.

This is not the place to undertake a comprehensive critique of Wallerstein, and the principal points of such a critique have already been made by several authors.[65] The following discussion will focus only on certain aspects of the approach, particularly the unit of analysis and its explanatory framework of causality. Wallerstein posed himself two questions: the criteria for determining historical stages, and the comparability of units across historical time. He responded with the abandonment of the sovereign state as the unit of analysis and adoption of a holistic overarching 'world-system'. The problem thus shifted to delineating 'the evolution of structures of the whole system'.[66]

Wallerstein introduced the distinction between a 'world-economy' and a 'world-empire' as two varieties of world-systems. Wallerstein's use of the term world, when in geographical terms he often means region is somewhat confusing. For instance, he says that in the sixteenth century, 'Europe was not the only world-economy at the time'.

Wallerstein's project encompasses a descriptive analysis of how one of these world-economies, the European, outstripped the others 'by embarking on the trajectory of capitalist development'. Wallerstein maintains that the European world economy was historically unique because it expanded without 'the emergence of a unified political structure', arguing that all the world-economies of the past had always been transformed eventually into 'world empires' such as China, Persia, and Rome.[67] Wallerstein begins with this contrast to the traditional empires, as described by S. Eisenstadt, which he says 'were a constant feature of the world scene for 5000 years'.[68] Wallerstein maintains that Europe's exceptionality depended on its economic rationality. According to Wallerstein, the strength of an empire 'lay in the fact that it guaranteed economic flows from the periphery to the centre by force (tribute and taxation) and by monopolistic advantages in trade. Its weakness lay in the fact that the bureaucracy made necessary by the political structure tended to absorb too much of the profit, especially as repression and exploitation bred revolt which increased military expenditure'.[69] He sees such political empires as a 'primitive means of economic domination'.

Wallerstein seems to underestimate the importance of the fact that within the time frame of such entities as 'China' or 'Rome', which was one of many centuries, there were long periods of rivalry in the regional states system prior to and subsequent to the fully consolidated hegemonic or imperial phase he denotes. In the case of Rome, the Mesopotamian and Persian area of the world-economy was never fully annexed into the world-empire but constituted the economic base of a rival power, first Parthia and later the Sassanians. The term 'China' is so general that it blurs the distinct phases of the East Asian order.

But it is not these distortions of historical time that are the real controversy, but rather Wallerstein's claim that the 'multiplicity of political systems' is the 'political side of the form of economic organization called capitalism'. Wallerstein argues, furthermore, that this political structure is the key to the flourishing of the capitalist mode of production on world scale. In Wallerstein's conceptual schematic, the world-economy is structurally differentiated into a hierarchy of strong 'core-states' and weak 'peripheral areas', between which is the semiperiphery, a zone with elements of core and periphery simultaneously. In Wallerstein's formulation of the relationship of state power to capital accumulation 'a state's strength correlates with the economic role of the owner-producers of that state in the world economy'. He gives five political indices of state strength:

> the degree to which state policy can directly help owner-producers
> compete in the world market (mercantilism); the degree to which
> states can affect the ability of other states to compete (military
> power), the degree to which states can mobilize their resources
> to perform these competitive and military tasks at costs that do
> not eat up the profits (public finance); the degree to which states
> can create administrations that will permit the swift carrying out
> of tactical decisions (an effective bureaucracy); and the degree
> to which the political rules reflect a balance of interests among
> owner-producers such that a working 'hegemonic bloc' (to use a
> Gramscian expression) forms the stable underpinnings of such a
> state. The last element, the politics of the class struggle, is the
> key to the others [The] modern history of the state [can be
> seen] rather as one long quest to create structures sufficiently
> strong to defend the interests of one set of owner-producers
> in the world-economy against other owner-producers, as well
> as, of course, against workers.[70]

Wallerstein's own treatment of the 'struggle in the core' from 1651
to 1763 makes it clear that the logic of inter-state competition can
nowhere be separated from that of the mode of production, particularly in transitional periods between the dominance of one mode and
another. The controversial aspect of this approach concerns causal
explanation, not necessarily the descriptive aspects of long cycles.

In discussing hegemony in the capitalist world-system, Wallerstein
indicates, following Perry Anderson, that there appears to be a
cyclical pattern of conflict:

> Class struggles in a capitalist world-economy are complex affairs
> and appear sinuously under many guises. The period leading
> up to the dominance of a hegemonic power seems to favor
> the intrastate form, as those that seek class advantage on the
> market seek to eliminate *internal* political constraints left over
> from earlier eras. The period of decline of hegemony seems to
> favor the interstate form, as those who seek class advantage
> on the market strive to eliminate *interstate* political constraints
> left over from earlier eras.[71]

Wallerstein recognises that as 'soon as a state becomes truly
hegemonic, it begins to decline' but he ascribes this decline as
due more to the relative gains of other states as opposed to purely

internally generated decline. This thesis depends on Wallerstein's particular definition of hegemony as more than mere core status, rather it is 'a situation wherein the products of a given core state are produced so efficiently that they are by and large competitive even in other core states, and therefore the given core state will be the primary beneficiary of a maximally free world market'.

Wallerstein considers such hegemony to be a rare condition and lists only Holland, Great Britain, and the United States as the powers who have been hegemonic in the capitalist world-economy, and each held that position for a relatively brief period. Holland held hegemony 'least plausibly because it was least of all the military giant of its era' and emerged as hegemonic upon the failure of Charles V to 'convert the world-economy into a world-empire'.[72] Hegemony and empire or 'world-empire' are thus two very different concepts for Wallerstein. Wallerstein's study of world historical processes in the era of capitalism led him to identify a cyclical pattern in the process leading to this 'exceptional' hegemony:

> Marked superiority in agro-industrial productive efficiency leads to dominance of the spheres of commercial distribution of world trade, with correlative profits accruing both from being the entrepôt of much of world trade and from controlling the 'invisibles' – transport, communications, and insurance. Commercial primacy leads in turn to control of the financial sectors of banking (exchange, deposit, and credit) and of investment (direct and portfolio).

> These superiorities are successive, but they overlap in time. Similarly, the loss of advantage seems to be in the same order (from productive to commercial to financial) and also largely successive. It follows that there is only a short moment in time when a given core power can manifest *simultaneously* productive, commercial, and financial superiority *over all other core powers*. This momentary summit is what we call hegemony.[73]

In this definition of hegemony, Wallerstein does not account for such structures of domination as those created by Spain and Portugal in America, Africa and Asia in the sixteenth and seventeenth centuries, nor that of Napoleonic France, the Third Reich, the Russian empire, the Austro–Hungarian empire, nor even of the Hapsburg empire in the age of Philip II or Charles V. His definition certainly has value, but it is not capable of explaining the majority of those historical 'hegemonic' or imperialist structures of domination that seem to derive their impetus more from the logic of state expansionism.[74]

Within the framework of the Wallerstein approach, several theorists have developed new empirical and theoretical arguments concerning general patterns or cycles in world historical development. Nicole Bousquet has attempted to identify temporal coincidence between cycles of competition among core states and secular trends or other long cycles (such as the Kondratieff) that are recurrent in the whole history of the world economy.[75] Bousquet's research has focused attention on 'the succession of periods of hegemony as defined by Wallerstein', by 'periods of competition at the center of the world economy'. Such core competition is defined by Bousquet as occurring when 'non-hegemonic core powers strive to regain or increase their share of the world-market'. Succinctly put, Bousquet argues that 'there appears to be a relationship between the rise to hegemony and an A-phase (be it secular or part of a Kondratieff cycle) on the one hand, and a B-phase and the return to a situation of competition on the other' but notes that conjuncture alone is not sufficient to explain major changes in the configuration of the core.[76] Bousquet observes a correlation between the initial phase of a hegemonic period and a process of decolonisation; the return to competition in the core is accompanied by a wave of colonisation and redivision of the periphery.

Bousquet argues that two trends characterise the production structure of the core: differentiation creates a polarisation of the centre into hegemonic and non-hegemonic powers; indifferentiation creates a return to 'a certain homogeneity' of the center: 'Production supremacy marks the end of the former, and competition in production marks the end of the latter.'[77] Bousquet concludes that changes in configuration at the centre are not in themselves cyclical nor the direct result of economic fluctuations but result from differentiation and indifferentiation, which are affected by conjuncture, 'but are in reality structural effects'. Differentiation and indifferentiation in the production structure are affected by conjuncture as follows: 'acceleration in an A-phase and deceleration in a B-phase'. Differentiation is propelled by a systematic bias in which one particular political entity adopts methods of production characterised by their economy of labour. When these most efficient production methods have been adopted in every sector of the economy, further growth poses an increase in labour costs and thus 'causes a crisis of capital accumulation' which precipitates a 'drastic transformation of the methods of production' which leads to production supremacy. The success of the hegemonic power creates a tendency for it to rely in the future on mere improvement in existing production methods and upon product and process diversification. In the non-hegemonic core powers there is a threshold or limit to relative decline which acts as the 'triggering point' to the process of emulation of the production structure of the hegemonic power. Nevertheless Bousquet views changes in the configuration at the centre 'as a kind of epiphenomenon, as a transformation of a superstructure stemming from an underlying economic process' and argues that 'national economic areas' are 'idiosyncratic in terms of the situation of the factors of production' and that the real dynamic is located at a centre-wide level, 'if not of the world economy' as a whole.[78]

The attempt to find temporal coincidence among different types of cycles has become a hallmark of the world-system approach. Albert Bergesen has outlined cycles of formal and informal colonial rule and generated the thesis: 'A multicentric core and formal core–periphery relations: a unicentric core and informal core periphery relations'.[79] Bergesen is fully committed to the world-system as the correct unit of analysis. In a debate with Robert Brenner, who criticises Wallerstein's emphasis on exchange relations in the core-periphery division of labour and de-emphasis of production relations and their concomitant class relations, Bergesen argues that it is the nature of world relations of production that 'determines the relations between various classes within national formations'.[80]

Among those theorists closely associated with the world-system approach, Christopher Chase-Dunn has defended a position that modifies the 'epiphenomenal causal explanation of much of the school'. Following Samir Amin, Chase-Dunn's analysis of the inter-dependent logic of the interstate system and the capitalist world-economy is an attempt to respond to the critique of Wallerstein as a reductionist whose approach reduces the states system's dynamic to a consequence of capital accumulation processes made by Modelski, Skocpol, Zolberg and Waltz, champions of the 'autonomy' of the states system *vis-à-vis* the world economy. Recognising the prior existence of states systems to capitalism, Chase-Dunn argues that 'both political–military power and the appropriation of surplus value through production and sale on the world market play an integrated role' in capitalist social formations.[81] In preference for a holistic theory, Chase-Dunn does not seek to establish a causal priority of the process of accumulation over political forms or vice versa. In

Chase-Dunn's formulation, 'the interstate system itself is the fundamental basis of the competitive commodity economy at the system level', but nevertheless continues to insist that the unit of analysis remain the 'system as a whole' rather than its parts, the 'national societies'. He also retains the Wallersteinian thesis that a multi-state system is a necessary condition for the reproduction and expansion of the capitalist mode of production and the corrollary that a 'world state' would probably bring the demise of the capitalist mode of production.[82] In this vein, Chase-Dunn addresses the question of why the Hapsburgs, Louis XIV, Napoleon, the Kaiser, and Hitler failed to convert the states-system into a 'world empire'. Chase-Dunn's explanation is pure Wallersteinianism: 'The transnational structures associated with the capitalist commodity economy operated to tip the balance in favor of preserving the state system'.[83] Chase-Dunn argues that the export of capital by a hegemonic power restrains it from imposing political 'imperium'. Interestingly, he implies in a footnote that geopolitical and strategic considerations are one of the keys to the logic of hegemonic competition. He sees the 'low overhead strategy' embodied in the 'Venetian model' as the one followed by the states that became hegemonic; the Netherlands, Britain, and the United States, in which a decentralised political apparatus of domination bears the costs of administration while surplus extraction is accomplished by trade. By contrast, the 'high overhead' 'land-oriented political centralizer', such as Germany and Russia, have been 'second-runner' in competition at the core.[84]

Within the literature of the World-System approach, particularly the Political Economy of the World-System Annuals, and in related volumes, a number of authors have published their disagreements with the approach from a more state-centric or 'autonomous' perspective.[85] Among these, David Rapkin has directly countered Chase-Dunn's arguments by contending that 'the materialist theory thus far advanced makes a stronger case for the dependence of world capitalism on the interstate political system than it does for the reverse dependency'.[86] Rapkin rejects the reliance of Wallerstein and Hopkins upon Walter Dorn for the 'uniqueness' thesis of the European multi-state system as 'patently incorrect', noting that the Chinese warring states, the Greek city-states, and ancient India all exhibited classic behaviour such as alliances, etc. He counters Chase-Dunn's rejection of the 'relevance of isomorphism with precapitalist systems' due to their instability and tendency to become world-empires by pointing out that it is unclear how the eventual historical 'demise' of these states systems into empires necessarily 'vitiates the counterargument linking the prior existence of the interstate political logic with the autonomy of the political realm'.[87] Rapkin rather cleverly reminds Chase Dunn that if Wallerstein's prediction that capitalism will be transformed into a unitary world socialism in 100–150 years is correct, 'this would give the modern interstate system a life span roughly comparable to that of the Chinese warring states system' – i.e., about five and a half centuries.[88] Rapkin critiques Chase Dunn's list of the factors that condition 'the rise and fall of hegemonic core states' as a list of factors which are all internally located within the state in question and none of which demonstrably derive from the so-called 'logic of the world capitalist system'.[89]

In a similar vein, James Lee Ray has pointed out that as a consequence of Wallerstein's general omission of International Relations sources in *The Modern World System* 'traditional politico–military conflict among states is ignored or the causes, as well as the effects, of that type of conflict are treated inadequately'.[90] Ray prescribes a synthesis of International Relations and 'world-system' analyses 'that will specify on which occasions and under which circumstances economic or political processes are more fundamental, or deserve theoretical priority, in chains of causal factors that are devised to explain outcomes in foreign policy or international politics'.[91]

The preoccupation with cycles and conjuncture has been accompanied by direct comparisons between the Wallerstein schema and other conceptions of 'World System time', such as that of Modelski. In particular, W.R. Thompson has pursued the comparative analysis of Modelski's cycles with Wallerstein's and used Modelski's long cycle schema to test traditional International Relations approaches to changing power configurations, such as that of Organski and Kugler.[92] Thompson has identified discrepancies in the Wallersteinian and Modelskian schema of cycles, pointing out that the A/B phases and the long cycles are not well synchronised. Likewise, Thompson concludes that 'Wallerstein's assertion of a relationship between B phases and core power conflict and warfare is not particularly well-supported in terms of the incidence of global wars'[93] since four sets of Modelski's global wars occurred during A phases, periods of economic expansion. Thompson identifies a lack of correspondence between the four phases of hegemony according to Wallerstein's Research Working Group on Cyclical Rhythms and Secular Trends: Ascending hegemony, Hegemonic victory, Hegemonic maturity, and Declining hegemony, and Modelski's long cycles, though he views the Wallersteinian 'hegemonic maturity' phase as roughly equating to Modelski's 'world power' concept.[94] Thompson questions Wallerstein's succession in the order of 'superiorities', arguing that 'it appears that military superiority preceded economic superiority in the Dutch and British eras of leadership'.[95] The argument that states system strategic logic is a determining factor of developments in trade rivalry has been further developed empirically by Gautam Sen, but this is quite outside the 'world system' discourse.[96]

An outstanding example of the eclectic synthesis prescribed by James Lee Ray between International Relations and World-System approaches to the study of power configuration is Raimo Vyrynen, who has argued in a seminal article 'Economic Cycles, Power Transition, Political Management and Wars Between Major Powers' that

> the combination of a structural and a cyclical perspective on international relations allows the identification of various historical sequences in the transformation of the international system. On the basis of these sequences it is, furthermore, possible to separate various historical systems from each other, to explore whether some of them have been more war-prone than others, and to ask what kinds of wars are waged in each period. Such a historical perspective thus provides an opportunity to rely on the comparative study of international systems. A *comparative historical approach* allows the conceptualization and analysis of dominant economic and diplomatic constellations and their consequences by the aid of some powerful variables.

He traces this perspective to Raymond Aron's historical sociology and its application to International Relations research.[97]

Raimo Väyrynen's analysis suggests that 'processes of power transition have an autonomous logic which can be modified, but not arrested, by the long waves of economic development', and contends that 'the factor of power transitions exerts greatest influence on the probability of major-power wars, and that the nature of management systems has a greater impact than the long waves of economic development'; viewing this as concordant with Bousquet's emphasis that differentiation and indifferentiation within the centre are more important than mere conjuncture in explaining rivalry and stability among major powers.[98] The question of conjuncture in cycles of war and economic growth has been the subject of an extensive empirical research project by Joshua Goldstein.[99] Goldstein concludes, on the basis of quantitative analysis, that the data strongly support a correlation of increased war among the great powers with periods of economic expansion or 'upswing'.

Following Wallerstein, Goldstein identifies three 150 year cycles since 1648, and argues for a correlation between the three 'hegemonic wars' of 1618–48, 1793–1815, and 1914–45 and secular price increases.

6.4   THE 'LSE SCHOOL'

The trend in Historical Sociology pioneered by Raymond Aron in addressing questions of war and peace has been taken up by both Michael Mann and John Hall, who might be referred to as the LSE school. Michael Mann emphasises 'geopolitical militarism' in which 'militarism derives from geopolitical aspects of our social structure which are far older than capitalism', and views militarism as only 'contingently associated with the rise of capitalism' having now become 'the general property of expansionist industrial societies' and no longer specific to capitalism.[100] Mann bluntly dismisses the Wallersteinian version of the necessary causal relationship between capitalism and the multi-state political form, countering that 'there is nothing in the capitalist mode of production which itself requires a multi-state system. The two are contingent . . . the multi-state system cannot be reduced to the requirements of industrial capitalism'.[101] Mann concurs with other critics of Wallerstein on the importance of the prior existence of the multi-state system to capitalism. In an echo of a view held by Martin Wight, Mann asserts that the fundamental source of war is in fact the existence of multi-state systems themselves.[102]

Beyond his contributions to the sociological interest in war and conflict, Mann has undertaken a research project on the 'history of power' on world historical scale.[103] In the first completed volume of this ambitious study Mann concludes with a chapter of generalisation entitled 'Patterns of world-historical development in agrarian societies'. In these conclusions, he denies any general 'historical materialism' or that history is a 'discontinuous succession of modes of production', or that class struggle is the 'motor of history'. He does, however, retain the belief that certain 'partial patterns' can be discerned in world historical development and that these patterns are explicable by 'historical, not comparative and abstract, structures and theories . . . situated in world-historical time'.[104]

Mann characterises 'power struggles' as the principal patternings of history. He sees a potentially cyclical or dialectical pattern of development in the oscillation between two historical variants of 'power configuration': the 'Empires of domination' character-ised by 'combined military concentrated coercion with an attempt at state territorial centralization and geopolitical hegemony' and 'multi-power-actor civilizations' in which 'decentralized power actors competed with one another within an overall framework of normative regulation'.[105] Mann recognises that certain empires of domination were in fact a sort of culminating development out of earlier multi-power-actor civilisations. He allows for complex contiguous interaction between the two types, such as the case of Phoenicia and Classical Greece in relation to the 'Near Eastern Empire'.

Mann poses the question whether there exists a dialectic between these two variants of power configuration in relation to each one's capability for innovation. He asks whether further social development was possible 'only when its polar opposite type arose to exploit precisely what it could not?' Mann's conjecture is that an affirmative answer would 'certainly entail a general theory of world-historical development'.[106] He senses a general pattern in world historical development in which the dynamic of multi-power-actor civilisations 'seems to have led toward its opposite, greater hegemonic centralization' and vice versa. The cycle of Hegemony and Rivalry? In Mann's dialectical formulation 'empires of domination' have 'unintentionally generated more diffuse power relations of two main sorts within their own interstices: (1) decentralized, property-owning landlord, merchants and artisans, that is, upper and middling classes; and (2) ideological movements'. Mann hypothesises that 'If these diffuse power relations continue to grow interstitially, a decentralized multi-power-actor civilisation may result, either from the collapse of the empire or from its gradual metamorphosis'.[107] Mann views 'the dialectic between them as the core of world-historical development' though he denies a claim that this dialectic is the 'essence of history'.

The oscillation between hegemonic consolidation and hegemonic entropy occurs in a unique historical continuum in which historical accident also plays a role; Mann thus resists attempting to force the historical data into overly formalistic or cyclical categories. It is this restraint that distinguishes his work most sharply from the world-system approach.

John Hall, following Raymond Aron, contends that 'economic systems do not explain the origin of warfare, which is instead the result of completely autonomous political factors'[108] and concurs with

Aron's critique of Marxist theories of imperialism. Unfortunately, Hall seems to have a strong predilection to erect a Marxist or 'Marxisant' strawman in the course of advancing his own positions. Hall's historical research project has focussed on the question of why Europe developed a multi-state system and why it came to dominate the world. He defends his sociological analysis explicitly as a philosophy of history and insists on the necessity of grounding theory in historical research of this type. Hall offers a Weberian-like emphasis on religion as a crucial causal variable in social development and relates the dynamic of religious culture to that of states-systems. He argues that the pre-modern states of Hindu India were 'custodial', and those of Islam were 'cyclical', and thus weak, on the basis of primarily religious-cultural considerations. He contrasts the 'weak' Islamic and Hindu states, and China's 'capstone' state to the 'strong' European states on the basis of 'considerable and ever-increasing infrastructural penetration'.[109] He, therefore concludes that in the European dynamic 'competition between strong states inside a larger culture encouraged the triumph of capitalism'.[110] Military competition in this context stimulated economic progress as a nationalisation of the economy made imperative by the emulative tendencies of the states in the system. In an argument related to Eisenstadt and Wallerstein, Hall says that in 'China, India and Islam the powerful influenced economic relationships, through bureaucratic interference or predatory rule' in contrast to Christendom's allowance for 'strong and autonomous power sources'.[111] Thus the 'European miracle' of the 'organic state' was born. Yet Hall's argument finally rests on tenuous and highly controversial assertions such as 'Christianity differs from Islam, as well as from Hinduism, since it did not "block" politics, and so did not encourage a climate of instability which limited the autonomy of market relationships'.[112] Despite his wide reading, Hall is not as systematic or conceptually rigorous in his analysis as Mann, and the neo-Smithian overtones of his thesis have an air of ideology about them.

6.5 CONCLUSIONS

Martin Wight's question concerning the succession of hegemonies seems to have moved to the centre of International Relations theory. The search for clues to the ordering principles of these successions of hegemony has inexorably pushed the historical parameters of

International Relations to encompass virtually the entire development of historical states systems. In its wake, this expansion of the subject has posed further research questions. For instance, do agrarian and industrial societies generate completely different types of political dynamic at the states system level? Do capitalist relations of production generate completely' different forms of political dynamic than pre-capitalist forms? Is there a definite break between such forms, agrarian versus industrial, capitalist versus pre-capitalist, or to what degree are there significant continuities in the behaviour of states systems throughout these transitions? Overall, the question of the comparability of widely divergent historical systems again moves to the forefront of theoretical debates.

Has the problem of historical parameters been resolved? Certainly not. Those theorists who insist on attributing law-like characteristics to 'cycles' as the determinant phenomena of states systems tend to fall err to a reification of the unit of analysis as a mechanism which determines the development of its constituent elements. The alternative to this type of reification is to be found in the recognition that world history is amenable to interpretation on the basis of certain 'patterned processes', but that the variation in these patterned processes is very considerable and precludes any universally valid causal explanation. Cycles have considerable heuristic value, but the preoccupation with the question of causality as attributed to cycles by some theorists is fraught with conceptual danger.

One of the most promising aspects of the dialogue between the three historical approaches to International Relations theory is the general recognition that there should be a wedding of analyses of high politics with close empirical study of changes in the structure of production and exchange. It is in this context, for instance, that the very important theoretical question of whether imperial states tend to constrict or promote economic expansion must be empirically addressed. The emerging tendency to differentiate between forms of imperium, exemplified in the distinction often made between 'hegemony' and 'empire', is a positive step forward. It leads to an interest in identifying the specific phases of development in systems of states, and generally should indicate that such phases entail both political management structures and production structures.

In my own view, hegemonic structures can best be understood when viewed as developing in a sequence of phases. The drive to create a hegemony or an empire is clearly not unrelated to the production structure, and its very essence may lay in the quest for surplus accumulation. Indeed, hegemony and empire can both be viewed as variant hierarchical structures not only of political and military power, but of surplus accumulation among states and their constituent classes. The general tendency for states systems to exhibit behaviour emanating from the struggle for hegemony seems to be universal. But are the motivations universal?

In answer to Wight's question, it would appear, at least tentatively, that there is no exception to the succession of hegemonies in any historical system of states, nor to the pattern wherein the 'balance of power' is evoked only as an attempt to counter an attempt at hegemony. In addition, it appears that taken as a general concept, 'centre–periphery' relations have existed in all historical systems of states, whether capitalist or pre-capitalist, agrarian or industrial, and in all its historical variants, this relationship has been a central element in the structure of hegemony.

The greatest research question remaining is that of what explains the shifts in the locus of power in states systems. These 'centre shifts' in the locus of power, at the heart of the succession of hegemonies phenomena, may rightly be seen as the real 'motor of history'. They are related to complex geographical and demographic factors, changes in the technical composition of the means of production and the relations of exchange, class struggle, the means of coercion and administration deployed by states, and to the overall juxtaposition of the constituent political entities of any states system as expressed in the distribution of capabilities and the conjuncture of phases in development. The full explanation of these centre shifts is fast becoming the central problematic of the International Relations discipline.

In response to the question of what motivates the drive for hegemony, I would argue that the answer probably rests in an analysis of the ultimate economic rewards accruing to the successful hegemonic state, and to its ruling class first and foremost. In the phase of 'Hegemonic Consolidation', one contender achieves predominance over its rivals, typically as a result of intense warfare. In my own reading of history, this consolidation is usually followed by a phase I would refer to as 'Infrastructural Integration'. It is in this phase that the hegemonic state seeks to take full advantage of the economic potential of the greater area now under its predominance. Investment is made in transportation, communications, and integrative reforms such as standardisation of weights and measures, currency reform, land reform, tax reform, and bureaucratic administrative reform are promoted. This is done precisely to encourage the overall economic productivity of the larger economic zone now under unified hegemonic direction in order to increase the hegemonic state's ability to extract surplus from it.

During the phase of 'Acute Rivalry' that usually precedes hegemonic consolidation, considerable resources are consumed in the rivalry process and the integration of the larger economic zone is often prevented or at least restricted as a function of political competition. The coming of 'hegemonic peace' allows the rechanneling of these resources to productive use or to consumption, and renders economic integration more feasible. Thus the eclipse of acute rivalry and the imposition of infrastructural and administrative reforms makes possible a phase of 'Hegemonic Prosperity'. It is in this phase that 'empire' and economic expansion seem most compatible. This prosperity phase seems to correlate closely with the political apex of the hegemon's power. In turn, the revenues resulting from the success of the infrastructural investment phase may coincide with further territorial expansion by the hegemon.

Inevitably, the prosperity phase begins to give way to the phase of 'Hegemonic Entropy'. This entropy appears to result from the fiscal consequences of over-extension, which entails heavy expenditure on the administrative and military apparatus, and from over-extraction, by which the revenue base is subjected to super-exploitation in order to finance these requirements. This over-extraction brings about an overall economic contraction. It is in this phase that 'empire' and economic prosperity seem to be least compatible. The fiscal crisis of the entropic hegemonic state is often exacerbated by the effects of a dual exploitation of the revenue base by competing elites. This competition for revenue between the propertied classes and the state is often accompanied by reconcentration of property holding by non-state elites and an attempt to deny revenues to the central state. Strong decentralising political pressure may be applied to the entropic hegemonic state, resulting in open de-consolidation of the hegemonic structure and its eventual disintegration.

The conjuncture of an entropic phase in one hegemonic structure with an ascendance, or consolidation, phase in another can contribute to a dramatic shift in the locus of power. An example of such a conjuncture can be seen in the interaction of the entropic phase of the Ch'ing dynasty in China with the ascendance of a new hegemonic order in Japan. In such a conjuncture of phases, the ascending hegemon typically takes advantage of the deconsolidation of the entropic hegemon to re-expropriate its periphery. The 'Hegemonic

Deconsolidation' phase is the ultimate result of an entropic phase that is not arrested by internal reform. It may manifest itself in the re-emergence of a multi-power system of states. This stage is crucial, for if reconsolidation under a new hegemon does not occur relatively quickly, usually within a few decades, then the reversion to a multi-state system may be quite long-lasting, persisting even up to several centuries depending on the specific conditions. The lack of any clear hegemon may again produce a period in which the several states of the system concentrate on consolidating their separate bases. This may produce a degree of economic stimulus, which is often accelerated as the pattern of acute rivalry reasserts itself. In the full-blown phase of 'Acute Rivalry' for hegemony, the resources governed by each state tend to be consumed in the rivalry process, thus constituting a counter-tendency to real economic expansion, despite heavy doses of state stimulus to production. A 'balance of power' behaviour pattern may emerge if an anti-hegemonic coalition is successfully maintained against the principal contender(s) for hegemony in the states system.

In terms of the factors conditioning the distribution of capabilities, in agrarian pre-capitalist social formations, as already indicated, the key factor appears to be the extent of territorial possession measured in the revenue it produces, and conditioned by the recurrent pattern of competition over this revenue base between the central state and the propertied classes. In capitalist industrial social formations, the linkage between rivalry for hegemony and the production structure is expressed in the competitive struggle among separate bodies of capital, both within and between state boundaries. As each state's capabilities ultimately depend on its ability to attain revenue through taxation of its national economy, both the absolute quantity of surplus value created and the apportionment of shares of surplus value between states are vital to the overall configuration of capabilities.

It is clear that the holism of history requires a holistic theoretical framework. Ahistorical, purely abstract conceptualisations have heuristic merits, but a historically grounded theory of general patterned processes of states systems seems to offer greater explanatory potential. While no ultimate synthesis of the three historical approaches to International Relations theory is likely, the eclecticism emerging from their common dialogue seems to be producing a new discourse, which may lead to ever more enriched and clarified expositions of the actual behavioural dynamics of historical systems of states. This is certainly a healthy development that will embellish the International Relations literature. In the end, the common discourse among these three approaches may serve to redefine International Relations theory itself. With traditional Realism manifestly moribund, the future of International Relations theory may lay in the reinvigoration of historically grounded theory of this kind.

NOTES AND REFERENCES

1. See: Martin Wight, 'Why is there no International Theory?' and 'The Balance of Power' in H. Butterfield and M. Wight (eds), *Diplomatic Investigations* (London: George Allen & Unwin, 1966), pp. 17–34, pp. 149–75; Martin Wight, *System of States*, Bull (ed.) (London: Leicester University Press in association with the London School of Economics, 1977); Hedley Bull and C. Holbraad (eds), *Power Politics* (New York: Holmes and Neier, 1978). See also Wight's pamphlet 'Power Politics' published by Chatham House in 1946. See also Brian Porter, 'Patterns of Thought and Practice: Martin Wight's "International Theory"', in Michael Donelan (ed.), *The Reason of States: A Study in International Political Theory* (London: George Allen and Unwin, 1978), Hedley Bull, *The Anarchical Society* (London: Macmillan, 1977), Hedley Bull and Adam Watson (eds), *The Expansion of International Society* (Oxford: Clarendon Press, 1984), and Hedley Bull, 'International Theory: the Case for a Classical Approach', *World Politics* (Vol. 18, No. 3, 1966) pp. 361–77, reprinted in Klaus Knorr and James Rosenau (eds), *Contending Approaches to International Politics* (Princeton, NJ: Princeton University Press, 1969) which contains replies to Bull. For a review of the 'Great Debate' see S. George, 'Reconciling the Classical and Scientific Approaches to International Relations', *Millennium: Journal of International Studies* (Vol. 5, No. 1, Spring 1976), pp. 28–40. See also, Hedley Bull, 'Martin Wight and the Theory of International Relations', *British Journal of International Studies* (Vol. 2, No. 2, 1976).

2. See Frederick J. Teggart, *Theory and Processes of History* (Berkeley, CA.: University of California Press, 1977) which is a reprinted edition of two works: *The Processes of History* (New Haven, CT.: Yale University Press, 1918) and *Theory of History* (New Haven, CT.: Yale University Press, 1925). Teggart criticised 'Eurocentric' history and championed the concept of a total 'Eurasian' history. In 'The Geographical Factor in History' in *The Processes of History* (1918) Teggart argued that, 'in their history, the two parts of Eurasia are inextricably bound together. Mackinder has shown how much light may be thrown upon European history by regarding it as subordinate to Asiatic . . . The oldest of historians (Herodotus) held the idea that epochs of European history were marked by alternating movements across the

imaginary line that separates East and West' (p. 248). Concerning the unit of analysis later chosen by Toynbee, the 'civilisations', it should be noted that Teggart preferred a rigorously comparative approach to the study of the origins of the state, emphasising geographical variables, and criticised the 'use of such vague and all-inclusive terms as "civilisation"' (p. 251). Teggart's thesis on the 'geographical' determinates of the origins of the state held that the areas of the emergence of primary states were 'termini of routes of travel' (pp. 251–52). Teggart's major study of European history, *Rome and China: A Study of Correlations in Historical Events* (Berkeley, CA.: University of California Press, 1939) was 're-discovered' for the IR discipline by Robert Gilpin in *War and Change in World Politics* (Cambridge: Cambridge University Press, 1981). Gilpin apparently accepts Teggart's thesis that Rome and China 'were functionally interdependent and were profoundly affected by the disturbances caused by the massive migration of the steppe nomads of Central Asia', but Gilpin qualifies this statement, adding that 'it would be absurd to regard Ancient China and Rome as parts of the same international system' (Gilpin, *War and Change*, p. 38). Gilpin likewise 're-discovered' Brooks Adams, *The Law of Civilization and Decay: An Essay on History* (New York: A. Knopf, 1943) which developed the thesis that trade and trade routes are the 'key to history'. For a negative critical reaction to Teggart's thesis on Rome and China see: Sir Mortimer Wheeler, *Rome Beyond the Imperial Frontiers* (Harmondsworth: Penguin, 1954), pp. 213–14.

3. Hedley Bull, 'Introduction: Martin Wight and the study of international relations', in Wight, *Systems of States*, pp. 2, 9, 16.

4. Wight, *Systems of State*. Hedley Bull notes this etymology in *The Anarchical Society*, p. 12.

5. Wight, 'De Systematibus civitatum', in *Systems of State*, p. 42.

6. Wight, *Systems of State*, p. 43.

7. Hedley Bull, *The Anarchical Society*, p. 15.

8. Bull, *The Anarchical Society*, p. 14.

9. Bull, *The Anarchical Society*, p. 21.

10. Bull and Watson (eds), *The Expansion of International Society*, p. 1. Bull's emphasis on 'order' generated an empirical research interest in diplomatic institutions. See: James Der Derian, *On Diplomacy: A Genealogy of Estrangement* (Oxford: Basil Blackwell, 1987).

11. This is from Bull and Watson's definition of 'international society', *The Expansion of International Society*, p. 1. For a defence of the concept of 'international society' as central to international theory, see: James Mayall, 'International Society and International Theory', in Donelan (ed), *The Reason of States: A Study in International Political Theory*.

12. Bull and Watson, (eds), *The Expansion of International Society*, p. 5. For an alernative historical analysis of the process of European impingement emphasising the technology of warfare, see William H. McNeill, *The Pursuit of Power: Technology, Armed Force, and Society since AD 1000* (Oxford: Basil Blackwell, 1982).

13. Bull and Watson (eds), *The Expansion of International Society*, pp. 6–7.

14. Bull and Watson (eds), *The Expansion of International Society*, pp. 7–8.
15. Gilpin, *War and Change*, pp. 2–3.
16. Gilpin, *War and Change*, pp. 37–8. For examples of attempts to do this see Robert Wesson, *State Systems: International Pluralism, Politics and Culture* (New York: The Free Press, 1978), Evan Luard, *Types of International Society* (New York: Free Press, 1976) and S. Eisenstadt, *The Political System of Empires* (New York: Free Press of Glencoe, 1963). See also Michael Doyle, *Empires* (Ithaca, NY: Cornell University Press, 1986).
17. Gilpin, *War and Change*, pp. 182–3. Gilpin quotes at length a passage by Toynbee from *Survey of International Affairs* (1931), p. 133, on the general pattern that Toynbee discerned among the states system of Renaissance Italy, the city-state system of classical Greece, and the Warring States system in China in relation to the enveloping 'ring' of greater powers that came to surround and overwhelm them in a sort of systemic 'implosion'. For an anthropologists formulation of a similar general evolutionary pattern see Elman R. Service, *Cultural Evolutionism*.
18. Gilpin, *War and Change*, pp. 42–3. For an excellent review of the international regimes literature see: Stephan Haggard and Beth A. Simmons, 'Theories of International Regimes', *International Organization* (Vol. 41, No. 3, Summer 1987), pp. 491–517.
19. Haggard and Simmons, 'Theories of International Regimes', pp. 106–8. For an example of a totally different approach to the explanation of ascendance and descendance based on organisation theory, see Mancur Olson, *The Rise and Decline of Nations: Economic Growth, Stagflation, and Local Rigidities* (New Haven, CT.: Yale University Press, 1982).
20. Haggard and Simmons, 'Theories of International Regimes', pp. 108, 110. See: Samir Amin, *Unequal Development: An Essay on the Social Social Formation of Peripheral Capitalism* (New York: Monthly Review Press, 1976). In Chapter one, 'The Precapitalist Formations', Amin discusses five modes of production: (1) primitive–communal (2) tribute-paying (3) slaveowning (4) simple petty–commodity, and (5) capitalist.
21. Gilpin, *War and Change*, p. 111.
22. Gilpin, *War and Change*, p. 144.
23. George Modelski, 'The Long Cycle of Global Politics and the Nation-State', *Comparative Studies in Society and History* (Vol. 20, 1978), pp. 214–35, 'Long Cycles of World Leadership', in William R. Thompson (ed.), *Contending Approaches to World System Analysis* (London: Sage Publications, 1983), pp. 115–41. See also in the same volume: 'Of Global Politics, Portugal, and Kindred Issues: A Rejoinder', pp. 291–98. For a recent critique of Modelski, see Richard Rosecrance, 'Long Cycle Theory and International Relations', *International Organisation* (Vol. 41, No. 2, Spring 1987), pp. 283–301. For other critiques of Modelski, see: Aristide R. Zolberg, '"World" and "System": A Misalliance' in Thompson

(ed), *Contending Approaches*, pp. 269–90, and Raimo Väyrynen, 'Global Power Dynamics and Collective Violence', in R. Väyrynen, Deiter Senghaas, and Christian Schmidt (eds), *The Quest for Peace: Transcending Collective Violence and War Among Societies, Cultures and States* (International Social Science Council, 1987).

24. Modelski, 'Long Cycles of World Leadership', p. 116.
25. See Fernand Braudel, *Civilization and Capitalism: 15–18th century, Vol. III, The Perspective of the World* (London: Collins, 1984).
26. Modelski, 'Long Cycles of World Leadership', p. 137.
27. See: George Modelski, 'Long Cycles, Kondratieffs, alternating innovations: implications for US foreign policy' in C.W. Kegley, Jr and P.J. McGowan (eds), *The Political Economy of Foreign Policy Behaviour* (Beverly Hills, Cal.: Sage Publications, 1981) and *Exploring Long Cycles* (London: Frances Pinter, 1987).
28. Zolberg, '"World" and "System"', pp. 227–78.
29. Modelski, 'Of Global Politics, Portugal and Kindred Issues: A Rejoinder', pp. 294–5.
30. V. Kubalkova and A.A. Cruickshank, *Marxism–Leninism and Theory of International Relations* (London: Routledge & Kegan Paul, 1980), pp. 13; 350. See also: *Marxism and International Relations* (Oxford: Clarendon Press, 1985).
31. See: Robert W. Cox, 'Social Forces, States and World Orders: Beyond International Relations Theory', *Millennium: Journal of International Studies* (Vol. 10, No. 2, 1981), pp. 126–55 reprinted with a postscript in R. Keohane (ed), *Neorealism and its Critics*, New York Columbia University Press, 1986), pp. 204–54.
32. Wight, 'Why is there no international theory', p. 25.
33. R.N. Berki, 'On Marxian Thought and the Problem of International Relations', *World Politics* (Vol. 24, No. 1, October 1971), pp. 80–105; p. 81.
34. Bob Jessop, *The Capitalist State* (Oxford: Basil Blackwell, 1982), p. xii. Ralph Miliband, 'Marx and the State' in Ralph Miliband and John Saville (eds), *The Socialist Register* (London: Merlin Press, 1965), reprinted in *Class Power and State Power: Political Essays* (London: Verso Editions and New Left Books, 1983), pp. 3–4.
35. Kubalkova and Cruickshank, *Marxism and International Relations*, p. 9.
36. Kubalkova and Cruickshank, *Marxism and Interantional Relations*, p. 23. See: Silviu Brucan, *The Dialectic of World Politics* (New York: Free Press, 1978), and *The Dissolution of Power: A Sociology of International Relations* (New York: Alfred A. Knopf, 1971), and Theda Skocpol, 'Wallerstein's World Capitalist System: A Theoretical and Historical Critique', *American Journal of Sociology* (Vol. 81, No. 5, March 1977), pp. 1025–90, Skocpol, *States and Social Revolutions* (Cambridge: Cambridge University Press, 1979), and Peter Evans, Dietrich Ruschemeyer and Theda Skocpol (eds.), *Bringing the State Back In* (Cambridge: Cambridge University Press, 1985). For a recent example of the trend to attribute more causal significance to the overarching states-system upon the socio-economic configuration

within states, see Gautam Sen, the *Military Origins of Industrialisation and International Trade Rivalry* (London: Frances Pinter, 1984).

37. For a review of the principal contributions to the (neo-) marxist study of IPE, see: Charles A. Barone, *Marxist Thought on Imperialism: Survey and Critique* (London: Macmillan, 1985), David Booth, 'Marxism and Development Sociology: Interpreting the Impasse', in Martin Shaw (ed.), *Marxist Sociology Revisited: Critical Assessments* (London: Macmillan, 1985), Anthony Brewer, *Marxist Theories of Imperialism: A Critical Survey* (London: Routledge & Kegan Paul, 1980), Magnus Blomstrom and Bjorn Hettne, *Development Theory in Transition: The Dependency Debate and Beyond: Third World Responses* (London: Zed Books, 1984), Ronald H. Chilcote, *Theories of Comparative Politics: The Search for a Paradigm* (Boulder, CO.: Westview Press, 1981), Chilcote, *Theories of Development and Underdevelopment* (Boulder, CO.: Westview Press, 1985), Peter Linqueco and Bruce McFarlane (eds.), *Neo-Marxist Theories of Development* (London: Croom Helm, 1983) Ian Roxborough, *Theories of Underdevelopment* (London: Macmillan, 1979), John G. Taylor, *From Modernization to Modes of Production: A Critique of the Sociologies of Development and Underdevelopment* (Atlantic Highlands, N.J.: Humanities Press, 1979), V.G. Kiernan, *Marxism and Imperialism* (London: Edward Arnold, 1974), I. Oxaal, T. Barnett and D. Booth (eds), *Beyond the Sociology of Development* (London: Routledge & Kegan Paul, 1975). See also: G. Kay, *Development and Underdevelopment: A Marxist Analysis* (London: Macmillan, 1975), Roger Owen and Bob Sutcliffe, *Studies in the Theory of Imperialism* (London: Longman, 1972), Julio Barso, 'An Analysis of Classical Theories of Imperialism' in Bertrand Russell Centenary Symposium, *Spheres of Influence in the Age of Imperialism* (Nottingham: Spokesman, 1972).

38. For the debate some of these new approaches have precipitated within the IR discipline, see: W. Ladd Hollist and James N. Rosenau, *World System Structure: Continuity and Change* (Beverly Hills, CA.: Sage, 1981), K.J. Holsti, *The Divided Discipline: Hegemony and Diversity in International Theory* (London: Allen & Unwin, 1985), Robert O. Keohane (ed.), *Neorealism and its Critics* (New York: Columbia University Press, 1986), Thompson (ed), *Contending Approaches*.

39. Booth, pp. 69, 73. See: Gabriel Palma, 'Dependency: A Formal Theory of Underdevelopment or a Methodology for the Analysis of Concrete Situations of Underdevelopment', *World Development* (Vol. 6, Nos. 7–8, 1978), Bill Warren, *Imperialism: Pioneer of Capitalism* (London: New Left Books, 1980), Ronald H. Chilcote and Dale L. Johnson (eds), *Theories of Development: Mode of Production or Dependency?* (Beverley Hills, CA: Sage, 1983), Ronaldo Munck, 'Imperialism and Dependency: Recent Debates and Old Dead Ends', *Latin American Perspectives* (Vol. 8, Nos. 3–4, Summer/Fall 1981), Ernesto Laclau, 'Feudalism and Capitalism in Latin America', *New Left Review* (No. 67, May–June 1971) reprinted, with a postscript, in Ernesto Laclau, *Politics and Ideology in Marxist Theory* (London: New Left Books, 1977), Robert Brenner, 'The Origins of Capitalist

Development: a Critique of Neo-Smithian Marxism', *New Left Review* (No. 104, July–August 1977), Aidan Foster-Carter, 'The Modes of Production Controversy', *New Left Review* (No. 107, January–February 1978). Harold Wolfe (ed.), *The Articulation of Modes of Production* (London: Routledge and Kegan Paul, 1980), Taylor, *From Modernization to Modes of Production*.

40. Robert W. Cox, 'Social Forces, States and World Orders: Beyond International Relations Theory' in Keohane (ed), *Neorealism*, pp. 214–15, originally published in *Millennium: Journal of International Studies* (Vol. 10, No. 2, Summer 1981).

41. Perry Anderson, *Passages from Antiquity to Feudalism* (London: New Left Books, 1974 and Verso, 1981), Anderson, *Lineages of the Absolutist State* (London: New Left Books, 1974).

42. Anderson, *Lineages of the Absolutist State*, pp. 11; 403–4.

43. For insight into the internal Marxist debate over central conceptual categories and other methodological issues see the debate outlined by Paul Q. Hirst in 'Anderson's Balance Sheet', continued in Paul Q. Hirst, *Marxism and Historical Writing* (London: Routledge & Kegan Paul, 1985), as follows: Louis Althusser and Etienne Balibar, *Reading Capital* (London: New Left Books, 1970), E.P. Thompson, *The Poverty of Theory and Other Essays* (London: Merlin Press, 1978), Anderson, *Passages from Antiquity to Feudalism*, *op. cit.*, Anderson, *Lineages of the Absolutist State*, Anderson, *Considerations on Western Marxism* (London: New Left Books, 1976), Anderson, *Arguments within English Marxism* (London: New Left Books, 1980), Barry Hindness and Paul Hirst, *Pre-Capitalist Modes of Production* (London: Routledge & Kegan Paul, 1975), Hindness and Hirst, *Mode of Production and Social Formation* (London: Macmillan, 1977), G.A. Cohen, *Karl Marx's Theory of History: A Defense* (Oxford: Oxford University Press, 1978), Alex Callincos, *Is there a Future for Marxism?* (London: Macmillan, 1982), and Andrew Levine and Eric Olin Wright, 'Rationality and Class Struggle', *New Left Review* (No. 123, September–October 1980). See also: Ralph Miliband's critique of Anderson's *Passages* and *Lineages*, 'Political Forms and Historical Materialism', reprinted in Ralph Miliband, *Class Power and State Power: Political Essays* (London: Verso Editions and New Left Books, 1983) and Anthony Giddens, *A Contemporary Critique of Historical Materialism, Vol. I, Power, Property and the State* (London: Macmillan, 1981), and *Vol. 2, The Nation State and Violence* (London: Polity Press, 1985), and the response to this critique by Eric Olin Wright, 'Gidden's Critique of Marxism', *New Left Review* (No. 138, March–April 1983), pp. 11–35.

44. See for instance: Geoffrey de Ste-Croix, *The Class Struggle in the Ancient Greek World: From the Archaic Age to the Arab Conquests* (London: Duckworth, 1981), Rodney Hilton, *et al.*, *The Transition from Feudalism to Capitalism* (London: Verso, 1978) which reprints a collection from the Dobb–Sweezy debate in *Science and Society* in the 1950s, *The Brenner Debate: Agrarian Class Structure and Economic Development in Pre-Industrial Europe* (Cambridge: Cambridge University Press, 1985), Karl Marx, *Pre-Capitalist Economic Formations*,

introduction by Eric Hobsbaum (London: Lawrence & Wishart, 1964), David McLellan, *Marx's Grundrisse* (St Albans: Paladin, 1971), Marx and Engels, *Pre-Capitalist Socio-Economic Formations: a Collection* (London: Lawrence & Wishart, 1979 and Moscow: Progress Publishers, 1979), V. Melotti, *Marx and the Third World* (London: Macmillan, 1977), L. Krader, *Formation of the State* (Engelwood Cliffs, N.J.: Prentice-Hall, 1968), Kradu, *The Asiatic Mode of Production: Sources, Development and Change in the Writings of Karl Marx* (Essen: Van Gorcum, 1976), Amin, *Unequal Development: An Essay on the Social Formations of Peripheral Capitalism*, Taylor, *From Modernization to Modes of Production*, Anderson, *Passages and Lineages*, and though quite dated now, it still repays a reading to see the works of Gordon Childe, *Man Makes Himself* (Mentor, 1951), and *What Happened in History* (Harmondsworth: Penguin, 1954). See also: S. Resnick and R. Wolff, 'The Theory of Transitional Conjunctures and the Transition from Feudalism to Capitalism', *Review of Radical Political Economy* Vol 2, No. 3, Fall 1979), and Nicos Mouzelis, 'Review Article: Modernization, Underdevelopment, Uneven Development: Prospects for a Theory of Third World Formations', *Journal of Peasant Studies* (Vol. 7, No. 3, April 1980).

45. N. Bukharin, *Imperialism and World Economy*, published in Russian in 1917, R. Hilferding, *Finance Capital*, published in German in 1910, J.A. Hobson, *Imperialism: A Study*, published in 1902, Karl Kautsky, 'Ultra-Imperialism', published in German in 1914, and Rosa Luxemburg, *The Accumulation of Capital*, published in German in 1913. A critique of Stalinism can be found in Herbert Marcuse, *Soviet Marxism: A Critical Analysis* (London: Routledge and Kegan Paul, 1958). See also: Kubalkova and Cruickshank, *Marxism-Leninism and Theory of International Relations*, op. cit.

46. Claudia von Braunmuhl, 'On the Analysis of the Bourgeois Nation-State within the World Market Context' in J. Holloway and S. Picciotto (eds), *State and Capital: A Marxist Debate* (London: Edward Arnold, 1978).

47. Martin Shaw, 'War, Imperialism and the State System: A Critique of Orthodox Marxism for the 1980s', in Martin Shaw (ed), *War, State and Society* (London: Macmillan, 1984), pp. 62–3. For the Poulantzas–Miliband debate see: Ralph Miliband, *The State in Capitalist Society* (London: Weidenfeld & Nicolson, 1969), Nicos Poulantzas, 'The Problem of the Capitalist State', *New Left Review* (No. 58, November–December 1969), Ralph Miliband, 'The Capitalist State – Reply to Nicos Poulantzas', *New Left Review* (No. 59, 1970), Nicos Poulantzas, *Political Power and Social Classes* (London: New Left Books, 1973) originally published in French in 1968, Ralph Miliband, 'Poulantzas and The Capitalist State', *New Left Review* (No. 82, November–December 1973), Ernesto Laclau, 'The Specificity of the Political: Around the Poulantzas–Miliband Debate', *Economy and Society* (Vol. 5, No. 1, February, 1975) Nicos Poulantzas, 'The Capitalist State: A Reply to Miliband and Laclau', *New Left Review* (No. 95, January–February 1975). For a later critique

of Poulantzas, see Erik Olin Wright, *Class, Crisis and the State* (London: New Left Books, 1978).

48.   See: G. van Benthem van den Bergh, 'The Interconnection between Processes of State Formation and Class Formation: Problems of Conceptualisation' (Institute of Social Studies, The Hague, Occasional Papers, No. 52, August, 1972), Cox, 'Social Forces, States and World Order: Beyond International Relations Theory', and 'Gramsci, Hegemony and International Relations: An Essay in Method', *Millennium: Journal of International Studies* (Vol. 12, No. 2, 1983), pp. 162–75, E. Krippendorff, 'Towards a Class Analysis of the International System', *Acta Politica* (Vol. 12, Jan. 1975), Ralph Pettman, *State and Class: A Sociology of International Affairs* (London: Croom Helm, 1979), Stephen Hymer, 'International Politics and International Economics: A Radical Approach', *Monthly Review* (Vol. 29, No. 1, March 1978), Samir Amin, 'Class and Nation Historically and in the Current Crises' *Monthly Review* (1980), Basso, 'An Analysis of Classical Theories of Imperialism', and see also Colin Barker, 'A Note on the Theory of Capitalist States', *Capital and Class* (4, Spring 1978), and 'The State as Capital', *International Socialism* (1, July 1978).

49.   Martin Shaw, 'War, Imperialism and the State System: A Critique of Orthodox Marxism for the 1980s', in Martin Shaw (ed.) *War, State and Society* (London: Macmillan, 1984), pp. 64–7.

50.   Kubalkova and Cruickshank, *Marxism and International Relations*, p. 19.

51.   K. Marx and Frederick Engels, *The German Ideology*, in K. Marx, F. Engels, V. Lenin, *On Historical Materialism: A Collection* (New York: International Publishers, 1974 and Moscow: Progress Publishers, 1972), p. 18.

52.   E.P. Thompson, 'Notes on Exterminism, The Last Stage of Civilisation', *New Left Review* (121, 1980). E.P. Thompson, *et al.*, *Exterminism and Cold War* (London: New Left Books/Verso, 1982), and the critique by Raymond Williams, 'The Politics of Nuclear Disarmament', *New Left Review* (124), p. 28, Mary Kaldor, 'Warfare and Capitalism', in Thompson, *et al.*, *Exterminism*.

53.   Michael Kidron, *Western Capitalism since the War* (London: Weidenfeld & Nicolson, 1968), Ernest Mandel, *Marxist Economic Theory*, Vol. 2 (London: Merlin, 1968).

54.   For a recent review of critical theory in IR, see Chapter 4 and Mark Hoffman, 'Critical Theory and the Inter-Paradigm Debate', *Millennium: Journal of International Studies* (Vol. 16, No. 2, Summer 1987), pp. 231–49. Hoffman lists the 'central core of authors' as Cox, John Maclean, Richard Ashley, Kubalkova and Cruickshank, Sylviu Brucan, Ekhart Krippendorff, and Andrew Linklater. See: Robert Cox, 'Social Forces, States, and World Order: Beyond International Relations Theory', John Maclean, 'Marxist Epistemology, Explanations of Change and the Study of International Relations' in B. Buzan and R.J. Barry Jones (eds), *Change in the Study of International Relations* (London: Frances Pinter, 1981), and 'Political Theory, International Theory and the Problem of Ideology',

Millennium: Journal of International Studies (Vol, 10, No. 2, 1981), Richard K. Ashley, 'The Poverty of Neorealism', *International Organisation* (Vol. 38, No. 2, 1984), pp. 225–86, Kubalkova and Cruickshank, *Marxism and International Relations,* Brucan, *The Dialectrics of World Politics,* E. Krippendorff, *International Relations as a Social Science* (Brighton: Harvester Press, 1982), A. Linklater, 'Realism, Marxism and Critical International Theory', *Review of International Studies* (Vol. 23, No. 2, 1986), pp. 301–12, and *Marxism and the Critical Theory of International Relations* (London: Macmillan, 1987) as cited in Hoffman, 'Critical Theory'.

55. Hoffman, 'Critical Theory', p. 244.

56. Robert Cox, *Production, Power, and World Order* (New York: Columbia University Press, 1987).

57. Fernand Braudel, *The Mediterranean and the Mediterranean World in the Age of Philip II,* 2 vols (Fontana, 1975).

58. Fernand Braudel, *Civilization and Capitalism: 15–18th Century,* 3 vols (London: Collins, 1984).

59. Fernand Braudel, *The Perspective of the World* (*Civilization and Capitalism: 15–18th Century, Vol. III*) (London: Collins, 1984), see the Introduction.

60. Braudel, *The Perspective of the World,* p. 55. See also Karl A. Wittfogel, *Oriental Despotism: A Comparative Study of Total Power* (New Haven, CT: Yale University Press, 1957).

61. Braudel, *The Perspective of the World,* p. 57.

62. Immanuel Wallerstein, *The Modern World-System I: Capitalist Agriculture and the Origins of the European World- Economy in the Sixteenth Century* (London: Academic Press, 1974).

63. Braudel, *The Perspective of the World,* p. 70.

64. Braudel, *The Perspective of the World,* p. 77.

65. See: Theda Skocpol, 'Wallerstein's World Capitalist System: A Theoretical Critique', *American Journal of Sociology* (No. 82, 1977), Aristide R. Zolberg, 'Origins of the Modern World System: A Missing Link', *World Politics* (Vol. 33, No. 2, 1981), and '"World" and "System": A Misalliance', in W.R. Thompson (ed.), *Contending Approaches,* P. Gourevitch, 'The International System and Regime Formation: a critical review of Anderson and Wallerstein', *Comparative Politics* (10, 1978), pp. 419–38, David P. Rapkin, 'The Inadequacy of a Single Logic: Integrating Political and Material Approaches to the World System' in Thompson (ed.), *Contending Approaches,* Peter Worsley, 'One World or Three? A Critique of the world-system theory of Immanuel Wallerstein', in R. Miliband and J. Saville (eds), *The Socialist Register* (London: Merlin Press, 1980), reprinted in David Held, *et al., States and Societies* (Oxford: Martin Robertson and The Open University, 1983), Brenner, 'The Origins of Capitalist Development: A Critique of Neo-Smithian Marxism', A. Aronowitz, 'A Methodological Critique of Wallerstein, *The Modern World System*', *Theory and Society* (Vol. 10, No. 4, 1980), and C.H. George, 'The Origins of Capitalism: a Marxist Epitome and a Critique of Immanuel Wallerstein's Modern World System', *Marxist Perspectives* (Summer, 1980).

66. Wallerstein, *The Modern World System I*, pp. 7–8.

67. Wallerstein, *The Modern World System I*, pp. 15–18.

68. See: S. Eisenstadt, *The Political System of Empires* (New York: Free Press of Glencoe, 1963), and *The Decline of Empires* (Engelwood Cliffs, NJ: Prentice-Hall, 1967), and 'The Causes of Disintegration and Fall of Empires: Sociological Analyses', *Diogenes* (No. 34, Summer 1961), pp. 82–107.

69. Wallerstein, *The Modern World System I*, p. 15.

70. Wallerstein, *The Modern World System II: Mercantilism and the Consolidation of the European World-Economy; 1600–1750* (New York: Academic Press, 1980), pp. 113–14.

71. Wallerstein, *The Modern World System II*, pp. 70–1. Wallerstein quotes from Anderson, *Lineages of the Absolutist State*, p. 55: 'For if the seventeenth century is the noon of turmoil and disarray in the relationship between class and state within the total system of aristrocratic political rule, the eighteenth century is by comparison the golden evening of their tranquility and reconciliation'.

72. Wallerstein, *The Modern World System II*, p. 38.

73. Wallerstein, *The Modern World System II*, pp. 38–9. For Wallerstein's recent views see: 'The States in the International Vortex of the Capitalist World-Economy' in Ali Kazancizil (ed), *The State in Global Perspective* (Aldershot: Gower/UNESCO, 1986), pp. 145–55.

74. However, the journal *Review* has published various analyses of ancient empires and 'world systems' such as M.I. Finley, 'Empire in the Graeco-Roman World', *Review* (Vol. II, No. 1, Summer 1978), Kajsa Ekholm and Jonathan Friedman, 'Capital, Imperialism and Exploitation in Ancient World-Systems', *Review* (Vol. VI, No. 1, Summer 1982), and Romila Thapar, 'Ideology and the Interpretation of Early Indian History' *Review* (Vol. V, No. 3, Winter 1982).

75. Nicole Bousquet, 'From Hegemony to Competition: Cycles of the Core?' in Terence K. Hopkins and Immanuel Wallerstein (eds), *Processes of the World-System* (London: Sage, 1980).

76. Bousquet, 'From Hegemony to Competition', pp. 48–9.

77. Bousquet, 'From Hegemony to Competition', p. 52.

78. Bousquet, 'From Hegemony to Competition', pp. 50–51; 83.

79. Albert Bergesen, 'Cycles of Formal Colonial Rule' in *Processes of the World System*, p. 21. See also: Albert Bergesen and R. Schoenberg, 'Long waves of colonial expansion and contraction, 1415–1969' (based on a data set compiled by O. Henige) in Albert Bergesen (ed.), *Studies of the Modern World-System* (New York: Academic Press, 1980), 'Long economic cycles and the size of industrial enterprise' in R. Robinson (ed.), *Dynamics of World Development* (Beverly Hills, CA: Sage, 1981), and '1914 Again? Another Cycle of Interstate Competition and War' in Pat McGowan and Charles W. Kegley (eds), *Foreign Policy and the Modern World-System* (Beverly Hills, CA: Sage, 1983), and 'Modeling Long Waves of Crisis in the World-System' in A. Bergesen (ed.), *Crisis in the World System* (Beverly Hills, CA: Sage, 1983).

80. Bergesen, 'Cycles of Formal Colonial Rule', pp. 123–4.

81. Christopher Chase Dunn, 'Interstate System and Capitalist World-Economy: One Logic or Two?' *International Studies Quarterly* (Vol. 25, No. 1, 1981), pp. 19–42, and in W. Ladd Hollist and James N. Rosenau (eds), *World System Structure* (London: Sage, 1981). See also: Amin, 'Class and Nation, Historically and in the Current Crisis'.

82. Chase-Dunn, 'Interstate System' pp. 35; 41–2 (in W. Ladd Hollist and James N. Rosenau).

83. Chase-Dunn, 'Interstate System, p. 48.

84. Chase-Dunn, 'Interstate System, pp.50–1.

85. For a review of part of the *Political Economy of the World-System Annuals* series see: Faruk Yalvac, 'World System Studies and International Relations', *Millennium: Journal of International Studies* (Vol. 9, No. 3, 1980).

86. David P. Rapkin, 'The Inadequacy of a Single Logic: Integrating Political and Material Approaches to the World System' in Thompson (ed.), *Contending Approaches*, p. 265.

87. Thompson (ed.), *Contending Approaches*, p. 254.

88. Thompson (ed.), *Contending Approaches*, p. 266: See also: Immanuel Wallerstein, 'The Withering Away of the States', *International Journal of the Sociology of Law* (6, 1980), pp. 369–78.

89. Wallerstein, 'The Withering Away of the States', pp. 263–5. See also, Christopher Chase Dunn, 'International Economic Policy in a Declining Core State', in W.P. Avery and D.P. Rapkin (eds), *America in a Changing World Political Economy* (New York: Longman, 1982), pp. 77–96.

90. James Lee Ray, 'The "World-System" and the Global Political System: A Crucial Relationship?' in Pat McGowan and Charles W. Kegley Jr, *Foreign Policy and the Modern World-System* (Beverly Hills, CA: Sage, 1983), pp. 29–30.

91. Ray, 'The "The World-System".

92. William R.Thompson, 'The World Economy, the Long Cycle, and the Question of World System Time', in McGowan and Kegley, *Foreign Policy*, and 'Succession Crisis in the Global Political System: A Test of the Transition Model', in Bergesen (ed.), *Crises in the World System*.

93. Thompson, 'The World Economy, the Long Cycle, and the Question of World System Time', pp. 48–9.

94. Thompson, 'The World Economy, the Long Cycle, and the Question of World System Time', pp. 52–3. See: The Research Working Group on Cyclical Rhythms and Secular Trends, 'Cyclical Rhythms and Secular Trends of the Capitalist World-Economy: some Premises, Hypotheses, and Questions', *Review* (Vol. II, No. 4, Spring 1979), pp. 483–500.

95. Thompson, 'The World Economy, The Long Cycle and the Question of World System Time', p. 57.

96. Gautam Sen, *The Military Origins of Industrialisation and International Trade Rivalry* (London: Frances Pinter, 1984).

97. Raimo Väyrynen, 'Economic Cycles, Power Transitions, Political Management and Wars Between Major Powers', *International Studies Quarterly* (27, December 1983), pp. 389–418. See also: 'Global Power Dynamics and Collective Violence' in Väyrynen, Senghaas, Schmidt

(eds), *The Quest for Peace: Transcending Collective Violence and War Among Societies, Cultures and States.*

98. Raimo Väyrynen, 'Economic Goals, Power Transitions, Political Management and Wars Between Major Powers', pp. 400, 409.

99. Joshua Goldstein, 'Long Cycles in War and Economic Growth', Vols. I and II (unpublished PhD dissertation, Massachusetts Institute of Technology, 1986). Goldstein's work is reviewed by Richard Rosecrance, 'Long Cycle Theory and International Relations', *International Organisation* (Vol. 41, No. 2, Spring 1987), pp. 283–301. Joshua Goldstein, 'Kondratieff Waves as War Cycles', *International Studies Quarterly* (29, December 1985).

100. Michael Mann, 'Capitalism and Militarism' in Martin Shaw (ed.), *War, State and Society* (London: Macmillan, 1984), pp. 28–9.

101. Mann, 'Capitalism and Militarism', p. 40. See also: Michael Mann, 'War and Social Theory: Into Battle with Classes, Nations and States', in Colin Creighton and Martin Shaw (eds), *The Sociology of War and Peace* (London: Macmillan, 1987), pp. 54–72. See also, 'The Autonomous Power of the State: Its Origins, Mechanisms and Results', *Archives Europeenes Sociologiques* (Vol. 25, 1984).

102. Mann, 'Capitalism and Militarism', p. 45.

103. Michael Mann, *The Sources of Social Power*, Vol. I, 'A History of Power from the Beginning to A.D. 1760' (Cambridge: Cambridge University Press, 1986). See also: 'States, Ancient and Modern', *European Journal of Sociology* (Vol. 18, 1977), pp. 263–98.

104. Mann, *The Sources of Social Power*, Vol. I, pp. 523; 531.

105. Mann, *The Sources of Social Power*, pp. 533–4.

106. Mann, *The Sources of Social Power*, pp. 535.

107. Mann, *The Sources of Social Power*, pp. 536–7.

108. John Hall, 'Raymond Aron's Sociology of States, or the Non-Relative Autonomy of Inter-State Behaviour', in Shaw (ed.), *War, State and Society*, p. 74.

109. John A. Hall, 'War and the Rise of the West', in Creighton and Shaw (eds), *The Sociology of War and Peace*, p. 48.

110. Hall, 'War and the Rise of the West', p. 49.

111. John A. Hall, *Powers and Liberties: The Causes and Consequence of the Rise of the West* (Harmondsworth: Penguin, in association with Basil Blackwell, 1985), p. 142.

112. Hall, *Powers and Liberties*, p. 143. See also John A. Hall, 'States and Economic Development: Reflections on Adam Smith', pp. 154–176, in John A. Hall (ed.), *States in History* (Oxford: Basil Blackwell, 1986) and J. Baechler, J.A. Hall and M. Mann (eds), *Europe and the Rise of Capitalism* (Oxford: Basil Blackwell, 1987), and John A. Hall, 'Religion and the Rise of Capitalism', *European Journal of Sociology* (Vol. 26, 1985).

7 The Political Culture of War and Nuclear Proliferation: A Third World Perspective*

Ali A. Mazrui

In this short study I am limiting my discussion of the nuclear age to two aspects which are seldom taken into account in deliberations of this kind:

- (a) Nuclear military power and cultural inequalities in the world;
- (b) Nuclear military power and sexual inequalities in the global military order.

In exploring the cultural imbalances I shall focus especially on the predicament of the *Muslim world* and of *Africa* in a world which has gone nuclear. In examining the issue of gender in the nuclear equation, I shall touch upon the psychology of *nuclear macho* and the fear of *nuclear castration* in the behaviour of nations. We shall of course pursue the policy implications of these issues, as well as their moral dimensions. What has happened to the *Jihad tradition* in Islam in the shadow of nuclear power? What has happened to the *warrior tradition* in Africa in the nuclear age?

7.1 ISLAM VERSUS THE NUCLEAR AGE

At least until the 1980s, the nuclear age has been bad news for Islam. The new science arrived at a time when Islam had been pushed to the periphery of technological civilisation and the margins of scientific know-how. Gone were the days when Muslims were so advanced in mathematics that the very numbers of calculation bore the name 'Arabic numerals'. Gone were the days when the Arabs led in pushing the frontiers of the metric principle. Who

155

even remembers that words like 'average', 'algebra', 'amalgam', 'atlas', 'cypher', 'chemistry' and 'zenith' were originally Arabic?

The arrival of the nuclear age in the twentieth century also coincided with the disappearance of the Islamic Caliphate in the world system for the first time in centuries. The Ottoman Empire had disintegrated after the First World War. Almost the entire Muslim world was under Euro-Christian domination – from Egypt to Indonesia, from Senegal to Malaya, from the Gulf states to Northern India. Never was the Muslim world more convincingly humbled. Ataturk's Turkey and Iran were just barely semi-independent. The rest of Islam was well and truly under Euro-Christian subjugation.

The world did not realise it at the time, but there were two super-powers about to establish a divided hegemony upon humanity following the Second World War. The Semitic factor was once again linked. One super-power was the United States – with a Jewish enclave which was destined to become one of the most important (if indirect) factors in the history of the Middle East in the twentieth century. The other super-power was of course the Soviet Union – with a Muslim enclave seemingly as *impotent* in influencing Middle Eastern trends as the Jewish enclave in America was decisive in the same role.

By the 1980s the Soviet Union had a Muslim population of well over 40 million in a total Soviet population of 250 million. The United States had a Jewish population of less than 7 million in an American population of 220 million. And yet the less than 7 million Jews of the Western super-power had more relevance for Islamic history than did the nearly 50 million Muslims in the Soviet Union. One reason was simply the fact that the Soviet Union was not a liberal democracy – and therefore electoral numbers counted less than they did in the United States. There is little doubt that had there been 50 million Muslims in the United States instead of the same number in the Soviet Union, the history of the whole world would have been more discernibly different. The Muslims in the United States would have begun to outweigh in some matters the influence of American Jews on American foreign policy towards the Middle East – for better or worse.

But of course this did not happen. The super-power which emerged as the nuclear leader in world politics was in any case the one with a 7 million Jewish enclave rather than the one with a 40 to 50 million Muslim enclave. The Islamic factor in the nuclear history of the world was doubly marginalised – not least because Western Jews were among the innovative giants of the nuclear age while Muslim scholars were scientifically peripheral in the twentieth century. The era of the atom was also the era of Albert Einstein, the most towering scientist of the twentieth century and one of the most famous Jews of all time. The stage was set for a future Jewish involvement in the nuclear age, against a background of global Muslim marginality. The *jihad* tradition in Islam was at a disadvantage.

In a sense we are back to the issue of a nuclearised Jewish state. No collective reincarnation in history has been more dramatic than the recreation of the Jewish state. The last Jewish state died 2000 years previously – only to be reborn in the full scientific glare of the nuclear age. The new state of Israel was born within three years of dropping the atomic bombs on Hiroshima and Nagasaki. A Jewish political entity which had died millennia ago in Biblical times was suddenly re-born and started blinking at the brightness of a 'nuclear dawn'.

Within a single generation the Jewish state itself became a nuclear power. That was bad news for the Arabs and for their supporters in the rest of the Muslim world. Without nuclear power, Israel's nuclear superiority could one day have been neutralised by Arab numerical preponderance – as the skill and organisational differential between Arabs and Israelis narrowed. But the acquisition of nuclear weapons by Israel has helped to create a potentially permanent military stalemate. Even when the Arabs become one day the equals of the Israelis in conventional weapons, and match the Israelis in nuclear capacity, the principle of the nuclear deterrent may work in the context of the Arab–Israeli conflict with greater certainty than it will necessarily continue to work in the East/West conflict. Israel just happens to have been created at a time when a nuclear stalemate could conceivably ensure its survival. That may be good for world Jewry – but it is not necessarily good news for the Muslim world if Jerusalem is lost forever to Muslim sovereignty.

But even in the realm of the peaceful uses of atomic energy, the nuclear age is potentially a disservice to Islam. It is oil rather than uranium ore which has recently given Islam new economic leverage in the world system. The Organisation of Petroleum Exporting Countries (OPEC) is primarily a Muslim organisation in composition and is Arab-led. The world has sometimes witnessed a kind of *petro-jihad* – as during the Arab oil embargo against the US in 1973. But will the world witness nuclearised *jihad* in the near future? In the short run, the prospects are fraught with difficulties.

7.2   THE CRESCENT OVER THE MUSHROOM CLOUD

If Islam gets nuclearised before the end of the century, two regional rivalries are likely to have played an important part in it. One is the rivalry between India and Pakistan; the other is the rivalry between Israel and the Arabs.

India may have decided to speed up its nuclear programme more because of China than because of Pakistan; but Pakistan's decision to speed up its own programme was almost certainly influenced if not inspired by India's explosion of a nuclear device in 1974.

The cultural rivalry of Muslims versus Hindus is also more relevant in Pakistani attitudes than in India's policies. Basically the attitude of the Indian government towards Pakistan has relatively little to do with the fact that Pakistan is a Muslim country. The Indian government deals with a variety of other Muslim countries on an entirely different basis. In contrast, the attitude of the Pakistani government towards India is presumably often clouded by a historic rivalry with Hindus. India itself is of course a secular state; Pakistan is an Islamic Republic. Perceptions of the state within Pakistan are conditioned by a cultural and religious self-consciousness. The pursuit of a new form of power like nuclear energy, and the quest for the new form of status as a member of the nuclear club, almost inevitably carries in Pakistan a sense of Muslim pride and cultural ambition. The basic dialectic in the Pakistani psyche between Islam as a religion 'in its own right and Islam as a negation of Hinduism is bound to have conditioned Pakistan's nuclear programme, as it has conditioned most other major directions of national, regional and global policies adopted in Pakistan. A special concept of *jihad* has been at work.

In reality Pakistan's nuclear ambitions go back to the late Prime Minister Zulkifar Ali Bhutto. And in his case, as in the minds of subsequent leaders, nuclear capability was seen as part of cultural and religiuos vindication. Prime Minister Bhutto was quoted as saying: 'There was a Christian bomb, a Jewish bomb, and now a Hindu bomb. Why not an Islamic bomb?'[1]

Pakistan's effort to match India's nuclear capability seems to have been considerably aided by the work of Dr Abdel Qader Khan, who worked for a while in a laboratory in Amsterdam and had access to a wide range of classified documents and scientific processes relevant for 'sensitive' nuclear research. According to reports he was even able to spend some time in Urenco Consortium's secret Uranium Enrichment Plant at Almelo near the border between the Federal Republic of Germany and the Netherlands. Dr Khan could thus observe the centrifuge process from close quarters.

It would seem that Khan originally accepted the job in the Netherlands purely as a means of livelihood prior to becoming a Dutch citizen (he was himself partly educated in Holland and was married to a Dutch woman) but reports imply that some time in 1974, presumably after India's explosion of its nuclear device and the impact this had on many Pakistanis still reeling from their defeat in the Indo–Pakistani War of 1971, Khan was persuaded to become a nuclear spy for Pakistan. Later on he left Holland to go back to his native country – and became in absentia the most controversial Third World scientist in recent international history. Holland was taken to task by its Urenco partners, Britain and West Germany. The Israelis lodged a vigorous protest to the Netherlands. The United States temporarily suspended most forms of aid to Pakistan; and much of the world speculated whether Libyan money and Pakistani know-how were together on their way towards nuclearising Islam.

While Pakistan's nuclear ambitions have been conditioned by rivalry with India, Libya's military ambitions are connected with its bid for leadership in the Arab world and its hostility towards Israel.

But a more likely Arab nuclear innovator than Libya might turn out to be Iraq, in spite of the setback of the destruction of its original reactor by Israel. International controversy erupted in the summer of 1980 concerning a French nuclear deal with the government of Iraq. Reports had it that a hundred technicians of the French government company Technitome, an arm of France's Atomic Energy Commission, were already in Iraq to install a powerful Osiris resurge reactor and a smaller Isis reactor under a contract which included supplying enriched uranium. The technicians were also scheduled to train 600 Iraqis to run the reactors. Voices of protest were heard, especially from Israel, Britain and the United States.

It was reported that the first shipment of approximately 33 pounds of highly enriched uranium (out of a total of some 158 pounds over three years) had left for Iraq in June 1980. Western scientists calculated that 158 pounds of the 93 per cent enriched uranium could enable Iraq to make between three and six nuclear bombs. It was estimated that it would take Iraq approximately five years to acquire this modest military nuclear capability.[2]

There was suspicion from quite early that the Israelis would attempt to abort the French-Iraqi deal even to the extent of committing murder and attempting sabotage. Important parts of one of the reactors were blown up in 1979 in a commando-style operation. And an Egyptian nuclear expert working for Iraq was murdered in Paris in June 1979. The French authorities and others strongly suspected Israeli involvement. And in the course of the controversy of the summer of 1980 western diplomats expressed fears about possible Israeli preemptive military action if and when intelligence revealed that Iraq was about to build nuclear weapons. As it turned out, Israel did not wait for such evidence before destroying Iraq's reactor in June 1981. Israel held the veto against the nuclearisation of Arab nationalism or Arab versions of Islamic Jihad.

The anxieties expressed by the Israelis carried a certain historical cynicism. After all, France had sold Israel a reactor without any inspection safeguards in the late 1950s. While Iraq has signed the Nuclear Nonproliferation Treaty, Isreal has not done so.

It has been reported that in the 1950s Israeli scientists at the Weizmann Institute perfected a new and cheaper way of making the heavy water that moderates the chain reaction in the nuclear reactor. Speculation has it that the Isrealis sold their secrets to France in exchange for a reactor. That reactor, situated at the secret Dimona Nuclear Plant, featured in a report of the United States Central Intelligence Agency (CIA) to the effect that Israel may already have between ten and twenty nuclear weapons.[3]

Whatever may be the extent of Israel's nuclear capability there is little doubt that the arms race in the Middle East, like the arms race between India and Pakistan, is a fundamental part of the background to the forthcoming nuclearisation of Islam. And even the peaceful uses of nuclear energy of the kind envisaged by President Richard Nixon for Egypt would, quite probably, be only a few years away from potential military uses accessible to a future government in Cairo, especially if political radicalism returns to Egypt.

How does all this relate to issues of leadership and politics at the global level? We should first note that the danger of nuclear war does come from two primary sources – vertical nuclear proliferation among the great powers and horizontal nuclear proliferation in the third world. Vertical proliferation involves greater sophistication and diversification of nuclear options and nuclear technology in the arsenals of the great powers. The same nuclear powers increase and diversify their destructive capabilities.

Horizontal proliferation, on the other hand, involves entirely new members of the Nuclear Club. The Nuclear Nonproliferation Treaty was in fact intended to deal with both the risk of vertical proliferation among the great powers and horizontal addition of new nuclear powers. The great powers were supposed to embark on effective steps toward disarmament, while at the same time helping to reduce the risk of more and more countries acquiring nuclear weapons. In reality, since 1968 when the Treaty struggled to be born, both vertical and horizontal proliferation have taken place. And the vertical variety among the great powers has escalated faster than the horizontal addition of new members to the nuclear club.

But what could effectively motivate the great powers not only to decelerate the arms race but also generally to declare nuclear weapons illegitimate and subsequently to start the process of conventional disarmament? It would seem that vertical proliferation has sometimes motivated the great powers to seek ways of containing the arms race. The Strategic Arms Limitation Treaties are in part a response to the stresses of vertical nuclear proliferation, a search for ways of containing the competition. And·yet for the time being vertical nuclear proliferation has not been adequate for the bigger goal of motivating the great powers to give up nuclear weapons altogether.

The question which arises is what sort of concern is likely to be effective enough to lead to the military denuclearisation of the world. One type of shock could be a somewhat limited accidental nuclear catastrophe of a military kind. The civilian accident at Three Mile Island in Pennsylvania did more for the anti-nuclear movement in the western world than almost anything else before the Soviet accident at Chernobyl. Had the accident gone out of hand, and a bigger catastrophe resulted, the revulsion against nuclear energy would have been even more dramatic.

Similarly, had the periodic computer errors in the United States about a Russian 'attack' resulted in a really precipitate American response, the disaster might have provided enough of a shock to create an irresistible anti-nuclear movement among the populations of the great powers themselves.

But one should not pray for disasters, however accidental. An alternative approach to shocking the world into nuclear renunciation is to take a risk with horizontal proliferation. There is still the possibility of a disaster, but at least not the certainty. The logic here is that a certain degree of nuclear proliferation in the world is bound to increase nuclear anxieties within the population of the great powers themselves, and strengthen pressures for the total abandonment of nuclear weapons by everybody. The great powers do not trust third world countries with those weapons.

That distrust could become an asset if the threat of nuclearisation of the third world creates enough consternation in the Northern hemisphere to result in a massive international movement to declare nuclear weapons illegitimate for everybody, and to put an end to nuclear arsenals in every country that has them. What this means is that although the greatest risks of nuclear war come from vertical proliferation in the Northern hemisphere and, secondarily horizontal proliferation in the Third World, the vertical variety in itself has not been enough to end this dangerous nuclear order. The 'vaccination' of horizontal nuclear proliferation might be needed to cure the world of this nuclear malaise – a dose of the disease becomes part of the necessary cure.

Here the Muslim world comes into relevance again. The most dangerous part of the third world from the point of view of global war is the Middle East. Modest horizontal proliferation in the Middle East would be more dangerous in *global* terms than a slightly higher level of proliferation in Latin America or Black Africa. This is partly because a regional war in the Middle East carries a greater risk of escalating into a world war than does a regional war in Latin America or Black Africa.

If, then, horizontal nuclear proliferation is a necessary vaccine against the existing nuclear order itself, proliferation in the heartland of the Muslim world should work faster than proliferation elsewhere. Although Brazil is much larger than Iraq, Brazil's nuclear capability would be less of a global shock than Iraqi nuclear bombs. Pakistan's explosion of a nuclear device would carry with it greater fears than a successful explosion by Argentina. Three nuclear powers in the Islamic world could be perceived as a greater threat to world peace than five nuclear powers in some other parts of the third world. In the total struggle against nuclear weapons in the world as a whole the Islamic world might well play a decisive role in the years ahead.

In this instance Islam might at first be playing a Russian nuclear roulette with two other civilisations – with Hinduism in South Asia and with Zionism and politicised Judaism in the Middle East. But out of the dangerous regional game might emerge an impetus for global reform; out of limited horizontal proliferation there might ultimately evolve global denuclearisation.

But where does Africa fit into these nuclear calculations? How have cultural and racial inequalities affected Africa in the nuclear age? It is to this theme that we must now turn.

7.3   AFRICA VERSUS THE NUCLEAR AGE

It is symbolic of the basic African condition that the first form of African participation in the nuclear age concerned a raw material. Uranium is of course as indigenous to Africa as 'the flame trees of Thika' or the baobab tree of Senegal. Africa in the 1930s and 1940s helped to provide the uranium which launched the western world into the nuclear orbit.

To change the metaphor, Africa was in attendance at the birth of the nuclear age. It was in part Africa's uranium from Zaire which helped to set in motion the first nuclear reactor in North America. And, for better or for worse, Africa's uranium may have gone into those dreadful atomic bombs which were dropped on Hiroshima and Nagasaki in August 1945. But of course Africa had no say in the matter. It was not an exercise in Africa's warrior tradition at all. An African resource had simply been pirated by others – and once again played a major role in a significant shift in Western industrialism.

Not that uranium was all that scarce even in the 1940s. What was significant was that outside the Soviet Bloc and North America, uranium seemed to be substantially available only in Black Africa. As Caryl P. Haskins put it way back in 1946:

> [Uranium] stands next to copper in abundance, is more abundant than zinc, and is about four times as plentiful as lead. . . However, the outstanding deposits are narrowly distributed, being confined to the United States, Canada, the Belgian Congo, Czechoslovakia and possibly Russia. The fact that the richest deposits of uranium ore occur in a fairly limited number of places make international control feasible; but it also foreshadows violent competitive struggles for ownership of the richest deposits (the struggle for oil greatly intensified).[4]

Of course since 1946 other reserves of uranium ore have been discovered in the world, including in different parts of Africa. African uranium has continued to fill many a reactor in the Western world, and to help create many a nuclear device.

The second service (after uranium supply) which Africa rendered to the nuclear age was also symbolic. Africa provided the desert for nuclear tests in the early 1960s. In this case Africa's nuclear involvement had slightly shifted from a purely indigenous resource (uranium) to a partially Islamic context of sovereignty (the Sahara). The transition was from providing indigenous nuclear material to furnishing a neo-Islamic laboratory in the desert for a Western bomb. At least two of the legacies of Africa's triple heritage were inadvertently involved – from the mines of Zaire to the sands of Algeria.

The third African point of entry into the nuclear age has been through the Republic of South Africa. For better or worse, South Africa has probably become a nuclear power or is close to it. This provides the third leg of Africa's triple heritage. Indigenous resources (Africa's uranium), a semi-Islamic testing laboratory (the dunes of the Sahara) and an actual Western productive capability (with South Africa's expertise).

A circle of influence developed. The progress of the French nuclear programme and its tests in the Sahara probably helped the Israeli nuclear programme. This was a period when France was quite close to Israel in terms of economic and technological collaboration. The French helped the Israelis build a nuclear reactor at Dimona and seemed at times to be closer to the Israelis in sharing nuclear secrets than even the Americans were. The evidence is abundant and clear – the French nuclear programme in the late 1950s and 1960s served as a midwife to the Israeli nuclear programme. And French tests in the Sahara were part and parcel of France's nuclear process and infrastructure in that period.

By a curious twist of destiny, the Israeli nuclear programme in turn came to serve as a midwife to the nuclear efforts of the Republic of South Africa in the 1970s and 1980s. Relations between the two countries cooled a little after the Sharpeville massacre of 1960 and when Israel briefly considered the possibility of extending aid to African liberation movements in Southern Africa. But by 1970 there were clear improvements in economic relationships. And after Black Africa's almost complete diplomatic break with Israel in 1973, cooperation between Israel and South Africa entered new areas, including the nuclear field. When a nuclear explosion occurred in the South Atlantic in September 1979, the question which arose was whether it was primarily a South African nuclear experiment undertaken with Israeli technical aid, or primarily an Israeli explosive experiment carried out with South Africa's logistical support. A cover-up policy was pursued by both countries, helped in part by their Western allies, especially the Carter Administration in the United States. The cyclical nuclear equation was about to be completed. The Sahara had aided France's nuclear programme, France had aided Israeli's nuclear design, and Israel had in turn aided South Africa's nuclear ambitions. Kwame Nkrumah's fear of a linkage between nuclear tests in the

Sahara and racism in South Africa had found astonishing vindication nearly two decades later. It was in April 1960 that Nkrumah addressed an international meeting in Accra in the following terms:

> Fellow Africans and friends: there are two threatening swords of Damocles hanging over the continent, and we must remove them. These are nuclear tests in the Sahara by the French Government and the apartheid policy of the Government of the Union of South Africa. It would be a great mistake to imagine that the achievement of political independence by certain areas in Africa will automatically mean the end of the struggle. It is merely the beginning of the struggle.[5]

It has turned out that Nkrumah's thesis of 'two swords of Damocles', one nuclear and one racist, was in fact prophetic. The Republic of South Africa is using nuclear power as a potentially stabilising factor in defence of apartheid. The old nuclear fall-out in the Sahara in the 1960s involved a linkage between racism and nuclear weapons which is only just beginning to reveal itself.

But the cultural and technological inequalities between white and black in Southern Africa affect other areas of security – conventional areas as well as nuclear domains. The Republic of South Africa has used its technological superiority to bully its Black neighbors into submission and into 'non-aggression' pacts. The sovereignty of Mozambique, Angola, Botswana, Swaziland, Lesotho, and perhaps even independent Zimbabwe has been violated from time to time, sometimes with utter impunity. European technological leadership in the last three centuries of world history has been inherited by people of European extraction operating in Africa – and has been used as a decisive military resource against Black Africans. South Africa's neighbours have begun to appreciate what it must feel like to be *Israel's* neighbour – for both South Africa and Israel have seldom hesitated to use blatant military muscle at the expense of the sovereignty of their neighbours.

Again cultural and technological inequalities have played a part in these politics of intervention. Israelis have enjoyed military pre-eminence for so long not because they are Jews but because a large part of their population is Western and European. Had the population of Israel consisted overwhelmingly of Middle Eastern Jews, the Arabs would have won every single war they have fought with their Jewish neighbour. Numbers would have counted. Middle Eastern Jews in Israel are often the most hawkish and eager to fight the

Arabs, but the military capability for assuring Israeli victory has come more from their European compatriots. Again culture has played a decisive role in deciding victory and defeat in military equations.

The danger both in the Middle East and Southern Africa lies in pushing the weak too far. We have already seen how desperate conditions in the two sub-regions can easily become fertile ground for different forms of terrorism. For the time being that terrorism in the two geographical areas has not yet gone nuclear. But if the cultural imbalances between Israeli and Arab, between white and black, continue to deepen the sense of desperation among the disadvantaged, we cannot rule out the possibility of their acquiring those nuclear devices one day from radical friends elsewhere. Powerlessness also corrupts – and absolute powerlessness can corrupt absolutely.

But there is one kind of powerlessness whose implications are particularly distinctive – the powerlessness of women on issues of war and peace. Related to this issue is the whole question of the psychology of *nuclear macho*. It is to these sexual questions of political culture that we must now turn.

7.4   THE GENDER OF NUCLEAR WAR

In societies which are vastly different from each other, war has so far been pre-eminently a masculine game. 'Our sons are our warriors' – this has been almost universal. Daughters have had different roles as a rule. Even countries like Israel, which involve women substantially in issues of war and peace, have tended to be protective of women in the allocation of combat duties.

If it is indeed true that there is a pronounced *macho* factor in the psychology of going to war, we cannot ignore the macho factor when we are discussing *nuclear* war. Perhaps that is indeed what is distinctive about war in the nuclear age – it has become too important to be left to men. The whole human species is at stake – men, women, and children. And while the human race has managed to survive for three million years in spite of the violent proclivities of the cave man, nuclear power requires the most fundamental of all human revolutions – a truly androgynised system of social and political power.

It is true that the most famous women rulers in the twentieth century have tended to be 'iron ladies' with a taste for nuclear credentials – Golda Meir, Indira Gandhi, as well as Margaret Thatcher. But for as long as most societies remain primarily male dominated, the women who succeed in the power game will tend to be approximations of what men regard as tough and heroic. We could only discover the true impact of women on decisions concerning war and peace when the power system as a whole has acquired true sexual balance, commensurate androgyny.

Am I assuming that women are generally less violent than men? The answer is 'Yes' – though the reasons may be more cultural than biological. Our information is inadequate about the causes, but there is no doubt about the correlation between violence and masculinity. The jails of crimes of violence are a solemn testimony; the wars across history; the concentration camps and their Mengeles. Of course the world has also produced brutal women. But while men and women have had an equal share in determining births, men have had an overwhelmingly larger share in determining deaths. Men and women are co-creators of the human race, but men have often been solo destroyers of large chunks of that race. The female of the species is the senior partner in the process of baby-making; the male of the species has been the senior partner in the business of corpse-making. In the twentieth century alone there has been no female equivalent of Hitler, or Stalin, or Pol Pot, or Idi Amin or the more brutal architects of *apartheid*.

In reality we cannot be sure that an androgynised power system on the world stage will in fact succeed in moderating the violent inclinations of states which have been so much a part of the globe for so long. But perhaps nothing short of a gender revolution can stand a chance of containing the nuclear threat to the species. If that does not work either, the future will be grim indeed for the human race as a whole as it faces its own escalating technological capacity for planetary self-destruction.

7.5 TOWARDS THE FUTURE

But for the time being the effects of both sexual disparities and cultural inequalities continue to condition the texture of world arrangements. In fact the two most revolutionary normative forces in the world are Marxism on the one side and Islam on the other. Marxism is a revolution of rising aspirations; Islam is a revolution of wounded memory. Marxism is an ideology of how the lowly have risen. Twentieth century Islam is a lament of how the mighty have fallen. Marxism is in search of proletarian internationalism. Marxism is still searching for a new order; twentieth century Islam is in search of an old order. At best Marxism is a cry for innovation; at its most obscurantist Islam is a whimper for restoration and revivalism.

The driving force of revolutionary Marxism is, in ideal conditions, class struggle. The driving force of revolutionary Islam is, in ideal conditions, *jihad*. But by the last quarter of the twentieth century, Marxist (or Soviet) military power globally has become a close second to the power of the first world of the West, whereas Islamic military power in the same period has receded to global marginality.

Of the two most revolutionary forces of the last quarter of the twentieth century – Marxism and Islam – Marxism is the more likely to want to preserve the status quo. Soviet leadership especially has virtually become one of the leading apologists of the existing state-system. Its main criticism of the United States is that Washington has become a destabilising force in the global equation, a threat to the military modus vivendi. In many ways Islam is the more frustrated of the two global revolutionary forces, and Islam is the more likely to take risks against the sanctity of the existing world order.

Islam, in desperation, may be forced to seek its own nuclearisation. One possibility would be to marry the financial resources of one part of the Muslim world with the scientific resources of another. Allah in His wisdom has made Egypt and Pakistan the scientific leaders of the Muslim world. Equally in His wisdom, Allah has made Saudi Arabia and other Gulf states the financial leaders of the Muslim world. A marriage of these two Islamic resources (science and money) could help narrow the gap between Islam as part of the third world, on one side, and the privileged credentials of a pro-Israel capitalist first world and a socialist second universe, on the other side.

All this is quite apart from the danger of pushing Islam not only to desperation, but to *despair*. Pushing Islam against the wall may arouse the ultimate martyrdom complex, the Kerbala syndrome in the case of the Shiites in emulation of the martyrdom of the Prophet's grandson, Hussein.

Islam in despair could be pushed to a nuclear terrorism as a version of *jihad*. Whatever Lord Acton may have meant, it is not only power which corrupts. It is also frustrated powerlessness. When powerlessness is frustrated absolutely, it can indeed corrupt absolutely. And a future case of Islamic nuclear terrorism – aimed probably against either Israel or the United States or both – may well be the outcome of the present Israeli-American insensitivity to the sense of honour of an alien Islamic civilisation.

There is one happy prospect that Black Africans can contemplate which the Arabs are denied. Black Africans can contemplate the prospect of inheriting the white bomb of the Republic of South Africa. Before the end of this century the Blacks of South Africa will probably succeed in overthrowing the regime of white supremacy. In the wake of the racial war which has to precede the Black victory, half the white population would have had to leave the Republic. But it seems almost certain that half the white population of South Africa would in the end also still remain behind. Partly through that other half, South Africa's nuclear capability would be transmitted from white control to black control.

It is therefore a fair question to ask whether the prospect of a nuclearised South Africa today is a blessing or a curse for the rest of Africa. Is it possible that white South Africa's nuclear bomb is a short-term nuisance for Black Africa but a long-term advantage? Are South Africa's Blacks going to be the legitimate heirs of South Africa's nuclear capability before the end of the century?

There is little doubt that white South Africa's bomb is irrelevant for the survival of apartheid. The main threat to South Africa's racist regime is *internal* to South Africa – and the regime is unlikely to use nuclear devices in the streets of Soweto. Such a use would in any case precipitate a white exodus – at least as serious a crisis for *apartheid* as the rebellion of Blacks.

But while nuclear power is of marginal significance in the fortunes of present-day South Africa, it may be more significant in the *post-apartheid* era of the Republic. As the new rulers inherit the white nuclear bomb, they will be transformed from the status of being the most humiliated Blacks of the twentieth century to the status of becoming the most powerful Blacks of the twenty-first century. Black-ruled South Africa will of course remain not only one of the richest countries in the world in terms of mineral resources, but also one of the most industrialised in the Southern hemisphere. The nuclear capability will remain part of a wider industrial complex.

But can such 'horizontal proliferation' be a cure to vertical proliferation? Again the underlying hope lies in creating the necessary culture shock for a serious commitment to *universal* nuclear disarmament. In any case, Black inheritance of South Africa's bomb will not be horizontal proliferation in the usual sense. No new *country* will have been added to the membership of the nuclear club – only a new *race*. For the first time the nuclear club will have a Black member. At the most, the horizontal proliferation will have been across the racial divide rather than state boundaries. And since Northern nuclear powers are more afraid of South African Blacks handling the bomb than of South African whites doing so, the new Black member of the nuclear club may well precipitate an agonising reappraisal as to whether the club should exist at all. The racial prejudices and distrust of the white members of the nuclear club may well serve the positive function of disbanding the club – and dismantling the nuclear arsenals in the cellars which had constituted credentials for membership.

But nuclear disarmament is not enough. There is need to reduce the risk of war. After all, once the genie of nuclear know-how is already out of the bottle, it can be re-utilised if war broke out – and a new nuclear arms race be inaugurated. The ultimate evil is man's proclivity towards war – and not merely the weapons with which he has fought it.

But what kind of fundamental revolution could stabilise the gains in nuclear disarmament and reduce the risk of war? In order to answer that question we need to ask that other question: What has been the most persistent characteristic of war in all societies, across all time, traversing all cultures?

No, the most persistent attribute of war has not been the consistency of motives – for men have fought for reasons which have ranged from greed to glory, from gold to God, from liberty to land, from sex to soccer. The motives have varied but war has continued.

The most recurrent attributes of war has not been its technology either – for we know that the technological range has been from the spear to the intercontinental missile.

Nor has war been a peculiarity of certain climates – for men have fought under the blazing sun as well as in snow drifts.

No, the most persistent attribute of war has not been its motivation, technology, organisation, goals or geographical context. As we have indicated, it has in fact been its *masculinity*.

But with the coming of the nuclear age, war has become too serious to be left to men. The power system of the world does indeed need to be androgynised. The most poignant of all paradoxes amounts to the following imperative: *If man is to survive, woman has to bear arms*.

NOTES AND REFERENCES

* This chapter is indebted to previous work by the author on nuclear proliferation and related issues, and on the political culture of world politics.

1. Cited by: C. Smith and Shyam Bhatia, 'How Dr Khan Stole the bomb for Islam', *The Observer* (London), 9 December 1979.

2. A United Press International report datelined Paris on some aspects of the French–Iraqi atomic deal was carried by many newspapers, including the *Ann Arbor News* (Ann Arbor, Michigan), 9 August 1980.

3. UPI report, and Smith and Bhatia, 'How Dr Khan Stole the bomb'. Consult also Ryukichi Imai and Robert Press, *Nuclear Nonproliferation: Failures and Prospects, A Report of the International Consultative Group on Nuclear Energy* (New York and London: The Rockefeller Foundation and the Royal Institute of International Affairs, 1980).

4. Caryl P. Haskins, 'Atomic Energy and American Foreign Policy', *Foreign Affairs* (Vol. 24, No. 4, July 1946), pp. 595–6. Consult also A. Boserup, L. Christensen and O. Nathan (eds.), *The Challenge of Nuclear Armaments* (Copenhagen: University of Copenhagen/Rhodos International Publishers, 1986).

5. Kwame Nkrumah, *I Speak of Freedom: A Statement of African Ideology* (London: Heinemann, 1961), p. 213. Consult also Ali A. Mazrui (ed.), *The Africans: A Triple Heritage* (London: BBC Publications, and Boston: Little, Brown & Co, 1986), especially Chapter 8 on 'Tools of Exploitation', and Sadruggin Aga Khan (ed.), *Nuclear War, Nuclear Proliferation and Their Consequences* (Oxford: The Clarendon Press, 1985).

8 Normative Theory and International Relations

Hugh C. Dyer

There is a broad literature in normative political theory, some explicit, much implicit, but for the most part this kind of theorising is marginal to the principal concerns of political theorists.[1] The condition is particularly acute in international political theory, with its own peculiar set of problems. This marginality is in itself an indicator of the dilemmas faced by those studying International Relations, that realm of human affairs lying beyond familiar national societies and relatively stable state institutions. The indication is that the mysterious and unpredictable nature of International Relations has led theorists to seek concrete truths about these relations with a desperation not found elsewhere. This search has been dominated by efforts to grasp some persistent reality; a reality beyond the scope of conventional political institutions, and thus felt to be beyond the reach of collective human will and only to be recognised, accepted, and where possible, managed. Hence, in the literature of International Relations one may discover idealists, where in national political relations one finds activists. The intent, here, is to indicate the problems arising from the dominance of positivistic, empiricist, scientistic ideas, and the resulting marginalisation of alternative perspectives, and to show what role there may be for normative theory – as one of these alternatives – in dealing with both the methodological issues and the subject matter of International Relations.[2]

The source of existing normative political theory is the need to know not simply what is done, but what ought to be done. The latter problem is sufficiently important to have led political thinkers seeking only descriptive knowledge of reality to also puzzle about how the exercise of will might bear on reality. In seeking to establish and measure interests and facts, they have been faced with the problem of values. As normative theory addresses values so it has crept into positivist undertakings, but naturally enough, only at the margins – only as required to address or dismiss an obstacle in the path to 'real' knowledge.

In the study of national societies value questions are seen to be sufficiently well understood by common sense not to require rigorous treatment, nor indeed is such treatment of long-term social factors required to proceed with the immediate task of describing and predicting the realities of daily politics.[3] Nevertheless, normative issues are considered a proper subject for philosophical reflection in as much as there is a natural curiosity about what is good and true about both individual and social existence. In the study of International Relations, however, common sense is out of its depth, and the immediate imperative of coping with the realities of daily politics simply overwhelms value questions. Nevertheless, the scale of conflict and the vast inequities of international political life engender some concern with normative issues. The marginalisation of normative theory thus results from the limited ability to comprehend over time, in national politics, and over time and space in international politics, the fundamental place of values in political life. It is not enough to say that theorists and practitioners take the course of least resistance; the problem of marginalisation is a problem of theoretical priority, and here a discussion of normative theory can begin.

Normative theory provides a tool not only for prescription but also for description. In its prescriptive role, it is significant enough as a means of discovering what ought to be done. Yet, for those who discount or dismiss the importance of human will, this feature of normative theory will be of little interest, since what ought to be done is, for them, dictated by straightforward interest calculations in the light of contingent events. In its descriptive role, it is more clearly a theoretical priority and can only be discounted or dismissed by taking unreasonably strong positions in long-standing debates of philosophy and social science. Beginning with the descriptive characteristics of normative theory will bring to bear central questions of International Relations.

A simple definition of norms as rules constituting social and political relationships will suffice for present purposes. It follows that normative theory is concerned to describe and explain these rules, and to evaluate the relationships they constitute. Normative theory is distinct from empirical or positivist theory by virtue of the subject matter being in the realm of ideas rather than of observable facts. The rules are not akin to physical laws, but are rather artifices of human invention. That they are none the less real for being so is the principal question upon which the importance of normative theory hinges. Consequently, an account of the descriptive role of normative theory will satisfy queries about the reality of norms and justify theorising about them.

The descriptive role of norms lies in their being necessary to the comprehension of social and political facts: Norms endow meaning, and thus take priority in any ascription of social or political reality. Explanation and evaluation are interdependent activities in as much as explanatory theory prescribes what is to be explained and how, and provides reasons for evaluative judgement. Such evaluation requires reference to propositions about social wants, needs and purposes which are thus necessary assumptions of an explanatory framework.[4] Hence evaluative, or normative theory underlies explanatory theory, providing the link between facts and values. The description of facts within an explanatory framework relies on a normative account of their meaning. It follows from this discussion that description and evaluation are closely linked, and hence also the descriptive and prescriptive roles of normative theory. Observations about what is done in social and political life can not be entirely distinguished from judgements about what ought to be done.[5] Having said this, it remains undetermined whether there are discoverable principles providing universal criteria for evaluation. All that can be said is that societies do establish such criteria through legal, moral and other social or political structures. These structures are comprised of rules which can be described by normative analysis. This carries us into a range of issues, central to normative inquiry, which relate to the philosophical foundations of these structures: ethics, rationality, meaning and language. These will be touched on tangentially here, and inevitably epistemological and methodological issues will also arise, although space does not permit dealing with them properly. Nevertheless, we turn now to a discussion of the prescriptive role of normative theory, before returning to an examination of how this kind of evaluative inquiry provides a tool for the description and explanation of social and political realities.

Prescriptive theory is directed to choice and action. It is theory intended to guide the exercise of human will. In the context of social and political existence it commonly takes the form of morality. It is instructive to note that morals are often referred to as normative ethics, and that the principal questions of metaethics and metaepistemology are similarly concerned with the logic of their respective subjects. Beyond moral theory referring to social experience there are also ideologies, religions and other belief systems which serve a similar purpose. All of these may fall under the rubric of normative theory, except where they incorporate some transcendental teleology. In this case, they exclude or transcend that rationality of historical, existential and ontological origins which is necessary to an effective prescriptive or evaluative theory.[6] This is a significant parameter not only for normative theory, but also for the social and political systems which it addresses. Clearly, it is possible to achieve social or political organisation on the basis of ideas which transcend conventional rationality, but such a system must nevertheless function as a rational system would function, and to that extent normative theory is applicable. The limits of normative theory exceed the limits of empirical or positivist theory in this respect, since it recognises the rule structures governing political organisation, and can cope with an idiosyncratic but internally consistent rationality. Nevertheless, the limits of a theory's explanatory ability coincide with the limits of successful social or political organisation, and coherent prescription is not possible where the grounds for choice are extrarational even within the context of an idiosyncratic normative structure. In practice this means that no theory can account for relations between two societies, for example, if one or both entirely opt out of a shared rationality. Of course, such an extreme situation is virtually impossible since, at the very least, existential experience will always provide some aspects of a shared rationality, as evidenced by the possibility of social life. (Truisms about the interdependence of the modern world would add weight to this position, but the reader will be spared.) No doubt individual human will may be exercised without rational grounds (as in the case of insanity), but the exercise of collective will in political action cannot escape the confines of social experience, and it is sufficient for a theory of politics to remain within these confines. Within a given social or political context normative theory can assess rule structures, and prescribe accordingly. How these prescriptions may be said to be true of the society to which they refer is a matter to be resolved, but once resolved, their worth is clear: They provide necessary guides for collective action, for policy. It follows that coherent collective action depends, in part, on the truth content of prescriptive statements; effective policy depends, in part, on the reality of values, and theories to account for them. The truth content of prescription is an INUS condition of policy (an insufficient but necessary component of an unnecessary but sufficient condition), since there are clearly other conditions, such as capability, but while any political structure is sufficient to generate policy, it must necessarily be the case that there are, for that polity, good grounds for choice of action.[7] Thus is revealed the role of normative theory in policy-formation. Also revealed is the need to address those issues relating to the foundations of social and political structures and the rules which both govern and define them. Again, the close connection between describing what is and prescribing what ought to be must be emphasised.

In discussing truth, or anything else for that matter, language is a necessity which cannot be escaped. Indeed, truth is generally held to depend on the coherence of the relationship between words and the world in which they are expressed.[8] Hence the meaning of words as settled by conventions of language is no small issue, although it may lie beyond the scope of the present discussion. What is more pertinent here is the relationship between words and statements and the world they correspond to. As an aside, it should be noted that the idea of truth being relational suggests this as a quality of all concepts, as distinct from independent meaning, and we may observe that viewing such important concepts as power, for example, as being relational gives the concept a subtlety which is too often denied it by absolute measures of the empirical variety. Furthermore, the idea of relationships accords with the essential nature of normative inquiry as a means of addressing rule-governed relations. Hence, in the context of these relations, the truth content of prescriptive statements depends on the coherence of these statements in relation to the world for which they prescribe. It is not adequate, of course, simply to measure the success of prescriptions since that would relegate policy-making to trial and error; a method often tried, and often in error. One must be able to judge the soundness, or truth, of prescriptions before acting. Truth, in this sense, depends on verification of a kind distinct from positivistic accounts of knowledge. The truth content is located in the relationship of the prescriptive statement to the rule structure of the society it addresses, and is measured by its correspondence to these normative structures. Simply put, there must be good grounds for making a prescriptive statement; grounds located, as for descriptive statements, in existing social and political arrangements.[9] This argument is not circular, since the criteria for sustaining the truth of prescriptive statements are not dependent on other prescriptive statements, but on descriptive ones. To say that the descriptive and prescriptive aspects of normative theory are based on the same social and political realities is not to say that what *is* also *ought to be*, or vice versa, but rather that prescriptive statements are grounded in the same value systems that underlie existing social institutions. If specific institutions, and the institutional facts they generate, are necessary to social and political existence then prescription can be derived directly from description of them; values can be derived from facts. If these institutions are themselves a matter of prior choice, the derivation is still valid for the duration of the institution. As long as it is accepted that some form of institution is necessary, although specific institutions may change over time, the argument is not circular, but possibly dialectic or 'dialogical'.[10] It is, of course, central to this argument that institutional facts be distinguished from physical facts; the former are determined by normative structures, where the latter are independent of social rules. Here we are concerned with social and political realities, and physical facts are relevant only in so far as they have social meaning. Nevertheless, living in a physical world means that many physical facts have social meaning, must necessarily be accounted for in language, and are consequently not ignored by normative analysis.

Given the preceding discussion of the descriptive and prescriptive aspects of normative theory, something may now be said of the usefulness of normative theory as a tool for the study of social and political relations. By calling attention to rule-governed behaviour, this kind of theory can avoid the problems that arise from seeking or asserting a concrete and static social reality. The inherited ideas of positivistic science are simply inadequate for explaining the vibrant complexities of social existence. Through a view of social and political relations as institutional facts subject to change, a more coherent explanation of social reality may be achieved.[11] From a more coherent descriptive basis, more effective policy prescriptions can be achieved. Hence a normative approach is not simply an aid to addressing strictly normative issues, but rather an holistic approach which is an aid to resolving practical political problems. As policy-makers well know, political problems are seldom 'cut and dried'. They are inevitably linked to a wide range of issues ordinarily viewed as distinct, particularly from the viewpoints of specific interest groups, and yet inexorably tied up with the totality of political life.[12] Positivistic theory will indicate the individual character of political problems, suggesting that they can be resolved independently of other political events.[13] Normative theory will indicate the location of specific events in the broad context of political relations, and its prescriptions will consequently be coherent with the totality of these relations.

Decision-makers will not, on this account, be able to inquire about the normative aspects of otherwise empirical problems since the present argument holds that politics *are* normative. In this sense, normative theory is not an ancillary undertaking intended to deal with extraneous value problems that plague the public conscience. If normative theory is restricted to addressing troublesome moral issues which interfere with otherwise efficient political choices then it will be, deservedly, marginalised. Moralising is not the point. If it were, then any number of value-noncognitivist theories might be employed to rule out moral considerations altogether, as is often the case in the study of international relations. This is not at all surprising when the dominant political theories are of the positivist, empirical, realist sort, since they do not recognise the normative essence of political relations. The point, then, is not to address strictly moral problems (as conventionally understood in terms of 'good' and 'evil') through normative political analysis, but all social and political problems.[14] In this respect policy-making is an activity which cannot be restricted to the merely contingent, but rather must be always concerned with the underlying common denominators of politics; the normative structure. This requires an escape from the conventional rationality which is predicated on specific goals relating to contingent events. The decision-making rationality of a normative approach requires the establishment of fundamental political goals, relating to the entirety of political and social existence, on which basis then and only then can contingent goals be coherently established. The values underlying political and social relations thus become the values which inform political choice, in the way that the descriptive and prescriptive roles of normative theory are connected through the fact–value relationship discussed earlier.

It follows that the establishment of political goals is a priority.[15] It is a complex undertaking, given that goals must be co-ordinated over wide-ranging issues, but a benefit of the undertaking is that means will not be easily confused with ends. Furthermore, means will be commensurate with the broadly defined goals and consequently not at odds with other contingent goals. Too often the second-order goal of acquiring the means to achieve a first-order goal is given priority, even at the expense of the first-order goal which provides its rationale.[16] Means cannot, then, be judged simply in terms of their efficacy in achieving the end to which they are directed, but must also be judged by their side-effects in the context of broadly based goals founded on normative systems. This discussion relates to the well-recognised difficulty of distinguishing between means and ends, where means can become ends in themselves, forming an endless chain.[17] By requiring a kind of cross-reference between means and a range of interdependent goals in a normative system, these means can be more readily assessed on the grounds of coherence, and are less likely to pass for goals in themselves. It is only when these fundamental reference points in the normative structure are unrecognised that the means-ends relationship is free to roam under the guise of empirical rationality.

In the area of International Relations the normative structure is particularly unfamiliar, and points of reference ill defined. Yet even where the familiarity of national political and social institutions is not available to provide convenient points of reference, coherence can still provide an indication of problematic policy choices. Where means of achieving one goal are at odds with other means or goals there is reason to suspect either means or goals, or both. A starting point for sorting out the international normative structure can be some generally accepted overriding goal, against which other ends and means may be judged. Such an overriding goal must, of course, be accepted (in one form or another) universally.[18] Measuring foreign policy goals, and means, against only national normative structures results in their being merely consistent with other foreign policy goals of the same nation. This is no guarantee of the policy's success in the face of conflicting normative structures elsewhere, unless one nation is able entirely to overwhelm the social experience of another. This is a virtually impossible feat, although power-political or *Realpolitik* theories have encouraged such attempts with resulting chaos or disaster. In the modern world, being highly interdependent, a tacit recognition of this constraint on foreign policy is evidenced in policy co-ordination and political co-operation of various kinds. The notion of sovereignty can be viewed here as being equivalent to independent national normative structures. Hence, one may observe coherent and successful policy based on an instinctive understanding of national normative structures, but only in so far as this policy is directed toward the political life of that nation, as founded on the same normative structures. What ought to be accords with what is, prescriptions for the society thus accord with descriptions of that society, and the values informing policy are the same ones that underlie the institutional facts at which policy is directed. Of course, the limits of national normative structures coincide with the limits of sovereignty. Whatever statements and actions may fly the sovereign flag there is no means of assuring their effect on international politics, given that the sovereign initiatives of others will be only coincidentally in accord. The measure of coherence to a normative structure is effective only within the bounds of the structure, and national value systems are not, as they say, the whole story. Foreign policy must thus be judged by its coherence in respect to a universal normative structure. Here the problem for policy-makers is a familiar one: mustering support for goals not directly related to national interests, and fitting the means of their support into national political programmes. The national normative structure must be meshed with the international normative structure. As suggested above, such a universal structure may be identified by locating universal goals, such as security, for example. If, as the present approach suggests, values and goals or interests are related, then whatever goals can be established as universal should also, by their coherence, indicate a normative structure.

No doubt such a universal normative system will be only vaguely perceived at first, but what is most significant in adopting a normative account of political relations is the perspective which it employs, and the consequences of adopting it. It may be that familiar features of International Relations will fall more readily into place under a normative theory than is at first expected. If the resulting organisation of observations about international relations is consistent and clarifying, then this approach will have fulfilled the requirements for a useful theory.

This wide-ranging, yet all too brief discussion might be taken to suggest that normative theory does not lend itself to the theoretical virtue of simplicity, but rather to complexity. However, while a normative approach militates against the oversimplification that so often plagues the policy process, such complexity as may be implied arises from the diverse applications of this approach rather than from its elemental significance. As this volume suggests, International Relations is a diverse field of endeavour, demanding general yet comprehensive theoretical foundations. Being well suited to meeting these demands, normative theory may yet take a more central role. At the very least, the insights of a normative approach deserve more than the marginal concern so common in the current study and practice of international relations.

NOTES AND REFERENCES

1. For a view on the avoidance of normative questions in Interanational Relations academia, and broad discussion of the subject, see˙ Chris Brown, 'Not My Department?: Normative Theory and International Relations', *Paradigms* (Vol. 1, No. 2, December 1987), pp.104–13. For an overview of the literature, see Mark Hoffman, 'Normative Approaches' in Margot Light and A.J.R. Groom (eds), *International Relations: A Handbook of Current Theory* (London: Francas Pinter, 1985). For recent examples of exploratory work in this area, see Mervyn Frost, *Towards a Normative Theory of International Relations* (Cambridge: Cambridge University Press, 1986), and the present author's review of this work in *Millennium: Journal of International Studies* (Vol. 16, No. 3, Winter 1987), pp. 551–2, and Chris Brown, 'The Modern Requirement: Reflections on Normative International Theory in a Post-Western World', *Millennium* (Vol. 17, No. 2, Summer 1988). For an inspired indication of the need for normative theorising, and a valuable reference, see Charles Beitz, *Political Theory and International Relations* (Princeton, N.J.: Princeton University Press, 1979). As background for normative issues in general see: F.M. Frohock, *Normative Political Theory* (Englewood Cliffs, N.J.: Prentice-Hall, 1974), especially Chapter 2; Edna Ullman-Margalit, *The Emergence of Norms* (Oxford: Oxford University Press, 1977); Georg Henrik von Wright, *Norm and Action: A Logical Enquiry* (London: Routledge & Kegan Paul, 1963).

2. On the issue of alternatives, and especially critical theory, Cox has said: 'To reason about possible future world orders . . . requires a broadening of our enquiry beyond conventional international relations, so as to encompass basic processes at work in the development of social forces and forms of state, and in the structure of global political economy. Such, at least, is the central argument of this essay.' Robert W. Cox, 'Social Forces, States and World Orders: Beyond International Relations Theory', *Millennium: Journal of International Studies* (Vol. 10, No. 2, Summer 1981), p. 130, and reprinted in Robert O. Keohane (ed.), *Neorealism and its Critics* (New York: Columbia University Press, 1986).

3. In this respect one may note, as Piaget does, the difference of method between philosophy and science, the former drawing objective knowledge from subjective verification, and the latter from ostensibly objective verification. See Jean Piaget, *Insights and Illusions of Philosophy* (Paris: Presses Universitaires de France, 1965; London: Routledge & Kegan Paul, 1972). On the issue of comparing domestic and international societies, see the thoughtful discussion in Hidemi Suganami, 'Reflections on the Domestic Analogy: The Case of Bull, Beitz and Linklater', *Review of International Studies* (Vol. 12, 1986), pp.145–58.

4. Charles Taylor provides an argument of this sort against positivistic political inquiry in 'Neutrality in Political Science' in P. Laslett and W.

Runciman (eds), *Politics, Philosophy and Society*, 3rd series (Oxford: Basil Blackwell, 1967).

5.   See, for example, Sidney Verba, *et al.*, *Elites and the Idea of Equality* (Cambridge IMA: Harvard University Press, 1987), p.113. In asking two basic questions about income inequality (how much is there?; how much should there be?), they note that 'the two questions – the empirical and the normative – are related to each other. . . In all societies, this suggests, the debate about income equality will involve at the same time questions of perception and questions of value'. Indeed, as von Leyden (and Bertrand Russell elsewhere) suggests, it may be that 'equality can be defined in such precise and technically restricted terms as to be almost totally inapplicable to the subject matter of politics'. W. von Leyden, *Aristotle on Equality and Justice: His Political Argument* (London: Macmillan, 1985), esp. Chapter 2, 'Two Definitions of Equality and Their Significance for Political Theory', p.26ff.

6.   A parenthetical comment by Kolakowski makes a similar point: 'There is no access to an epistemological absolute, and there is no privileged access to the absolute Being which might result in reliable theoretical knowledge (this last restriction is needed, as we may not *a priori* exclude the reality of mystical experience that provides some people with this privileged access; but their experience cannot be re-forged into a theory). This double denial does not need to end up with pragmatic nihilism; it is compatible with the belief that metaphysical and non-pragmatic insight is possible as a result of our living within the realm of good and evil and of experiencing good and evil as one's own.' Leszek Kolakowski, *Metaphysical Horror* (Oxford: Basil Blackwell, 1988), p. 98. The whole of this small book is highly recommended.

7.   In discussing the necessity of the Absolute (a self-rooted reality), Kolakowski writes: 'One may argue, in the Humean spirit, that this experience, when expressed in metaphysical parlance, is no more than a tautology: once the assumption is made that everything needs a ground or sufficient reason, then whatever is contingent must by definition be referred to something that is self-grounded; but the assumption is arbitrary.' *Metaphysical Horror*, p. 17–8.

8.   See G.J. Warnock, *Morality and Language* (Totowa, N.J.: Barnes & Noble, 1983), p. 88.

9.   How and why prescriptions are actually followed is, of course, another matter. Note the argument in Friedrich Kratochwil, 'Norms and Values: Rethinking the Domestic Analogy', *Ethics and International Affairs* (Vol. 1, 1987), p.153, that regime strength 'does not seem to result from the logical neatness of relating rules and higher principles to each other, but . . . from the acceptance of norm-regulated practices. In other words, the crucial variable here is institutionalisation.'

Also recommended to the reader is Kratochwil's discussion of knowledge in the social sciences in his forthcoming article 'Regimes, Interpretation and the "Science" of Politics: A Reappraisal', *Millennium: Journal of International Studies* (Vol. 17, No. 2, Summer 1988).

10. See the distinction between 'monological' and 'dialogical' in Richard K. Ashley, 'Untying the Sovereign State: A Double Reading of

the Anarchy Problematique', *Millennium: Journal of International Studies* (Vol. 17, No. 2, Summer 1988), and a similar piece by Ashley in Hayward R. Alker, Jr, and Richard K. Ashley (eds.), *After Neo-realism: Anarchy, Power and International Collaboration* (New York: Columbia University Press, forthcoming).

11.   Again with respect to regimes Kratochwil, 'Norms and Values', p.152, argues: 'Actors are not only programmed by rules and norms, by their practice they also reproduce and change the normative structures by which they are able to act, share meanings, communicate intentions, criticize claims, and justify choices. Thus, one of the most important sources of change . . . is the practice of the actors themselves'

Note also a central argument in Brian Fay, *Social Theory and Political Practice* (London: Allen & Unwin, 1975), pp. 90–1, concerning the characterisation of interpretive and critical social science, as being respectively conservative and potentially innovative respectively. Following Fay's distinction, one might consider the two aspects of normative theory as having similar characteristics: as descriptive theory it may be necessarily conservative in describing the status quo order (though nevertheless sufficiently insightful to allow for immanent change), while as prescriptive theory it may allow for alternative inter-pretations of the reality it addresses, since choices must be made.

12.   This is not to suggest that norms and values are the only con-siderations, or that all of political life can be reduced to these categories. As noted above, effective policy depends only *in part* on the reality of values. Verba, *et al. Elites*, p.17 thus state: 'Even if one accepts our position that values are autonomous – that they are not mere superstructure or rationalization of one's economic self-interest – their causal relation to policy would be comprehensible only in the context of a wide range of other political and economic factors'.

13.   Elsewhere in this volume Mark Hoffman (Chapter 4) notes one kind of response to a critique of Realism: 'Waltz by accepting that he has engaged in problem solving'. As an aside on the inter-paradigm debate, it might be said that the conventional division of International Relations theory along 'Kuhnian' paradigmatic lines seems to reflect differences in the estimation of human nature: the Realist, Liberal, and Structural camps are respectively pessimistic, optimistic and deter-ministic, (though few in any camp would accept these characterisations without argument). It is perhaps because the latter category, following this scheme, is relatively non-judgemental on the matter of human nature and concerned, rather, with exploring the human condition that it fares better in providing new insights. Of course Kuhn himself expresses some surprise at the way in which his theory of change in natural science found adherents in social science, and indeed this characterisation of the division of International Relations theory may not be entirely appropriate. See the 1969 postscript in Thomas S. Kuhn, *The Structure of Scientific Revolutions*, 2nd. edn., enlarged (Chicago and London: University of Chicago Press, 1970), p. 208.

14.   As an example of confusion on this point, one might point to George Kennan's view of morality in his article, 'Morality and

Foreign Policy', *Foreign Affairs* (Vol. 64, No. 2, Winter 1985–6), p.217. Kennan raises the 'question as to whether there is any such thing as morality that does not rest, consciously or otherwise, on some foundation of religious faith, for the renunciation of self-interest, which is what all morality implies, can never be rationalized by purely secular or materialistic considerations'. This is an understanding of morality which does not admit an enlightened self-interest founded on the recognised benefits of long-run co-operation. The relationship of normative theory in the study of International Relations to the more familiar concerns of ethical thought is obviously close, but also uneasy. Moralism in international affairs has acquired, and perhaps deserves, a bad name. Yet this is not the point of normative theory. Uneasiness notwithstanding, to the extent that ethics is concerned with value systems and the direction of human will (individually and collectively) it is an integral part of the normative approach, and in this respect contributes to the fundamental epistemological and methodological role that normative theory plays in understanding International Relations.

15.   Kratochwil 'Norms and Values', p.159) discusses '[t]wo polar models of society . . . one which is largely attitudinal and value-based – a communitarian model – and one which emphasises rights and rules – a liberal model. . .' While the international domain is a far cry from an unregulated or anarchical state, value considerations providing the foundations for the generalized attitude toward socially recognised "others" are rather weakly articulated. . . . In other words, it is a community which is, at best, based on a mutual recognition of rights and united by common practices, but is not based on a vision of a common good or a common way of life'. Establishing political goals coherent with an international normative structure would clearly require some such vision.

16.   For an interesting and useful discussion of difficulties in determining self-justifying interests, and related problems of establishing goals, see Vernon van Dyke, 'Values and Interests', *American Political Science Review* (Vol. 56, September 1962), pp. 567–76. Van Dyke proposes 'a perspective from which values and interests can be viewed . . . [as] virtually synonymous'.

17.   See, for example, Fay, *Social Theory*, p.49.

18.   This does not (at least, is not intended to) beg the question of 'necessary' versus 'contingent', since contingency is accepted here. However, not seeking (or remaining silent on the question of) an absolute does not mean that the contingent world cannot achieve some order, even if that order is itself contingent (though denying an absolute *might* mean this). On these issues see again Kolakowski, *Metaphysical Horror*, p. 18–21.

Of course, this does beg the question of what the universal goals are (contingent or otherwise), or *should be*, which in turn leads to issues of moral philosophy, the central problem of which is the 'is–ought' question, and the related questions of whether *logical form* or *substantive content* is the distinguishing aspect of moral judgements and whether there is a logical distinction between statements about facts and moral judgements. This may be problematic for the present argument, since it implicitly criticises positivistic realism for confusing the logic of morality with the logic of facts, and yet seeks to draw an intimate relationship between facts and values. For elaborations and debates on these issues see W.D. Hudson (ed.), *The Is-Ought Question* (London: Macmillan, 1969), Edward Regis Jr (ed.), *Gewirth's Ethical Rationalism: Critical Essays with a reply by Alan Gewirth* (Chicago, Ill.: University of Chicago Press, 1984), and Morton White, *What Is and What Ought To B Done: An Essay on Ethnics and Epistemology* (Oxford: Oxford University Press, 1981).

Part II
Country and Regional Approaches

9 Studies on International Relations in Brazil: Recent Times (1950-80)*

Gelson Fonseca, Jr

Anyone wishing to examine the present state of the social sciences in any country in the world comes up against the difficult but unavoidable problem of delimiting the area of study covered by International Relations. This brief study seeks to evade interminable methodological discussions by adopting a highly selective criterion which identifies, in the case of Brazil, the study of International Relations with the debate on foreign policy. For Brazil this criterion is acceptable, because by concentrating on analyses of the state's external actions very few specialists in International Relations will be left out of the purview of our survey.[1]

A preliminary observation of this field of study will reveal that research into International Relations within the context of Brazilian academia presently constitutes a relatively dynamic sector which, although now expanding, is still limited and lacking in solid traditions. Few university-level institutions are dedicated to the study of international relations. Aside from the diplomatic academy belonging to the Ministry of External Relations (the Rio Branco Institute) there is only one university that offers an undergraduate degree in International Relations and a few centres that offer graduate studies.[2] Any specialisation beyond a master's degree is therefore usually obtained at universities abroad (the United States, Great Britain, France or Mexico). Specialised publications do not yet appear as regularly as might be desired. Few scholars devote themselves full-time to research in the field of International Relations, a situation which is reflected by the scanty literature available.[3]

Another problem is that because of the newness of the field, professionals find few job opportunities outside academic spheres. The Ministry of External Relations has a corps of diplomats

189

composed solely of candidates who have passed an entrance exam
and outside consultants.

Nevertheless, despite the embryonic and limited nature of the
research involved, which began to gain depth only in the 1970s,
studies of International Relations in Brazil deserve our attention, at
the very least because of two factors. First, although the discipline still
does not cover the broad spectrum of Brazilian diplomatic activities,
it is a fact that intellectual reflection has kept up with the priorities
established in foreign policy: the 'anguish' of the researcher remains
close to the anguish of the policy-makers. As a result, an analysis of
scholarly production is always greatly revealing with regard to the
state's activities. The 'Irrelevancy Syndrome' mentioned by Herz
does not occur in Brazil.[4] Second, the very manner in which
the problems are approached theoretically is of interest in itself
– particularly if seen from the perspective of the first world –
because the research involved is, to a great extent, ostensibly
prescriptive. The analyst does not eschew values in a search for a
perfectly neutral scientific attitude. On the contrary, as a rule the
analysis leads in a natural way to participation and criticism; with-
drawal to an ivory tower does not exist as an intellectual option.[5]

It must also be noted that although the 'Brazilian Way' to
reflect on International Relations is essentially characterised by a
search for an understanding of the major Brazilian foreign policy
trends and decisions, it is also true that a more careful examination
of the field reveals a number of important theoretical stays, and is
thus broader and more abstract in scope than would at first appear.

The best examples of this perspective are provided by the
analyses based on dependency theory which address the integration
of the country into the worldwide capitalist system and which
constitute the most important Latin American contribution to an
understanding of that international system. Well-known founders
of this school are Fernando Henrique Cardoso and Teotonio dos
Santos.[6] On the other hand, and closer to the classical tradition
of thought in International Relations, is Celso Lafer, whose fine
studies are strongly coloured by Arendtian overtones.[7]

After this very general presentation of the field it would be
useful to mention the historical context in which Brazilian specialists
in international relations work. The modern issues facing Brazilian
diplomacy were first delineated during the early years of the twentieth
century, when the country freed itself from its traditional dependence
on Europe, introduced a new model of relations with the United

States, and solved its border disputes with its South American neighbours. This agenda – relations with the United States and Latin America was enriched through the years, but the issues are fundamental and permanent. With regard to relations with the United States the policies proposed by the intellectuals ranged from a position defending pan-American alignment to one of confrontation at all levels; the solutions suggested for relations with South America ran the gamut from the need for Brazilian hegemony to the quest for a Bolivian integration scheme. At the same time, and beginning early in the century, there was a perception of the possibility that because of the geographic dimensions and economic potential involved, Brazil's role would necessarily have to be unique. It was clear at all times that Brazil will not just be shunted around the international chessboard.

A third topic (after relations with the United States and relations with Latin America) was thus placed on the agenda: what should Brazil's role on the world scene be? The first answers indicated that at some point in time Brazil should take its rightful place as a Western power, standing shoulder-to-shoulder with the United States. (An early and significant expression of this 'pride' arises late in the 1920s when Brazil resigned from the League of Nations because it was unable to secure a permanent seat on the Council.) Of course, as time went by, and most especially after the decolonisation process in the 1950s, other possible world roles are envisioned for Brazil, such as the leadership of a third world coalition or the guardianship of Latin American stability.

What interests us, however, is to examine how these problems concerning Brazil's integration into the modern world take on analytic shape, and how they have been dealt with conceptually by scholars over the last three decades.

Here we see that the debate during all this period did not centre on how to construct *the best theory* on International Relations (as was true during the 1950s in the United States) but on what *the best foreign policy for the country* would be. And although the intellectual debate regarding these issues shows significant variation, it can be said that the arguments and analyses which were produced conform in a general fashion to two basic models of interpretation.[8]

The first model would characterise Brazil as 'the incomplete nation'. Its conceptual basis is formed by the various versions of the theory of imperialism: the first step in the analysis is to demonstrate that the Brazilian nation *per se* is incomplete as a nation because the dominant culture and the reigning values in

Brazil are imported from the *metropole*; the domestic economy is shaped by forms of production which do not take the society's real needs into account but instead serve the interests of central capitalism.[9] Within this conception the theoretical foundations for the connection between the nation and the external world will vary from author to author according to the perceived nature of ties with the central powers; the most recent versions of the model consider dependency theory to be the theoretical framework which best allows the process of International Relations in Brazil to be understood as part of the imperialist world system. At this point it would be of interest to enquire just what the consequences would be (in terms of foreign policy) if the 'incomplete nation' model were adopted.

Let us briefly extrapolate some of these possible scenarios. First, foreign policy, especially the game of diplomacy, is seen here as irrelevant when compared to the international elements which under this model are already embedded *within the nation* (domestic culture is alienated, dynamic economic forces are foreign, multinational firms shape the productive structure in a way that is not adapted to local reality, etc.). In political terms this model necessarily points the way to a nationalistic platform proposing the renewal of authentically Brazilian cultural values, leading to greater state control over the economy, changes in the pattern of political domination and so forth. The resulting prescriptions for action might have more or less radical overtones, but what is always really being proposed is the possibility of 'corrective national action', usually to be carried out by 'an enlightened class' or by the state itself in order to remedy the problems created by the 'evils' of the mode of integration into the international capitalist system. The solution for the international problems is therefore defined at the *national* level. Within these parameters the model is primarily concerned with transformations in the capitalist system and only very indirectly with strategic conflict. The second point is that with the above as a background, diplomatic action in the 'incomplete nation' is seen as pre-determined by the dependent nature of society, and as a result the dominating classes will use diplomacy to ratify and reinforce the links with the imperialist metropolises. Third, regional policies will be an extension of the country's dependent status; for example, in Latin America Brazil might play the role of a policeman for the United States, acting in other words as a sub-imperialist power; activity in Africa might be 'mercantilistic'; international fora might be used as mere cover-ups for the servile performance of Brazilian diplomacy. In short, in terms of policy this model tends to be extremely critical of any advances toward the West which are perceived as a continuation of dependence; suggestions will be made instead for nationalistic courses of action to be followed, including greater foreign policy independence, the adoption of nonaligned attitudes, and more 'third-worldism'.

The second model used to characterise Brazil's role in the world is based on Morgenthau-like realism expressed above all by the 'geopolitical schools of thought'. This model sees Brazil as a 'bulwark of the West'. Here the debate and the analyses are composed within the framework of strategy: integration in the capitalist system is apparently less important than the stand taken in the East–West conflict. This world view, adopted primarily by military analysts and some civilians,[10] does not command the same following among scholars as the previous theory, which has clearly been the model of choice among social scientists. In analytic terms, a simple version of the second model would include the following four elements: (1) In the international world order the key relations are strategic, and there are two basic ways to identify world powers: one which uses definitions in terms of amounts of power and the other in terms of ideological options. (2) Within the context of the East–West conflict, both because of geographical circumstance and because of ideological identification, Brazil should act as a bulwark of the Western world. The foundation underpinning Brazil's International Relations should be a concept of 'loyal exchanges' with the United States, by which Brazil would obtain strategic and economic advantages as a result of its diplomatic position in defending Western values and interests. (3) Intellectual analyses should therefore concentrate on defining Brazil's contribution to restraining communism, and the government's policies should vary according to the varying diagnoses of the perceived communist threat (external, internal, worldwide, regional, subversive or conventional). (4) Because of the vast scope of its geographic situation Brazil should play a role in the security of the Western hemisphere, participating in and reinforcing the mechanisms of continental security in the Americas and defending the idea of a South Atlantic Organisation.

This model therefore leads to a basically pro-Western attitude which would involve, to a greater or lesser degree, policies of alignment with the United States. The Third World would be considered as an arena being disputed by East and West, with Latin America constituting a stage for power struggles between 'democracy' and 'totalitarianism'.

The two models above thus represent polarised views of Brazilian foreign policy which (as was also true of the idealist schools of thought in Europe between the two world wars), were *criticised by the facts*, or belied by reality. (However, in the Brazilian case no invasion of Abyssinia was necessary.) In fact, Brazilian reality became more complex than the theories and many of the expectations built into the models were frustrated by the options which characterised Brazilian diplomacy in the middle 1970s.

Let us examine just how this has occurred. From the point of view of the 'incomplete nation model', a paradox was created: the strengthening of ties between Brazil and the capitalist system coincided with the initiation of a broad area of conflict, both economic and political in scope, between Brazil and the bastion of capitalism itself, the United States (e.g., including the refusal to sign the Non-Proliferation Treaty, the law establishing a 200 mile extension for territorial waters, the proposals regarding the reformation of the world economic order and the disputes regarding protectionism). Foreign policy no longer ratified 'dependence', it went on to question it. This forced international political analysis to admit that diplomatic action was worthy of some attention in its own right. Another element that was not foreseen by the model was the fact that despite the distortions in the distribution of domestic social benefits, dependence did not necessarily mean stagnation. On the contrary, the country grew economically.

From the point of view of the 'Western Bulwark' model, another paradox was established: if the rise of the military caste led at first to a position of automatic alignment with the United States, later, and most especially after 1974 (although important harbingers did appear as early as 1967), foreign policy displayed characteristics reminiscent of the period 1961-64 when the government tended to lean almost to the left (after all, the movement of 1964 was created to counter the allegedly communist stance adopted by President Goulart). Under the Geisel administration, Brazilian diplomacy adopted a position of pragmatism and non-alignment, as a foil to the forms of ideological association and alliance with the United States which were characteristic of Brazilian diplomacy for the period between 1964 and 1974.

For the academic analyst this 'criticism by the facts' (the implicit denial of the theoretical models by real-life diplomacy) led to more modest and careful propositions than the previous theoretical models. Brazil's foreign policy refused to fit into simple categories and deterministic models of interpretation could no longer be used. The country's position as a member of the third world did not necessarily limit its autonomy nor its development and it displayed an advanced degree of urbanisation and industrialisation (In the 1970s, Brazil had the eighth largest GNP in the Western world.) The characteristic of being a Western country was insufficient to avoid the beginning of a number of disputes with the United States ranging from differences in political matters to quarrels over specific issues. Brazil adopted an openly pro-Arab position in Middle Eastern affairs, was strongly anti-apartheid and was one of the first to recognise the MPLA Government in Angola. And since the beginning of the 1970s, innumerable economic disputes have arisen, culminating in current American pressure which seeks Brazilian modification of a law establishing market reserve for informatics.

Foreign policy thus becomes a sort of 'conceptual enigma'. As a result the focal point of scholarly analyses shifts precisely to those efforts which seek to define the 'essence' of Brazilian foreign policy. In order to solve the enigma, traditional paradigms are reconsidered and new lines of investigation open up. We will try to briefly review some of these and in this way identify the central concerns of contemporary studies carried out by Brazilian specialists in International Relations.

In a brief outline of what has occurred it can be said that the former models characterising Brazil's world role are being revised at four levels.

The level of the understanding of global movements

This approach seeks to undo the dichotomy which described the international systems as an arena for strategic or economic confrontation. One of the pioneering efforts along these lines is that of Araujo Castro, a diplomat who doubled as an intellectual. Castro endeavours to sever Brazilian foreign policy options from the straitjacket of the superpower model. He shows that under certain circumstances the superpowers tend to come closer together, 'freezing the power' in the system and thus effectively barring the way to rising countries such as Brazil, which should therefore follow paths traced out independently.[11]Recently several other analysts have begun working with the notion of a 'crisis in the system', which also displaces simplistic descriptions, especially when seen from the view point of someone like Celso Lafer, who attributes the current world crisis to 'a disjunction between order and power' in the international sphere which opens up new possibilities for medium-size powers, natural and credible proponents of alternative ways to construct a new international order.[12]

The level of diplomatic traditions

The revision of classical models leads to new versions and accents in Brazilian diplomatic history. Getulio Vargas' 'pendulum diplomacy' in the 1930s – a time when Brazil tried to make its own way in the world by taking advantage of the German-American dispute for influence in South America – is rediscovered. Marcelo Abreu, Ricardo Seitenfus and Gerson Moura produce new interpretations of this period, and the latter puts forth a significant formula to help understand the process of diplomacy in the 1930s: 'autonomy within dependence'.[13]

The level of relations between domestic and foreign policy

The classical models did not produce sophisticated analyses of the interaction between the domestic and foreign spheres of policy. One of the first things that a revision of these models showed, as Carlos Estevan Martins noted, was that the differing types of hegemony during the apparently monolithic military period (1964–1974) gave rise to separate and distinct diplomatic proposals. The identification of authoritarianism with geopolitics also proves to be analytically poor. Helio Jaguaribe, the dean of Brazilian political scientists, in an encompassing study that includes multiple approaches to the problem of the Brazilian international presence, also points out the multiple possible diplomatic itineraries that would follow from different Brazilian development scenarios.[14]

The level of characterisation of foreign policy

Faced with the new complexity of the diplomatic process and the 'enigmas' it brings forth, some lines of analysis concentrate on the definition of just what the 'essence' of Brazilian foreign policy is. Here one finds a number of approaches. There is much discussion, as in Sardenberg, regarding the proper way to conciliate the 'third worldist' and Western dimensions of Brazilian diplomacy. Other analyses speculate on how Brazil will use its new-found potential, whether in a hegemonic fashion or not, and here the studies of Antonio Carlos Peixoto produce some interesting hypotheses. Monica Hirst re-examines modern Brazilian diplomatic history and describes the varying situations and arenas in which it is played out. And in a recent study Maria Regina Soares de Lima uncovers another facet of Brazil's 'complexity' by discussing the different positions adopted by Brazil at various diplomatic meetings held simultaneously – sometimes dependent, sometimes hegemonic, sometimes from a position of equality between partners.[15]

In short, despite the brief time span and small sample of authors covered by this study, one can clearly see that reflection on International Relations has become firmly established in Brazil. Studies in this area can now avail themselves of finely honed analytical tools which go beyond simplistic one-sided schemata. Without any loss to their critical capacity, studies in this field now enjoy the use of suitable concepts with which to meet the challenges of a reality that is both complex and unique, the very first challenge which confronts anyone who truly wishes to understand Brazilian life.

NOTES AND REFERENCES

*   Any opinions contained herein are exclusively personal. The study has been translated by Maria Luiza Ligiero.

1.   This criterion does not highlight the most important analysis produced by Latin America of the system of International Relations; in other words, 'dependency theory'. Since dependency theory is far more than an attempt to explain foreign policy (its objective is to reach an understanding of the exact causes of the under (or distorted) development of Latin American countries), it is touched upon only briefly in this study. The contributions of economists and lawyers, who have a well-established tradition of commentary in this field, are also ignored. The concern here is mostly with political science studies.

2.   The Rio Branco Institute, which is the diplomatic academy belonging to the Ministry of External Relations, is exclusively dedicated to giving professional courses for diplomats. The University of Brasilia offers an undergraduate degree in International Relations. Within the academic world, aside from the regional studies centres such as the Centre for Afro–Asian Studies at Cândido Mendes University, there is also an Institute of International Relations which was set up by the Catholic University of Rio de Janeiro some years ago which now offers a master's programme in International Relations. For an attempt, although preliminary, to introduce the institutional

panorama in this area, see Alexandre Barros, 'El Estúdio de las Relaciones Internacionales en Brasil', in R.N. Perina (ed.), *El Estúdio de las Relaciones Internacionales en América y el Caribe* (Buenos Aires: Grupo Editor Latinoamericano, 1985). An interesting note on the expansion of the field in Brazil was the recent election of a Brazilian scientist, Clovis Brigagão, to the Executive Secretariat of the International Peace Research Association.

3. For a complete survey of the literature on Brazilian foreign policy which also covers studies by foreigners, see Maria Regina Soares de Lima and Zairo Borges Cheibub, *Relações Internacionais e Política Externa Brasileira: Debate Intelectual e Produção Acadêmica* (Rio de Janeiro: IUPERJ, 1983). As for specialised magazines, the most traditional publication, the *Revista Brasileira de Política Internacional*, has been published only sporadically over the last few years. For a geopolitical focus, one should see *Política e Estratégia*, which first began to be published in 1983 and also *Contexto Internacional*, published by IRI-PUC-RJ.

4. For the issue of irrelevance in the context of the Western World, see John Herz, 'Relevancies and Irrelevancies in the Study of International Relations', in J.H. Herz (ed.), *The Nation-State and the Crisis of World Politics* (New York: David Mckay, 1976).

5. The attitude of the intellectual world would thus, if we use Morgenthau's categories, be close to 'prophetic confrontation', without, however, involving connotations as dramatic as those in Morgenthau's concept. Especially after the middle 1970s, a consensus was reached in society regarding the basic guidelines of foreign policy and 'intellectual criticism' is more apt to propose a slight change in bearings than radically new positions. See Hans Morgenthau, *Truth and Power* (New York: Praeger Publishers, 1970), pp. 17–18.

6. See Fernando Henrique Cardoso and Enzo Falletto, *Dependencia y Desarrollo en América Latina* (Buenos Aires: Siglo Veintiuno Editores, 1971); Theotonio dos Santos, *Imperialismo y Dependencia* (México, DF: Ediciones Era, 1978) and Vilma Figueiredo, *Desenvolvimento Dependente Brasileiro* (Rio de Janeiro: Zahar, 1978).

7. See Celso Lafer, *Paradoxos e Possibilidades* (Rio de Janeiro: Editora Nova Fronteira, 1982), and *O Brasil e a Crise Mundial* (São Paulo: Editora Perspectiva, 1984), as well as a study that espouses a modern return to idealism, L.A. Bahia, *Soberania, Paz e Guerra* (Rio de Janeiro: Zahar, 1978).

8. A classic presentation of this dichotomy can be found in Helio Jaguaribe, *O Nacionalismo na atualidade Brasileira* (Rio de Janeiro: ISEB, 1953). For an analysis of this dichotomy see Keith L. Storrs, 'Brazil's Independent Foreign Policy, 1961–1969: Background, Tenets, Linkage to Domestic Politics and Aftermath', Latin American Studies Program, Dissertation Series, Cornell University (No. 44, 1973). To verify how persistent and current the debate between the 'Internationalists' and 'Nationalists' is with regard to the foreign debt problem, see Abraham Lowenthal, 'Brazil and the United States', in *Headline Series* (New York: Foreign Policy Association, 1986), pp. 32–41.

9. For typical analyses following this model, see Paulo Schilling, *O Expansionismo Brasileiro* (São Paulo: Global, 1987) and Ruy Mauro Marini, 'Brazilian Sub-Imperialism', *Monthly Review* (Vol. 23, No. 9, 1 February 1972). Also worthwhile are the three issues of *Política Externa Independente* which during the period between 1965 and 1966 based its criticisms of Brazilian diplomacy on this model.

10. Some examples of the model: Golbery do Couto e Silva, *Geopolítica do Brasil*, 3rd edn (Rio de Janeiro: Livraria José Olympio Editora, 1981); Carlos de Meira Matos, *Brasil Geopolítica e Destino* (Rio de Janeiro: Livraria José Olympio Editora, 1975). See as well the articles by Oliveiros Ferreira in several editions of the magazine *Política e Estratégia* (Vol. 2, Nos. 2, 3 and 4, 1984). For an analysis of this school of thought, see: G. Lamazière, 'Pensée Géopolitique et Politique Extérieure au Brésil, 1952–1979', (Paris: Mémoire de DEA d'Etude Politique de Défense, Université de Paris). And Shiguenoli Myamoto, *Do Discurso Triunfalista ao Programa Econômico: Geopolítica e Política Externa no Brasil pós 64*, doctoral thesis, University of São Paulo.

11. See R. Amado (ed.), *Araujo Castro* (Brasília: Editora da UNB, 1982).

12. For an analysis of the concept of 'crisis', see Lafer's *O Brasil e a Crise Mundial*, and Gerson Moura, Paulo Kramer and Paulo Wrobel, 'Os Caminhos Difíceis da Autonomia: as Relações Brasil-EUA', *Contexto Internacional* (No. 2, July–August 1985).

13. Three important analyses of Getulio's diplomacy are by Marcelo .de Paiva Abreu, *Brazil and the World Economy, 1930-1945*, PhD dissertation, University of Cambridge, 1977; Gerson Moura, *Autonomia na Dependência: Política Externa Brasileira de 1935 a 1942* (Rio de Janeiro: Edit. Nova Fronteira, 1980); and Ricardo D.S. Seitenfus, *O Brasil de Getúlio Vargas e a Formação de Blocos, 1930–1942* (São Paulo: Cia. Editora Nacional, 1985).

14. For an analysis of the relations between variables in domestic policy and diplomatic practice see C.E. Martins, 'A Evolução da Política Exterior Brasileira na Década 64–74', *Estudos CEBRAP* (Vol. 12, 1975); C.E. Martins, 'Brazil and the United States from the 1960s to the 1970s', in J. Cotler and R. Fagen (eds.), *Latin America and the United States: The Changing Political Realities* (Stanford, CA: Stanford University Press, 1974). For a broad analysis of Brazil's International Relations, see Helio Jaguaribe, *Novo Cenário Internacional* (Rio de Janeiro: Edit. Guanabara, 1984).

15. For an analysis of the relations between power and hegemony, see A.C. Peixoto, 'La montée en puissance du Brésil: concepts et realités', in *Revue française de science politique* (Vol. 30, No. 2, April 1980). For an analysis of the process of diversification in foreign policy, see Monica Hirst, 'Pesos y Medidas de Política Externa Brasileña', in Juan Carlos Puig (ed.), *America Latina: Políticas Exteriores Comparadas* (Buenos Aires: Grupo Editora Interamericana, 1984). For an attempt at providing a global characterisation of foreign policy, see R. Sardenberg, 'A Política Externa do Brasil e a América Latina', text presented during the Seminar on New Problems and

Conditioning Factors in International Relations in Latin America (Rio de Janeiro: the Catholic University, 1980) and 'A Política Externa do Brasil no Mundo em Mudanças', *Defesa Nacional* (No. 687, January–February, 1980); Maria Regina Soares de Lima, *The Political Economy of Brazilian Foreign Policy: Nuclear Energy, Trade and Itaipu*, PhD dissertation, Vanderbilt University, 1986.

10 'Whose World is it Anyway?' International Relations in South Africa*

Peter Vale

This chapter's central thesis finds its source in the organic link between ideology and social science. As with other ideologies, South Africa's corrodes the study of International Relations. This is not surprising: in almost all cases, the discipline concerns itself with questions which are of some interest to governments.

If the tools of academic trade (and the fruit of academic labour) reinforce a state's *raison d'être*, governments, and their supporters, exploit scholarship; this often happens with the agreement of the compliant scholar. In this event, International Relations, and its easily-abused supporting lexicon, serves narrow political or diplomatic ends.[1] Deployed thus, the study is not an academic but a missionary exercise, used to promote partisan interests.[2] This has happened in South Africa.

South Africa's contribution to the development of International Relations has been poor. This does not mean that individuals have made unimportant contributions to the discourse on facets of the discipline's 'stuff'; rather, taken as a whole, the country report is unimpressive. It is interesting to note, in contrast, that some South Africans who live – by fiat or choice – outside its borders have strongly contributed to the development of International Relations.[3]

The chapter traces the implantation of International Relations into South Africa and discusses how it took institutional root. It classifies the main approaches to the study within the country, demonstrating its preoccupation with, and in, the establishment. Finally, some ideas are advanced which may assist in liberating International Relations from its infatuation with South Africa's minority.

10.1   THE ESTABLISHMENT'S WORLD

Seventeenth century Dutch trading ambitions first brought Euro-
peans to what is now called South Africa, but the permanence
of whites[4] was only secured by British power at the end of
the nineteenth century.[5] These were events of great international
significance for they had the effect of incorporating, as a glitter
in the dominant power's vision of an ideal world, the southern
tip of distant Africa into the mainstream of contemporary international affairs. The afterglow – South Africa's whites – were left
with a strong cultural affinity for foreign lands; an international
condition of no small consequence. The study of International
Relations in South Africa, therefore, derives from two separate,
imported sources: one Continental, the other British.

The first dominated the field until the Second World War
when in parallel with developments in the study of International
Relations elsewhere, its influence waned. It retains, nevertheless, a
symbolic importance. Why? The first codified law in South Africa
was Roman–Dutch, and it remains the touchstone of South Africa's
legal system. It was of course within this tradition that Grotius (and
others of his School) made powerful advances in international law
two decades before the landings at the Cape of Good Hope. South
Africa's legal system springs, therefore, from the same fountain as
international law, and successive South African governments have
made much of this; International Law features strongly in official
approaches to global questions. (It is an instructive aside to note
that each of the country's Foreign Ministers has had legal training.)

However, the currency of South Africa's approach to International
Law has been debased in the years since the Second World War.
Given the minority's deepening crisis of legitimacy, South Africa's
international lawyers – with few, but important, exceptions[6] – have
been unsympathetic to the strengthening position of natural law.
The growing emphasis on human rights and the deprecation of
state sovereignty understandably threatens minority power. Thus,
while international law retains a place within international studies
in South Africa[7] – it is, for example, taught in all the country's
law schools – its selective application and positivist setting is
used chiefly to justify *apartheid's* view of its international position.[8]

The study's British source, which was inspired by the Chatham
House 'ideal', flowered after the First World War. Notwithstanding
powerful forays by American methodology[9], it continues to colour

the study of International Relations in South Africa.

Various reasons account for the success of this model. The Union (of South Africa) played an active role in the events leading up to the creation of the League of Nations;[10] indeed, the First World War was the fledgeling state's first major foreign policy adventure. As important, was the cultural and economic congruence between South Africa's ruling establishment[11] and those who championed the idea which was to become the Royal Institute of International Affairs.[12] For example, South African money was directly involved in the creation of Chatham House: 'Sir Abe Bailey, the South African mining magnate, gave the Institute a perpetual endowment of 5,000 (pounds sterling) per year'.[13] (The link between capital, especially mining capital, and the study of International Relations is a strong one in South Africa.[14]) These factors, plus the belief that South Africa had an African 'destiny', led to the creation of 1934 of the South African Institute of International Affairs (SAIIA).

Firmly cast in the Chatham House mould,[15] the SAIIA has set the agenda for International Relations in South Africa for more than fifty years. All serious efforts to engage the study – within the universities and in the broader society – have been touched by its activities. An examination of its publications and conference programme reveals, however, that the arc of the SAIIA's (and South Africa's) interests has been limited. This selective focus has been sharpened by two important constraints under which the SAIIA operates: its pool of financial support and the Chatham House ethos.

Given the absence of (American-type) foundation support and a determined refusal to take money from South Africa's government, the SAIIA's funding comes from the country's private sector. (The mining houses were especially generous in the Institute's formative years). This is clearly not a clientele without an interest in their own – and South Africa's – future; the SAIIA is charged with responding to these interests. In this, it is no different from other Institutes of International Affairs. However, in the apartheid context there are fundamental limitations imposed by the nature of the polity.

The Institute's role within the establishment has been further entrenched by constraints which flow from the Chatham House idea; one such is the complex question of relations with incumbent governments – again, an area of some consequence in South Africa. As sister institutes have fostered ties with governments, so this has happened (at times uncomfortably) in South Africa. Members of the governing National Party (including State President P.W.

Botha), opposition parliamentarians and senior bureaucrats (from the Departments of Foreign Affairs, Defence and (the former) Information) have appeared on Institute platforms.

Faced with the challenge of catering for multiple audiences in a deeply divided society, the SAIIA has been unable (some have said, unwilling) to engage some fundamental International Relations issues – Human Rights and the waning legitimacy of the white-ruled state, for example – which have fallen so obviously within South Africa's compass since 1945. These issues have not been entirely neglected by the Institute; indeed, recent work suggests a discovery of their urgency, but the chief thrust of the SAIIA's work is towards an establishment of which they are, undeniably, a part.

Periodically, the Institute has gone further than its founders might have intended; it has, for example, opened windows through which its clientele could view developments within their country. A sympathetic observer describes this role:

> [t]he oval mahogany table in the Board Room of Jan Smuts House has witnessed . . . countless smaller and less formal meetings, often with foreign visitors present, where people from all sectors and groups of South African society have discussed the difficult interlinked questions of domestic politics and South Africa's external relations in a changing world.[16]

Like sister Institutes, the SAIIA is prevented by its constitution from taking a 'party' political position, and this has saved it from exploitation, enabling it to sustain international recognition for its professionalism and objectivity. Jan Smuts House has vigorously defended itself against any moves which could erode its acceptability outside, and its accessibility within, the country. In short, it has not been used in establishment crusades.

This appears to be understood by those – in business and in government – who are drawn to the idea that International Relations should be used for missionary purposes: they have set about developing institutions which are employed in the defence of *apartheid*. By osmosis, International Relations in South Africa has been influenced by these institutions.

A discussion of four such efforts[17] distinguishes their role from that of the SAIIA. The South Africa Foundation, established in the early 1960s, is intended to be a 'group to combat the cold war against' South Africa. Its aims to present 'South Africa's case at home and overseas'.[18] This institution operates offices in Washington, Paris,

Bonn and London, and shrouds its propaganda activities in academic jargon and feigned objectivity; it is, however, a tightly-controlled international lobbyist for South African business. Its quarterly journal, *South Africa International*, has scholarly pretensions and some academics have contributed to it; strictly speaking, however, it is a propaganda organ. An idea of how close the ties are between the business community and government in crusades of this kind is illustrated by the fact that the Foundation's chief executive officer was formerly the country's Ambassador to the United Nations.

In the early 1970s, the white government through its (then) Department of Information established a short-lived quasi–academic propaganda organisation, the Foreign Affairs Association (FAA). One of its architects gives this candid appraisal of its activities:

> The FAA brought many top political and academic figures from the Western world to South Africa, and information which the FAA published or disseminated at its overseas conferences found its way into political offices, public libraries, business organisations and universities all over the world.[19]

After a Commission of Enquiry into irregularities within the sponsoring department, the FAA was disbanded. In a less blatant form, however, its work continues through an organisation calling itself The Southern African Forum.

A discussion of two further institutions of the crusading species deepens their contrast with serious scholarship: these are the Institute for American Studies at the Rand Afrikaans University and the University of Pretoria's Institute for Strategic Studies. The first is directed by a former South African Information Attache to Washington, and its work reveals a preferred appraisal of currents within US politics, especially on the South African issue.[20] The second is (probably) sponsored by the South African Defence Force – certainly, a serving Staff Officer has sat on the Board of Control. This Institute demonstrates a partisan understanding of contemporary strategy which results from its preoccupation with tracking South Africa's position in southern Africa.[21]

The tension between academic International Relations and its use for crusading purposes is also to be found elsewhere on South Africa's campuses.[22] With varying degrees of interest (and success), a course in International Relations can be found on all nineteen of South Africa's universities. In most cases, these courses are offered as component parts of the curricula in the respective university's Department of Politics (or Political Science, the term preferred in South Africa). In three universities – the (correspondence) University of South Africa, the University of Pretoria and the Potchefstroom University for Christian Higher Education – a sub-Department of International Relations exists. In the case of the first and third, a separate Chair has been founded. The University of South Africa also boasts a sub-Department of Strategic Studies headed by a Professor. The preoccupation of this Chair appears to be in servicing the post-graduate requirements of the South African Defence Force and, recently, theses submitted to the university from this Department have been placed under a total embargo for 'security reasons'.[23] This narrow, partisan use of International Relations has been recognised and condemned by the country's political science fraternity.[24]

A self-contained Department exists in only one of South Africa's universities, Witwatersrand. Its head occupies the Jan Smuts Chair of International Relations. Established in 1957, this was intended as the teaching wing of the South African Institute of International Affairs. However, the goals of the original design have faded with time and institutional rivalry.

This department has also sought to use International Relations to promote sectional interests. In the early-1980s, under the imprimatur of the Jan Smuts Professor, a proposal for the establishment of the 'South African Foreign Affairs Research Institution' was confidentially circulated to the country's business community. Before arguing that 'there are several reasons for believing that academics and scholars might succeed where others have failed in analysing the realities [*sic*] of the South African situation', the document proposed 'to bring overseas scholars directly into contact with the South African situation in such a way that they find themselves committed to research and publishing on South African questions, with a particular focus on South Africa's external dilemmas'.[25] After some discussion in the press, the idea was (apparently) abandoned.

Most of the published work in South Africa is in the Realist[26] or neo-Realist genre; and departures from this convention – transnationalism[27] or peace research,[28] for example – are not encouraged within its conservative culture. An analysis of the published work reveals five underlying symptoms: limited focus; an absence of interest in world order issues; the strong pull of political polemic; scant attention to theoretical rigour;[29] and a neglect of what Martin Wight called 'international theory'. A discussion of these symptoms gives an insight into the anatomy of International Relations in South Africa.

With one exception,[30] theoretical concerns have not engaged South African scholars. There have, however, been two efforts to ignite a local debate on these issues. The first aimed to work along the lines of the original British Committee on the Theory of International Politics, but faded after three meetings. The second, held in 1986, saw 23 of South Africa's younger scholars meet, together with three foreign visitors, in a two-day workshop. A follow-up meeting is planned, and the proceedings of the first gathering will shortly appear.[31]

This failure to engage theory has not only weakened the overall quality of South African International Relations but – as importantly – showed that the study was immune from the (new) revisionist school, which in the early- and mid-1970s, transformed South (and southern) African studies.[32] There have been some interesting International Relations contributions to this revisionist work, but these have mainly been made by scholars drawn from outside the discipline.[33]

The serious academic in South Africa faces two structural restraints: an oppressive academic sub-culture and the difficulty of access to policy-making.[34] Notwithstanding their disciplines, the former is faced by all academics; the latter is especially important to those with an interest in policy issues.

The white state is worried by those interested in such questions and limits their access. For example, research into sensitive areas, like nuclear questions, is restricted.[35] Moreover, access to the archives of the Department of Foreign Affairs has been withdrawn. The free flow of information has also been debilitated by 'emergency' regulations which have savaged the press.

On the other hand, there have been formal exchanges between the Department of Foreign Affairs and other 'interested parties' (read academics) over the years. The frequency of such exchanges has recently increased as, it appears, has the number of those invited to attend them.[36] In addition, the South African Defence Force consults regularly with select academics.[37]

Notwithstanding problems of access, most South African work is in the policy studies field. Here pioneering work has been done by scholars on the decision-making process, initially in foreign affairs[38] and, more recently, in the country's security apparatus.[39]

This is work of world class standard. In ways more real than illusory, it demonstrated that modern South Africa was not a liberal state with authoritarian tendencies, but an authoritarian state with moribund liberal institutions. This has huge implications both for foreign and regional policy. While the work focuses on the ruling establishment it, arguably, does not advance its cause. In other words, it is not crusading work.

What of the pull of polemic? An index on the work published by South Africans reveals that a considerable amount of ink has been spilt discussing the Soviet Union's policy toward South, and southern, Africa. The idea that Moscow (and various of its allies) have fairly specific goals in the region arises from the conjuncture of four factors: the (now largely discredited) belief that the Cape Sea Route is a prize to be valued; the inconclusive debate over the importance of South Africa's mineral resource endowment; the reassertion of knee-jerk anti-communism by the Reagan Administration and Mrs Thatcher; and the imputed influence played within the African National Congress (ANC) by the South African Communist Party. All of these factors have been raised by the South African government in support of its domestic, regional and international policies.

The work on this topic which emanates from South African-based pens is boldly sectarian and crudely simplistic. It is characterised by inchoate drawings from Soviet rhetoric which are presented as authoritative declarations of intent. The cumulative effect is one of archaic reasoning, unsubstantiated impressions and arcane deductions. (Much of it ironically – though not surprisingly – reads like some contributions to the Moscow-based journal, *International Affairs*.)[40] More than any other work, its vulgar anti-Marxist message demonstrates the missionary nature of International Relations in South Africa: the white government has enthusiastically embraced this message.[41] Thus it is that members of the academic community have played a role in supporting *apartheid's* anti-Communist crusade.

In response to the crudity of this work (and out of a genuine interest in Soviet policy), at least two published articles have tried to open counter-arguments.[42] Of more enduring importance, however, may be the transformation within the Institute for Soviet Studies (formerly the Institute for the Study of Marxism) at the University of Stellenbosch. Perhaps, the name change signifies a deepening maturity in approach and an acknowledgement that, in the words of the Institute, some issues 'have . . . received little attention in the academic community in South Africa, namely the dynamics and constraints of Soviet policy-making with regard to Africa'. This raises an intriguing question: Can crusading institutions (and crusaders) rehabilitate themselves?

Although the United Nations is taught in university courses, there is little interest in the UN and its institutions. This is not surprising. The United Nations is publicly portrayed – even within the country's schooling system – as an institution which is bent – as, indeed, it is – on the total, absolute destruction of minority rule and of dislodging South Africa from Namibia. Probably because of this, there is little interest in wider world order problems.

The underlying theme of this chapter holds that a preoccupation with the miseries which *apartheid* has visited on South Africa has retarded the study of International Relations. So much intellectual energy has been spent on analysing the plight of the establishment that little capacity has remained to analyse other questions, although stimulating work has been done on the southern African region, especially in the wake of the liberation of Mozambique and Angola. This falls into three distinct schools:[43] episodic, revisionist and technical.

A review of South African research publications confirms that, with the exception of one publicist-type pamphlet,[44] the primary international issue – arms control – has been ignored. South African interest in the exciting and innovative work on international political economy has been confined to economists.[45] (As a rule, interdisciplinary approaches to international questions have been eschewed in South Africa.) North–South issues, despite the oft cited assertion that South Africa is a 'microcosm' of the conflict between the first and third worlds,[46] has been almost entirely neglected;[47] although the Lomé regimes have been researched[48] The dynamics of alliances – especially the historically-significant new thrust towards a post-alliance world – have only been touched in a carom fashion.[49] The single work on Antarctica – an issue of some importance to South Africa – has been done by a non-South African geophysicist resident in the country.[50]

Perhaps, South Africa's International Relations scholars can be forgiven for this lack of diversity: after all their ranks, while growing, are still sparse. But one thing is unforgivable – the almost total neglect of the world within which their fellow countrymen operate. To this we now turn.

10.2   THE OTHER WORLD

A revealing – and for International Relations, disturbing – paradox runs through the deliberations on the international position of South Africa. Although *apartheid's* embattlement flows from the exclusion of its majority from the mainstream of political life, systematic attention has been paid only to the position of the white-ruled state in the international system. Therefore, South Africa's majority have been the object of discussion in International Relations, not subjects in that discussion.[51] On the surface this appears to be eroding, especially on the sanctions issue, where the opinion of blacks is constantly canvassed.[52] But the central focus of this interest remains the state, and black opinion forms only the sub-text of a desire to put pressure on *apartheid*.

South Africa's majority, however, does have a rich international experience which will affect the country's future. The decisions – both by the ANC and the Pan Africanist Congress – to go into exile and take up arms against minority rule had immensely important international consequences; equal in magnitude to those which first brought whites to southern Africa. These liberation movements – particularly the ANC – have an impressive diplomatic record and shaped views on innumerable international questions – from arms control to Antarctica.[53]

Moreover, blacks within the country are not only preoccupied with domestic issues – the tension between survival and the struggle to end *apartheid* – but have clear positions on a range of international issues. Indeed, a remarkable feature of recent years has been the appearance of powerful subterranean messages from South Africa's majority which are directed towards the international community.[54] Despite the importance of these, only one serious effort has been made (by a South African in voluntary exile) to understand what the country's majority feel – in their own right, not in response to pressure on the white state – on a range of international questions.[55]

Although a lack of access may account for this lacuna, a more probable explanation lies in the inability of the majority to believe that the study of International Relations is at all relevant to them.[56]

A glance at the 'International Relations' programme at one of South Africa's (black) universities, Zululand, confirms the point. (The choice is an extreme case, to be sure, but it succeeds in supporting the argument.) The syllabus outlines these sub-topics: 'Nationalism, National Power, Foreign Policy, Diplomacy, War,

Peace and Neutrality'.[57] All are perfectly respectable (although somewhat timebound) topics, but in the syllabus' published expatiation not one touches Africa,[58] nor inter-state relations in Africa;[59] nor wars of national liberation; nor non-alignment. Moreover, none of the interesting books by Africans on these themes are prescribed. They are remote, distant and of no direct consequence to the international experience and aspirations of those they are intended to reach – they describe a world through white (almost colonial) eyes.

There is a growing body of opinion which suggests that Africa has – and will continue to have – a discreet approach to International Relations.[60] This is driven by Africa's experience, by the continuing effects of colonial domination and by the anger (and humiliation) which all Africans – black and white – feel about *apartheid*. This African approach will affect, and be affected by, the political changes which will come to South Africa.

* * *

No longer do South Africa's majority believe that they are mere objects in the debate on their international future. They have begun to chart the course both for a post-*apartheid* state and a foreign policy which will be influenced by African, Third World and non-aligned values. Therefore, it is a matter of serious concern that the only article on the prospects for this foreign policy was written and published in Britain.[61]

Given the enormity of the South African issue, it is not surprising that the country's International Relations scholars face daunting challenges. They can salvage their discipline from *apartheid's* corrosion by promoting, instead, its engagement with the intellectual and moral imperative of a new society forged upon the same anvil worked by the discipline's founding fathers. But academic liberation will prove a more troublesome alloy to cast.

NOTES AND REFERENCES

*   A draft of this chapter was presented to colleagues in early December 1987. Their comments – for which I am grateful – shaped some thoughts, but it retains its original thrust.

1.   Vale's Axiom holds that a state's sense of diplomatic security is inversely proportional to its use of the International Relations lexicon. So British diplomats are not prone to draw from this to justify Britain's standing (although a content analysis of Foreign Office

'briefings during the Falkland's War will validate the Axiom); the Americans – who suffer from a close linkage between the scholar and the practitioner (witness Kissinger) – are more inclined to use shorthand to justify their actions. Insecure states – South Africa, Taiwan, Chile – seem to use it all the time.

2. The thrust of this contribution will leave the intelligent reader with no doubt as to where its author stands politically and professionally. With many others, I believe that there is a healthy tension between scholarship's central goal of enlightenment and the goal of politics, liberation. The chapter, therefore, is informed by a specific reading of South Africa's current reality and is supported by a distinct understanding of its future.

3. C.A.W. Manning was Montague Burton (formerly Cassel) Professor of International Relations at the London School of Economics from 1930 to 1962. His work includes *The Nature of International Society* (London: Bell, 1962) and *Peaceful Change and International Problems* (London: Macmillan, 1937). Others are Jack Spence, Professor of Politics, University of Leicester and author of *Republic Under Pressure: a study of South African foreign policy* (London: Oxford for the Royal Institute of International Affairs, 1965) and the exiled Sam Nolutshungu (currently) at the University of Manchester, author of *South Africa in Africa: a Study in Ideology and Foreign Policy* (Manchester: Manchester University Press, 1975).

4. A comment on the nomenclature of *apartheid*: people of mixed race are classified as 'Coloured'; Asian people are classified as 'Indians'; Blacks are classified according to a legally-defined 'ethnic group' – say, 'Zulu', 'Xhosa' or 'Tswana' – but it is common especially in academic work, to refer to Blacks as 'Africans'. In recent years, the generic terms, 'blacks', is used to include 'Africans', 'Coloureds' and 'Indians'. Although I use these terms, this does not denote approval of the system of racial classification.

5. Of course, Africa's southernmost tip was first 'rounded' by Portuguese sailors in the fifteenth century, but only with the end of Portuguese colonialism in the late 1970s did Lusitanian culture play a role in South African life. Other European peoples settled in South Africa and brought their culture with them: French Huguenots, for example, are mainly responsible for South Africa's excellent viticulture. While on these matters, it is important to debunk a popular myth about European settlement in South Africa. European settlers did not find an empty, largely unpopulated country. Blacks, destined to become *apartheid*'s victims, were settled on the continent's southernmost tip.

6. One exception is John Dugard, of the University of the Witwatersrand, author of – among other works – *Human Rights and the South African Legal Order* (Princeton: Princeton, N.J. University Press, 1978). With other legal academics, Dugard is responsible for the founding of the *South African Journal on Human Rights*. Human Rights questions have always interested lawyers more than non-lawyers in South Africa.

7. For a decade the *South African Yearbook of International, Law* has been published by the VerLoren van Themaat Centre for International

Law, University of South Africa. The journal's editorial policy is unwaveringly traditional, but it does carry some interesting primary sources.

8. See, for example, two books written by a former advisor to the Department of Foreign Affairs who is the son of the (present) Minister of Constitutional Development and Planning. Jan C. Heunis, *The Coventry Four* (Johannesburg: Perskor, 1985) and *United Nations versus South Africa: a legal assessment of UN and UN related activities in respect of South Africa* (Johannesburg: Lex Patria, 1986).

9. See, for example, Koos van Wyk, *Elite Opinions on South African Foreign Policy* (Johannesburg: Research Project on South African Foreign Relations, Occasional Paper No. 1, 1984).

10. See, Sara Pienaar, *South Africa and International Relations between the Two World Wars: The League of Nations Dimension* (Johannesburg: Witwatersrand University Press, 1987).

11. Some colleagues who read this essay in draft were troubled – unduly, in my opinion – by the notion of an 'establishment' and insisted that a definition should be provided. As used elsewhere, the establishment means simply those who exercise economic, political and social power. Often such power is invested by the establishment itself and, as often, it is largely unchallenged.

12. See, A.L. Bostock, *A Short History of the South African Institute of International Affairs* (Braamfontein: The South African Institute of International Affairs, 1984).

13. Bostock, *A Short History*, p. 3.

14. South Africa's economic prosperity has turned on its mining industry. With the rise of Afrikaner power, direct political influence eluded the wealthy and powerful mining houses and they have, periodically, indulged themselves in efforts to shape public opinion on a range of political and social issues. One such exercise, which recently took the country's establishment by storm, is a simplistic effort at scenario–building and political extrapolation which draws a distinction between a 'wasteland' and 'winning nations'. Its central inspiration is a rudimentary form of 'free market' economics. It was sponsored by the giant Anglo–American Corporation. See Clem Sunter, *The World and South Africa in the 1990s* (Cape Town: Human Rousseau Tafelberg, 1987).

15. The SAIIA, for example, encourages the use of the name of its headquarters, Jan Smuts House, interchangeably with its institutional name as does Chatham House.

16. Bostock, *A Short History*, p. 99.

17. This chapter discusses a few of South Africa's institutions. We should note, however, that the proliferation of Institutes concerned with social, political, economic and international issues appears to have replaced an old principle of South African politics: 'Avoid a problem, establish a government Commission of Inquiry'. There is a good discussion of research Institutes concerned with international questions in Deon Geldenhuys, *The Diplomacy of Isolation: South African Foreign Policy Making* (Johannesburg: Macmillan for the South African Institute of International Affairs, 1984), pp. 168–171.

18. Louis Gerber, *Friends and Influence: the Diplomacy of Private Enterprise* (London: Purnell, 1973), p. 8.
19. Eschel Rhoodie. *The* Real *Information Scandal (Pretoria: Orbis SA (Pty) Ltd, 1983), p. 269.*
20. See, for example, P.H. Kapp and G.C. Olivier (eds), United States–South Africa Relations: Past, Present and Future (Cape Town: Tafelberg for the Human Sciences Research Council, 1987).Two words of explanation are necessary: firstly, the second editor, Olivier, formerly a Professor of Politics at the University of Pretoria, is now with South Africa's Department of Foreign Affairs. This is a rare feat: there is not a strong tradition of mobility between academia and bureaucracy – especially in the foreign affairs field. The former South African Ambassador to London, Denis Worrall, was also an academic, but his move to diplomacy was a reward for service to the Nationalist Party. Diplomats have more easily become politicians, as the career record of South Africa's Minister of Foreign Affairs shows. One person, Stoffel van der Merwe, currently a Cabinet Minister, has been particularly adventurous: aviator, diplomat, academic and politician! In 1980 Dr. Neil Barnard, formerly Professor of Politics at the University of the Orange Free State, became the chief bureaucrat in the (civilian) Department of National Security (DONS). See his PhD thesis, *Die Magsfaktor in Internasionale Verhoudinge* (The Power Factor in International Relations) (Bloemfontein: University of the Orange Free State, 1975). Not surprisingly, this department has strong links with DONS. (See note 26 below.) Only John Barratt, of The South African Institute of International Affairs has successfully moved from diplomacy to academia.
    Secondly, HSRC stands for the Human Sciences Research Council which is the South African version of the U.S. Social Science Research Council. Its work is funded by the South African government and, in the light of this, periodic questions are raised as to whether it can truly be a disinterested purveyor of funds in an emotionally-charged situation.
21. Some outside commentators, like Robert Davies from Eduardo Mondlane University, Mozambique, have pointed out that this Institute (known by the acronym ISSUP) is 'to some degree a "think-tank" for the military's strategic planners' (*Journal of Southern African Studies* (Vol. 12, No. 2, April 1986), p. 314). This is a sound conclusion.
22. A word on South Africa's universities is necessary. The 1959 'Extension of University Education Amendment Act' segregated the country's four liberal English-speaking universities, Cape Town, Witwatersrand, Rhodes and Natal. As a consequence, four new ethnically-based universities were established, Western Cape (for Coloureds), Westville (for Indians), the North and Zululand (for Africans). (An older black university, Fort Hare, was henceforth incorporated with these new universities.) Despite protest, the liberal universities were effectively white only for almost twenty years. Gradually a number of black students were allowed back on these

campuses and today each has about 20 per cent black enrolment. South Africa's Afrikaans universities did not readily accept people of colour and were less affected by the 1959 legislation.

Recently, the South African government has launched another attack on the universities. This time the government has tied its subsidies – all South Africa's universities receive upwards of 70 per cent of their revenue from the state – to a university's responsibility to 'maintain law and order' on the campus. The effect will be that the universities will be forced to become custodians of the state's order, or face bankruptcy. In early 1988 the universities of Cape Town and Western Cape successfully challenged these plans in the courts. This forced the government to rethink, but the Universities remain threatened.

23. Two such theses are: J.C.K. van der Merwe, *n Ondersoek van Aspekte van die ontstaan en verloop van die insugensie in Owamboland tot 1983* (An enquiry into aspects of the origins and course of the insurgency in Ovamboland until 1983) (unpublished MA thesis, University of South Africa, 1986); J.K. Cilliers, *An Analysis of Problems related to Combating Urban Insurgency, with special reference to the South African Defence Force, 1975–1985* (Unpublished D.Litt et Phil thesis, University of South Africa, 1987). (Dr Cilliers is a Major in the South African Defence Force.)

24. At their bi-annual Congress, held at Stellenbosch, in October 1987, the Political Science Association of South Africa adopted the following resolution:

> The Political Science Association of South Africa is deeply concerned with developments threatening the integrity of the system of external examination of work submitted for degree purposes at South African universities. The integrity of the system of external examination is crucial to the general health of universities, as it also is crucial to international accreditation of locally-conferred degrees. On these grounds, we find it in principle unacceptable that theses submitted for examination at South Africa's universities are, for security reasons, labelled as classified information and consequently, (a) submitted for external examination only to academics who have security clearance and (b) that such theses and dissertations are not subject to inspection by the general academic community.

25. Document entitled Proposal for the Establishment of the South African Foreign Affairs Research Institution (SAFARI) – affiliated with the Department of International Relations. The University of the Witwatersrand (Johannesburg) (undated), pp. 4–5.

26. There is South African strain of Realism, 'Afrikaner Calvinist Realism' which flourished in the late 1950s and early 1960s. Associated with the University of the Orange Free State and Potchefstroom University for Christian Higher Education, this work is published in Afrikaans and is largely inaccessible to foreign audiences. Its influence in some policy-making circles may still be fairly potent. (See note 20 above.)

27. The only piece written in the style of the transnational school is Peter Vale, 'South Africa and the Changing International Community:

interpreting the future in the light of the past', in Robert Schrire (ed.), *South Africa: Public Policy Perspectives* (Cape Town: Juta, 1981), pp 340–67.

28. Andre du Pisani's forthcoming PhD thesis to be titled *A Critical Evaluation of Conflict Resolution Techniques: From Workshops to Theory* (University of Cape Town), promises to be an exception. Another will be the project 'Research on Militarization' launched under the aegis of the Association for Sociology in Southern Africa.

29. In the early 1970s, G.C. Olivier presented a PhD thesis on South Africa's foreign policy to the University of Pretoria which was strongly grounded in theory. The work was republished as *Suid-Afrika se Buitelandse beleid*. (Pretoria: Academica, 1976). (For further details on Olivier see footnote 20, above.)

   Some younger South Africans are strongly drawn to theory. See, for example, Garth L. Shelton, 'Theoretical Perspectives on South African Foreign Policy Making', *Politikon* (Vol. 13, No. 1, June 1986), pp. 3–21. Its author is with the University of the Witwatersrand's Department of International Relations. His writing proves that it is possible to free oneself from the straitjacket of one's undergraduate training.

30. Mervyn Frost, *Toward a Normative Theory of International Relations* (Cambridge: The University Press, 1986). It is sometimes argues that General Smuts's book *Holism and Evolution* (London: Macmillan, 1926) is, *inter alia*, a home-grown theory of International Relations. I think not.

31. Mervyn Frost, Peter Vale and David Weiner, *International Relations Methodology: Some facets of an ongoing debate* (Pretoria: Human Sciences Research Council, 1988).

32. This work is associated with the names of Shula Marks, Stanley Trapido, Gavin Williams and Charles van Onselen. For any understanding of South and southern African studies, it must be read. Its essence is neatly captured in Fredrick Johnstone, ' "Most Painful to our Hearts": South Africa through the eyes of the new school', *Canadian Journal of African Studies* (Vol. 16, No. 1, 1982), pp. 5–26.

33. See, Alf Stadler, *The Political Economy of Modern South Africa* (London: Croom Helm, 1987); Duncan Innes, *Anglo: Anglo American and the rise of modern South Africa* (traditionlly published in Johannesburg: Ravan Press, 1984); Martin Legassick and Duncan Innes 'Capital Restructuring and Apartheid: A Critique of Constructive Engagement', *African Affairs* (Vol. 76, No. 305, October 1977), pp. 437–482. The annual publication called *South African Review* traditionally published in Johannesburg by Ravan Press invariably carries less weighty work of this type.

34. This difficulty of access to decision-making, makes a nonsense of an illusion that at least one of South Africa's serious International Relations scholars, Deon Geldenhuys, is the 'theorist' for the South African government's policy of regional destabilisation. See, for example, Joseph Hanlon, *Beggar Your Neighbours: Apartheid Power in Southern Africa* (London: Catholic Institute of International Affairs in

.Collaboration with James Curry, Indiana University Press, 1986), p. 309. In my opinion, Geldenhuys is descriptive, and not concerned with theoretical structures. As a general rule, he seems to touch on these issues where existing theory is able to shed light on aspects of description: In Geldenhuys's work – as in the work of other South Africans – there is little effort to develop new, innovative theoretical paradigms.

35: See, however, G.H. Barrie, 'South Africa and nuclear energy – national and international legal aspects', *Tydskrif vir die Suid-Afrikaanse Reg (Journal of South African Law)* (No. 2, 1987), pp. 153–174.The author was formerly legal advisor to the Department of Foreign Affairs.

36. Who, and why, individuals are invited to attend these is a matter for speculation. This writer, for example, has never been invited. I have, however, encouraged colleagues to attend, believing that it is important to point out to bureaucrats the consequences of policy actions. This is especially so with regard to southern African issues where the South African Defence Force has wreaked such havoc. Colleagues who attended a recent conference reported that 'a great deal of time was taken up by formal presentations' (presumably) by the Department of Foreign Affairs.

37. At the Rand Afrikaans University there is a research and teaching 'Department of National Security' headed by General Hein de V. du Toit formerly Director of Military Intelligence.

38. See, Geldenhuys, *The Diplomacy of Isolation*.

39. See, Deon Geldenhuys and Hennie Kotze, 'Aspects of political decision-making in South Africa', *Politikon* (Vol. 10, No. 1, June 1983), pp. 33–45; Deon Geldenhuys and Hennie Kotze, 'P.W. Botha as decision maker: a preliminary study of personality and politics', *Politikon* (Vol. 12, No. 1, June 1985), pp. 30–42; Philip Frankel, *Pretoria's Praetorians: civil military relations in South Africa* (Cambridge: Cambridge University Press, 1984).

40. See, for example, M. Hough. 'Sowjet-betrokkenheid in Suidelike Afrika: Implikasies vir RSA' ('Soviet involvement in southern Africa: Implications for the Republic of South Africa'), in *Papers Delivered at a Symposium Organised by the Institute for the Study of Marxism, (14 March 1983)* (Stellenbosch: Institute for the Study of Marxism, 1983, Occasional Publication 1), pp. 30–50; Dirk T. Kunert. 'Windows of peril: Africa, the world and the 1980s', *South Africa International* (Vol. 11, No. 1, 1980), pp. 1–20; Dirk T. Kunert, *Africa: Soviet Strategy and Western Counter-strategy* (Johannesburg: Southern Africa Forum, 1981, Occasional Paper 1); Dirk T. Kunert and Colin Vale, 'The Chimera of the "Zimbabwe Solution"', *Strategic Review* (Vol. 12, No.3, 1984), pp. 23–36; G.S. Labuschagne, *Moscow, Havana and the MPLA takeover of Angola* (Pretoria: Foreign Affairs Association, 1976, Study Report No. 3).

41. The work of the Jan Smuts Professor of International Relations, appears to have 'impressed none other than the prime minister' (now the State President). Geldenhuys, *The Diplomacy of Isolation*, p. 171.

42. Robert Schrire. 'Russian Policy in Sub-Saharan Africa – past achievements and future prospects', *Optima* (Vol. 31, No. 1,

1983), pp. 2–17 and John Barratt, *The Soviet Union and South Africa* (Johannesburg: SAIIA, 1981).

43. I have used this categorisation in Peter Vale, 'Regional Policy: The Compulsion to Incorporate', in Jesmond Blumenfeld (ed.), *South Africa in Crisis* (London: Croom Helm for The Royal Institute of International Affairs, 1987), pp. 176–194. Briefly, the 'Episodic School' has chronicled events of episodes in southern Africa without giving attention to the development of a strong framework. (See, for example, Deon Geldenhuys, 'Recrossing the Matola Threshold: the "Terrorist Factor" in South Africa's regional relations', *South African International* (Vol. 13, No. 3, 1983), pp. 52–71; John Barratt, 'Foreign Policy 1983–1985 – the regional context', in D.J. van Vurren (ed.). *South Africa: a plural society in transition*, (Durban: Butterworth, 1985), pp. 414–478; Peter Vale. 'South Africa's regional foreign policy: a search for the *status quo ante*', *New Zealand International Review*, Vol. 7, No. 5, (1982), pp. 15–18.) The 'Revisionists' have, as the name suggests, used a strong revisionist paradigm. (See, for example, Robert Davies and Dan O'Meara. 'Total Strategy in Southern Africa: an analysis of South African regional policy since 1978', *Journal of Southern African Studies* (Vol. 11, No. 2, 1985), pp. 183–211; Robert Davies, *South Africa Strategy Towards Mozambique in the Post–Nkomati Period: A Critical Analysis of Effects and Implications* (Uppsala: Scandinavian Institute of African Studies, Research Report No. 73); Renfrew Christie, *Electricity, Industry and Class in South Africa* (London: Macmillan, 1984.) The Technical School has been limited to making important inventories of technical and economic issues. (See, for example, Gavin Maasdorp, 'Squaring Up to Economic Domination: Regional Patterns', in Robert Rotberg, *et al.* (eds), *South Africa and its Neighbours: Regional Security And Self-Interest* (Lexington: Lexington Books, 1985), pp. 91–135; Gavin Maasdorp. *Transport Policies and Economic Development in Southern Africa: A Comparative Study in Eight Countries* (Durban: University of Natal, Economic Research Unit, 1984).)

44. Peter Vale and Wally Kopp, *A Layman's Guide to Arms Control and Nuclear Arms* (Johannesburg: SAIIA, Special Study Series, 1982).

45. See, for example, Vishnu Padayachee, 'Apartheid South Africa and the International Monetary Fund', *Transformation* (3, 1987), pp. 31–57; Trevor Bell, 'International Competition and Industrial Decentralisation in South Africa', *World Development* (Vol. 15, No.10–11, pp.1291–1307).

46. The notion of 'development' has a particular meaning in South Africa. It means, the transfer of resources from the central (essentially white-based) core of the South African economy to the poor rural and homeland areas. Some of this is, indeed, 'international' in the sense suggested in note 51 below.

47. The exception is Marthnus G. Erasmus, *The New International Economic Order and International Organisations: Towards a special status for Developing Countries* (Frankfurt: Haag & Herchen, 1979).

48. See, J.D. Matthews, *The Association System of the European*

Community (New York: Praeger, 1977); Peter Vale, *Six and Eighteen; Nine and Forty-Six: The Road from Rome to Lome* (unpublished MA thesis, University of Leicester, 1976).

49. Peter Vale, *The Atlantic Nations and South Africa: Economic Constraints and Community Fracture* (Unpublished PhD Thesis, University of Leicester, 1980).

50. Maarten J. de Wit *Minerals and Mining in Antarctica: Science and Technology, Economics and Politics* (Oxford: Clarendon Press, 1985).

51. In a restricted (and illegal) fashion a debate on the 'international' role of blacks has taken place, but this has been within the context only of the South African government's homeland policy. The granting of 'independence' to four of these ethnic structures has been supported by the trappings of an 'international' relationship. By a unique feat, South Africa has become one of the few states to conduct international Relations with itself!

52. See, for example, Mark Orkin, *The Struggle and the Future: What Black South Africans Really Think* (Johannesburg: Ravan Press, 1986).

53. An insight into Nelson Mandela's thoughts on some international issues is offered in Samuel Dash, 'A Rare Talk with Nelson Mandela', *New York Times Magazine* (7 July 1985), pp. 21–2.

54. Three examples demonstrate the point: At the funeral of four black activists in July 1985, in the small Eastern Cape hamlet, Cradock, a Soviet flag was unfurled. Emergency detainees in the St Albans Prison (near the City of Port Elizabeth) staged a hunger strike in memory of Mozambique's Samora Machel. When wardens tried to break the strike they were resisted, resulting in violence. In October 1987, as a result of Mrs Thatcher's obdurate stand against sanctions and her disparaging remarks about the ANC, the United Democratic Front, the ANC's non-violent ally, broke all contacts with Britain.

55. David Hirschmann, *Changing Attitudes of Black South Africans Towards the United States of America* (Grahamstown: ISER, Development Studies Working Paper No. 34, 1987).

56. Wilmot James, one of South Africa's gifted young sociologists, is reported as commenting:

> There is an aversion to studying international relations among blacks . . . . This aversion is exacerbated by the fact that IR is dominated by the Afrikaner universities. Furthermore, no effort has been made to train blacks. Only now are people beginning to think how a new generation will run a new, majority-ruled South African state.

Cited in Witney W. Schneidman, *The Study of International Relations in South Africa: A Trip Report*, presented to The United State–South Africa Leadership Exchange Program (mimeo, November 1986) p. 12. (Confidential Report. Cited with the permission of the sponsoring body.)

57. University of Zululand, Faculty of Economic and Political Sciences. Course CPS 225 'International Relations' (mimeo, no date).

58. Some South African scholars have dealt strongly with African questions. See, for example, Annette Seegers, 'The Development of the

Armed Forces in Mozambique', *Studies in Marxism* (No. 3, November 1984), pp. 23–57; Andre du Pisani, *South West Africa/Namibia: The Politics of Continuity and Change* (Johannesburg: Jonathan Ball, 1986).

59. Here to some responsible work has been done by South Africans. See, for example, Annette Seegers, 'South African Liberation: Touchstone of African Solidarity' in B.E. Arlinghaus (ed.), *African Security Issues: Sovereignty, Stability and Solidarity* (Boulder, Col.: Westview Press, 1983), pp. 185–202.

60. See, Ali A. Mazrui, *Africa's International Relations: The Diplomacy of Dependency and Change* (London: Heinemann, 1977). Also O.J.C.B. Ojo, D.K. Orwa and C.M.B. Utete, *African International Relations* (London: Longman, 1985).

61. Barry Buzan and H.O. Nazareth, 'South Africa versus Azania: The Implications of Who Rules', *International Affairs* (Vol. 62, No. 1, Winter 1985–86), pp. 35–40.

11 The Study of International Relations in France*

Marie-Claude Smouts

11.1 A DUAL CHARACTERISTIC

For many years analysis of international relations within the French academic community has been – and to a large degree remains – a specialisation subsumed within the more traditional and well-established disciplines of Law, History and Economics. Those writers who, in the 1960s, introduced International Relations into academic debate within France came predominantly from one of these three backgrounds. The majority of these scholars remained within the framework of these well-defined disciplines and their degrees, careers and clearly articulated curricula. It was under these conditions in the 1960s and 1970s that a number of International Relations textbooks were published, which though presented as new, were little more than up-to-date variants of traditional scholarship in the subjects of international public law and international organisation already offered to students of Law.

This largely institutional approach had nothing in common with what, at the same time, was being called 'International Relations' in the United States. However, the line between the development of contemporary international public law and international politics is blurred, and the contribution of French legal scholars to the understanding of International Relations has not been insignificant. In particular the *Annuaire français de droit international* (French Annual of International Law) has proved a remarkable research tool for International Relations scholars, with articles on topical questions going well beyond strict legal analysis, as well as a rich critical bibliography which is not restricted to purely legal literature. Furthermore, the annual symposium of the *Société française sur le droit international* (French Society for International Law), which

221

brings together legal scholars, diplomats and even political scientists, considers subjects which exist on this blurred line between law and politics: for example, the European Economic Community (EEC) or the crisis confronting international organisations.

Some historians have sought to develop the study of International Relations by employing the methods and accepted norms of their own discipline. This development has essentially followed two diametrically opposed paths, on the one hand that of the *Ecole des Annales* – typified by the work of Fernand Braudel and his followers – and on the other hand the work associated with the study of the *'forces profondes'*[1] established in the inter-war years by Pierre Renouvin, J.B. Duroselle being his best-known intellectual heir.

Finally, among economists, the analysis introduced by François Perroux in the form of the radical 'external critique' was followed up by neo-Marxist writers, giving it a wide-ranging audience. In developing an analysis specifically around economic power, they had a far-reaching influence on the portrayal of power relations between the countries of the North and those of the South. Moreover, the *Institut d'étude du développement économique et social* (IEDES), along with the *Revue Tiers-Monde*, has been the largest purveyor of the centre–periphery problematic as well as of the work carried out by the dependency schools during the 1970s. The Institute remains an essential tool for the generation and dissemination of knowledge on the economies of third world countries and the problems of development.

Over the same period, fewer scientists actually decided to opt for Political Science, this at a time when the discipline was beginning to strengthen its credentials after a prolonged period of uncertainty. For the remaining pioneers, four frameworks existed within which these studies could be pursued:

1. The *Fondation nationale des sciences politiques* (FNSP) along with the *Institut d'études politiques* (IEP) in Paris, several IEPs in the provinces, the *Centre d'études et de recherches internationales* (CERI) (a large research centre in Paris created in 1952) and the *Centre d'études d'Afrique noire* (CEAN) (a centre for more specialised research in Bordeaux).

2. The legal and political science sections at the *Centre national de la recherche scientifique* (CNRS) which divided into two distinct sections, thereby giving recognition to Political Science, only in 1982.

3. The research teams and laboratories of CNRS, of which the most important is the *Centre de recherches et d'études sur les sociétés méditerranéennes* (CRESM).

4. The political science *Unités d'enseignement et de recherche* (faculties[2]) existing within the university system, of which a few offered a *diplôme d'études approfondies*[3] (DEA) in International Relations at the postgraduate level.

Insofar as International Relations has existed at all in France as a specific field of study, it has effectively been closely bound with Political Science. Specialists who have adopted this field of study have not claimed any autonomy for the subject as they believe this to be an illusion, given the difficulty the latter has had in separating itself from public law and being accepted in and of itself. Of course International Relations is based upon the postulate that interactions between social groups are different to those that would exist in the absence of national boundaries, yet it asks the same fundamental questions as Political Science and also deals with the phenomena of power, organisation, conflict and co-operation. On the level of epistomology and within the constraints of feasible aspirations, both suffer from the same methodological and theoretical uncertainties.

The introduction of International Relations into the sphere of Political Science has led to a considerable amount of confusion over defining the parameters of the field of study. The boundary between what does and what does *not* strictly count as the field of International Relations is full of uncertainty. A mistaken but deep-rooted French tradition distinguishes Political Science as applied to the *Hexagone*[4] from Political Science as applied to, as it were, all the rest; foreign countries or transnational forces. Contrary to what is happening in academic circles in other countries, area studies ('*aires culturelles*') are not separated from International Relations. Country or regional specialists who use the methods of Political Science to analyse the political nature of societies other than French society, are considered – perhaps mistakenly – to be International Relations scholars and are grouped in the same research centres as those who are interested in phenomena reaching across national boundaries. Moreover, this latter group of scholars is far less numerous than the former.

This dual characteristic – of being influenced by traditional disciplines drawing upon Political Science, and of lacking the distinction between area studies and international relations – gives research in France a peculiarly French complexion. It explains, to a large degree, the subject's strengths – and weaknesses.

11.2 'HEXAGONALE' OR ORIGINAL?

Scholars of International Relations in France were not confronted with the scholastic rivalry between 'Idealists' and 'Realists' which split the American scientific community in the 1950s, nor by the 'Thirty Years War' which continues to contrast the 'Traditionalists' with the 'Behaviouralists'. Generally speaking, they have remained on the sidelines of the debates stirred up by their Anglo-Saxon colleagues. Impervious to the systems theory of M. Kaplan, indifferent to K. Waltz, sceptical of the successive versions of 'transnationalism' (Functionalism, Integration, Interdependence, etc.), the fellow countrymen of General de Gaulle probably felt American imperialism over the discipline a good deal less than their German and Scandinavian counterparts. At present, even though the use of concepts originating from across the Atlantic has given scientific discourse on International Relations a caricatured 'franglais' tone, and bibliographies are still very American, this has not stimulated rejection, for the simple reason that there has been no sense of domination. It is, however, worth noting in this respect that the chapter devoted to International Relations in the monumental treatment of Political Science by M. Grawitz and J. Leca, was written by a bicultural American specialist, Stanley Hoffmann (perhaps just a hint of a complex).

If there has been a notable stimulus, it has come from the paradigms elicited by Raymond Aron and the Marxist influence on North–South relations, but this is more a question of recent developments due to the emergence of a new generation of scholars than of an intellectual revolution.

Concentrating upon the principal weaknesses of Morgenthau's work – the imprecise nature of his concept of 'power' and the ambiguity of his notion of national interest – Aron closely studied the Realist approach, taking into consideration those aspects which were most open to criticism. As an alternative, he offered a more qualified and acceptable version which dominated, and still leaves an indelible mark upon, the French approach to International Relations. It is readily agreed that International Relations cannot be a normative science as there are too many variables to construct a 'theory' for universal explanation or prediction. Realist paradigms are largely accepted: the international society is seen as an anarchic one, in which the central issue remains peace or war and the principal actors are states. Foreign policy studies, quite limited until the 1980s, have been notable for this approach and have put emphasis on diplomatic action and strategy. Only in the last few years has the analysis of decision-making begun to be applied to foreign policy, and the role of the overall environment been taken into consideration. However, the significance of economic and social forces in the formulation of foreign policy is still given little attention. Analyses of international actors can be both extremely traditional and underdeveloped. The study of international organisations is essentially undertaken by legal scholars, and is more concerned with the mechanisms and creations of law than the phenomena of power and the role of the new actors on the international stage. There is a paucity of research on the EEC. Outside of the civil service only four or five specialists can adequately analyse what is at stake and what the consequences are of what goes on in Brussels. There are many good studies of multinational corporations, but these are conducted by economists and hitherto have been neglected by political scientists.

Narrowly conceived, International Relations in France has not achieved the 'critical mass' which would have provided it with firmer foundations. The discipline remains fragmented, with a few strong points but with some considerable gaps. Conversely, the study of interactions on this or that side of national boundaries has developed in a quite original fashion. The penetration of Political Science into area studies and the gradual process of assimilation between International Relations scholars themselves and specialists of foreign systems has naturally exploded the *'aronien'* frameworks of analysis. This phenomenon is particularly noticeable where the relationship between the internal and external forces in third world countries is concerned, and in the role of transnational forces.

The study of the political role of Islam is, for example, a strong point in French research, largely due to the quality of Orientalists and Africanists. At present, a new direction in research looks at questions of the autonomy of the state and cultural identity within developing countries. This problematic goes beyond that of the centre–periphery model of the 1960s and 1970s. Without ignoring the structural inequalities between North and South, this new research recognises a significant margin of autonomy within the political societies of the third world, and examines how these societies can adopt and adapt values, norms and externally derived models, whether from East or West.

This entirely innovative approach, looking at the influence of the international system on Third World countries finds is based on a development of comparative studies. Increasingly, specialists in a language or civilisation use both the tools of Political Science and anthropology. Not only are political systems being studied, but also the extra-institutional aspects of the political dynamic: language, music, and custom, which collectively form 'popular modes of political action'. Despite some reservations, research by a new generation of political scientists is leading to a transformation of the study of foreign societies: it is no longer considered an 'exotic' specialisation. The regrouping of specialists from different fields around the same questions of Political Science, at the confluence of the internal, the international and the comparative, has give rise to diverse research on totalitarianism, democracy and the conditions under which representative and pluralist governments are established. This has deepened understanding of the Latin American, African and Asian countries, which has in turn enriched Political Science itself.

This relatively recent phenomenon illustrates a trend which will continue, but which is increasingly applied to the study of the South rather than of industrialised countries. Research on the latter remains very weak in France, and this lack of knowledge about her neighbours and Western partners can be ascribed to an insufficient number of specialists; paradoxical in a country which wishes to be seen as a European superpower.

11.3 SCATTERED RESEARCH EFFORT

Academic institutions with the means to undertake long-term research projects, and ensure a cumulative and regular output, are few and far between. Research within the university system, while often of high quality, is only maintained by the efforts of a few individuals operating without adequate funding or co-ordination. Political scholars interested in International Relations are even more isolated than their scholarly counterparts in Economics, History and Law.

IFRI (*Institut français de relations internationales*, comprising a dozen research fellows) has a particular vocation, similar to that of the Royal Institute of International Affairs or the Council on Foreign Relations. It publishes a review aimed at an informed but general audience, *Politique étrangère*, and an annual report on the state of the international political economy (*Ramses*).

The two laboratories of the *Fondation nationale des sciences politiques* (CERI, with 47 research fellows, and CEAN, with 26) and CRESM (23 research fellows) are the largest research centres. They publish some thirty books and over 200 articles a year. By organising research programmes spread over several years, and often of an inter-disciplinary nature, these centres function as 'umbrella organisations' for scholarly research.

However, political scientists do not have a monopoly on the debate on international relations (nor on anything else, for that matter). In the midst of these scholars, sometimes with them and sometimes against, there are a range of alternative sources of knowledge about International Relations. Studies on defence and strategy commissioned by the Ministry of Defence, for example, are partly from experts and organisations outside the ambit of the academic world. At the same time, a few specialists, from CERI, IFRI, the major daily newspapers, ministerial *cabinets*[5] and the civil service regularly get together for discussions. Even though this field is the speciality of no more than twenty experts, all from differing backgrounds, together they define the content and substance of French thought on defence and disarmament.

In the field of international political economy one also finds groups of experts meeting informally. While these are not strictly speaking 'think tanks', they have regular and frequent colloquia followed by publications in which virtually the same senior civil servants from the Ministry of Planning or the Treasury, 'captains of industry', journalists and research fellows appear time and time again.

Therefore, though one cannot speak of a 'French school of International Relations', there is a definite acceleration in the generation and circulation of ideas, which augurs favourably for the development of a discipline which is still incomplete, but very much alive.

2. The UER were created by the 1968 *loi d'orientation de l'enseignement supérieur* (of 12 November), partly as a means of stimulating inter-disciplinary study.

3. Although there is no strict equivalent, this certificate approximates to a Masters degree within the British university system.

4. Figurative term used to describe France, derived from its physical shape on the map (hexagonal).

5. Each minister of the French government has his/her own *cabinet* (group of advisers). It does not refer to the British example of the Cabinet (comprising senior ministers of the government, on the Westminster model).

12 The Study of International Relations in the Soviet Union*

Margot Light

Political Science is a relatively young subject in the Soviet Union, and International Relations is an even newer branch of it. While Western scholars were contending methodological approaches to the study of international politics, their Soviet colleagues were arguing that Political Science and International Relations should be established as independent fields of enquiry.[1] The official position under Stalin, and for a number of years after his death, had been that Marxism-Leninism *was* Political Science and provided a ready-made theory of International Relations. Books and articles were written on International Relations, but they were the works of historians, international lawyers, exegetists of Marxist–Leninist doctrine. It is only in the last twenty years that the profession of *mezhdunarodnik* (specialist in International Relations) has emerged. There are well-staffed research Institutes, a large publishing programme which produces books in editions of thousands (and sometimes even hundreds of thousands), and learned journals of International Relations. In other words, with one curious exception, International Relations has all the paraphernalia of an academic field which is recognised, respected and well-established. The exception is that there are very few undergraduate programmes in which people can specialise in International Relations.

Despite an extensive academic infrastructure and the enviable institution of a relatively large number of posts for professional researchers whose sole task is to research and write, there have been regular complaints at the quinquennial Congress of the Communist Party of the Soviet Union (CPSU) about the kind of research that is done in the Soviet Union on questions of politics and International Relations. Social scientists have been exhorted to produce better and more relevant work.[2] On the one hand, these complaints could signify that the struggle for the establishment of an independent academic field of enquiry unfettered by ideological demands has succeeded so well that the leaders of the CPSU are anxious to reimpose the connection between academic work and the needs of the state and the Party. On the other hand, they could mean that constraints, whether self-imposed or handed down from above, still affect the direction and quality of research.

The products of their research may be criticised, but some *mezhdunarodniki* are thought to have considerable impact on Soviet policy. Perhaps the most spectacular example is A.N. Yakovlev, who was promoted from the directorship of the Institute of World Economy and International Relations (called IMEMO from its initials in Russian) to become the Central Committee secretary responsible for ideology, propaganda and culture in 1986 (in June 1987 he also became a full member of the Politburo).[3] It is difficult to reconcile the perceived shortcomings of the field with the responsibility entrusted to some of its major proponents.

This study will begin with a brief account of the development of International Relations as an academic discipline in the Soviet Union and its present institutional organisation. It will then describe the one undergraduate Institute and the structure of one of the postgraduate Institutes attached to the Academy of Sciences. The nature of published research will be examined, to try to illuminate some of the reasons why dissatisfaction is expressed so regularly about the work produced by Soviet social scientists. The concluding section will consider the implications of Gorbachev's 'new political thinking' for the study of International Relations.

12.1 THE DEVELOPMENT OF INTERNATIONAL RELATIONS AS AN ACADEMIC DISCIPLINE

Given the late emergence of the social sciences, including International Relations in the Soviet Union, it is ironic that one of the early acts undertaken by the Bolsheviks in the field of education was the establishment of a Socialist Academy of Social Sciences (renamed the Communist Academy in 1923). However, its role was soon envisaged as extending beyond scholarly work. It was to be an 'ideological Gosplan' to provide the Marxist expertise required by the government in every walk of life. In fact, it was not the Communist Academy that produced the first research in foreign policy, but the Association of Oriental Studies, set up to study Eastern countries. But by the end of the 1920s Soviet orientalists had been accused of bourgeois influence, and the principle that academic work should be closely related to the needs of the Party and the state had become firmly established in the Soviet Union.[4]

From then until 1936, foreign policy research was concentrated in the Institute of World Economy and World Politics, directed from 1927 by Eugene Varga who was for many years close to Stalin.[5] The Institute's purposes were to train specialists in world economy and international politics, collect contemporary, relevant data for the government and Party, conduct research, develop Marxist–Leninist theory to counter the left and right opposition at home and abroad and to popularise policies of the day. An associated teaching Institute, the Institute of Red Professors for World Economy and World Politics was also established. In 1936 the Communist Academy was dissolved. The USSR Academy of Sciences became the umbrella organisation for Varga's Institute, as well as for the Institute of Oriental Studies (established in 1929) and the Pacific Institute (established in 1942).

Varga lost Stalin's support during the war for failing to produce an accurate assessment of the German war capability. But the two men fell out irretrievably over Varga's optimistic study of the new-found strengths of the capitalist economies which had resulted from the war. He amended his book, but was dismissed from his post and the Institute and its journal were closed down.[6] The Oriental and Pacific Institutes were merged, but very little research was done in Stalin's last years. It could be argued that there was very little Soviet foreign policy in those years, so that from a practical point of view there was correspondingly little need for foreign policy research. In fact, however, the cult of personality turned Stalin into the acknowledged expert in all fields. If an official Stalinist line was imposed on subjects like linguistics and genetics, what hope could there possibly be for independent research in International Relations? And Varga's fate made it clear what the penalties were for disagreeing with Stalin.

When Stalin died and Soviet foreign policy was revived, the shortage of information on which to base policy was immediately felt. At the 20th Congress of the CPSU in 1956, complaints were voiced that Soviet scholars were lagging seriously behind. They did not 'study facts and figures deeply'.[7] Varga's Institute (now called IMEMO) was re-established under the directorship of A.A. Arzumanyan, followed by a number of other institutions: the

Institute for Chinese Studies (1956), united in 1960 with the Institute of Oriental Studies; the Africa Institute (1959); the Institute of Latin America (1961); the Institute of the Far East (1966); the Institute of the USA and Canada (1968); and the Institute of the International Workers' Movement (1968). Two of the present features of the study of International Relations in the Soviet Union became apparent as the number of Institutes grew: they did not have undergraduate programmes and they were multidisciplinary area studies Institutes organised on a geographic basis and divided internally by discipline.[8]

The burgeoning of interest in, and facilities for, the study of International Relations was initiated by Khrushchev but, as the dates make obvious, continued by Brezhnev. Nevertheless, Soviet *mezhdunarodniki* still did not feel that they belonged to a recognised field. Nor did social scientists believe that they could study questions 'whose answers are not known beforehand'.[9] And the Soviet leadership continued expressing dissatisfaction with their research output. Foreign policy research ceased to be the sole preserve of the Academy of Sciences Institutes. Institutions which had previously restricted themselves to teaching (for example, university area studies departments and the Moscow State Institute of International Relations, which will be described in greater detail below) also became actively involved in research. Moreover, academics, whether from the teaching or the Academy Institutes, were not the only people publishing works on International Relations. Although it is unlikely that Andrei Gromyko was personally responsible for the innumerable books that appeared under his editorship, many serious and scholarly works were published by staff members of the two departments of the Central Committee Secretariat which deal with foreign affairs.[10] Judging by the volume of books and articles, the source of the complaints voiced at successive Party Congresses could not have been quantity of work.

12.2 UNDERGRADUATE AND POSTGRADUATE STUDY OF INTERNATIONAL RELATIONS

A brief look at the pre-Gorbachev internal organisation, first, of the only Institute which teaches an undergraduate degree, and second, of one of the major research Institutes, would probably help to indicate the differences and similarities between the study of International Relations in the Soviet Union and in the West.

It will also provide a basis for understanding the changes which are taking place under Gorbachev.

There are still very few major undergraduate programmes in International Relations in the Soviet Union.[11] The largest and most important full programme is run by the Moscow State Institute of International Relations (known by its Russian acronym MGIMO), which is attached to the Ministry of Foreign Affairs. Founded in 1944, its function is to train diplomats, international lawyers and journalists. After graduation they are placed not only in the Ministry of Foreign Affairs, but also in the Ministry of Foreign Trade, the Central Committee apparatus, TASS or the major newspapers. In other words, they are intended to become prac-titioners rather than scholars of International Relations. In recent years, however, the Institute has become more research oriented and some of its graduates go on to teach (many of the current teaching staff are MGIMO graduates) and do research.[12]

In the context of Soviet education, it is less odd than it might seem that the Institute is attached to the Ministry of Foreign Affairs. For one thing, it is rare in the Soviet Union for a student to enter tertiary education without a clearly specified profession in mind. Education is generally far more explicitly vocational than it is in the West. For another, Soviet ministries each have control over a gigantic field of endeavour and function rather like giant monopolies. It is usual for them to sponsor and control educational establishments designed to train the specialists they need. Thus while the State Committee for National Education (*Goskomnarobr*, formerly the Ministries of Higher and Specialised Education and of General Education which were combined into this one State Committee in April 1988) is entirely devoted to education, other ministries are primarily concerned with other spheres of national endeavour, but they frequently fund and supervise Institutes to serve those spheres.

There are four faculties in the Institute of International Relations: International Relations, Law, International Economic Relations (the largest faculty) and Journalism. All students are obliged to study two foreign languages and the length of the degree programme depends on the languages: in common with most teritiary institutions, a degree programme takes five years, but students of Eastern languages study for a sixth year. Although International Relations is taught through-out the Institute, the proportion differs from faculty to faculty. Students in the faculty of International Relations study general sub-jects like the history of International Relations and Law, Economics,

Current Affairs and the theory of International Relations (Western as well as Soviet), but specialise in a particular country or region. There is no undergraduate course which corresponds to Western courses in Strategic Studies (postgraduate students, however, study Soviet military doctrine and can take courses in strategy). The syllabus for all subjects is decided centrally by the ministry (which also decides on student numbers depending on need), but individual departments and teachers are said to have some leeway in interpreting it.

The Institute runs a three year graduate programme consisting partly of taught courses and partly of a research project. Postgraduate students have to pass examinations in a foreign language, Marxist–Leninist philosophy and political economy (these requirements are identical for all postgraduate students in all disciplines), in addition to one or two related to their field of specialisation. After submitting a dissertation and defending it publicly, the student becomes a Candidate of Historical, Philosophical, Legal or Economic Science (depending on the research topic). Later he or she can become a Doctor of one of the sciences by defending a longer and more substantial dissertation. There is no such qualification as Candidate of Political Science or International Relations. Although the reason is almost certainly historic, the absence stands perhaps as a symbol of the difficulty of establishing these disciplines independently from Marxism–Leninism or from more traditional subjects like History and Law.

The Institute of World Economy and International Relations, like the other Institutes attached to the Academy of Sciences, is entirely devoted to postgraduate and post-doctoral research. It publishes the major scholarly journal of International Relations *Mirovaya ekonomika i mezhdunarodnye otnosheniya*. It is divided into two sections, Economics and International Relations, of which economics is by far the larger. Until recently there were two major departments (International Organisation and International Affairs) within the the International Relations section, each divided into sectors. The 65–70 people who work in the Department of International Affairs belonged to one of three regional sectors – Western Europe, the Far East and the United States – or to one of two theoretical sectors – Strategic Studies or Theoretical problems of research and prognosis in international affairs. In 1983 a sector was established to study arms control and international security. The theoretical problems sector has undertaken critical studies of Western International Relations theory. It has also attempted to apply quantitative methods to International Relations.[13]

Among the staff of Institutes like IMEMO there are likely to be a few with first degrees in International Relations, but there are unlikely to be graduates of Politics or Sociology. The vast majority are graduates of History, Law and Economics. The geographic designation of the area studies institutions suggests a far more rigid division between areas of the world as far as research is concerned than exists in fact. There are overlaps and shared interests and there is considerable cross-fertilisation between Institutes, with combined seminars, symposia and research projects. Perhaps the most surprising discovery that Western scholars make about Soviet *mezhdunarodniki* is the amount of Western literature with which they are familiar, even when that literature has not been translated and does not appear in the catalogues of the major libraries. It is not only that they all read one or more foreign languages, but also that unobtainable works are somehow acquired (for those who do not succeed, Soviet institutions offer extensive abstracting services).

While this brief description of how the Institutes are organised highlights some of the differences between International Relations East and West, it does not offer a *prima facie* reason for the dissatisfaction which the leadership frequently expresses with the research output, nor for the more muted discontent of the *mezhdunarodniki* with the status of their profession. Earlier it was suggested that the problem could either be that the leaders of the CPSU feel that the connection between academic work and the needs of the state and Party has grown too lax or, on the other hand, it might be that ideological constraints still operate which affect the direction and quality of research. A consideration of some of the features of published material might give some insight into the nature of the problem.

12.3 INTERNATIONAL RELATIONS: THE PUBLISHED WORK

Mainstream Soviet writing on International Relations has, like its Western counterpart, been dominated by an implicit rational actor model. The nation state is the basic unit of analysis and action. One Western scholar noted more than 15 years ago that 'Western and Soviet perspectives on the basic structure of the modern international system are essentially similar'.[14] This has remained true. But in the Soviet case, the unitary rational actor is guided by the hand of inevitable historical process, causing imperialists to behave aggressively and socialists to act in the interests of the working class. The final outcome (a socialist world) is predetermined (though short-term zig-zags need to be explained) and it depends not upon International Relations, but upon endemic domestic class conflict within capitalist societies.

Most of the International Relations works published in massive editions have been historical narratives. As is the case in other branches of history, leadership change has tended to be followed by the rewriting of the history of foreign policy. In the process of this rewriting, the Soviet state has become more reified. As the names of discredited leaders have been removed from history, so past actions have increasingly been attributed to the Soviet state or government. One looks in vain, for example, for mention of Khrushchev's name in accounts written in the Brezhnev era about events which occurred from 1953–64.[15] On the other hand, although Khrushchev was publicly criticised when he was dismissed from power, his foreign policy has never been openly scrutinised by Soviet scholars. The foreign policy of the CPSU and the Soviet state has been uniformly correct.

In fact, there has rarely been mention of mistakes in Soviet policy in the published work on International Relations, and there have been no officially published works which are critical of past or present policy. Stalin, for example, was criticised for his conduct of the war, but not for his conduct of foreign policy. It has also been rare to find alternative explanations for particular events in one work, or even in works published over a number of years. This is not to imply that there have been no variations in interpretation over time, but to point to the fact that the same interpretation has tended to be offered by the entire profession at any one time. And even when it has been obvious that the interpretation is new, explanations have not been offered about why the change has occurred.[16]

If, as Welch and Triska put it, 'narrative is king' in mainstream Western writing about Soviet foreign policy, the same has been true of mainstream Soviet work.[17] And it is difficult not to conclude that as far as historical accounts are concerned, many of the ideological fetters have remained and the official line has continued to reign.

In effect, the plea to be able to study questions 'whose answers are not known beforehand' (see note 9) was recognition and rejection of these fetters. But it was also the prelude to a methodological debate which was not dissimilar to the one which had already taken place in the West. The proponents of a new methodology called for more 'sociological and interdisciplinary research'.[18] Two parallel trends became evident in Soviet 'Behavioural' literature. There were books and articles of critical comment on 'bourgeois' theory.[19] There was also a discussion about the utility of sociological and quantitative methods in the study of International Relations, and some attempts were made to apply new methods.[20] The efforts to introduce new methods continue, but it has proved difficult to dislodge the 'conservative alliance of ideologists and legal specialists'.[21]

In fact, however, the argument between Soviet traditionalists and social scientists concerned *how* International Relations should be studied, not *what* should be studied. And it did not really touch upon the crux of the problem: the relationship of International Relations research to the Party line. In other words, the origin of the discontent on both sides has to do with the relationship between the role of the *mezhdunarodniki* as scholars, and the service they owe to the Party and the state. The latter has frequently acted as a constraint on the former (and not only under Stalin), to the detriment of both. The plea to be able to consider questions to which the answer is not known beforehand refers, on the one hand, to methodology. But on the other hand, and perhaps more importantly, it can also be understood to refer to history, to the relationship of the Party to its past and, most important of all, to the research agenda and what happens when an answer is reached which does not fit the Party line. If Soviet International Relations researchers are to be more relevant and useful, they must first be able to reach their own conclusions about the past in order to apply the lessons of the past to the present and future. And they must also feel free to admit to answers that might contradict the official line.[22]

12.4 THE 'NEW POLITICAL THINKING' AND THE STUDY OF INTERNATIONAL RELATIONS

The introduction of reconstruction (*perestroika*) and openness (*glasnost*) suggests that Gorbachev understands both the problems of Soviet society in general, and those of the relationship between the study of the social sciences including International Relations, and the practice of Soviet policy in particular. The terms *perestroika* and *glasnost*, and the associated package of ideas called the 'new political thinking', are very much in vogue. What implications do they have for the study of International Relations?

The 'new political thinking' covers both the practice and the study of Soviet foreign policy. As far as practice is concerned, it is primarily concerned with the central strategic relationship between the Soviet Union and the United States. Various spokesmen have stressed different aspects, but there are six principles of contemporary International Relations which all of them mention: (1) the interdependence of survival; (2) the need to reduce the level of military confrontation; (3) the impossibility of ensuring security through military–technical means alone; (4) the indivisibility of national and international security; (5) the need for more flexible foreign policies and the readiness to compromise; and finally, the need for a comprehensive approach to security problems, including the willingness to tackle difficulties in the military, economic, political and humanitarian spheres.[23]

None of these ideas is entirely new. Most have been voiced from time to time in the academic International Relations literature in recent years. Nor is the call for reconstruction and *glasnost* entirely novel. Successive Party Congresses have called for improvements in productivity, in the quality of workmanship and in accountability, all major features of *perestroika*. Moreover, the term 'criticism and self-criticism' which is not entirely different from the way in which *glasnost* seems to operate, has a long history in the CPSU (although there has always been great selectivity in who can criticise and from whom self-criticism is expected). What is new is calling them the 'new political thinking' and sanctioning them at the highest level of the political leadership. Moreover, the six principles have begun to be applied to Soviet policy. At the most obvious level, the previous Soviet reputation for intransigence has been overturned by the speed with which arms control proposals have been modified to incorporate Western fears (and some efforts have been made to modify the stance on human rights, whether to satisfy the West or to gain the support of the Soviet intelligentsia). There have also been sweeping changes in the foreign policy establishment. The 'new political thinking' is being presented and practised by new diplomats and officials in the Ministry of Foreign Affairs and the International Department of the Central Committee. Arms Control has emerged as an important area of research. A new Academy of Sciences Institute devoted to European Affairs is to be established.[24]

In May 1986 a foreign policy conference discussed the implementation of the policy adopted at the 27th Party Congress. Although the proceedings were not publicly reported, the implications of the 'new political thinking' for the teaching of International Relations to future practitioners studying at MGIMO and the Diplomatic Academy were on the agenda.

A year later Shevardnadze referred to a scrupulous examination in May and June of 1986 of 'serious shortcomings in the training and re-training of diplomatic cadres in our educational Institutes'. The outcome had been a decision to reconstruct the educational process to fulfil the practical requirements of the Ministry. This entailed improving both the standards of entrants and the educational syllabus. In September 1987 he noted some improvement, but lamented that 'inert and conservative forces' within MGIMO and the Diplomatic Academy still held sway.[25]

At the time of the foreign policy conference in May 1986, Primakov, the new director of IMEMO, proposed a programme for International Relations research in the Soviet Union. Scholars should concentrate less on the contradictions between the socialist and capitalist social systems, and pay more attention to their unity and interdependence, in particular to the effects on the socialist economies of events in the world economy and the common processes which occur irrespective of social system. *Mezhdunarodniki* should study and develop the concept of international economic security, both as it should operate between the capitalist centre and its periphery and between East and West. The processes by which socialism is built should be investigated, with particular reference to the effect of the level of economic development from which it is begun. As far as the study of capitalist society is concerned, particular attention should be paid to the extent to which internal contradictions have served as a new source of development causing, for example, the internationalisation of production and capital, and the formation of 'transnational monopoly capital'.[26]

But the 'new political thinking', it was recognised, required more than personnel changes, new area studies Institutes, reconstructed syllabi and the establishment of civilian arms control departments. An examination of Soviet foreign policy and a new look at old history were prerequisites for 'new political thinking'. Scholars, one academic complained, seemed to find it easy to analyse mistakes in the economic and social spheres but they fell into 'hypnotic silence' about 'sacred cows' of Soviet foreign and defence policy. In fact, however, 'analysis of lost battles is no less useful for the present and future than pathetic descriptions of victories that have been won'. New mistakes can only be avoided if those of the past are examined. If International Relations claims to be scientific, *mezhdunarodniki* should understand that in true science 'there can be no forbidden themes or closed areas'.[27]

Primakov's article ended by emphasising the vital contribution expected from Soviet social scientists to the successful implementation of the 'new political thinking' at home and abroad:

> The modern world is more complex, interdependent, dynamic and contradictory than ever before. That is why scientific cognition, the application of the Marxist-Leninist dialectic and a systemic approach to analysing social phenomena are particularly important. This dictates the special role and responsibility . . . of the social sciences, including economics, philosophy, sociology, political science.[28]

Whether Soviet *mezhdunarodniki* will be able to fulfil this responsibility, however, depends partly upon the contents of the 'new political thinking'. But it also depends upon opening the historical archives and upon the way in which *glasnost* operates. For the crux of the problem remains the same. If the 'new political thinking' becomes the only permissible thinking, it will become a constraint on the study of International Relations. The consequence will serve neither International Relations as a discipline, nor the needs of the Soviet state.

NOTES AND REFERENCES

*   I am grateful to Neil Malcolm for his helpful comments on the version of this paper that was published in *Millennium: Journal of International Studies* (Vol. 16, No. 2, Summer 1987) and to Dennis Ogden and David Wedgwood Benn for drawing my attention to new, relevant material.

1.   For accounts of the debate and its results see William Zimmerman, *Soviet Perspectives on International Relations 1956–1967* (Princeton, N.J.: Princeton University Press, 1970), Ronald J. Hill, *Soviet Politics, Political Science and Reform* (Oxford: Martin Robertson; and New York: M.E. Sharpe, 1980), pp. 1–19, Neil Malcolm, *Soviet Political Scientists and American Politics* (London: Macmillan in association with the Centre for Russian and East European Studies, University of Birmingham, 1984), pp. 5–12, Archie Brown, 'Political Science in the Soviet Union: A New Stage of Development', *Soviet Studies* (Vol. 36, No. 3, July 1984), pp. 317–44, and Allen Lynch, *The Soviet Study of International Relations* (Cambridge: Cambridge University Press, 1987). The nearest to a political science Institute, the Institute

of State and Law, concentrates on legal and institutional studies. A Soviet Political Science Association was established in the 1960s. Nonetheless, there is still no easily identifiable field of Political Science. Nor is there a Soviet International Studies Association.

2. See, for example, Leonid Brezhnev, *Otchetnyi doklad Tsentral'nogo Komiteta KPSS XXIV S"ezdu Kommunisticheskoi Partii Sovetskogo Soyuza* (Moscow: Politizdat, 1971), pp. 106–7; Brezhnev, *Otchetnyi doklad Tsentral'nogo Komiteta KPSS XXV S"ezdu Kommunisticheskoi Partii Sovetskogo Soyuza* (Moscow, Politizdat, 1976), p. 88; Brezhnev, *Otchetnyi doklad Tsentral'nogo Komiteta KPSS XXVI S"ezdu Kommunisticheskoi Partii Sovetskogo Soyuza* (Moscow, Politizdat, 1981), pp. 105–6.

3. The movement between academia and responsible political positions is not always from the former to the latter. Arbatov, for example, was head of the USA section of the International Department of the Central Committee for three years before assuming the directorship of the influential Institute of the USA and Canada. And Yakovlev was deputy chief of the Central Committee Propaganda Department for several years before being 'exiled' to the post of Soviet Ambassador to Canada. He was brought back to IMEMO after Brezhnev's death.

4. See Oded Eran, *The Mezhdunarodniki* (Ramat Gan: Turtledove, 1979), pp. 9–29 (quote on p. 13) on the founding and early role of the Academy and the harnessing of academic work to state purposes.

5. Eran, *The Mezhdunarodniki*, p. 41, calls Varga 'the emperor of Soviet foreign policy studies until World War Two'. But he was also a sound and respected academic.

6. Evgeny S. Varga, *Izmeneniya v ekonomike kapitalizma v itoge Vtoroi mirovoi voiny* (Moscow, Gospolitizdat, 1946). For an account of the Varga dispute, see Jerry Hough, *The Struggle for the Third World: Soviet Debates and American Options* (Washington, D.C.: Brookings Institution, 1986), pp. 106–14.

7. See Malcolm, *Soviet Political Scientists*, pp. 4–5, for the background to the revival. The quote, from Mikoyan's speech at the Congress, is on p. 4.

8. The Institute of the International Workers' Movement shared the second of these features, although it was not geographically based.

9. F.M. Burlatsky, 'Politika i nauka', *Pravda*, 10 January 1965, cited in Malcolm, *Soviet Political Scientists*, p. 7.

10. The two departments are the International Department and the Department for Liaison with Communist and Workers' Parties of Socialist Countries. Perhaps the best known of Gromyko's edited works is the standard *History of the Foreign Policy of the USSR*, which has appeared in regular new editions: A.A. Gromyko and B.N. Ponomarev (eds), *Istoriya vneshnei politiki SSSR* (Moscow: Nauka, 1971, 1976, 1981). Examples of works by high ranking officials of the Central Committee Secretariat are K.N. Brutents, *National Liberation Movements Today* (Moscow: Progress Publishers, 1977); B.N. Ponomarev, 'Sovmestnaya bor'ba rabochego i natsional'no–osvoboditel'nogo dvizhenii protiv imperializma, za

sotsial'ny progress', *Kommunist* (No. 16, 1980), pp. 30–44; G. Shakhnazarov, *The Coming World Order* (Moscow: Progress Publishers, 1984). Malcolm, *Soviet Political Scientists*, p. 13, suggests that all the foreign policy Institutes are primarily responsible to the International Department of the Central Committee. Many of them spend up to 25 per cent of their time on policy-relevant work assigned by higher political authorities. See Jerry F. Hough, 'The Foreign Policy Establishment', in Robbin F. Laird and Erik P. Hoffmann (eds.), *Soviet Foreign Policy in a Changing World* (New York: Aldine, 1986), pp. 150–1.

11. There are individual undergraduate courses in International Relations in other institutions, but not an entire degree programme.

12. For the early history of this Institute, see Hough, 'The Foreign Policy Establishment', pp. 148–9. Future diplomats also attend the Ministry's Diplomatic Academy for further training and re-training. There are, of course, diplomats who have not graduated from this Institute, just as there are graduates of the Institute who have not become diplomats.

13. For example, V.I. Gantman (ed.), *Sovremennye burzhuaznye teorii mezhdunarodnykh otnoshenii* (Moscow: Nauka, 1976). The description of the Institute comes from an unpublished paper, Michael Banks and Margot Light, 'Behaviouralist and Bikhaiveristski: A Report on a British–Soviet Dialogue on the Theory of International Relations', 1974. For the establishment of the arms control sector, see Pat Litherland, 'Gorbachev and Arms Control: Civilian Experts and Soviet Policy', *Peace Research Report No. 12* (Bradford: School of Peace Studies, University of Bradford, November 1986). A description of the way the Institute of the USA and Canada is organised is given by Malcolm, *Soviet Political Scientists*, pp. 15–16.

14. Zimmerman, *Soviet Perspectives*, p. 94. It should be noted, however, that this assertion is vehemently rejected by Soviet scholars.

15. See, for example, the various editions of Gromyko and Ponomarev (eds), *Istoriya*.

16. The repetition of the word 'published' here is intended to suggest that Soviet decision-makers must have less selective and tendentious work available on which to base their decisions. The use of the past tense reflects the fact that Gorbachev's policy of *glasnost* has begun to change the situation. The 'blank spots' in Soviet history (see Gorbachev's speech to senior media personnel in *Kommunist* (No. 4, 1987), pp. 20–27) have begun to be filled in.

17. William Welch and Jan F. Triska, 'Soviet Foreign Policy Studies and Foreign Policy Models', *World Politics*, (Vol. 23, No. 4, 1971), pp. 704–33.

18. D.V. Ermolenko, *Sotsiologiya i problemy mezhdunarodnykh otnoshenii* (Moscow, IMO, 1977), p. 12.

19. See, for example, S.A. Petrovskii and L.A. Petrovskaya, 'Modernizm' protiv 'traditsionalizma' v burzhuaznykh issledovaniyakh mezhdunarodnykh otnoshenii', *Voprosy filosofii* (No. 2, 1974), pp. 39–54 and Gantman, (ed.) *Sovremennye burzhuaznye teorii*.

20. See, for example, F.M Burlatsky and A.M Galkin, *Sotsiologiya: Politika: Mezhdunarodnye otnosheniya* (Moscow: IMO, 1974); E.A.

Pozdnyakov, *Sistemnyi podkhod i mezhdunarodnye otnsheniya* (Moscow: Nauka, 1976). There is a very good analysis of the Soviet 'behaviouralists' in A. Lynch, *The Soviet Study*.

21. D.E. Powell and P. Shoup, 'The Emergence of Political Science in Communist Countries', *American Political Science Review* (Vol. 64, No. 2, 1970), p. 194.

22. The one field where this was possible even before Gorbachev came to power was Third World research. See, for example, Elizabeth Valkenier, *The Soviet Union and the Third World: An Economic Bind* (New York: Praeger, 1983), and Hough, *The Struggle for the Third World*.

23. These principles were included in Gorbachev's Congress report, M.S. Gorbachev, 'Politicheskii doklad Tsentral'nogo Komiteta KPSS XXVII S"ezdu Kommunisticheskoi Partii Sovetskogo Soyuza', *Pravda*, 26 February 1986. See also A.F. Dobrynin, 'Za bes"yadernyi mir, navstrechu XXI veku', *Kommunist*, (No. 8, 1986), pp. 18–31 and E. Primakov 'XXVII s"ezd KPSS i issledovanie problem mirovoi ekonomiki i mezhdunarodnykh otnoshenii', *Mirovaya ekonomika i mezhdunarodnye otnosheniya* (No. 5, 1986), pp. 3–14.

24. For a more detailed analysis of the personnel changes, see M. Light, '"New Thinking" in Soviet foreign policy?', *Coexistence*, (Vol. 24, No. 3), pp. 233–43. For the growth of a civilian arms control community, see Litherland, 'Gorbachev and Arms Control'. A report on the proposed Institute of European Affairs was published in *The Guardian* (18 November 1987).

25. E.A. Shevardnadze, 'Perestroika v sovetskoi diplomatii', *Vestnik Ministerstva inostrannykh del SSSR* (No. 1, 1987), a shortened version of which is reprinted in *Argumenty i Fakty* (No. 36 (361), 12–18 September 1987), pp. 1, 4–5 (quotes on p. 5).

26. Primakov, 'XXVII s"ezd'.

27. P. Cherkasov, 'Ne tol'ko propaganda', *Novyi Mir* (No. 10, 1987), pp. 262–4 (quotes on p. 263).

28. Primakov, 'XXVII s"ezd', p. 14.

13 The Study of International Relations in the Federal Republic of Germany

Ulrich Albrecht

The circumstances that the study of International Relations and other fields of academia must contend with have changed greatly in the atomic age, if compared to conventional wisdom in this and other fields of academia. As Ernst Bloch, the grand old man of Marxist philosophy noted:

> It is known that learning is not to serve school or science, not solely for this purpose, but for so-called life. In our time, the bitter addendum is required, for survival.[1]

After the student revolt of 1968 (which brought a number of its proponents into prominent teaching positions), and especially after the rise of the peace movement to a scale unprecedented in Germany history, the community of scholars devoted to the field of International Relations experienced a deep split. The major grouping tried to continue with the pre-eminent paradigm, Morgenthau's Realist approach. The centre of this school, by now called 'Neorealism', is found in Munich. But a number of scholars did not join in this mainstream. Some felt an obligation to the re-education background, which strongly influenced German Political Science after the Nazi period. Political Science, at least as long as it dealt with domestic issues, was equated with 'science for democratisation' (*Demokratisierungswissenschaft*). Scholars of International Relations have asked to what extent the *arcanum* of state power, the decision to go to war, or foreign policy in general might possibly be democratised (such developments can also be traced in Austria). The findings of most of the scholars are markedly resigned: representative democracy renders few possibilities for greater democratic participation in foreign relations in the atomic age.[2]

A second line of development, closer to the centre of political opinion in post-war Germany, is concerned with the peace problem in Europe. There is discussion about a 'special responsibility' or a 'special task' for Germans, after launching two world wars in this century, to contribute to enhancing peace. The late president of the Federal Republic, Gustav Heinemann, a former staunch supporter of neutralist stances, demanded in his inaugural address the formal establishment of peace research in West Germany. A number of research institutions were rapidly established both in and outside universities. Scholars of International Relations have dominated German peace studies throughout the years. The conservative parties, after taking over from the social democratic–liberal coalitions, made the government support for peace research a key issue to indicate political change (*Die Wende*). The Bavarian prime minister, Franz- Josef Strauss, personally intervened to bring government support for peace research to a halt: it is truly a unique that a party leader should be so concerned about particular academic developments. However, it is quite possible that Strauss was more interested in fighting the Social Democratic Party (SPD), than in a special school in International Relations. Nevertheless, the consequences of this blow were disastrous. Much funding of empirical research was discontinued despite attempts by the *Deutsche Forschungsgemeinschaft* (roughly comparable to the United Kingdom's ESRC) to accept grant applications by scholars who formerly were supported by peace research funds. Today, public money (for empirical political studies) in West Germany is available solely for research into third world conflict and East–West relations.

This was particularly troublesome for a third strand of academic engagement in International Relations. After the student unrest in 1968 and the renewed interest in Marxist studies, the inputs into the emerging field of International Political Economy were numerous, especially in Germany. First, the outstanding peace researchers Johan Galtung and Dieter Senghaas transferred an important school of thought into Germany, namely the '*dependencia*' debate about dependencies inherent in North-South relations. Second, there was a growing consensus about the rise of importance of economic issues in international affairs, in part stimulated by the expanding role of West Germany in international economics; the Federal Republic surpassed the United States as the world's largest exporter. This induced anlaysts to stress an old question: how is economic strength being translated into political power? The simple self-portrait preferred in Bonn, that Germany remains an economic giant and a political dwarf at the same time, had been challenged before the conservatives came to power. Criticisms were supported by penetrating studies about the political impact of West Germany's flourishing economy on international affairs. Dr Strauss's intervention interfered with all studies about an alleged German military–industrial complex, about arms race dynamics in West Germany and about Germany's subtle financial means of dominating the European Community.

It may be premature to make substantial statements about how this politico-economic approach to International Relations survived the political change in Germany. Two features, however, appear likely to survive, despite the cut of government support by grants. The first is work about international debts and their political repercussions. Given the long pre-eminence of German lenders on world markets of finance (for example, German banks financed one half of the weapons airlift to both Israel and Egypt during the Yom Kippur War which was not covered by public money on both sides), it is quite understandable that West German academics pioneer European investigations into such matters.[3] The other feature of ongoing study of politico-economic affairs is related with the international trade in arms. The level of debate on West German arms transfers remains unique, compared to the unconscientious approach of other academic communities. The contemporary rise of Krupp as a gun-maker – in contrast to popular knowledge about an intimate relationship between the Hohenzollerns and the firm – was facilitated by third world exports, violating British and other trade barriers, thus helping Krupp to recover the entry costs into what hitherto was the domain of the Prussian (public) Arsenal. The historical function of German arms trafficking, together with other contributions by technology to the international reputation of Germany in the past, has recently encouraged a number of studies. History of science, which also covers technological application and political impact, has not been a common subject in the German tradition.

Given the overwhelming influence of America in post-war cultural and scientific affairs in West Germany, the evolution of Political Science is a notable deviation. While comparable social sciences, following the US path, underwent a course of heavy mathematisation, this single branch abstained. Modern economics in West Germany are based on heavy doses of demanding mathematics, and students of subjects such as psychology cannot bypass a certain amount of training in statistics. But the typical German diploma political scientist has no formal education in quantitative methods. The history of ideas approach, bits of systems theory in the Karl Deutsch tradition, historicism and heuristic approaches of the classical type still dominate the field.

The reason for this remarkable resistance against mathematisation can be found in looking into the academic background of the first generation of professors in Political Science after the Nazi period. Few scientists with a background in the Political Science of the Weimar Republic had survived in Germany. The *Deutsche Hochschule für Politik*, a third-level teaching institution oriented towards the socialists and some of the bourgeois parties (which today forms the basis of the Department of Political Science of the Free University of Berlin) was abolished by the Nazis. Hence most of the first generation of Political Science teachers after the war were noted journalists (e.g., Richard Loewenthal, Eugen Kogon), or had a background in Public Law or History. It is understandable that these people, despite all enthusiasm for American accomplishments, did not command the skills to go into mathematical analyses of foreign policy. On the contrary, they passed a legacy of methodological conservatism along to their pupils. Today there is thus only a very small group of political scientists employing quantitative tools of analysis in the Federal Republic of Germany, most of them trained in the United States.

This celebrated old generation of German Political Science was helpful, however, in the troublesome process of converting the level of political analysis from a dominant Cold War view of the world into a more appropriate perspective, especially in the field of international studies. The shift can be dramatically demonstrated in the field of studies related to East Germany and the Eastern bloc. Until the mid-1970s, area studies and East-West studies in general were given the task of comparing the Western and Eastern systems (with the inherent bias that the former would always emerge as the superior one). Furthermore, such studies needed to be mindful of the obligation set out in the Federal Republic of Germany's constitution that reunification was the ultimate objective of all German political efforts. In the legalistic German tradition, this constitutional principle is still in force, but it has lost its overriding priority in teaching and research in politics.

International Relations was also studied in order to give advice to the government and to influence administrative and political decisions. A narrow understanding of the interrelationship between science and politics had inhibited innovation in analysis during the early years of the Federal Republic's existence. By the mid-1970s a team of political scientists, headed by the late Peter C. Ludz, advocated the study of other societies according to their immanent self-understanding. This process was regarded as a revolution. The team succeeded in gearing the official government-issued publications about East Germany to the new methodological approach, and this was reflected in the innovation commonly phrased as *Ostpolitik* within academia. Later versions of the documents, after heavy controversies in government and political circles, mitigated this methodological purity. But the last decade of studies in international affairs, as far as East European and communist societies are concerned, is markedly distinct from earlier writings.

This does not imply that the study of International Relations in Germany – after some manoeuvring in order to catch up with after the Nazi and Cold War period – is now more or less comparable to activities in other countries, and in line with standards common in the Western world. Ideological issues, especially theories of totalitarian regimes in the East and in Third World countries, still enjoy a disproportionate level of attention. Studies in decision-making processes, group theories and other innovations in methodological debate tend to be less common in West Germany than elsewhere. Mainstream thinking in International Relations in Germany still looks more for innovation from abroad, rather than contributing to international debate on further development of the discipline. The mainstream dissidents, the analysts of political economics and the scholars who consider the international system as a structured power hierarchy, i.e., those who are interested in 'low politics' (in contrast to diplomatic 'high politics'), apparently have more to tell the international academic community than the watchdogs of established German priorities, who stress issues ranging from reunification to methodological conservatism.

NOTES AND REFERENCES

1. Quoted from (one of the numerous activities of this kind) *Verantwortung für den Frieden (II)* (Responsibility for peace), a series of

lectures at Aix-la-Chapelle (Aachen) Technical University, Preface, p. 7.
2. I have given an overview to this debate in the book *Internationale Politik: Einfuhrung in das System internationaler Herrschaft* (International Politics: An Introduction to the System of International Dominance) (Munich: Oldenbourg, 1986).
3. This is a cross reference to studies *e.g.*, by Elmar Altvater and Alexander Schubert, published in German and Romance languages.

14 The Study of International Relations in Japan*

Takashi Inoguchi

14.1 THE DEVELOPMENT OF THE STUDY OF INTERNATIONAL RELATIONS IN JAPAN

The development of the study of International Relations in Japan is best understood in historical perspective. Prior to 1945 the study of International Relations was conceived as an amalgamation of Law, History and Economics in the international arena.[1] It is indicative of this conception of the study of international relations that one of the oldest existing journals for the study of International Relations, *Kokusaiho gaiko zasshi* (Journal of International Law and Diplomacy), appeared as early as 1902. At its inception, the study of International Relations in Japan was largely understood as Diplomatic History and International Law. These two fields of study were deemed essential for the appropriate handling of International Relations as practised by the Western powers. After all, the gunboat diplomacy of the Western powers in the mid-nineteenth century forced a long-secluded Japan to open its doors. Then, as Japan emerged as a military power and acquired colonial possessions, military studies and colonial studies were added to the field. From this, it is clear that the study of International Relations was shaped by the practical needs of the newly modernising state in East Asia. In other words, the study of International Relations in Japan was a reflection of *raison d'état*. The dominance of such practical considerations implies that the study of International Relations was academically weak as a discipline. The same can be said of the study of politics. As a matter of fact, Political Science in Japan did not exist prior to 1945.[2] What did exist was known as *Staatslehre*, or the study of the state, which was intended to satisfy the practical needs of the governing elite corps.

The defeat in 1945 brought about some modifications in the study of International Relations in Japan. During the period of the Allied Occupation (1945–52) both Political Science and International Relations were introduced in the curriculum of universities. However, the actual content of the curriculum of International Relations did not change overnight, as Diplomatic History, International Law and Economics retained – and continue to hold – major weight. At the same time, two new phenomena should be noted. First, the American approach to the study of International Relations has steadily permeated the curriculum. Second, American-style area studies have slowly expanded. The global expansion of Japan's external economic activities have contributed to both. Although International Relations has come to be regarded as a discipline, its fragmented structure, both intellectual and institutional, has not changed much. In this respect, Political Science is not very different from International Relations. As the intellectual structure of the discipline will be dealt with later on, it is necessary to summarise the institutional structure of International Relations here. To accomplish that task, it is necessary, if briefly, to touch upon the institutional structure of Political Science.

Indicative of the tenuous institutional foundation of Political Science and International Relations is the code scheme of academic disciplines used in the Ministry of Education for Scientific Research Grants-in-Aid (equivalent to the American National Science Foundation research grant programme). In it, Political Science is only one of the five fields of Law. Furthermore, International Relations does not exist as a category or sub-category! Those who submit proposals for research grants use such categories as History, Sociology, Anthropology, Geography, Economics or Political Science. No less indicative of the weak institutional foundation is the small number – in absolute terms – of departments of International Relations or of Political Science now existing in Japan. There are only a few Political Science Departments in Japan with the autonomous capacity to hire teaching staffs. About half of Political Science professors are members of Law Departments, where they are obliged to spend a more or less dependent, if not humiliating, existence. This is the legacy of the past *Staatslehre* tradition. Although there are more than a few International Relations departments in Japan, most of them suffer from a very fragmented character. Most typically, such departments are composed of those specialising in contemporary history, area studies, foreign languages, international economics and business, international law and international politics.

Despite all this, both Political Science and International Relations have their own academic associations: the Japanese Political Science Association (Nihon Seiji Gakkai) has about 1000 members, while the Japanese Association of International Relations (Nihon Kokusai Seiji Gakkai) also boasts a membership of about 1000. It appears that about 300 individuals have dual membership.[3] The relatively large size of these associations is essentially a reflection of the large number of Japanese universities and colleges – which amount to more than 400 with half of them concentrated in the greater Tokyo area.

The steady expansion of International Relations on campus has been attributed primarily to the rapid growth of general interest in international affairs that has accompanied the expansion of Japanese external economic activities. Its driving force seems to be rooted in the practical needs of government and the private business sector. It is thus not surprising to find that the research departments of the government ministries and leading business firms have contributed to the development of International Relations. Leading think-tanks which have close associations with various ministries such as the Japan Institute of International Affairs (Ministry of Foreign Affairs), the Research Institute for Peace and Security (Defence Agency), the Institute of Finance and Economics (Ministry of Finance), the Institute of Industry (Ministry of International Trade and Industry) and the Institute of Economic Research (Economic Planning Agency) produce books and papers with academics, business analysts and bureaucrats also participating in research projects. The same is the case with leading think tanks of private business firms such as the Nomura Research Institute and the Mitsubishi Research Institute. The same can be said of the National Institute for Research Advancement, the funding agency for think tanks.

14.2 MAJOR STRANDS OF INTELLECTUAL TRADITION IN INTERNATIONAL RELATIONS

Before discussing the intellectual structure of International Relations, it is necessary to touch on the following four major strands of intellectual tradition in the field that continue to affect its intellectual structure.[4] First, the *Staatslehre* tradition has remained strong even after 1945, and its major manifestation in International Relations is reflected in the emphasis on rich descriptive detail. In this tradition, top priority is given to supplying rich historical–institutional backgrounds and describing events and their consequences in detail. The purpose behind this is to help analyse signs of major international changes that might affect Japan's foreign relations. Pre-war period military studies and colonial studies were very much influenced by this tradition. Even after 1945, however, the bulk of area studies have continued along this tradition, especially when such studies are conducted by government-related think-tanks. However, most area studies as practised on university campuses are often 'excessively' humanistic, rather than social- scientific or policy-relevant.

Second, the Marxist tradition was very strong in International Relations from the 1920s through the 1960s. This is associated with the conception of social sciences as the *Oppositionswissenschaft*, or 'opposition science'. As if to counter the *Staatslehre* tradition, the strong Marxist tradition was clearly discernible during the period of the 1920s to the 1960s. Marxist categories of political analysis imparted a critical colouring to the observation of political events and the recognition of the ideological biases of the observer. In the 1920s, when the phrase 'social science' first came to be used, it often denoted Marxism, thus rendering the social sciences as synonymous with Marxism. Marxist influence became widespread after 1945, and from the immediate post-war period to the mid-1960s, the major social sciences – Economics, Political Science, and Sociology – were often led by Marxists or Marxist-leaning scholars. International Relations was no exception: Given the strong *Staatslehre* tradition and the continuation of one party dominance for more than three decades since the mid-1950s, it is considered natural or desirable for academics and journalists to be critical of government conduct as a sort of countervailing power.

The third strand is the historicist tradition. This tradition has been very strong, and renders the bulk of scholarship in International Relations akin to historical studies, a branch of humanistic studies rather than that of social science. This tradition is different from that of *Staatslehre* in that the historicist tradition does not pay much attention to policy relevance and that the topics covered tend to involve events and personalities prior to 1945. Somewhat similar to the Rankean conception of History, '*wie es eigentlich gewesen*' – or in Japanese parlance 'let the facts speak out' – characterises the spirit that tends to dominate much of International Relations. Cautious fact-finding and careful reconstruction of sequences and causes and effects constitute a large portion of these studies.

The fourth, and final, strand is the recent introduction of perspectives and methodologies from American Political Science. In the pre-war period the absorption of European social scientific thought – in the form of the works of Max Weber, Emile Durkheim, Leon Walras, and Alfred Marshall – constituted an antidote to the strong Marxist influence in the social science. After 1945 American social sciences played a similar role while American-style International Relations has many components, of which two are most important: being conscious of theories – i.e., attempting to formulate or to verify them – and being vigorous in empirical testing. This strand of intellectual tradition has become much stronger in the 1970s and 1980s.[5]

14.3 INTELLECTUAL STRUCTURE OF THE DISCIPLINE

The most important characteristic of the field of International Relations studies in Japan is its fragmented structure. As is clear from the preceding account of its development and major intellectual strands, Japanese International Relations has many faces and undercurrents. However, the following succinct profiles of the sub-fields of Japanese International Relations, and their respective publications, should enable the reader to grasp this complexity. The sub-fields are discussed in the following order: (1) international theories, (2) behavioural studies, (3) international political economy, (4) international organisations, (5) strategic studies, (6) peace research, (7) diplomatic history, and (8) area studies.

International Theories

A glance at college textbooks of International Relations enables one to grasp the flavour of Japanese treatment of theories of International Relations.[6] First, most textbooks tend to be historically oriented. Instead for instance, of tackling with major theoretical questions on the nature of the international system head on, most textbooks thus treat them in historical perspective. Indicative of this is the widespread proclivity of citing the works of certain types of major authors of International Relations textbooks. Only moderately theoretical authors are favoured. The works of K.J. Holsti provide such an example. Next in order of preference are historically oriented works, such as those of E.H. Carr, and those which are theoretical but not filled with excessive jargon, such as Hedley Bull. Second, the range of theories covered in textbooks is fairly wide. Those mainly American theories of International

Relations such as interdependence, state autonomy, hegemonic stability, transnational relations, world-systems theory, and policy co-ordination are often touched on. Needless to say, more traditional topics such as power, nation–states, war and peace, sovereignty, international law, and the international system are more comfortably treated therein. Also, explanations of such concepts as dependency, structural violence, deterrence and compellence, and mutually assured destruction are often given some space.

To sum up, the overall interest in 'big' theories is not very great. It seems that they are seriously considered only in so far as they are deemed useful in explaining or understanding certain empirical realities under investigation. One can easily get the false impression that Japan has absorbed the vast bulk of American International Relations by looking at the frequency of American authors appearing on Japanese studies of International Relations. But this mirage is rather due to the overall passivity of Japanese theoretical scholarship.

Behavioural Studies

This is a sub-field in which the American influence is manifested most clearly. About a dozen mostly American-trained Behaviouralists have published works on such subjects as the cognitive map of Japanese foreign policy makers, the exit-voice model of third world responses to dependency, US Congressional legislative behaviour, explanatory and predictive models of Soviet–Japanese fishery negotiations, and Chinese conflict behaviour.[7] The number of those engaged in this kind of research has been gradually increasing. Still the overall acceptance of American Behavioural studies is not very high.

International Political Economy

This sub-field has been growing steadily. One such indication is that works on a wide range of related subjects have been published in the 1980s. Included among these recent studies are: game-theoretic analysis of economic policy co-ordination, cost–benefit analyses of Pax Americana and Pax Britannica, state-centred frameworks of international political economy, world-systemic analysis of US policy toward the Eastern Mediterranean, the structural properties of the emerging international system, Japan–United States economic conflicts, the political economy of Japan's international relations.[8]

It is clear that the foremost attention has been paid in this sub-field to such questions as the nature of the international system, past, present, and future, and Japan's role therein. Moreover, the American influence is easily discernible in this sub-field.

International Organisation

From the immediate post-war period until the mid-1960s, the United Nations was a favoured topic among those specialising in International Relations and Law. Although Japanese enthusiasm for the United Nations has subsided since that time, major works in this sub-field include those dealing with third world solidarity in UNCTAD, UN voting behaviour, and international law covering arms control.[9]

Strategic Studies

There are two major factors which have long stifled Strategic Studies in Japan. First, the widespread pacifism or the inhibition originating from the defeat in the Second World War has long discouraged the development of strategic studies. Anything that smacks of war and military affairs has been stifled. Constitutionally and otherwise, this barrier has been very significant. Second, even as the psychological inhibition has slowly subsided, the fact that Japan's strategy has been predicated upon its alliance with the United States has seemed to discourage serious studies by Japanese analysts on their own initiative. Only recently has Japan become more interested in Strategic Studies. One can argue that the most noteworthy accomplishment in this field is the annual publication of *Asian Security* by the Research Institute for Peace and Security.[10] This annual survey provides a quite detailed and reasonably balanced assessment of international security matters in the Asia–Pacific region, leaving global East–West strategic issues for publications of other noted institutions such as the International Institute for Strategic Studies and the Stockholm International Peace Research Institute. Also noteworthy is the increasing contribution from Japan to the debate on international security management.[11]

Peace Research

As pacifism has been a dominant factor in the psychology of the Japanese people after 1945, it is not difficult to fathom the reason for the fact that peace research has been one of the relatively important sub-fields of International Relations studies in Japan. The underlying concern of much of the peace research seems to have been concerned with how to avoid the kind of situation which might lead Japan to another war. Its favourite topics are, to take a few examples, East–West relations, Japanese defence build-up, structural violence in the third world, opposition to United States bases, Japanese barbarism in Asia during the Second World War, human rights under developmental authoritarianism, and Japan's economic aid and its negative consequences.[12] In terms of its theoretical foundation, however, Japanese peace research has been largely content to absorb innovations from abroad, such as those of Johan Galtung, Dieter Senghaas, Samir Amin, and Anatol Rapoport, rather than producing its own creative ideas.

Diplomatic History

This sub-field is the oldest pillar in the edifice of the Japanese study of International Relations. Not only those trained in History, but also a large share of those originally from Political Science or International Relations, are drawn into the study of diplomatic history. The most popular subjects have been modern Japanese diplomatic history, and United States–Japanese and Sino-Japanese relations between the mid-nineteenth century through the Occupation period of 1945–52. Although many studies have been made, few have ventured to write broad-gauged pieces on topics such as war and peace in the twentieth century.[13] Rather, most diplomatic historians work meticulously on absorbing details of diplomatic history, always driven by the search for more new documents. Yet, because the Japanese government holds its diplomatic documents longer than other governments, such as those of the United States or the United Kingdom, many Japanese diplomatic historians are frustrated in their work. As for the study of diplomatic history outside the realm of immediate concerns, Japanese contributions have not been very great. Notable exceptions are the work of the late Masataka Banno on mid-nineteenth century Chinese diplomatic history, and Akira Iriye's American diplomatic history.[14]

Area Studies

The fact, mentioned above, that Area Studies is not differentiated from International Relations is interesting in and of itself. In this respect, Japanese International Relations is similar to that of France.[15] In fact, Area Studies specialists account for more than one third of the membership of the Japanese Association of International Relations, with less than one third considered theoreticians and less than one third considered diplomatic historians. Of all the regions of the world, East Asia – comprising China, Korea and Vietnam – enjoys the largest number of specialists. Works on such topics as Chinese local politics, Chinese defence and the People's Liberation Army, the Chinese political system in transition, Chinese political elites, developmental authoritarianism in Taiwan, Vietnam's independent foreign policy, and Korean democratisation movements have recently been published.

Southeast Asia follows East Asia in terms of the size of its corps of specialists. Works on such topics as the nature of Southeast Asian patrimonial states, Indonesian nationalism, ethnic relations in Indochina, and the Japanese in Southeast Asia during the Second World War are noteworthy. The fact that both East Asia and Southeast Asia are, for geographical and historical reasons, closer to Japan is the primary factory for the relative popularity of area studies on these two regions.

It might come as a small surprise to find that Japanese specialists on the Soviet Union and the United States are not particularly numerous. The relative paucity of Japanese Soviet studies seems to be proportional to the Japanese sense of dependence on the US security umbrella, aimed as it is, primarily against the Soviet Union. In other words, the relative lack of Soviet security threat perceived by the Japanese people has not encouraged them to study the Soviet Union very seriously. More recently, however, a few serious solid works have emerged with a focus on Stalinist politics, post-war Soviet political elites, and Soviet military policy.

The poverty of American studies in Japan has been attributed to the comfort of dependence of Japanese Americanists *vis-à-vis* institutional-cum-financial ties with the United States. There have been no vigorous efforts at enlarging the corps of Americanists as if the size of membership and the amount of benefit from such membership go against each other. It is not surprising, given the steady economic integration between both countries, to find that non-Americanists, whether they are academics or businessmen or bureaucrats, who are forced to know about the economy, politics, law and society of the United States, have a deeper, more accurate knowledge of the subject than many Americanists. Aside from the distinction between Americanists and non-Americanists, various works have been published on such topics as American neo-conservatism, Congressional legislative staffs, Congressional elections at the grass roots level, and American agriculture as a pressure group.

Japanese Europeanists do not fare any better than the Americanists or Sovietologists. Some noteworthy recent works among them include: an Anglo–Japanese comparison of local politicians, German–Japanese comparison of political leadership in the immediate post-war period, and a comparative historical sociology of Europe.

Japanese area studies on the Middle East, Latin America, South Asia, Africa and Australia cannot boast of much accomplishment either. Of these, the Middle East and Latin America have been given significant attention by Japanese area specialists recently if only because of the Japanese economic interest therein.

It is clear from the admittedly rough sketch of Japanese area studies that they are stronger *vis-à-vis* areas geographically adjacent to Japan in East and Southeast Asia, rather than other developing areas, a fact that is explained largely by the geographical-historical affinity and close economic interactions with these areas. Also clear is the fact that they are not particularly strong on North America or the Soviet Union – a fact which can be explained by the peculiarities of the perception of security threat from the Soviet Union and the pervasive need to adapt to the economic interdependence with the United States respectively.

14.4 CURRENT DIRECTIONS

Two major concerns underlie the recent Japanese Study of International Relations. One involves the nature and properties of the emerging international system and the other involves the role and responsibility of Japan therein. The rapid devolution of Pax Americana – from the height of American power in the mid-1960s to the recent low in terms of the value of the dollar, industrial competitiveness, financial indebtedness, and military prowess – has led many students of International Relations in Japan to probe into these questions, inasmuch as Japan's position in the international system is largely predicated upon its friendship with the United States both in terms of economics and security. Four long term scenarios now being discussed in Japan may help to convey the atmosphere of such discussions.[16]

The first scenario is called the 'Pax Americana - Mark Two'.[17] This scenario forecasts the comeback of a strong America shortly after the current difficulties are largely overcome, anticipating vigorous technological innovation, economic recovery, and the skilful use of American power in the international arena. This scenario is most palatable to many Japanese in that international security tasks continue to be shouldered largely by the United States. The second scenario is that of 'Bigemony' or 'Amerippon'. This scenario extrapolates the current trend of a massive economic integration between two economies into the future. In this scheme, the United States and Japan constitute a largely integrated economy (the 'NichiBei economy', or the 'United States–Japan economy' in the singular form) and exert joint world leadership according to some form of appropriate division of labour. This scenario is no less comfortable to many Japanese for the same reason as above. The third scenario is that of 'Pax Consortis', or world management through myriad consultations and co-ordination among major world peers, including the United States. This scenario captures the imagery of policy co-ordination in international economic affairs, while assuming tacitly that strategic nuclear arsenals will cease to be a major factor in International Relations in the future. The fourth scenario is that of 'Pax Nipponica'. This scenario tends to focus on rapid Japanese advances in the countries of international economic activities, and tacitly assumes the declining significance of the use of military, especially nuclear, power in international relations.

Needless to say, most academic studies are devoted to the description and explanation of various aspects the historical and contemporary international systems and their components. The point here, however, is that although these concerns are kept inside, they are surely one of the major factors which has led many students of International Relations in Japan to move more vigorously in the expansion and consolidation of Japanese International Relations, however fragmented and feeble its institutional and intellectual structures are. It would be most interesting to see whether or not the field is shifting out of its preoccupation for 'practical' concerns toward an emphasis on theory-building of sorts, something that might be expected from scholars in an increasingly important world power like Japan.

NOTES AND REFERENCES

* The author gratefully acknowledges the comments on an earlier draft by Brian Woodall.

1. For pre-1960 development, see Kawata Tadashi, *Kokusai kankei gairon* (Outline of International Relations) (University of Tokyo Press, 1958). For later development, see, *inter alia*, the Japanese Association of International Relations (ed.), *Sengo Nihon no kokusai seijigaku* (International Relations Studies in Japan since the Second World War) (Yuhikaku, 1979), and Institute of International Relations, Sophia University (ed.), *Nihon niokeru kokusai kankei kenkyu, chiiki kenkyu no jittai hokoku* (International Relations and Area Studies in Japan) (National Institute for Research Advancement, 1986).

2. For the pre-1945 development, see Royama Masamichi, *Nihon ni okeru Kindai seijigaku no hattatsu* (The Development of Modern Political Science in Japan) (Jitsugyo no Nihon sha, 1949). For the more recent development, see Takashi Inoguchi, 'Japan', in William G. Andrews (ed.), *The International Handbook of Political Science* (Westport, Conn.: Greenwood Press, 1982), pp. 207–18; Takashi Inoguchi, 'Tradition and Adaptation in a Segmented Community: Development and Institutionalization of Japanese Political Science Since 1945', paper prepared for presentation at the Symposium on the Development and Institutionalisation of Political Science, Helsinki, 2–8 October, 1985; Takashi Inoguchi, 'Nihon no seijigaku community' (Japanese Political Science Community), *University Press* (Spring 1986), pp. 22–31; Takashi Inoguchi, 'Kiro ni tatsu Nihon no shakaikagaku' (Japanese Social Science at a Crossroad), *Chuo koron* (June 1981), pp. 222–36; Takashi Ingouchi, 'Kokusaika jidai no koto kyoiku' (Higher Education at a Time of Internationalization), *Chuo koron* (November 1985), pp. 282–304.

3. See Takashi Inoguchi, 'Nihon no seijigaku community', and 'Tradition and Adaptation in a Segmented Community'.

4. See Takashi Inoguchi, 'Japan', and 'Tradition and Adaptation in a Segmented Community'.

5. See Takashi Inoguchi, 'International Relations', in *An Introductory Bibliography for Japanese Studies in Social Sciences 1981–1985* (Bonjinsha forthcoming, 1988); Takashi Inoguchi, 'Nihon ni okeru nikaku seijigaku no hatten to tenbo' (Comparative Politics: Its Development and Prospect), *Nihon seiji gakkai nempo* (Annals of the Japanese Political Science Association), (Iwanami shoten, 1988).

6. K.J. Holsti compares the study of international relations in Japan with those in other countries in his *The Dividing Discipline: Hegemony and Diversity in International Relations* (London: Allen & Unwin, 1985). It must be noted that his methodology of systematically counting authors' names cited in representative International Relations textbooks gives some limit to his observations, especially on Japan. The selection of textbooks happens to include mostly outdated ones. My own

selection would include: Kawata Tadashi, *Kokusai kankei no seiji keizaigaku* (The Political Economy of International Relations) (NHK Books, 1980); Takashi Inoguchi, *Kokusai seiji keizai no kozu* (International Political Economy) (Yuhikaku Publishers, 1982); Eto Shinkichi *et al.*, *Kokusai kankeiron* (International Relations) (University of Tokyo Press, 1982); Urano Tatsumi, *Kokusai kankeiron no sai kosei* (Reconstructing International Relations) (Nansosha, 1985).

7. Yamamoto Yoshinobu and Tani Akira, 'Ninchi to seisaku kettei' (Cognition and Policymaking), *Nihon seiji gakkai nempo* (Annals of the Japanese Political Science Association) (Iwanami shoten, 1984), pp. 67–88; Kuniko Inoguchi, 'Exit and Voice: The Third World Responses to Dependency Since OPEC's Initiative', in Charles W. Kegley and Patrick McGowan (eds), *The Political Economy of Foreign Policy Behavior* (Beverly Hills: Sage 1981), pp. 255–76; Kuniko Inoguchi, 'Third World Responses to OPEC: The External Dimension', in Harold Jacobson and Dusan Sidjanski (eds), *The Emerging International Economic Order: Dynamic Processes, Constraints, and Opportunities* (Beverly Hills: Sage, 1982), pp. 171–206; Ikuo Kabashima and Hideo Sato, 'Local Content and Congressional Politics: Interest Group Theory and Foreign Policy Implications', *International Studies Quarterly* (Vol. 30, No. 3, September 1986), pp. 295–314; Takashi Inoguchi and Nobuharu Miyatake, 'The Politics of Derementalism: The Case of Soviet–Japanese Salmon Catch Negotiations, 1957–1977', *Behavioral Science*, (Vol. 23, No. 6 (November 1978), pp. 457–469; Takashi Inoguchi and Nobuharu Miyatake, 'Negotiation as Quasi- Budgeting: The Salmon Catch Negotiations between Two World Fishery Powers', *International Organization* (Vol. 33, No. 2, Spring 1979), pp. 229-256; Akihiko Tanaka, 'China, China-Watching and CHINA- WATCHER', in Donald A. Sylvan and Steve Chan (eds), *Foreign Policy Decision-Making: Perception, Cognition and Artificial Intelligence* (New York: Praeger, 1984), pp. 123–39; Tanaka Akihiko, 'Internal–External Linkage in Chinese International Conflict Behavior: A Macro-Model', *Journal of North-East Asian Studies* (Vol. 11, No. 1, March 1983), pp. 53–65.

8. Koichi Hamada, *The Political Economy of International Monetary Interdependence* (MIT Press, 1985); Sakamoto Masahiro, *Pax Americana no kokusai system* (The International System of Pax Americana) (Yuhikaku Publishers, 1986); Takashi Inoguchi, *Kokusai seiji keizai no kozu* (International Political Economy) (Yuhikaku Publishers, 1982); Yui Daizaburo, *Sengo sekai chitsujo no keisei: Amerika shihonshugi to higashi chichukai chiiki 1944–1947* (The Construction of the Postwar World Order: American Capitalism and the East Mediterranean, 1944–1947), University of Tokyo Press, 1985; Inouchi Kuniko, *Post-haken system to Nihon no sentaku* (The Emerging Post-Hegemonic System and Choices for Japan) (Chikuma shobo, 1987); Sato Hideo, *et al.*, *NichiBei keizai funso no kaimei* (Japan–US Economic Conflicts) (Nihon keizai shimbunsha, 1983); Kusano Atsushi, *NichiBei Orange kosho* (Japan–US Negotiations on Citrus Import) (Nihon keizai shimbunsha, 1985); Takashi

Inoguchi, *Kokusai kankei no seiji keizaigaku: Nihon no yakuwari to sentaku* (The Political Economy of International Relations: Japan's Roles and Choice) (University of Tokyo Press, 1986).

9. Sato Yukio, *Gendai no kokusai soshiki: Kokuren senmon kikan no seijika to Daisan sekai no taiyo* (Contemporary International Organisations: The Politicisation of UN institutions and the Third World) (Ningen kagakusha, 1982); Kurosawa Mitsuru, *Gunshuku kokusaiho no atarashii shiza: kakuheiki fukakusan taisei no kenkyu* (New Perspectives on International Law Covering Arms Control: A Study of Non-proliferation of Nuclear Weapons) (Yushindo, 1984); Ryo Oshiba, 'Budgetmaking in the United Nations Development Program', *International Studies Quarterly* (Vol. 29, No. 3, September 1985), pp. 313–326.

10. It is published by *Asagumo shimbunsha* annually in English and in Japanese separately.

11. Recent ones include: Masashi Nishihara, *East Asian Security and the Trilateral Countries* (New York: New York University Press, 1986); Yukio Sato, 'The Evolution of Japanese Security Policy' (London: International Institute for Strategic Studies, Adelphi Paper No. 212, 1986); Hisahiko Okazaki, *Strategic Thinking* (London: Brassey's, 1987); Takashi Inoguchi, 'Trade, Technology and Security: Implications for East Asia and the West' (London: International Institute for Strategic Studies, Adelphi Papers No. 218, 1987), pp. 39–55.

12. Shindo Eiichi (ed.), *Heiwa senryaku no kozu* (Peace Strategy) (Nihon hyoronsha, 1986); Sakamoto Yoshikazu (ed.), *Boryoku to heiwa* (Violence and Peace) (Asahi shimbunsha, 1982); Tanaka Naoki, *Gunkaku n. hikeizdigaku* (Anti-Economics of Military Buildup) (Asahi shimbunsha, 1982); United Nations University and Institute for Asian Studies of Soka University (eds), *Asian Refugees* (Ochanomizu shobo, 1986); Bamba Nobuya, *Chikyu bunka no yukue* (Whither World Culture?) (University of Tokyo Press, 1983); Nihon Heiwa gakkai, *Heiwagaku* (Peace Research), 4 vols, (Waseda University Press, 1983–1987).

13. Iriye Akira, *20 seiki no senso to heiwa* (War and Peace in the Twentieth Century) (Tokyo: University of Tokyo, 1986).

14. Masataka Banno, *China and the West 1858–1861: the Origins of the Tsungli Yamen* (Harvard: Harvard University Press, 1964); Akira Iriye, *After Imperialism: the Search for a New Order in the Far East, 1921–1931* (Harvard: Harvard University Press, 1965); Akira Iriye, *Pacific Estrangement: Japanese and American Expansion, 1897–1911* (Harvard: Harvard University Press, 1972); Akira Iriye, *Power and Culture: the Japanese-American War, 1941–1945* (Harvard: Harvard University Press, 1981).

15. See Professor Smouts's study (Chapter 11 in this volume). The limit on length forces me not to give citation to those works mentioned under the rubric of area studies.

16. Takashi Inoguchi, 'Tenkanki Nihon no kadai' (Japan's Tasks at a Time of Transition), *Nihon keizai shimbun* (1, 8, 15, 22, 29 November, 1987). See also Takashi Inoguchi, 'Japan's Images and Options: Not a Challenger, But a Supporter', *Journal of Japanese*

Studies (Vol. 12, No. 1, Winter 1986), pp. 95–115; Takashi Inoguchi, 'Japan's Foreign Policy Background', in Herbert J. Ellison, (ed.), *Japan and the Pacific Quadrille: The Major Powers in East Asia* (Boulder, Col.: Westview Press, 1987), pp. 81–105; Takashi Inoguchi, *Tadanori to Ikkoku hanei shugi o koete* (Beyond Free Ride and 'Prosperity in One Country') (Toyo keizai shimposha, 1987); Takashi Inoguchi, 'The Ideas and Structure of Japan's Foreign Policy', in Takashi Inoguchi and Daniel I. Okimoto (eds), *The Political Economy of Japan, Vol. II: The Changing International Context* (Stanford: Stanford University Press, 1988) pp. 23–63, 490–500.

17. These scenarios are drawn from the works of such authors as Robert Keohane, Murakami Yasusuke, C. Fred Bergsten, Zbigniew Brzezinski, Robert Gilpin, Inoguchi Kuniko, and Ezra Vogel.

15 The Study of International Relations in the United Kingdom

Christopher Hill

The notion of a 'British school' of International Relations has become common currency over the last decade, certainly among the British themselves. Roy Jones has strongly attacked the illusions of the English approach (*sic*), with its supposed emphasis on the existence of a discrete international society; Steve Smith has written on the contrast with American approaches (and encouraged colleagues on the same path), and Gene Lyons has reviewed recent literature from the United Kingdom for readers of *World Politics*.[1] They all assume the existence of a distinctive British perspective and school of thought on International Relations, although none are so naive as to pretend that this school does not overlap with other national traditions, or that it does not have internal divisions of its own.

Given, then, that the problems of discussing a British school have been dealt with extensively, there is no need to cover the same ground. It is clear to any reasonable observer:

1. That a sufficiently homogeneous intellectual grouping exists among British students of International Relations for us to be able to distinguish it at least from the other two major national traditions in the West, namely those of France and the United States.

2. That the British have made an important intellectual contribution to the development of the subject, even if they have increasingly been swamped, in terms of quantity of output, by the vast American academic machine;.

3. That there are signs of the enduring concerns of British writers on International Relations attracting general interest again, after two decades in which the tide of fashion has been running against them. This is paralleled by an increasing

willingness in Britain itself to assimilate aspects of the American approach, now that the duel of honour between 'scientific' and 'traditional' methodologies has passed into history.

The important question following from these three pre-suppositions, will be taken to be: what is happening in British International Relations circles at present? Three different dimensions will be considered in the attempt at an answer – the disciplinary, relating to the areas of current preoccupation and new thinking among professionals in the subject; the sociological, dealing with the relations between International Relations and other subject disciplines, as well as its status in British universities, and the way it is taught; and the political, in terms of the importance (or lack of it) of the academic subject to British attitudes on foreign policy and the wider world, both at the popular and decisional levels.

The most important level to consider is clearly the intellectual. What contribution is British scholarship making to the development of the subject of International Relations? No amount of well-taught courses or well-designed textbooks can substitute for significant input in terms of new ideas, if we are to presume to a place near the centre of the International Relations community and not to be relegated to the service industry periphery. This will be an uphill struggle. There is no point in pretending that British writers on International Relations have so far made as much of an impact on their foreign colleagues as have their equivalents in the arts, or other areas such as political philosophy. Apart perhaps from E.H. Carr, the path-breakers in the field, from Morgenthau and Deutsch, through Waltz and Allison to Keohane and Nye, have been primarily American. This is inevitable to a degree: countries smaller than the United States are, in the way of things, only going to throw up the occasional giant in the field, such as Raymond Aron in France. Moreover, many excellent books get swamped in the sheer tide of material (some of it ethnocentric) which distracts American students from outside work. F.S. Northedge, Joseph Frankel, Roy Jones and others are not read as much outside these shores as their ideas deserve.

Despite the structural difficulties, there are signs that work is being done in Britain which will turn out to have made a notable contribution to the evolution of International Relations as a subject, when the intellectual histories come to be written in the next century. This is the case mostly in terms of refining or extending existing lines of enquiry, rather than suggesting a new paradigm. One might be forgiven for thinking that those who strain for newness above all things are bound to be forced back into rediscovering the wheel, such is the febrile pace of academic fashion-mongering. It is not a fault, for example, that the steadily more important British school of foreign policy analysis takes many of its cues from American literature (although there is a certain circularity here; Kenneth Boulding, Colin Gray and others are, like Cary Grant and Bob Hope, English exports). It is a sign of confidence that writers like William Wallace, James Barber and Steve Smith have been able to draw on transatlantic work without either reacting defensively against it, or swallowing it wholesale. The work that has already been completed, or is in the process of being done, on pressure-groups and foreign policy, on the implementation process and on the significance of belief-systems is worth attention beyond the British circuit.

The study of international institutions continues to be a major branch of International Relations activity in Britain, admirably resisting the dictates of intellectual fashion. The accumulation over decades of expertise on the history, administration, and constitutions of international organisations (IO) has in recent years been supplemented by sophisticated work on their behaviour and functions. This owes something to decision-making analysis, and something to the 'regimes' approach of Nye and Keohane, but because of the existing tradition onto which it is grafted, it has a solid historical and philosophical base.

The area of strategic studies in Britain is even more well-integrated with its American counterparts than is foreign policy analysis, while still retaining its identity. The founding and continued success of the International Institute for Strategic Studies (IISS) in London, and the Arms and Disarmament Information Unit in Sussex (ADIU), together with the international reputations of several individual scholars, ensures that the British perspective is not ignored. This is an area, like many in International Relations, where politics and academe come close together. There is scope for a distinctive British (increasingly West European) contribution to strategic thinking partly because of the fault-lines in the Atlantic Alliance itself, just as the articulation of a European tradition of thinking about war will itself have policy implications. This has been particularly evident in recent debates about arms control on the one hand, and deterrence on the other. To put it at its lowest, there is in Britain an established tradition of writing on the role of force in modern international society, and of its place in the history of strategic thought, from

Sun Ziu to Clausewitz and Liddell Hart. The debate is calm and rational, resisting (on the whole) both technical obscurantism and political posturing. It is of vital importance that such thinking is not confined to the think-tanks in Washington and Moscow, and Britain certainly provides a vital alternative point of reference.

One should not exaggerate the extent to which institutions like the IISS are independent of American intellectual influences. One of the main concerns of IISS is, after all, to make the strategic debate transnational. This is also increasingly true of the Royal Institute of International Affairs (RIIA), which is beginning to chafe under the constitutional restriction of limiting its membership to British citizens alone. At the intellectual level it is clearly concerned not to be restricted to parochial British concerns. Nonetheless, the RIIA, together with university institutions like the London School of Economics and the School of Oriental and African Studies in London, provide the United Kingdom with a rich source of specialised knowledge on those parts of the world with which the British have historically had most to do (which is to say, a large part of the earth's surface). The tradition of area studies is particularly well-developed in Britain, and makes possible easy co-operation between both experts in the internal affairs of individual countries, and those whose focus is more the pattern of international relations of an entire regional sub-system. Although government cuts in public expenditure are beginning to threaten this comparative advantage, particularly with respect to Latin American and African politics, there is still immense strength across a range of different areas and cultures. The practical, let alone intellectual importance of such a tradition has been brought home by the Islamic resurgence, which has highlighted the knowledge and skills of many otherwise neglected British experts, and the belated recognition by the present government that the United States is luring away from this country the best part of a generation of experts on Soviet foreign policy.

The richness of regional specialisms within British international studies is closely connected to the strength of scholarship on the third world, which also arises from the Imperial past and the Commonwealth present. There can be little doubt that within the field of development studies, which is obviously difficult to keep distinguished from parts of International Relations, such centres as the Institute for Development Studies at Sussex, and both the Institute of Commonwealth Studies and the Overseas Development Institute in London, are among the most active groups. The nature of foreign aid has perhaps been debated more effectively in Britain (for example by Bauer, Cassen, Hayter, and White) than elsewhere, while the still neglected subject of the external relations of developing states has been stimulated largely by the writings (and doctoral supervisions) of British academics such as Christopher Clapham and James Mayall.

So far, the emphasis has been on scholarship with a clear practical relationship to the world of policy, rather than on work of a more general, theoretical, kind. It is true that many of the strengths of the British approach to International Relations lie in the areas of clear-sighted empiricism. However, it would be foolish to stop at this point, with a seeming confirmation of the stereotype of British academics, like politicians, being wedded to pragmatism and distrustful of ideas. This would be only a half-truth, if truth it be. One of the most innovative areas in modern British scholarship in International Relations has been precisely concerned with the broad brush, and alternative conceptualisations of international relations – namely that of international political economy (IPE). This relatively new subject, now spawning courses and degrees after years in the ante-rooms of the conference circuit, owes a good deal to Susan Strange and her determination to challenge the American liberal orthodoxies on international economic relations.

The acceleration of interest in international political economy throughout the academic community, not excluding the United States, has some important origins in the United Kingdom partly because the British tradition makes a virtue of the proximity of political science to politics proper. Instead of trying to emulate the natural sciences with their supposedly value-free methods of analysis, British writers of most ideological persuasions have accepted that their work is always going to reflect some kind of preference-ordering, whether or not it is designed to influence the events of the day. This has meant that it has been more natural for the British school than for more hard-edged social scientists, to tackle directly the semi-normative debates involved in the study of such phenomena as imperialism, the international trading order, mercantilism, or the demands for economic justice. Under the auspices of the British International Studies Association (which is a relatively small but close-knit and intellectually active grouping), a team of specialists has emerged over the last fifteen years which is likely to be as influential as any in setting the terms of the debate in this important sub-area of International Relations, as it continues to grow during the 1990s.

It has been argued so far that the most active areas of discussion in the International Relations community in Britain are currently foreign policy analysis, IO, strategic studies, regional studies, and IPE. There are, however, other important strands to the British tradition, which extend more widely and have more to do with the connections which International Relations makes with other academic subjects. This brings us to the second, sociology of knowledge, aspect of our main theme. The inherently multidisciplinary nature of International Relations, with its huge scope and myriad loan-words, has been positively embraced in the United Kingdom. Subject rivalries exist – IPE for instance has not yet managed to do more than attract the odd dissident from mainstream Economics – but in general there is a good deal of cross-fertilisation with other disciplines. This has been particularly true with regard to History, Law and Political Theory, and is beginning to be so with Sociology. So far as History is concerned, the fact that many British teachers of International Relations were themselves trained as historians, together with the strong awareness of Britain's past as a great power, has tended to reinforce the existing historical orientation of the subject here. This is both a strength and weakness: sensitivity towards context and change is balanced out by a continued resistance in some quarters to a comparative or conceptual approach – for example, in the areas of integration theory, or decision-making analysis.

International law has been at the heart of thinking about International Relations right from the beginning of International Relations as an academic subject, whether in Britain, the United States, or continental Europe. Since the 1920s the relationship between the two subjects has varied a good deal over time and place, but it has not been broken. In the United Kingdom the connection with international law has remained strong and fruitful at both direct and indirect levels. Scholars like Rosalyn Higgins and Adam Roberts work at the interface of the subjects, in the tradition of Louis Henkin, showing how law affects foreign policy through setting norms, expectations, and practical frameworks. Indirectly, through the work of Charles Manning, and those variously influenced by him, such as F.S. Northedge and Alan James, legal considerations have also been an important influence on those conceptions of an 'international society' which are so central to the British school of writing on International Relations. On this view, a community of states (and indeed peoples) cannot rest solely on formal rules and obligations: it is impossible in any case to get agreement on the establishment of such rules, let alone their observance. But equally, without the capacity to formalise those agreements which are to be kept, or to have disputes adjudicated, the political institutions of international society will work less effectively. The general adherence to this line of argument in the British school has therefore led not just to the study (sometimes stigmatised as 'traditionalist') of arrangements like the balance of power, diplomacy, and various principles of 'order', but also to an extensive tradition of writing about actual international negotiations, drawing on law, political science and history. In both halves of the equation British expertise is well-developed. If the pattern of American oscillation between idealism and introspection ever settles down into a Grotian compromise, then the work done in the United Kingdom will come into sharper focus.

The development of 'international theory', in the sense of a normative and speculative debate about the nature of international politics and the dilemmas it throws up, has been especially marked in Britain. Closely connected to the discussion of international law has been a receptivity towards political philosophers and what they have to say about inter-state relations. Hobbes, Rousseau, Kant, Hegel, Marx, Mill and the like have thus been pressed into service as the founding fathers of the subject of International Relations on this side of the Atlantic. If this has risked anachronism at times, it has brought with it the benefit of an appreciation of the intellectual history underlying the present states system, and a proper level of preparation for the discussion of perennially important ideas like justice, autonomy and statehood. For those (and they are a growing number) who feel that the great issues of political theory are increasingly played out in the international realm, the ground has been well-prepared by the British school of what Butterfield and Wight called 'diplomatic investigations'.

The last area of inter-disciplinary activity on the British scene worth noting relates to sociology. Max Weber, the elite theorists, and those concerned with organisational behaviour have been assimilated into the study of foreign policy-making in Britain as elsewhere. What is perhaps more striking is the importance of figures such as Ernest Gellner, in stimulating discussions on such matters as the nature of nationalism, and John Burton, who gathered round him a group (the Centre for the Analysis of Conflict) dedicated to relating the analysis of international conflict to the analysis of conflict in general. This latter group draws on a wide range of literature in their anatomy of a 'world society', which is seen as including but also transcending, relations between governments. In recent years there has also been the emergence of considerable interest in 'historical sociology'. The lead of Wallerstein and Braudel has been followed in Britain by sociologists like Michael Mann and John Hall, who find an increasing number of interlocutors within mainstream International Relations.

Before leaving the theme of International Relation's academic relationships, it is important to say something about the current status of the subject in British universities. Here the news is mildly encouraging, despite the general paucity of funds and jobs from which all higher education in the United Kingdom currently suffers. Whereas for decades those working in the field of International Relations have had to put up with, in its benign form, patronising supervision, and more malignly, imperialism or sabotage from longer established subject-areas such as History or Political Science, the contemporary atmosphere is far more positive. It is true that (where it exists at all) International Relations struggles to achieve a separate departmental identity. Mostly it operates within the broad structure of Government or Political Science departments. But occasionally an 'International Studies' formulation brings together different departments on equal terms, as at Birmingham, while independent departments of International Relations (in rough order of size) exist at the LSE, Aberystwyth, North Staffordshire Polytechnic, and Keele. International Relations is also a significant force at Aberdeen, Cambridge, Cardiff, City, Coventry Polytechnic, East Anglia, Kent, Lancaster, Oxford, St Andrews, Southampton, Surrey, Sussex, Trent Polytechnic and Warwick. In other words, the subject is now well-established and has survived the worst of times in better shape than most.

This is partly the result of there being very strong interest in the subject from consumers, that is students, and practitioners such as civil servants, journalists and businessmen. While the social sciences in general have given ground before neo-conservative scepticism, International Relations has flourished. At the LSE it ranks with Law and Accountancy as the subjects most in demand with students. This is broadly the state of affairs around the country, and there must be many university finance committees which have looked with relief at the ability of International Relations courses to attract foreign students and their fees. To some extent this is caused by the fact that public interest in global problems is at last beginning to develop. But it is also a reflection of the very real strengths of the teaching of the subject in this country. The kind of eclecticism described above, with practical wisdom, theoretical range and normative debate all highly valued, is a stimulating combination, while the emphasis placed in most British faculties on good teaching and personal contact with students reaps its own reward. It should also not be forgotten that Commonwealth contacts are still important (although not to be taken for granted, as shown by Malaysia's redirecting of its students to the United States after a recent clash with Britain). Together with the advantage of the English language, this means that British writings on International Relations, and courses in our colleges, find a ready market in many countries of the world. The reputation of the BBC External Services, on which some academics broadcast, helps not a little in this regard.

The last part of the triad of the analysis – the political significance of scholarship in International Relations – need not detain us long. As suggested above, decision-makers responsible for the conduct of British external relations have, over the last decade or so, shown a much higher level of interest in professional International Relations, as opposed to individual professors of Government or History with a taste for contemporary foreign policy. Some International Relations students have started to appear in the ranks of the Diplomatic Service and Ministry of Defence (MOD), while both the Foreign and Commonwealth Office and the MOD send members regularly to academic conferences or seminars. The latter also sponsors several lectureships in defence studies around the country. It is clear that at least the newer generation of officials and politicians appreciates the need both to absorb some of the special expertise available in the universities (if mostly of the empirical variety) and to be well-informed about the nature of the academic debate on international relations, which may in the long run have a profound effect of public perceptions of foreign policy. F.A. Hayek once said that he preferred to work in the realm of ideas because ultimately that was the way to exercise real power. It looks as if practitioners in Britain, who have always been resistant to the discussion of theory and concepts, are now at least half-persuaded of this argument in the context of international relations.

At the popular level, it cannot really be said that there is much awareness of the work being done by International Relations scholars in Britain, even if the general will is being indirectly influenced in the way just suggested. A relatively small proportion of the population goes to university, and International Relations is a minor subject within the system of higher education as a whole. Yet gradually, through the frequent appearances of academics on the more serious radio and TV programmes, and through the work of many International Relations-trained staff in polytechnics, colleges and schools, an awareness of the issues at stake is beginning to seep down through society at large. The Open University in particular has shown a positive interest in the dissemination of the International Relations literature, and has produced excellent materials of its own. An 'A' level examination for 18-year-olds in International Relations is at last in prospect, although whether the subject is appropriate for that level is questionable (in any case, it may not survive the imminent reform of the tertiary examination system).

It will take a generation or more for the preoccupations of International Relations scholars to start being more widely shared in British society, even if terms like 'interdependence', 'perception', and now 'cognitive dissonance' are beginning to appear in the everyday language of the educated. Yet it has taken 60 years for the subject to become accepted as a legitimate form of serious scholarship in the university world itself, and we should not be surprised if our efforts do not seem to be immediately appreciated by politicians or public opinion. The pace of change in the wider world, and Britain's total immersion in it, will slowly compel certain changes in consciousness. In any event, it falls to the academic to forswear glory today for influence tomorrow, and at least International Relations in Britain is now in a position to have some long-term effect.

NOTES AND REFERENCES

1.   See Roy Jones, 'The English School of International Relations: A Case for Closure', *Review of International Studies* (Vol. 7, No. 1, 1981), pp. 1–13; Steve Smith (ed.), *International Relations: British and American Perspectives* (Oxford: Basil Blackwell in association with the British International Studies Association, 1985); Gene Lyons, 'The Study of International Relations in Great Britain: Further Connections', *World Politics* (Vol. 38, No. 4, 1968), pp. 626–45.

16 The Study of International Relations in Hispanic America

Mark S.C. Simpson and Paulo Wrobel

It is not an easy task to attempt an overview of the state of the International Relations discipline in Hispanic America. The first obstacle to such an undertaking is the heterogeneity of the countries involved – namely, all former Spanish colonies south of the Rio Grande. With this in mind we have chosen to concentrate on those countries where the study of International Relations is most developed, namely Argentina, Chile, and Mexico, understanding these to be representative of developments in the region as a whole, even though we do not deal with each of these in detail. The second obstacle, which is inherent to the discipline itself and is not peculiar to Hispanic America alone, has to do with the difficulties of defining what does or does not belong to the field. If in the very academic centres where the study of International Relations was first developed there is a great deal of effort still being expended in attempting to define the subject matter, one can imagine to what degree this problem is compounded in a region where the social sciences as a whole have not acquired the level of specialisation that one sees in Europe and North America.

Under such conditions there has been a tendency for International Relations to be treated as an appendage of Sociology, Political Science and Economics, International Relations being understood simply as the study of the international aspects of the essentially 'domestic' subject matter of the former. The specificity of the field and its unique research agenda is still to be acknowledged, although, as will be indicated below, great progress has been made in the last two decades.

16.1 INSTITUTIONAL SETTING

The first conditioning factor to bear in mind when attempting to explain the institutional development of the field is the nonparticipation of Hispanic America in the First World War. The cataclysm which served as midwife for the birth in Great Britain and the United States of the first centres dedicated to the study of the causes of war and conditions of peace did not affect the region.

The inter-war period, however, saw many Hispanic American countries joining the League of Nations, providing them with their first substantive links with the international community besides their traditional reference points, namely the United States and the Great Powers of Europe. After the Second World War all joined the United Nations as founding members, within the confines of which they witnessed the dramas of decolonisation and their implications for an increasingly complex international system. Together with the institutionalisation of the inter-American system, in the form of the Organisation of American States in 1948, these developments forced governments to recognise the interdependence of the post-war world and the importance of the international arena for their individual national projects, as well as prompting them to raise the professional standard of those directly involved in statecraft.

The establishment of teaching and research centres specifically dedicated to international studies is, however, a much more recent phenomenon, resulting from government policies of the 1960s which aimed to raise the standard of social science in Hispanic America through the training of personnel in European and North American universities. This was a reflection of the instrumentalist view of the social sciences held by all governments in the region, and is understandable given the dominance of 'developmentalist' ideas during this period.

However, as a result of the paucity of funds available for this training programme and the lack of infrastructural support for the returning scholars, many were forced to straddle more than one field. This was obviously detrimental to a fledgling discipline such as International Relations, which tended to lose out to the older and stronger sibling disciplines in the struggle for government funding. Notwithstanding these problems, the first institute in Hispanic America geared specifically to the study of International Relations was founded in 1966: the *Instituto de Estudios Internacionales* of the University of Chile in Santiago; a project which was brought to fruition with the assistance of the Royal Institute of International Affairs in London. The reasons for the breakthrough can be attributed to the unique concentration of professionals attached to the research agencies of the United Nations located in Santiago, such as ECLA (the Economic Commission for Latin America) and INTAL (the Institute for the Integration of Latin America).

Once initiated, the process gained momentum and centres were soon established in Argentina and Mexico and both countries now have at least two Institutes concerned with the study of International Relations, as well as area studies centres. The growth of institutes has also been paralleled by the proliferation of publications. Chile has its *Estudios Internacionales*, Mexico its *Foro Internacional*, *Relaciones Internacionales* and *Estudios de Asia y Africa*, while Argentina has its *Revista Argentina de Relaciones Internacionales*.

An important step in strengthening the field was taken in 1973 with the establishment of RIAL (International Relations in Latin America), a body funded by the UN which aimed to bring together the various Institutes throughout the region. The first work produced by RIAL was a report on the New International Economic Order (NIEO) from a Latin American perspective. Located in Santiago, Chile, RIAL has attempted to co-ordinate research in the field and provides for an exchange of views among Latin American scholars by organising annual conferences.

16.2 THEMATIC OVERVIEW

The first point to note as far as the intellectual debates in the field are concerned is the influence of nineteenth century Hispano–American writings on the predicament of the region. These tended to see the Hispanic American states as victims of powerful extra-continental forces rather than actors in their own right. These ideas flowed into the populist political movements of the twentieth century. In Argentina for example, Peronism called for a struggle of 'national liberation' aimed at allowing the country to reach its true 'power potential' and increase its capacity for autonomous action in the international system.

The theme of victimisation was partly taken up by ECLA in the 1950s under the direction of the Argentinian economist Raul Prebisch. The importance of ECLA's attempts at explaining the causes of Latin American underdevelopment and the weakness of states in the region lies in the fact that the organisation went beyond the simplistic guilt attribution exercises of the earlier periods which linked all problems to '*Imperialismo Yanqui*'. It attempted to situate the Latin American experience within the wider context of the processes of the international economy, as well as placing it in a historical perspective. The whole coterie of concepts developed by ECLA, such as that of declining terms of trade and the stratification of the world into centres and peripheries, thus represented the first attempt at explaining the problems of the region at a systemic level.

The impact of ECLA's body of thought can be measured by the continuing importance given to the development problematic within the academic communities concerned with international affairs in Hispanic America. These ideas found resonance among the national elites of Hispanic American countries who were concerned with initiating a process of modernisation, providing them with both a diagnosis of the problem and a blueprint for the future. On a secondary level, they also addressed a felt need to strengthen the capabilities of their states so as to permit them a more active role in international affairs. These objectives were seen to be interconnected: development was linked to an increase in national power and sovereignty.

By the 1970s, ECLA's approach had branched off in a number of directions. On the one hand, concentration was given to the study of foreign policies of different states at the expense of a wider systemic approach. Furthermore, researchers tended to limit themselves to the study of relations between particular Hispanic American countries and the United States. On the other hand, the normative evaluation of the existing unequal distribution of power in the international system, which was an integral part of ECLA's approach, was taken up by 'dependency' theorists.

Though undoubtedly a highly original approach, dependency theory, in the view of the authors, was not an unqualified blessing as far as the development of the discipline in the region was concerned. The reasons for this are many, but one should note that dependency theory was primarily a product of sociologists and aimed at explaining the essentially domestic manifestations of underdevelopment. Consequently, there were very few attempts to link the ideas of dependency theory with the wider questions which have been the traditional concerns of International Relations, such as explanations of the causes of war, the phenomenon of international organisations and law, or foreign policy analysis. At its worst it tended to 'freeze' the international system and was overly deterministic. Since it was not an attempt to explain the external behaviour of states in the region, its contribution to the wider questions of International Relations was limited.

A third spin-off from ECLA has been the attention given by

International Relations circles in Hispanic America to integration studies, since the pooling of resources in order to accelerate economic development was central to the organisation's policy prescriptions. Economic integration was also seen as a means of uniting a 'Balkanised' region in face of the high degree of American penetration, both economic and military, so as to ensure the survival of the parts. The historical roots of this theme arguably precede ECLA and can be traced to Bolivar's vision of a united Spanish America in the wake of the Wars of Independence. The contemporary manifestations of this quintessentially Spanish American idea are to be found in the many attempts at economic integration, such as the Andean Pact. The enormous amount of academic effort devoted to the study of these enterprises has, however, impacted negatively on the field as a whole to the extent that in certain circles International Relations has tended to be equated solely with the relations between countries of the region, and even more specifically with the integration process in Hispanic America.

One can detect a fourth current of thought in the region which is intimately linked with the military, particularly in Chile and Argentina – namely, geopolitics. The output of military think-tanks stresses the 'national vocation' of the specific countries in question, e.g., Chile seen as an actor in the South Pacific zone and Argentina as the dominant power in the South Atlantic.

16.3 CONCLUSION

In attempting a somewhat impressionistic evaluation of the state of the discipline in Hispanic America, a number of observations can be made. First, in Hispanic America there is not a discipline of International Relations in the traditional European or North American sense – that is, an academic community doing 'normal science', demonstrating a consensus on basic postulates and methodology. If we can divide the development of a discipline into three stages – the establishment of a research agenda specific to the field, the production of case studies and flowing from this, a stage of theory building – then one can say that Hispanic America is still in the process of transition from the first to the second stage.

If, however, one were to divide the field into paradigms – the Realist, Interdependence and World Systems/Dependency approaches – as is customary in most recent literature, it could be argued that these schools of thought are represented in Hispanic America. In general terms one can equate Realism with the geopolitical thinking of the military and right wing civilian counterparts, interdependence with the liberal/nationalist elements in Hispanic American politics who support the process of economic integration, and finally the World Systems/Dependency approach with the left. It seems to be the case however, that in general those involved are unaware of the richness and variety of their respective adopted paradigms.

Finally, one could add that the development of the International Relations discipline will depend largely on the capacity of existing institutions to break away from their concentration on conjunctural problems that the states in the region are facing. Though a long-term project, it is essential that the academic centres establish their independence from state interests in determining their research agendas.

17 The Study of International Relations in the United States

Neil R. Richardson

To characterise the study of International Relations in the United States entails a reflection upon the work of hundreds of scholars across several academic disciplines and housed in hundreds of institutions. While a relative few of these organisations are 'think tanks', the remainder are colleges and universities offering undergraduate instruction in the field. Scores of them also train graduate students. Describing these activities coherently necessitates some considerable degree of generalisation.[1]

With this in mind, I will attempt in the following pages to do justice to the task. The discussion will begin with a consideration of directions of International Relations theorising in the United States, and then turn to institutional contexts in which International Relations scholarship is produced and disseminated. In contrast to the variety of scholarship and teaching that will be described, I will conclude that a great deal of continuity underlies these twin processes, forming a reasonably secure platform for speculation about the future of International Relations scholarship in the United States.

17.1 THEORY

International Relations began to emerge as a disciplined academic focus in the United States in early decades of this century, at a time when international law had come to rival diplomatic history as a dominant mode for the study of world affairs. This legalistic focus was, of course, entirely compatible with the theory of Idealism, which asserted that prevailing international conflict could be remedied by altering the institutions and rules that governed political discourse and shepherded conflict into peaceful resolution.

281

The failure of the League of Nations, however, gave rise to realism as an antidote. Appearing in the late 1930s, realism claimed to capture the essence of International Relations by positing the primacy of the nation state and its pursuit of power in service of the national interest. Idealism, meanwhile, was in intellectual disrepute nearly everywhere on the heels of the Second World War, even though its remaining adherents quickly attached new hope to the fledgling United Nations. During the 1940s and 1950s, realism had a monopoly on the US academy.

By the later 1950s, however, theoretical work began to appear that addressed some of Realism's lacunae. In particular, the appearance of – and favourable reception to – Kaplan's *System and Process in International Politics* and Snyder, Bruck, and Sapin's *Foreign Policy Decision-Making* can be understood as frontal responses to gaps in Realism's account of international politics.[2] The succeeding three decades have witnessed a profusion of research directions, foreshadowed in these two works, that in varying degrees depart from Realism's central tenets.

Decision-making studies, for example, take apart the twin assumptions of unitary and rational state choice. Allison's examination of the Cuban missile crisis remains a cogent statement on the fragmentation of the process, carefully documenting how a multitude of agencies are enlisted to contribute to a final choice of action, each of them engaging in myopic routines and, eventually, coming to compete with each other.[3] Moreover, these same organisational and bureaucratic processes also jeopardise the faithful implementation of the chosen option.

Allison's highly influential analysis not only documented the potential effects of state fragmentation, it thereby also exposed systematically some of the organisational and human frailties that routinely undercut rational decision-making. Steinbruner's emphasis was rather the reverse.[4] Here, the focus is on individual cognitive processes, often cybernetically simplified, by which the human mind reduces complexity to manageable proportions. On a scale of aggregation, a midpoint between Allison's organisations and Steinbruner's individuals is found in considerations of decision-making by small groups. Among them, Janis's *Victims of Groupthink* is an innovative example. Drawing from social psychology, he shows in a series of cases how the interactions within a group can produce social dynamics that blunt and distort individuals' better judgements in reaching foreign policy decisions.[5]

Throughout this same period of the 1960s and 1970s, Kaplan's book triggered further thoughts that confronted realism from the opposite direction. Kaplan abstracted six international system types, five of which depict conditions of anarchy in keeping with a realist assumption. However, he departed from realism's exclusive focus on nation state autonomy as he specified 'essential rules' of behaviour for these system members. The rules make clear that nation states are to strive not only for their particularistic interests, they are also to restrain themselves from actions that might disturb an important element of the system itself. For example, in Kaplan's multipolar balance of power system, the actors are to 'fight rather than pass up an opportunity to increase capabilities' yet 'stop fighting rather than eliminate an essential national actor'.[6] Notice that, while the first of these rules is a Realist prescription, the second is not. The second rule specifies that actors are to restrain themselves from fighting a war that would reduce the number of poles – the latter a characteristic of the system rather than any of its members.

Kaplan's inclusion of systemic determinants of state behaviour opened a new vein of theorising. In the mid-1960s, seminal articles by Waltz and by Deutsch and Singer proposed theories that, together, constitute a debate about whether a bipolar or a multipolar system is more susceptible to (destabilising) war between major powers.[7]

The role of the state was subjected to theoretical challenge by students of international integration, reflecting the liberal tradition expressed earlier in Idealism.[8] Spurred by the early successes of the European Community, Haas, Deutsch, and others theorised about the conditions and processes that encourage nation states and their citizens to surrender some degree of sovereignty to supranational institutions, a phenomenon unanticipated by Realism.[9] Integration theorising lost most of its impetus by the end of the decade. One reason is that theorists could not consensually decide what distinguishes integration as process from integration as status. Moreover, European integration had reached an apparent plateau in qualitative terms, while efforts to mimic the process elsewhere – for example, in Central America – were decidedly unsuccessful.

Thus, the half-life of integration theory was rather short. Yet, a number of its driving ideas live on in the efforts of those who study interdependence, transnationalism, and international regimes. Keohane and Nye are central figures here. Since the appearance of their *Transnational Relations and World Politics* in 1972, many scholars have continued to explore the interplay between state and non-state actors, the latter including entities both private and public.[10] Their explicit theoretical thrust was, again, to challenge Realist assumptions.

Most obviously, they emphasised the growing importance of transnational processes and organisational structures that regulate a diverse range of international transactions. This concern most often led to a substantive focus on international political economy, then highlighted by the collapse of fixed currency exchange rates, an enormous change in the world oil market, and Third World demands for a New International Economic Order (NIEO). Economic interdependence was a forceful reality that propelled theoretical development.

Realism assumes that states' policy-makers are considerably unfettered as they choose ways to advance their respective national interests. Interdependence, on the other hand, denotes a mutual reliance of nations upon each other. Another point of divergence thus concerns the relatively restricted range of choice available to policy-makers in interdependent countries. For them, certain options will entail costs in the form of damage to mutually beneficial ties they have to others. Deficit spending in the US may ease unemployment at home, but it can also raise interest rates in Canada. Furthermore, the growing complexity of interdependence is a consequence of multiple issue-areas of salience to actors (that is, in addition to realist devotion to military security). In turn, these issue-areas are sometimes linked together, thereby increasing the chances that options available with reference to any one issue will impinge upon other facets of International Relationships. In a recent retrospective, Keohane and Nye propose that the web of interdependence is becoming so dense that it constitutes a systemic element in theory.[11]

Transnationalism and interdependence has borrowed, too, from the focus on subnational processes pioneered by earlier students of decision-making. Keohane and Nye's *Power and Interdependence* exemplified the assertion that international interdependence has brought a larger, more diverse array of individuals and groups into the foreign policy arena.[12] This development includes a proliferation of both private parties and public agencies whose policies have international content. Two consequences follow, they believe. On the one hand, it is increasingly difficult to try to identify a truly 'national policy' with respect to a given issue in view of the number of diverse policies these sub-national actors adopt and pursue (sometimes in opposition to, and/or ignorance of, each other). Furthermore, policy (and pressure on officials) develops from transnational alliances of counterpart members of different societies and states. Needless to say, this conception of contemporary world politics not only characterises new types of actors, it explicitly departs from assumptions of unitary and rational decision-making once again.

Such discussions of multiple types of actors, transnationalism, and interdependence are the genesis of theoretical and empirical studies of international regimes that have come to the fore in the last decade. Invariably, different scholars bring different questions and conceptions to the matter. For example, Stein and Young have explored the creation of regime.[13] Keohane has theorised about the conditions under which the value of regimes in promoting a sustained pattern of co-operation outweighs the costs of more *ad hoc* arrangements.[14] In turn, Snidal investigated the distribution of costs entailed in regime creation and maintenance under conditions in which there is no hegemon.[15]

Frequently, the study of regimes is thus couched in the larger theory of hegemonic stability. The latter has enjoyed a renaissance in recent years. For some, it constitutes a genuinely cyclical theory of the rise and fall of world leadership over the centuries.[16] The theory speaks to the likelihood of major power war as a hegemon's predominance in the international system wanes. But, during its years of ascension and dominance, the hegemon arrogates to itself the role of creator and sustainer of regimes that constrain other countries and serve the hegemon's (and probably some others') interests.

Attention to the theory of hegemonic stability has risen precisely as the leadership of the United States in the post-war order has declined. This is to say that most of the recent research effort, while clothed in the larger theory, in fact concerns post-war regime maintenance and the decline of the United States in particular; only scant heed is paid to earlier periods witnessing the decline of Spanish, Dutch, or British supremacy.[17]

Snidal's regime article exemplifies a methodological strain of 'public choice' research that has been emerging in US political science for many years now. Although Rousseau wrote of the stag hunt, and Riker's early book, *Theory of Political Coalitions*, devoted some attention to military alliances, public choice research has only more recently begun to appear with regularity in International Relations writings.[18] This research is formally deductive, frequently game-theoretic, often lacking in systematic empiricism, and is commonly devoted to understanding why actors may choose to engage in the provision of collective goods such as alliance protection, multilateral trade liberalisation, or joint benefit from seabed use or pollution abatement. The intersection of regimes with collective goods provision is something of a natural fit, particularly when choice is conceived as being repetitious behaviour between actors.[19]

If interdependence, transnationalism, and regime theory are mainly concerned with international political economy and reflect liberal thought, questions of war and peace in the realist tradition have hardly been forgotten. Brodie, Schelling, and their successors have relentlessly explored deterrence theory and practice under conditions of ever-changing weapons technology.[20] In the footsteps of Richardson and Wright, Singer remains central to a younger generation of scholars who explore the correlates of war informed by large data sets.[21]

A very different genre of research is embodied in the World Order Models Project (WOMP).[22] Those associated with this project are exploring the reconception of world politics through the prism of a global society. While their numbers are few, their ideas are sufficiently bold in the era of nuclear threat, growing economic disparity, and ecological degradation that they have generated fairly widespread interest since the 1970s.

Finally, neo-Marxist theory constitutes a separate realm of research. Its reinvigoration in the United States began about two decades ago, triggered by Latin American scholars' formulation of dependency theory.[23] Some US theorists were quickly drawn to it.

By the 1960s, it was apparent that development strategies were insufficient and, in the view of increasing numbers of observers, often damaging. Resentment was thus growing. Under the aegis of the United Nations, UNCTAD was created; its work made early contributions to the theory of dependency that was entering academic discussions. The theory seeks to explain how and why poor societies have been not simply stultified but, more correctly, distorted as participants in the liberal post-war international economic regime that contributed to prosperity elsewhere.

Dependency theory, as a response to the failure of efforts prescribed by neoclassical development theory, is therefore not a direct alternative to realism or other orthodox theory of International Relations.[24] Furthermore, its analysis rests on social class relations, relegating inter-state relations to nearly epiphenomenal status. Accordingly, dependency theory and orthodox International Relations theory seem to defy synthesis.[25] Indeed, it has proved exceedingly difficult even to test propositions derived from dependency theory by the conventional empirical methods of Behavioural research that North Americans and others soon brought to its questions.[26]

Dependency theory has been eclipsed by world systems theory in the last decade. Also neo-Marxist, this newer work characterises the global system as one organised by capitalism, wherein there is a division of labour between interactive core and peripheral societies.[27] Like dependency theory, it portrays poor ('peripheral') societies as victims of exploitation at the hands of the wealthy, industrialised ('core') centres of capitalism. Also for both theories, the agents of this exploitation are transnational elite allies who use trade, aid, and multinational corporate investment for personal gain under rules created by the core in the wake of the Second World War.

World systems theory's contribution, then, lies in its more comprehensive spatial domain when compared to dependency theory and, relatedly, in its claim to a more profound attribution of cause in the capitalist system that now encircles the globe. Although both dependency and world system theorists disagree on a number of points, including whether a distorted society at the periphery can escape its circumstance, it bears repeating that these theories stand intellectually apart from more mainstream International Relations theory for reasons of both epistemology and units of analysis.[28]

In sum, US scholars bring to the study of International Relations a panoply of philosophical traditions and, accordingly, their research reflects dispositions to place different questions on their respective agendas.[29] They also disagree about appropriate units of analysis and even about the research methods that are most fruitful. These profound differences do not, however, prevent them from sharing institutions and students with each other.

17.2 INSTITUTIONS

As an academic field, International Relations is ordinarily treated as a specialisation within the institutional framework of Political Science departments. The evolution of International Relations studies from diplomatic history to international law was redefined as distinctly political by realist theory. As Hans Morgenthau, realism's most distinguished American proponent, phrased it, '[i]nternational politics, like all politics, is a struggle for power'.[30]

Meanwhile, Political science was likewise experiencing a newly found identity in colleges and universities throughout the country, usually breaking away from history departments. As in the case of International Relations, Political Science was a discipline strongly propelled by normative issues and history and most attentive to questions of political institutions. The two infant disciplines were strikingly similar, and these parallels doubtless hastened the day of their merger. Since the Second World War, International Relations as a field of study in the US has largely been folded into political science programmes.

The merger has benefitted the study of International Relations in the sense that its scholars have been encouraged to reflect upon the domestic contexts and consequences of foreign affairs. In addition, political scientists were, in general, well ahead of International Relations specialists in broadening their attention so as to include political behaviour as companion to political institutions as a focus of legitimate (indeed, compelling) concern. While International Relations scholarship has not consequently abandoned legal and historical analysis, it has nevertheless adopted the positivistic social science emphasis on a search for nomothetic statements about classes of cases and their expected similarities in behaviour.

As in social science more generally, International Relations scholarship has enjoyed substantial research support from the US government and private foundations. The 1960s were the heyday of research funding, subsidising among other things the collection and analysis of large data sets on domestic and international violence, economic and social attributes of nation states, diplomatic interactions, and the like. Such efforts continue, but on a smaller scale since the 1970s, when a measure of disenchantment with early results together with macroeconomic tightening produced a serious decline in extramural funding support.

Another consequence of the social science caste of International Relations studies has been less salutary, at least in the short run of the last three decades. This is the near-orphanage of international law. Its study has been progressively relegated to secondary status in the United States, making notable appearances in both Political Science and legal research, to be sure, yet overwhelmed by others as its separate institutional (if not intellectual) identity in the academy has largely evaporated. Only quite recently, in the new clothes of regime theory, has the study of international law begun to ascend in mainstream US studies of International Relations.

Undergraduate student interest in international relations is by all accounts flourishing these days. There are no systematic surveys available, but in hundreds of colleges and universities enrolments in introductory and advanced International Relations courses are robust and, in many instances, burgeoning. What accounts for this?

In the United States, many people's first thought is that Ronald Reagan's 'high profile' foreign policy posture has kindled students' awareness of world affairs. Although this may be germane to students, there are yet other reasons at once more self-serving and more profound that are probably of greater importance and longer duration than the stance of any particular US administration.

It is entirely fair to say that many undergraduates find international studies very relevant to their futures. Now, for most this is decidedly not the 'relevance' sought by an earlier generation committed to bettering the human condition, although there is a substantial portion for whom this is still true. Rather, the perceived relevance of International Relations for so many of today's students is borne of an appreciation of the fact that a growing number of employers desire college graduates having some familiarity with – and sensitivity to – the global context of their professional activities. Growing proportions of government agencies and private businesses alike find themselves routinely engaged in transnational, even interdependent, working relationships. This they communicate to college career advisors.

Reinforcing this student self-interest is the changing content of typical International Relations curricula. Reflecting theoretical shifts away from strict Realism, particularly by the 1970s, are undergraduate courses and texts that are no longer preoccupied with Realism's 'high politics' of power balances and military security. Students today are thus still instructed in the politics of force; entire courses are devoted to military security and international conflict. But they typically also learn as much about the interdependent international political economy through courses on oil politics or third world debt. While developments in both theory and the real world explain the expanding content of the typical curriculum, student interest sustains it. Indeed, a number of schools are joining the ranks of what were once the few to offer an International Relations curriculum that cuts across departmental boundaries, combining ingredients from Political Science, Economics, History, and foreign languages.

Unsurprisingly, graduate programmes in Political Science also feature large contingents of advanced degree students for whom International Relations is the chosen specialisation. A recent annual report indicates that, among eight categories, about 24 per cent of 1987's PhDs in political science (85 from a total 358) are specialists in International Relations.[31] Similarly, the monthly national listing of available academic positions currently posted reveals that, from nine categories of specialisation, International Relations is the specified field for about 20 per cent of the openings (34 of 172).[32]

Of particular interest to graduate students are qualitative features of graduate programmes. A small share of them attend International Affairs Institutes. These few interdisciplinary programmes include prominently the Fletcher School of Law and Diplomacy at Tufts University, the School of Public and International Affairs at Columbia, the Woodrow Wilson School of Public and International Affairs at Princeton, the School of Foreign Service at Georgetown University, and Johns Hopkins' School of Advanced International Studies. Each has a very small PhD programme, emphasising instead terminal MA degrees for the large bulk of their students.

These programmes were, for many years, unique in attempting to balance academic rigour with pragmatic, vocational training suited to a variety of careers in the public and private sectors. Instruction is routinely offered by academics and practitioners alike. Two developments have begun to erode their unique mission, however.[33] One change is in the market for their graduates. Here, new openings in the public sector have largely vanished owing to cutbacks in the federal budget. Simultaneously, private sector positions with banks and other multinational corporations are being flooded by the mushrooming numbers of MBAs coming from the swelling business school graduate programmes nationwide. Furthermore, there are signs that business schools are developing interdisciplinary curricula while Political Science departments are more interested in policy analysis than before, thereby encroaching from both sides on the character of training that had long been the almost exclusive province of these international affairs programmes. Nevertheless, these few institutions retain, for now at least, a special identity.

Much the greater share of graduate students enrol in Political Science departments instead. Their preferences among departments are driven by a school's prestige, convenience, and cost. Yet many are also propelled by the substantive, theoretical, and methodological inclinations of the faculty with whom they will study.

In large departments, the International Relations faculty are usually diverse. Thus, at the University of California (Berkeley), Michigan, Minnesota, and Princeton, to name but a few, the intellectual menu is broad. On the other hand, some departments have reputations deriving from a greater emphasis on some aspect of international studies. In the area of international political economy, Chicago and Yale come quickly to mind. For strategic studies, one might think first of Harvard or Stanford. In methodological terms, Michigan is known for quantitative empirical research, the State University of New York at Rochester is identified with deductive theorising, and the University of Virginia is seen as offering training in historical methods of International Relations analysis.

Of course, these are but a few, impressionistically drawn illustrations. What Hill has dubbed 'the vast American academic machine' includes scores of universities having MA and PhD programmes.[34] US scholars – including many at strictly undergraduate institutions – publish hundreds of books and journal articles each year on all conceivable facets of International Relations. As many as one thousand of them convene annually at International Studies Association meetings.[35] In a variety of ways, then, they become known to undergraduates contemplating advanced degree programmes.

The institutional base of US scholarship thus offers instruction to many thousands of undergraduates who elect each year to concentrate their studies in International Relations. Most of them immediately enter the work force, but many hundreds enrol in International Relations graduate school programmes instead. Dozens annually complete a doctoral programme in International Relations and most of them assume faculty positions thereafter.

17.3 CONCLUSION

What coherence is to be found in the study of International Relations in the United States? Many would despair at this point. As McKinlay and Little have persuasively shown, the divergent philosophies of Realist, Liberal, and Socialist thought continue to underpin rival theories of International Relations today.[36] What appears to one group as a solution to an international problem is therefore a problem from the perspective of a rival theory. Add to this the wide and still expanding range of research methodologies employed, the various units of analysis scrutinised, and the likelihood that the next generation of scholars will considerably reflect current training, and one could easily be tempted to conclude that intellectual coherence is even more elusive today than it has ever been, and that it will continue to be so.

Superficially appealing, such a conclusion is nevertheless imbalanced. To say that scholarly work is nothing but fragmented is to ignore some of its important features. In the wake of the Behavioural revolution of the 1950s and 1960s, the animus between Behaviouralists and Traditionalists has been supplanted by a large measure of mutual respect – or, at least, mutual tolerance. In addition, Holsti makes a strong case for the view that the overwhelming number of theoretical departures from Realist assumptions are not so different after all. [37]Despite the attention given to substantial and subnational actors, despite the shift away from military security to political economy, despite, in other words, the imagination revealed by theorists, by far the largest share of International Relations research continues to take for granted (at least implicitly) the transcendent importance of war and peace issues, the sustained essentiality of the nation state actor, and thus an image of world politics as a system still comprised most fundamentally of interactions among them. This is not a portrait of stagnation, but one of adaptation.

Whether one accepts precisely this formulation is, of course, unimportant. What cannot be gainsaid is the fact that International Relations scholars in the United States continue to devote most of their effort to understanding inter-state relations in an environment that is assumed to be orderly. Alternatives such as neo-Marxism receive some attention, but they show no signs of seriously eroding the hegemonic position of this conception among US scholars. Moreover, discourse in this country is almost autarchically insulated from scholarship in other countries (see note 1). There is every reason to believe that theoretical and methodological evolution will continue; after all, scholars are rewarded for thinking! But a revolution in theory is more likely to follow real world politics than to lead it. Meanwhile, it is highly probable that the dominance of the interstate conception of world politics in the United States academy will live on in the next generation of its scholars.

NOTES AND REFERENCES

1. The task of generalising about US scholarship is only slightly eased by the disturbing fact that this activity occurs in rather unsplendid isolation from most of the research conducted in other countries. Many have made this observation and at least one empirical study

lends this impression great credence. See K.J. Holsti, *The Dividing Discipline: Hegemony and Diversity in International Theory* (Boston: Allen & Unwin, 1985), chapters 5 and 6.

2. Morton A. Kaplan, *System and Process in International Politics* (New York: Wiley, 1957); Richard C. Snyder, H.W. Bruck, and Burton Sapin, *Foreign Policy Decision-Making* (New York: The Free Press, 1963).

3. Graham I. Allison, 'Conceptual Models and the Cuban Missile Crisis', *American Political Science Review* (Vol. 63, No. 3, 1969), pp. 689-718.

4. John D. Steinbruner, *The Cybernetic Theory of Decision: New Dimensions of Political Analysis* (Princeton, NJ: Princeton University Press, 1974), esp. Part I.

5. Irving Janis, *Victims of Groupthink* (Boston, MA: Houghton Mifflin, 1972).

6. Kaplan, *System and Process*, p. 23.

7. Kenneth N. Waltz, 'International Structure, National Force, and the Balance of World Power', *Journal of International Affairs* (Vol. 21, No. 2, 1967), pp. 215–231; Karl W. Deutsch and J. David Singer, 'Multipolar Power Systems and International Stability', *World Politics* (Vol. 16, No. 3, 1964), pp. 390–406. Waltz's 'Neorealist' *Theory of International Politics* (Reading, MA: Addison-Wesley, 1979) is at once a more ample and more cogent revision of his original argument.

8. See R.D. McKinley and R. Little, *Global Problems and World Order* (London: Frances Pinter, 1986) for an illuminating overview of the Liberal, Realist, and Socialist traditions in international theory.

9. Ernst B. Haas, *The Uniting of Europe* (Stanford, CA: Stanford University Press, 1964); Karl W. Deutsch *et al.*, *Political Community and the North Atlantic Area* (Princeton, N.J.: Princeton University Press, 1957).

10. Robert O. Keohane and Joseph S. Nye, *Transnational Relations and World Politics* (Cambridge, MA: Harvard University Press, 1972). See also Robert O. Keohane and Joseph S. Nye, 'Transnational Relations and International Organizations', *World Politics* (Vol. 27, No. 1, 1974), pp. 39–62.

11. Robert O. Keohane and Joseph S. Nye, '*Power and Interdependence* Revisited', *International Organization* (Vol. 41, No. 4, 1987), pp. 745-749.

12. Robert O. Keohane and Joseph S. Nye, *Power and Interdependence: World Politics in Transition* (Boston, MA: Little, Brown, 1977).

13. Arthur A. Stein, 'Coordination and Collaboration: Regime in an Anarchic World', *International Organization* (Vol. 36, No. 2, 1982), pp. 277–97 and Oran R. Young, 'Regime Dynamics: The Rise and Fall of International Regimes' *International Organization* (Vol. 36, No. 2, 1982).

14. Robert O. Keohane, *After Hegemony: Cooperation and Discord in the World Political Economy* (Princeton NJ: Princeton University Press, 1984).

15. Duncan Snidal, 'Coordination versus Prisoners' Dilemma: Implications for International Cooperation and Regimes', *American Political Science Review* (Vol. 79, No. 4, 1985), pp. 923–42.

16. George Modelski, 'The Long Cycle of Global Politics and the Nation-State', *Comparative Studies in Society and History* (Vol. 20, No. 2, 1978), pp. 214–35; Robert Gilpin, *War and Change in World Politics* (Cambridge: Cambridge University Press, 1981).

17. Gilpin, *War and Change*, is one exception. A broader yet similar argument is made by Ekkehart Krippendorff, 'The Dominance of American Approaches to International Relations', *Millennium: Journal of International Studies* (Vol. 16, No. 2, 1987), pp. 207–14, reprinted in this volume.

18. William H. Riker, *The Theory of Political Coalitions* (New Haven CT: Yale University Press, 1962).

19. An important recent study of iterative bargaining is Robert Axelrod, *The Evolution of Cooperation* (New York: Basic Books, 1984).

20. Bernard Brodie, *Strategy in the Missile Age* (Princeton, N.J.: Princeton University Press, 1959); Thomas C. Schelling, *The Strategy of Conflict* (New York: Oxford University Press, 1960). Useful analysis of these and more recent efforts are Patrick M. Morgan, *Deterrence: A Conceptual Analysis* (Beverley Hills, CA: Sage, 1977) and Robert Jervis, 'Deterrence Theory Revisited', *World Politics* (Vol. 31, No. 2, 1979), pp. 289–324.

21. Lewis Fry Richardson, *Statistics of Deadly Quarrels* (Pittsburgh, PA: Boxwood Press, 1960); Quincy Wright, *A Study of War* (Chicago, IL: University of Chicago Press, 1942); J. David Singer and Melvin Small, *The Wages of War, 1816–1965: A Statistical Handbook* (New York: Wiley, 1972). For a provocative theory of rational war calculations, with data-based tests, see Bruce Bueno de Mesquita, *The War Trap* (New Haven, CT: Yale University Press, 1980).

22. See, for example, Richard A. Falk, *This Endangered Planet* (New York: Random House, 1979); Rajni Kothari, *Footsteps into the Future* (New York: The Free Press, 1974).

23. For example, Fernando H. Cardoso and Enzo Faletto, *Dependencia y Desarrollo en America Latina* (Mexico: Siglo Veintiuno editores sa, 1971, 3rd edn); Andre Gunder Frank, *Development and Underdevelopment in Latin America* (New York: Monthly Review Press, 1968).

24. Holsti, *The Dividing Discipline*, pp. 63 ff.

25. A most articulate discussion of this point is James A. Caporaso, 'Dependence, Dependency, and Power in the Global System: A Structural and Behavioral Analysis', *International Organization* (Vol. 32, No. 1, 1978), pp. 13–43.

26. A vigorous denunciation of such efforts is written by one of the theory's principal architects; see Fernando Henrique Cardoso, 'The Consumption of Dependency Theory in the United States', *Latin American Research Review* (Vol. 12, No. 3, 1977), pp. 7–24.

27. See Immanuel Wallerstein, *The Capitalist World Economy* (Cambridge: Cambridge University Press, 1979) for the most complete presentation of world system theory.

28. On the debate over escape from the world system compare Immanuel Wallerstein, 'The Rise and Future Demise of the World Capitalist System', *Comparative Studies in Society and History* (Vol. 16, No.

4, 1974), pp. 387–415, to the somewhat more optimistic Samir Amin, 'Accumulation and Development: A Theoretical Model', *Review of African Political Economy* (Vol. 1, 1974), pp. 9–26.

29. This is a central theme of McKinlay and Little, *Global Problems*.
30. Hans J. Morgenthau, *Politics Among Nations: The Struggle for Power and Peace*, 5th edn, revised (New York: Knopf, 1978), p. 29.
31. American Political Science Association, 'Doctoral Dissertations in Political Science', *PS* (Vol. 20, No. 4, 1987), pp. 1039–65.
32. American Political Science Association, *Personnel Service Newsletter* (Vol. 32, No. 4, 1987).
33. I borrow here from a useful overview of the status of these interdisciplinary MA programmes by Roger S. Leeds, 'Graduate Education in International Affairs: A Discipline in Transition', *SAIS Review* (Vol. 6, No. 2, 1986), pp. 205–18.
34. Christopher Hill, 'The Study of International Relations in the United Kingdom', *Millennium: Journal of International Studies* (Vol. 16, No. 2, Summer 1987), p. 301, reprinted this volume.
35. See, for example, the annual convention report, 'Washington 1987 A Record-Setting Success', *International Studies Newsletter* (Vol. 14, No. 4, 1987), p. 1. The International Studies Association has a predominantly US (and Political Science) membership. It usually meets in North America (although the 1989 meetings will be held in London).
36. McKinlay and Little, *Global Problems*.
37. Holsti, *The Dividing Discipline*.

18 The Study of International Relations in Nigeria

Olajide Aluko

At the outset it is important to make the distinction between International Relations and international politics. In many institutions, especially in North America, these terms are used interchangeably. Yet while 'International Relations' refers to all forms of ties across national boundaries, ranging from politico–diplomatic, security–military and economic–developmental to sociocultural relations, 'international politics' refers specifically to the political aspects of such relations.

Here we will examine the study of International Relations, rather than the political aspects only, including the growth of International Relations in Nigeria, the approach to the study, the problems facing the discipline, and its prospects.

18.1 GROWTH OF THE STUDY

Although Nigeria did not become independent until 1960, as early as 1956 the Balewa government introduced to the pre-independence parliament Sessional Paper No. 11 which provided, among other things, for the training of future Nigerian diplomats. Such training was to be carried out in overseas institutions, such as the London School of Economics, Oxford University and the School of Diplomacy at the Hague, as institutions for such training were not available in Nigeria in the late 1950s.

The impetus for the study of International Relations was provided by the Nigerian government when it established the Nigerian Institute of International Affairs (NIIA) in 1961, with the following objectives:

1. to encourage and facilitate the understanding of international affairs, and of the circumstances, conditions, and attitudes of foreign countries and their peoples;

2. to provide and maintain means of information upon international questions, and promote the study and investigation of international questions by means of conferences, lectures, and discussions, and by the preparation and publication of books, records reports . . . so as to develop a body of informed opinions on world affairs.[1]

The Institute was also enjoined by the government to promote the scientific study of international politics, economics, and jurisprudence. Its purpose is also to provide information and advice to the government and members of the public on matters concerning International Relations and 'to provide facilities for the training of Nigerian diplomats and personnel and those of other countries whose vocations relate to international affairs'.[2] Finally, it is to 'promote and encourage the study and research into all aspects of international affairs'. The Nigerian government appointed Dr Lawrence Fabunmi, who completed his PhD in International Relations at the London School of Economics, as its first Director-General. He was supported by a number of research staff and other auxiliary staff.

The Nigerian government strongly believed that Nigeria by its sheer size, population (about 25 per cent of the whole of Africa) and vast and varied natural and mineral resources, was destined to play an active leadership role in Africa, and to take a vigorous initiative in the international arena. However, in spite of the vision that marked the founding of the NIIA and the measures taken, very little research came out of the Institute during its first five years, that is, until the January 1966 *coup d'état*. There were two main reasons for this. First, the Balewa government by 1962 was weighed down by a dauntingly complex internal political crisis which diverted its attention away from external issues, and by extension the Institute. Second, during the immediate years of independence the country lacked a sufficient number of academic specialists in International Relations who could have carried out basic and applied research at the Institute.

From early 1966 until the end of the civil war in January 1970, the NIIA became more of a centre for finding practical solutions to actual political crises and conflict rather than a research institute in international affairs. However, from 1970 onwards a new life has been brought to the Institute's research activities. Apart from providing the government with draft memoranda such as the one that led to the sudden recognition of the MPLA government in Luanda late in November 1975, it has turned out a number of books, monographs and articles. Its quarterly journal, the *Nigerian Journal of International Affairs*, carries articles on various aspects of International Relations, ranging from area studies and the foreign policies of individual countries, through economic matters to security problems.[3]

The study of International Relations in Nigerian universities began during the second half of the 1960s. The University College of Ibadan (now University of Ibadan), which was the only university in the country upon independence in 1960, did not offer any courses in international relations until the early 1970s. Even then, this was within the Department of Political Science. Indeed, the Universities of Nigeria, Nsukka and Ife took the lead. In 1965, the University of Nsukka began offering some courses such as comparative government, the foreign policies of the Great Powers, as well as those of some African states including Nigeria. In 1966 the University of Ife signed an agreement with the Nigerian government to train its external affairs officers, however, the political crisis and conflict that gripped the country from late 1966 until January 1970 made it extremely difficult to implement this agreement.

In 1971, the University of Ife established postgraduate courses in International Relations and in March 1976 it established the first Department of International Relations in Nigeria. In 1977, the University of Ife established the first Chair in International Relations in Nigeria, and in the whole of black Africa. In 1982, the University began its undergraduate programme in international relations. In 1980, the Ahmadu Bello University in Zaria had introduced a separate undergraduate programme in international studies within the Department of Political Science. Although the other universities have not gone as far as Ife and Zaria in having separate departments and undergraduate and graduate programmes in International Relations, almost all of them run a number of courses within their various departments of Political Science. Other institutions in which International Relations courses have been taught since the late 1970s include the Command and Staff College in Jaji, the Nigerian Institute of Policy and Strategic Studies and the Foreign Service Academy of the Ministry of External Affairs, Lagos.

Many of the books and articles now being used are the result of the research activities carried out by Nigerian students of international relations. In spite of these, however, we still rely heavily on materials published by Western scholars. Nonetheless, compared with the pre-civil war days, the advance made in the teaching and research in International Relations in Nigeria has since the early 1970s been spectacular. Two major factors contributed to this development. The intervention of numerous foreign powers in the Nigerian civil war brought home to Nigerian leaders and students of international relations that Nigeria's security and territorial integrity could be gravely endangered by external forces. Secondly, the Nigerian economy was very strong in the 1970s thanks to the oil price hikes of 1973–74 and 1979–80. From the revenue generated by the oil boom the Nigerian government made funds available to universities to intensify the study of International Relations and also to establish some military institutions, and other non-university-based institutions for International Relations teaching and research.

In short, one can say that the study has left its infancy in Nigeria, but has yet to reach maturity.

18.2 APPROACH TO THE STUDY

While the study of International Relations in Nigeria has been spared guerrilla warfare between the Traditional and the Scientific writers, such as that between Hedley Bull and Morton Kaplan in the 1960s, Nigerian academics have differed in their approach to the subject. Most of those who have made significant contributions to the understanding of International Relations in Nigeria follow the traditional, Realist approach. However, a very tiny group of Nigerian Marxist writers such as Segun Osoba of the University of Ife, Ikenna Nzimiro, and O.C. Eze of the Imo State University in Owerri, and a few non-Nigerian writers such as Timothy Shaw have preferred the political economy approach. They condemn the overwhelming majority of other scholars for being super-structural and state-centric, and mistaking the states in the developing world for autonomous actors.

While these writers may have some points, their writings are not helpful. As long as we live in an anarchical society, foreign policy will continue to focus on the nation state. In many developing countries in Africa and Asia, the question of national unity cannot be taken for granted. There are vast ethnic, regional, and religious differences which have been weakening the already minimal commitment to national cohesion. In such places it is imperative that the study of International Relations be more state-centric, for then it can serve the purpose not only of uniting the country, but also of assisting such countries in playing a more realistic role in the world.

It is not that the Scientific or Behavioural approach is not useful in the study of international affairs, but it is the general consensus in Nigeria that its usefulness must not be exaggerated. For in International Relations we are dealing with a large number of complex, unquantifiable and unverifiable variables. Moreover, in many developing countries, there are not sufficient data to generate the level of hypotheses that are made in either the United States or in the Scandinavian countries. No theories of peace research or conflict studies have thus been developed in Nigeria.

18.3　PROBLEMS FACING THE STUDY

The appointment of the present Nigerian Minister for External Affairs, Dr A.B. Akinyemi, and that of his predecessor Dr Ibrahim A. Gambari, both of whom are academic specialists in International Relations, show that the Nigerian government has come to recognise the value of such specialists. However, three main problems confront the study of International Relations in Nigeria: finance; access to raw data; and the resistance of the top civil service to intellectuals.

Up until 1981 financing was not a serious problem in the study of international affairs of Nigeria. But with the virtual collapse of the oil market in July 1981, the question of funding became a major problem. Since the early 1970s crude oil has accounted for about 97 per cent of Nigerian foreign exchange earnings, and about 85 per cent of the government's revenue. The problem has been exacerbated by the virtual collapse of agriculture, combined with large-scale corruption among public officials, and utter mismanagement of the economy. It has therefore been very difficult for the government to release more money for employment of teaching and research staff in International Relations and for the acquisition of essential books, journals, and other relevant documents. Indeed, since 1982, subventions to the various universities and other institutions engaged in the study of international affairs have been dwindling. Not only have the university libraries been unable to order new publications in International Relations, but they have also been unable to renew their subscriptions to relevant international journals since 1982. This financial straitjacket has led to massive reductions in the number of international conferences on international affairs in Nigeria, and also in the number of Nigeria scholars travelling abroad for similar conferences.

Access to raw data by students of International Relations has been very constrained. The Official Secrets Oaths Act imposes a moratorium of 30 years on all classified government papers. There is also a lack of mutual trust between the top federal civil servants and the academics. The type of periodic interchange of staff between them that is found in the United States rarely takes place in Nigeria. Indeed, top federal civil servants resist the 'invasion' of their special preserve. Finally, there are very few memoirs or biographies of former leaders or ambassadors from which students can glean information. The notable exception is Kola Balogun's *Mission to Ghana* (1963) written by Nigeria's first High Commissioner to Ghana from 1959 to 1961.

18.4 FUTURE PROSPECTS

The future prospects for the study of International Relations are not bright. Crude oil has not recovered to its pre-1981 price level. In September 1986, the government, by introducing the Second Tier Foreign Exchange Market (SFEM) effectively devalued the currency by about 400 per cent against the US dollar. This means that the total external debt of the country which stood at Naira 29.3 billion[4] in 1985 has now risen to about Naira 117.2 billion. The foreign reserves have been virtually depleted to less than one month's import bill. Although agriculture has recently shown some slight improvement, it has yet to recover to its pre-1966 level of output. The upshot of all this has been a reduction in government expenditures of about 25 per cent across the board in 1987. This has of course been damaging to all branches of academic study.

Repealing the Official Secrets Oaths Act is not one of the priorities of the present Nigerian government. Indeed, the recent proscription of the weekly magazine, *Newswatch* in April 1987 by the Babangida government indicates that the government is bent on preventing information from getting to the public, perhaps more so than the Buhari government.

If the economy were to improve substantially, if foreign capital was to begin flowing into Nigeria on a large scale, and if international confidence in Nigeria's economy and management suddenly returned, then the outlook would not be as bleak. If the Official Secrets Oaths Act were reviewed, if the top civil servants were to become less hostile to academics, and if the Nigerian government offered enlightened leadership on the side of serious intellectual pursuit, then one could hope for better prospects in the long-term future. However, in the short term, the prospects for the study of International Relations in Nigeria are likely to be poor.

NOTES AND REFERENCES

1. For details see Decree 35, *The Nigerian Institute of International Affairs Decree, 1971* (Lagos).
2. From the above, we can see that its functions are in some respects different from those of the Royal Institute of International Affairs in the United Kingdom. The difference is understandable: the NIIA Publications is entirely financed by the government.
3. Among its Publications are: A.B. Akinyemi, *Readings in Nigerian Foreign Policy* (Lagos 1978); G. Olusanya and B.A. Akindele, *Twenty-Five Years of Nigerian Foreign Policy* (Lagos 1986).
4. *Annual Report and Statement of Accounts for the year ended 31 December 1985* (Lagos: Central Bank of Nigeria, 1986), p. 90.

19 The Study of International Relations in Israel

Aharon Klieman

Foreign affairs specialists visiting Israel for the first time from Western Europe or North America invariably register surprise at finding the local academic scene so professionally similar to their own. Perception matches reality, for the Israeli study of international relations does not differ in its basic outline and contours from the leading centres of teaching and research elsewhere.

Aside from the expected variance in specific topics of national and scholarly concern, the core curriculum at Israeli institutions of higher learning is essentially the same as in other Western countries. Each of the theoretical contructs, dominant approaches and methodologies – from the traditional to the most Behavioural and *avant garde* – is represented. So, too, do members of the Israeli branch of the profession share the continuing twofold preoccupation with the larger search for identity and the problem of direction.

That Israel is today in the mainstream of the discipline rather than a provincial eastern Mediterranean backwater should not be taken so easily for granted. A constant struggle has been made both to forge strong professional links overseas and to reach, and maintain, high professional standards. What I have been told sometimes strikes the bemused outside observer as characteristic Israeli hyperactivism is really a deeper, almost compulsive effort – both individual and institutional – at countering physical distance along with Arab exclusionary campaigns aimed against Israeli nationals. If mediocrity and isolation (geographic or political) obsess all Jewish Israeli intellectuals this holds true especially for the circle of scholars whose concentration on international affairs of necessity dictates a global orientation. It is this quest for recognition which perhaps best accounts for the high ratings of Israeli colleagues in virtually every category of professional activity: from associa-

303

tion membership, conference attendance and paper presentation
to journal and other scholarly publication.

19.1   ISRAEL AMONG THE NATIONS

External political developments being of constant and direct
immediacy for community-conscious Israelis, little effort is required
to convince students in an introductory world politics course of the
subject-matter's relevance. Wider public awareness has been height-
ened by a sequence of four singularly dramatic events during the past
twenty years. First, the Six Day War of 1967, which, in retrospect, may
have enhanced Israeli security but complicated its foreign relations.
This was followed by the traumatic 1973 Yom Kippur War, exposing
structural and procedural defects in national policy-making while at
the same time discouraging complacency by arguing for greater citizen participation in the debate over policy issues and options bearing
on their individual lives. Then came the Sadat initiative in November
1977, that generated renewed hope in peace prospects together with
public as well as scholarly interest in the mechanics, or 'modalities',
of how states make the transition from enmity to amity. The last
formative event took place in 1982, with the military intervention
in Lebanon teaching the limits of coercive diplomacy and the
imperative for a more integrated, subtle politico–military strategy if
in fact Israel is to achieve a durable peace within the next decades.

In Israel's case its prospects for normalcy, for security and for
economic strength as an industrialising yet small, solitary Jewish state
deficient in natural resources will hinge on developments beyond
the country's immediate borders as much as on domestic variables.
One senses the younger generation in particular has taken this
message to heart, with the universities being the main beneficiary.

19.2   UNIVERSITY PROGRAMMES OF INTERNATIONAL
RELATIONS STUDY

The study of international affairs is one of the growth areas in
Israeli academia. Indeed, it has experienced a major transformation,
emerging in the 1980s as a recognised field of specialisation in
addition to becoming a more disciplined discipline. Signposts of
this increased demand for understanding and expertise are found

in each of the following: student enrolment, course offerings, faculty rosters, and postgraduate employment opportunities.

The origins of the profession date back to the pre-state period of the British mandate for Palestine. Following the establishment of the Hebrew University in Jerusalem in 1925 courses were taught on the history, philosophy and jurisprudence of the nation state and its external relations by such distinguished names as Benjamin Akzin, Nathan Feinberg, Leo Kohn and Meir Verete. This unstructured pattern continued until 1969. In a landmark decision, after a previous attempt in the early 1960s had failed, the Hebrew University opened a separate Department of International Relations built around scholars like Saul Friedlander, its first director, Michael Brecher, Yehoshafat Harkabi and Nissim Bar-Yaakov.

The Hebrew University remains the only institution offering three programmes in International Relations, including one at the undergraduate level. Nearly 600 students at present are working on bachelor degrees in the Department of International Relations; about 300 new students are admitted each year. At the more advanced level approximately 100 graduates are studying for their master's degree, with nearly a dozen in various stages of PhD work.

At the three other universities International Relations is taught within departments of Political Science.[1] Tel-Aviv University offers a required first-year 'Introduction to World Politics' which then serves as the prerequisite for a large number of International Relations-related elective lecture courses. Graduate students may specialise in international politics and foreign policy, international economics, or strategic studies, aside from public administration, political theory and comparative politics. Some 35 graduates, or one-third of those enrolled in the MA program, are pursuing one of the former three fields; six of the twelve approved doctoral dissertation topics likewise fall within the category of International Relations. A comparable distribution exists at both Haifa University and Bar-Ilan University. In the latter, figures indicate that International Relations is the second most preferred area of graduate concentration (after public administration): about 30 out of 70 registered MA students, and three out of ten PhD candidates.

Special mention should be made of the Open University. Founded in 1976, it has shared in this larger effort at bringing the theme of 'Israel among the nations' to a wider audience. As part of its diverse programme of external studies it offers courses on 'Basic Concepts of International Relations',[2] 'Selected Problems in Israeli Foreign

Policy', 'The Emergence of the Modern Middle East', 'The Politics of Africa'. The Open University has extended its activities into broadcasting radio lectures on the above topics, organising one-day public seminars, translating basic International Relations readings into Hebrew and editing a well-received book on Israeli statecraft.[3] The Command and Staff College, like the National Defence College, while catering to a much more select audience of middle-echelon career officers, also exposes them to a battery of intensive courses on Middle East and international affairs led by university guest lecturers.

19.3   FACULTY MEMBERS: A PROFILE

This demand for International Relations courses and expertise in turn has stimulated a parallel increase in the teaching staff. At Tel-Aviv six of the 17 full-time positions in Political Science are held by International Relations specialists. Haifa has four such slots; so, too, Bar-Ilan. Hebrew University's Department of International Relations reports 21 positions: fourteen tenured and seven untenured. Even these figures do not fully reflect the number of people lecturing in the field. For one thing, there are some professors, in particular regional or country specialists, whose courses in comparative politics fall within the scope of world affairs yet who don't necessarily see themselves as limited solely to International Relations. Similarly, due to university politics and structuring, even in Jerusalem not all course offerings in world affairs are concentrated in the Department of International Relations. One finds a wide selection of listings taught by members of other departments: Russian studies, the Institute of Asian and African Studies, American studies and of course Political Science. At Tel-Aviv a comparable division of labour prevails, with current regional affairs dealt with by the Department for Middle Eastern and African history and its sister Department of Russian history responsible for covering Soviet policy – both located in the School of History, as opposed to the Political Science Department across the campus in the Faculty of Social Science. Separate spheres of influence, especially if not accompanied by regularised consultation and co-ordination, have not always made for the most integrated, consistent or effective university teaching programme.

The community of International Relations scholars lends itself to a composite profile in which essentially three waves or generations can be identified on the basis of the two variables of age and professional training. In the initial stage, bridging the pre-state period and the post-1948 era of statehood until the late 1960s, lecturers for the most part tended to be Jewish emigrés from central or eastern Europe whose approach mirrored their continental schooling, with its solid grounding in the classics and strong emphasis on law, history and normative theory. The pioneer educators have since passed from the scene, but only after laying the foundations for serious Israeli scholarship.

Their place was taken by the second generation which has overseen the rapid development of separate International Relations programmes at each of the universities throughout the 1970s and 1980s. With few exceptions this generation received its professional training abroad, either in western Europe, primarily British, universities or else in the United States. Representatives of the European school include senior people like David Vital (Oxford), Dan Horowitz (Oxford), Saul Friedlander (Geneva), Yair Evron (London School of Economics), Amnon Sella (Edinburgh), Gabriel Sheffer (Oxford), Uri Bialer, Yossi Heller and Avner Yaniv – all three London School of Economics graduates.

Israeli professors with American degrees include: Yehezkel Dror, Saadia Touval and Michael Handel (Harvard), Gabriel Ben-Dor (Princeton), Avraham Ben-Zvi (Chicago), Nissan Oren (Johns Hopkins), Shai Feldman (California, Berkeley), Eytan Gilboa (Harvard), Nimrod Novik (Pennsylvania). Their ranks were swelled by a third sub-group comprised of individuals either who held extended appointments (Michael Brecher, Alan Dowty) or who have settled here permanently from the West. This includes Galia Golan (The Hebrew University), Aharon Klieman (Johns Hopkins, SAIS), Edy Kaufman (Paris, Sorbonne), Mark Heller (Harvard), Dore Gold (Columbia), Gerald Steinberg (MIT); and from the United Kingdom, Stuart Cohen (Oxford), Raymond Cohen (Oxford, Lancaster and Hebrew University), Norman Rose (London School of Economics).

Now, toward the end of this decade, it becomes possible to speak of a third generation of younger, Israeli-born specialists with a slightly more pronounced inclination toward the newer, more quantitative and Behavioural approaches. Some have received appointments as teachers or researchers after successfully completing doctoral work abroad, including Ze'ev Maoz (Michigan), Efraim Inbar (Chicago), Uri Ullman (Indiana), Ariel Levite (Cornell), Immanuel Adler (Berkeley), and Amikam Nachmani (Oxford). Others, though, have been awarded doctorates here in Israel, thus suggesting the capacity of the local International Relations academic programme to be at once attractive and self-sustaining. Among this latter group are Yaakov Vertzberger and Yaakov Bar-Siman-Tov of Hebrew University, and Efraim Karsh of Tel-Aviv University. This younger generation is already beginning to make its mark, and is counted upon to play a significant role in determining the course of the Israeli discipline in the years to come. An immediate concern though, is that the growth experienced in the last decade or so – manifested in both programme expansion and recruitment – may have peaked. The serious budgetary constraints facing all the institutions of higher learning is one factor; another is the priority given by the several departments of political science to strengthening their other, non-International Relations sub-fields.

The private and public sectors at present are a more promising job market for graduates in foreign studies. The large banks compete with companies engaged in the export-import business for applicants showing language aptitude, country specialisation or degrees in either international law or economics. This trend should continue as Israel's commercial and diplomatic relations extend into regions like eastern Europe and the Far East previously closed to it.

19.4 FIELDS OF ACADEMIC INTEREST

Our earlier profile of Israeli scholars categorised them along generational lines and by academic training. A third feature is cross-cutting; it distinguishes between International Relations generalists and those with narrower, especially regional or individual country expertise. Thus, for example, an entire group of prominent Middle East affairs specialists is exempted from discussion here, yet is worthy of separate treatment in its own right.

We are reminded by Holsti and others[4] that fields of scholarly interest in any given country largely reflect the spectrum of its national themes and immediate concerns. This bias certainly shows up in Israeli research and teaching emphases; but at the same time it has stimulated an enormous amount of original work. Brecher's major contribution to decision-making and crisis analysis, based on the Israeli case, comes immediately to mind.[5]

My point is that unfortunately for Israel it has provided, together with the larger Middle East sub-system, a principal testing ground for new weaponry and applied military doctrines. By the same token, however, Israel also offers an extraordinary opportunity for testing conventional political wisdom and for exploring new directions. In turning political adversity into scholarly advantage the Israeli community of International Relations researchers tends as a whole more toward the state-centric approach than to the transnational one; to concentrate somewhat less on the thematic, or theory and methodology, and more on substantive aspects usually of direct concern to Israel.

Two noteworthy considerations act as reinforcement. First are the pressures to which the scholar and expert are often subjected: to show commitment and to be policy-relevant. Calls by the media for analysis of fast-breaking world developments, requests to participate in Arab–Israel simulation exercises, speaking invitations to discuss current events, even annual military reserve duty spent drafting position papers or scenarios – these are but a few of the forces which return even the theoretically-inclined academic back to existing realities.

A second consideration stems from the part-time affiliation of many senior lecturers on International Relations with one or another of the Research Institutes that have proliferated over the last ten–fifteen years.[6] Listed by city there is the Jewish-Arab Center in Haifa; Tel-Aviv boasts of the Jaffee Center for Strategic Studies, which publishes the annual *Middle East Military Balance* and a monograph series, and the Dayan Center, sponsor of the yearly *Middle East Contemporary Survey* and occasional papers in Hebrew and English on Arab history and politics; Jeruslaem-based institutions include the Leonard Davis Institute for International Relations, the Van Leer Foundation and the Truman Peace Research Institute.

Scholars are encouraged in this association by a complex of motives beginning in the conviction that research and teaching are mutually inclusive, and ending in the slightly less prosaic inducements of prestige, salary increments or publishing outlets. Nevertheless, what matters here is that from the standpoint of the Institutes themselves their common interest lies in being policy-oriented. It follows therefore that they serve as primary contractors for project studies investigating contemporary issues relating to Israeli foreign affairs and security broadly defined rather than those of a more heuristic or theoretical nature. Often the final product suggests something of a compromise between two opposite pulls: the one, of broad generalisation and universal application; the other, of empirical case studies, if not restricted to Israel then certainly applicable to it.

A survey of the major scholarly work done by Israelis indicates distinction in several specific areas. Ten such 'clusters' include the following: superpower regional contests;[7] crisis management and conflict resolution;[8] big power–small state (patron–client) relationships;[9] decision-making and domestic–external linkages;[10] perceptual models of nationality and irrationality;[11] defence economics and national security policy;[12] intelligence and strategic surprise;[13] conventional and nuclear deterrence strategies;[14] international law and organisations;[15] modern diplomatic practice, with specific reference to Israeli foreign policy.[16]

The benefits of this systematic thinking and insight are mostly under-exploited, however. Which is another way of saying that the International Relations specialist as educator, in the larger sense of the concept, is still unappreciated in the context of Israel. The individual scholar may have both an impressive list of publications and what Hoffmann also discerns in American academics as the tendency 'to want to be useful, not only as a scientist, but as an expert citizen whose science can help promote intelligently the embattled values of his country'[17] not to mention the extra incentive, in the instance of Israel, where the country itself is embattled. And yet the primary target audience is certainly not the Israeli public at large; with the possible exception of a very small civilian and military elite the audience is a foreign one.

The most common explanation for this paradox ascribes it to the 'two cultures', i.e. to the 'great divide' found in many western societies between the scholar and the practitioner.[18] But possibly size is even more of a factor. Israel is too small to sustain more than a few scholarly publications, meaning there is virtually no access to the Hebrew-speaking audience other than through brief radio commentary or TV appearances, or perhaps an occasional op-ed piece in the Hebrew press. The only Hebrew-language political science journal is *Medina, Mimshal v'Yachasim Bein-Leumiim* (State, Government and International Relations), a quarterly with a limited readership. Similarly, the monthly survey, *Skira Khodsheet*, caters chiefly to a military readership. There are two journals of note published in Israel in English: *The Jerusalem Quarterly* and the *Jerusalem Journal of International Relations*; but they merely confirm the point being argued here with a subscription drive aimed at the overseas reader. Merely add the professional factor (publication as the criterion for promotion and tenure) and one is able better to understand the preference of scholars working in Israel to have their research findings appear in prestigious journals abroad and announced by the leading university presses or publishing houses in the US and Western Europe.

19.5 THE STATE OF THE SCIENCE IN ISRAEL

Choice of audience – academic or layman?, at home or abroad? – is but the first of several dilemmas now confronting the study of International Relations in Israel. Rather than ending this survey on a self-congratulatory note it seems only appropriate in the context of a Jewish–Israeli branch of the profession to conclude by beginning with its shortcomings. These final remarks may also serve as an agenda for what specifically might be done in the coming years to further strengthen the discipline.

Parochialism

Concern with immediate, pressing issues centring on Israel, while understandable, nevertheless, has deflected us from a broader, systemic view of global-wide political issues. The allegiance of Israeli colleagues may be divided, but only marginally so. Their concern is for the state of the nation, and considerably less with the state of the discipline or with the state of the world. They have thus not really taken up as yet the challenge of struggling with larger theoretical questions. There is much room for generalisation and for conceptualising at higher levels of abstraction.

To be sure, the absence of foundation support or of government enthusiasm are retardants, discouraging heuristic exercises as well as new and original course design. Until now, of the range of functions open to the Israeli specialist, all four – description, analysis, prescription and even prediction – have been preferred to theorising. What needs to be done is to supplement the existing pattern of narrow, problem-directed, Israel-oriented teaching and research in order to strike a better balance between theory and praxis, between systemic and country-specific phenomena.

Neglected Areas

Because Israeli international studies are not informed by a dominant school of thought or single acknowledged leading thinker they have evolved in eclectic fashion, based on individual preference and national developments. Suffice it to note the growth of interest in international terrorism in response to the sudden rash of air hijackings and terrorist actions in the late 1960s and early 1970s related to the Arab–Israel conflict.

As a consequence, the tendency has been for some sub-fields to receive thorough treatment in the classroom and in scholarly publication – indeed, some are perceived of as Israeli areas of expertise; whereas others are seriously neglected. The following table suggests this disparity in emphases.

Treated	*Neglected*
Israeli and Middle East political history	modern diplomatic history
Middle East regional politics	Middle East (and international) economics
Arab-Israel conflict patterns	other conflict situations
strategic studies arms race dynamics	diplomatic practice arms control and disarmament
force capabilities	political geography and defence economics
crisis decision-making	non-crisis decision-making
conflict management	conflict resolution and peace studies
single-country foreign policy (Israel, United States, Britain, Soviet Union)	comparative foreign policies
American studies; the third world	European politics
international law	international regimes, world organisations
methodology (simulation, game theory, quantitative)	broad-range theory

This criticism should not be misinterpreted as implying total neglect of entire topics or gaping holes in Israeli scholarship. The cross-listing merely suggests that much more can be done to round out course offerings, to guide recruitment and to generate further research.

Institutional Rivalries

Israeli teachers of world politics, to their credit, have avoided replicating the debilitating American battle of the literates versus the numerates.[19] Yet neither do they benefit from a sense of community. This absence of group solidarity is as surprising as it is necessary given common concerns, mutual research interests and limited resources at their disposal.

Historians and social scientists, for example, do not often talk to each other – in the scholarly sense – despite working on similar subjects, although from different perspectives. When they do get together the discourse usually confirms they are not using the same language, arguing particular events against paradigms. Similar bridges are lacking between the several universities and between the handful of departments offering International Relations courses. There is little inter-disciplinary research or team teaching. Few collaborative efforts have been undertaken along the lines of a common textbook or introductory world politics syllabus, or of edited works with Israeli contributors drawn from the several departments. There is, in short, no real conscious attempt at pooling intellectual, manpower or monetary resources.

This tradition ought to be abandoned in favour of wider frameworks: inter-university, inter-departmental and, in particular, inter-personal. There is great untapped potential here. And it can be fostered through increased participation at all three levels in each other's scientific projects, seminars, workshops and conferences. Virtually the sole meeting-ground until now have been the yearly one-day meetings of the Israel Political Science Association; only at this late date is there a move afoot to organise an Israeli branch of the International Studies Association which might serve as a vital umbrella under which scholars labouring in the same vineyard can come together to share teaching experiences as well as research problems.

Marginal Policy Input

A final irony is that despite whatever prospects for objectivity have been sacrificed in pursuit of relevance, nothing in the Israeli experience quite compares to the American model for scholar-turned-statesman. There is little movement back and forth between academia and government, thereby reinforcing 'the great divide' between the scholar and national policy-makers.[20] Each side remains fairly self-contained in its respective sphere of competence and thus free to deprecate the other's narrowness and shortcomings.

To some purists this prevailing situation of mutual misunderstanding may be satisfactory; the author disagrees. So long as the gap remains it is fair to conclude that both professions stand to lose. Government leaders forfeit what the International Relations scholar has to offer by way of unconventional thinking, alternative policy recommendations, historical and theoretical perspectives – the larger picture. Similarly, the academic is deprived by this state of alienation and lack of communication from grasping the real world of foreign policy, in particular the complex of operational constraints at work on decision-makers. It is an invaluable experience which the 'ivory tower' scholar might later be able to draw upon in his or her lecturing and research.

There is, and always will be room for self-improvement in the Israeli discipline. Yet nothing can detract from what the very study of International Relations in itself already symbolises. What better conveys the profound revolution which has taken place in the history and status of the Jewish people in modern times, especially since 1948, than the emphasis given in Israel to global affairs? It reflects the transition of the Jews from homelessness to sovereignty, from powerlessness to national power and from being an international anomaly to an important player in the game of nations. This renewed involvement lies at the heart of the intense public as well as professional, scholarly interest in international politics and foreign policy one finds in Israel at present.

NOTES AND REFERENCES

1. The Technion University specialises in the physical sciences. Ben-Gurion University of the Negev offers a sub-field in political science as part of its Faculty of Social Science.

2. The course is accompanied by twelve extensive reading units thus far published on fundamental issues such as 'the nature of the international system', and 'foreign policy-making'.

3. Benjamin Neuberger (ed.), *Diplomacy and Confrontation: Selected Issues in Israel's Foreign Relations, 1948–1978* (Tel-Aviv: Everyman's University, 1984).

4. K.J. Holsti, *International Politics* (Englewood Cliffs: Prentice-Hall, 1967), pp. 22-23.
5. Michael Brecher, *The Foreign Policy System of Israel* (New Haven: Yale University Press, 1972); Michael Brecher, *Decisions in Israel's Foreign Policy* (London: Oxford University Press, 1974); Michael Brecher, *Decisions in Crisis: Israel 1967 and 1973* (Berkeley: University of California Press, 1980).
6. A description of the research activity of the leading non-governmental institutions at the start of the decade is provided by Mark Heller, 'International Relations Research in Israel', *Orbis* (Fall 1982), pp. 757–64.
7. Yair Evron, *The Middle East: Nations, Super-Powers and War* (London: Elek, 1973); Edy Kaufman, *The Superpowers and Their Spheres of Influence* (New York: St Martin's Press, 1976); Avraham Ben-Zvi, *The American Approach to Superpower Collaboration in the Middle East, 1973–1986* (Boulder, Col. and Jerusalem: Westview Press and The Jerusalem Post, 1986), Jaffee, Center for Strategic Studies Study No. 5. Three important studies of Soviet policy are: Galia Golan, *Yom Kippur and After: The Soviet Union and the Middle East Crisis* (Cambridge: Cambridge University Press, 1977); Yaakov Roi, *The Limits to Power: Soviet Policy in the Middle East* (London: Croom Helm, 1979); Amnon Sella, *Soviet Political and Military Conduct in the Middle East* (London: Macmillan, 1981).
8. Raymond Cohen and Stuart Cohen, *Peace Conferences: The Formal Aspects* (Jerusalem: The Hebrew University's The Leonard Davis Institute for International Relations (hereafter 'Davis Institute')); Yaakov Bar-Siman-Tov, *The Israeli–Egyptian War of Attrition: A Case Study of Limited Local War* (New York: Columbia University Press, 1980); Alan Dowty, *Middle East Crisis: United States Decision-Making in 1968, 1970, and 1973* (Berkeley: University of California Press, 1984). A significant addition to the literature on crises is the special issue of *The Jerusalem Journal of International Relations* 'on Studies in Crisis Behavior', Michael Brecher (ed.) (Winter–Spring 1978).

How to mediate and then resolve conflict is the focus of Saadia Touval, *The Peace Brokers: Mediators in the Arab–Israeli Conflict 1948–1979* (Princeton, N.J.: Princeton University Press, 1982); also Nissan Oren (ed.), *Termination of Wars: Processes, Procedures and Aftermaths* (Jerusalem: The Magnes Press, 1982). Further representative of studying international conflict through the prism of the Arab–Israeli struggle is Shmuel Sandler's *Israel, the Palestinians and the West Bank* (Lexington: Lexington Books, 1984). Zeev Maoz enlarges the frame of reference in his quantitative study, *Paths to Conflict: International Dispute Initiation 1916-1976* (Boulder, Col.: Westview Press, 1982). Of interest methodologically is Eytan Gilboa, *Simulation of Conflict and Conflict Resolution in the Middle East* (Jerusalem: Davis Institute, 1980).
9. The first to look closely at great power–small state relationships was David Vital in his two studies, *The Inequality of States* (Oxford: Clarendon Press, 1967) and *The Survival of Small States* (Oxford:

Oxford Clarendon Press, 1971). Often cited in the literature is Yehezkel Dror, *Crazy States* (Lexington: D.C. Heath, 1971). Several younger scholars have built upon this earlier work. Representative are: Michael Handel, *Weak States in the International System* (London: Frank Cass, 1981); Efraim Inbar, *Outcast Countries in the World Community* (Denver: University of Denver, 1985); Efraim Karsh, *The Cautious Bear: Soviet Military Engagement in Middle East Wars in the Post-1967 Era* (Jerusalem: Jaffee Center for Strategic Studies, 1985); Avraham Ben-Zvi, *Alliance Politics and the Limits of Influence: The Case of the United States and Israel 1975–1983* (Jerusalem: Jaffee Center for Strategic Studies, 1984); Shlomo Slonim, *United States – Israel Relations, 1967–1973: A Study of the Convergence and Divergence of Interests* (Jerusalem: Davis Institute, 1974); Eytan Gilboa, *American Public Opinion Toward Israel and the Arab–Israel Conflict* (Lexington: D.C. Heath, 1987); Yaakov Bar-Siman-Tov, *Israel, the Superpowers and War in the Middle East* (Boulder, Col.: Westview Press, 1987).

10. Linkage theory and the decision-making approach inform the work of Michael Brecher. See his *The Foreign Policy System of Israel: Setting, Images, Process* (London: Oxford University Press, 1972); also Yaakov Bar-Siman-Tov, *Linkage Politics in the Middle East: Syria Between Domestic and External Conflict, 1961–1970* (Boulder: Westview Press, 1983).

11. Cognition and perception play an important role in the work of such Israeli scholars as: Yehoshafat Harkabi, *Arab Attitudes Toward Israel* (London: Vallentine, 1972) and *The Bar Kochba Syndrome: Risk and Realism in International Politics* (Chappaqua, New York: Rossel Books, 1983); Nissan Oren (ed.), *Image and Reality in International Politics* (New York: St Martins Press, 1984); Raymond Cohen, *Threat Perception in International Crisis* (Madison: University of Wisconsin Press, 1979). See also Yaacov Vertzberger, *Misperception in Foreign Policy Making: The Sino-Indian Conflict, 1959–1962* (Boulder, Col.: Westview Press, 1984).

12. Michael Handel, *Israel's Political–Military Doctrine* (Cambridge: Harvard University. Centre for International Affairs, 1975); Dan Horowitz, *Israel's Concept of Defensible Borders* (Jerusalem: Davis Institute, 1975); Zvi Lanir (ed.), *Israeli Security Planning in the 1980s* (New York: Praeger, 1984); Yair Evron, *War and Intervention in Lebanon: The Israel–Syrian Deterrence Dialogue* (London: Croom Helm, 1987). Two recent works are by Avner Yaniv, *Deterrence Without the Bomb: The Politics of Israeli Strategy* (Lexington: Lexington Books, 1986) and *Dilemmas of Security* (New York: Oxford University Press, 1987). One of the few scholars dealing with the economic dimension in world politics is Alfred Tovias of the Hebrew University. Two of his studies are: *Tariff Preferences in Mediterranean Diplomacy*. (London: St Martin's Press, 1977); and Seev Hirsch, Ruth Arad and Alfred Tovias, *The Economics of Peacemaking: Focus on the Egyptian–Israeli Situation* (New York: Macmillan, 1983).

13. A great amount of research on intelligence and surprise has been generated by the 1973 war, including that of Avraham Ben-Zvi,

'Hindsight and Foresight: A Conceptual Framework for the Analysis of Surprise Attack', *World Politics* (Vol. 28, No. 3, April, 1976), pp. 381–95; Michael Handel, *The Diplomacy of Surprise* (Cambridge: Harvard University, 1981); Ariel Levite, *Intelligence and Strategic Surprise* (New York: Columbia University Press, 1987).

14. Yehoshsfat Harkabi, *Nuclear War and Nuclear Peace* (Jerusalem: Israel Program for Scientific Translations, 1966); Yair Evron, *The Role of Arms Control in the Middle East* (London: International Institute of Strategic Studies, 1977); Shai Feldman, *Israel's Nuclear Deterrence* (New York: Columbia University Press, 1983); Avraham Ben-Zvi, *The Illusion of Deterrence* (Boulder, Col.: Westview Press, 1987).

15. Merely reflective of the international legal approach are: Nissim Bar Yaacov, *The Israel–Syrian Armistice* (Jerusalem: The Magnes Press, 1967); Yehuda Blum, *Secure Boundaries and Middle East Peace in Light of International Law and Practice* (Jerusalem: The Magnes Press, 1971); Ruth Lapidoth, *Freedom of Navigation, with Special Reference to International Waterways in the Middle East* (Jerusalem: Davis Institute, 1975).

16. Raymond Cohen, *International Politics: The Rules of the Game* (New York: Longman, 1981); Uri Bialer, *'Our Place in the World': Mapai and Israel's Foreign Policy Orientation 1947–1952* (Jerusalem: Davis Institute, 1981). Abba Eban, Israel's scholar-statesman, has written an important commentary on contemporary diplomatic practice, *The New Diplomacy: International Affairs in the Modern Age* (New York: Random House, 1983). See also the present author's two studies of aspects of Israeli diplomacy: Aaron S. Klieman, *Israel's Globan Reach: Arms Sales as Diplomacy* (New York and London: Pergamon–Brassey's, 1985), and *Statecraft in the Dark: Israel's Practice of Quiet Diplomacy* (Jerusalem: Jaffee Center for Strategic Studies, 1988). A new contribution is the study of Israeli diplomatic ties in the initial years by Uri Bialer, *Between East and West: Israel's Foreign Policy Orientation* (Cambridge: Cambridge University Press, forthcoming).

17. Stanley Hoffmann, *Janus and Minerva: Essays in the Theory and Practice of International Politics* (Boulder and London: Westview Press, 1987), p. 10. The reader interested in comparing the state of the discipline in other countries will find most useful the chapter 1, on 'An American Social Science: International Relations' (pp. 3–23).

18. Norman D. Palmer deals with this 'great divide' in his article, 'The Study of International Relations in the United States', *International Studies Quarterly* (Vol. 24, No. 3, September 1980), pp. 343–363. The existence of such a communication problem between Israeli politicians and intellectuals is cited by Lewis Brownstein, 'Decision-Making in Israeli Foreign Policy: An Unplanned Process', *Political Science Quarterly* (Vol. 92, No. 2, Summer 1977), pp. 259–279.

19. The terms are borrowed from Hoffmann, *Janus and Minerra*, p. 17. It is perhaps instructive that at the height of the famous exchange in the mid-1960s between Morton Kaplan, representing the 'Scientific' school, and Hedley Bull on behalf of the 'Traditionalist' or classical approach, it was an Israeli scholar, David Vital, who felt moved to respond

with a critique of both protagonists for encouraging an artificial and ultimately dysfunctional polarisation. David Vital, 'On Approaches to the Study of International Relations, Or, Back to Machiavelli', *World Politics* (Vol. XIX, No. 4, July 1967), pp. 551–562.

20. The two closest examples which come to mind in recent years of International Relations scholars being appointed to government posts are Professor Shlomo Avineri who took a temporary leave of absence from the Hebrew University's political science faculty to serve as director-general of the Ministry for Foreign Affairs from 1975 to 1977; and Dr Nimrod Novik, a senior researcher at Tel-Aviv University's Jaffee Center for Strategic Studies, who has been key political advisor to Shimon Peres, first Prime Minister and then Foreign Minister under the National Unity Government since 1984. These, however, are more in the category of exceptions proving the rule.

20 International Relations Scholarship in the People's Republic of China

Michael B. Yahuda

The development of International Relations as an academic discipline is still at a very early stage in the People's Republic of China.[1] Indeed the social sciences as a whole in China are still in the process of rebuilding after the ravages of the Cultural Revolution of 1966–76, and the limited roles accorded to them even before that time.

International Relations was not among the social sciences that had been well established in China before 1949. To be sure, among the hundreds of Chinese scholars who had been educated in the 1930s and 1940s, to the highest standards in some of the best centres of learning in the West, were those with interests in the allied subjects of International Law, Political Science and International Economics. In view of the paucity of International Relations departments in the West in those years, it is hardly surprising that the subject attracted little attention from Chinese scholars of the time. Perhaps even more importantly, unlike subjects such as History, Literature or Political Philosophy, International Relations could not draw on a legacy of more than two millennia of traditional scholarship.

Following the Communist victory in 1949, Chinese education and scholarship were totally reorganised roughly along Soviet lines. Higher education in general and the social sciences in particular were deemed to be heavily influenced by the West and in need of a Marxist reorientation; some subjects such as Sociology and Political Science were effectively abolished as academic disciplines in 1952. The Soviet practice of largely separating teaching and research was followed, with universities focusing mainly on teaching under the Ministry of Higher Education, while the research-oriented Academy of Sciences was under the direct authority of the State Council. With some modifications this binary structure is still in place today.

It was not until May 1977 that a separate Chinese Academy of Social Sciences (CASS) was established, drawing upon the former Department of Philosophy and Social Science of the Academy of Sciences. That department's six social science disciplines (Philosophy, History, Political Economy and the somewhat less developed Law, International Economics and Politics, and Minority Nationalities Studies) were expanded to include between 30 and 40 Institutes. At the time CASS was established, it was made clear that the pledge to modernise science and technology (as one of the 'four modernisations') also included the social sciences. In November 1978 the authoritative *People's Daily* (in a reversal of nearly thirty years' orthodoxy) declared that the 'laws' of social science, like those of the natural sciences, were independent of the desires or standpoint of any individual or class. In early 1979 Deng Xiaoping finally removed the remaining official stigma on intellectuals by announcing that they too were members of the working class.

Before considering the ensuing development of International Relations in China, two further points need to be made about the social sciences as a whole. First, contemporary Chinese scholarship has acquired a more genuine academic character than at any previous stage since 1949. Debate is settled by rigorous argument or by reference to empirical data rather than by the intervention of political leaders or by reference to unchallengeable textual authorities. Second, the new scholarship has the official purpose of serving the modernisation of the country. As with the goal of modernisation itself, China's social sciences and associated disciplines are supposed to aim at being both socialist and Chinese. However, owing to the need to be policy-relevant, and because of new beginnings after the baleful legacy of the Cultural Revolution and previous years of isolation from the main developments in the social sciences elsewhere in the world, Chinese scholars are unlikely to contribute to general social science theorising in the immediate future. Unlike their Soviet colleagues, Chinese scholars have not been charged with the duty of developing so called 'genuinely scientific studies' in contrast with the allegedly 'bourgeois scholarship' of the West. However, even as they absorb eclectically from scholarship elsewhere in the world, Chinese social scientists have developed independent positions in their analysis which reflect China's particular perspectives and needs. As we shall see this is true even of the nascent discipline of International Relations.

20.1 THE SCOPE OF INTERNATIONAL RELATIONS

Chinese scholars have yet to define what they mean by International Relations. There is a clear outline neither of the scope of the subject nor of the philosophical approach or methodology by which it should best be studied. In fact the subject has something of the vagueness suggested by the English term 'international studies'. The nearest official delineation is provided by the subject index of the quarterly journal *International Studies* for its eight issues of 1985 and 1986, including 79 articles in all.[2] They were divided into three broad headings. Under the first, 'General and Theoretical Aspects', were included twenty articles on 'International Relations', eight on 'the World Economy', four on 'International Law' and one on 'International Organisations'. The bulk of those on International Relations were concerned with analyses of contemporary international problems involving the two superpowers (eleven included either or both in the title), while others focused on the Asian Pacific, Japan, Western Europe, Yugoslavia and prospects for peace. The articles on the world economy included discussions of North–South issues, problems and prospects of the Western economies, and the price of oil. The second broad heading, entitled 'International Countries and Regions', included three articles on China's foreign relations, seven on the United States, seventeen on Western Europe, and fifteen on Asia and Africa. Those on China's foreign relations included an explanation of China's stand on disarmament, an exposition of China's role in the Asia Pacific region, and background on the Sino-Indian dispute. The articles on the other countries and regions were non-polemical accounts of economic, social and political developments in the countries concerned. The final broad heading, 'Miscellaneous', included a review of a Chinese book on disarmament, a lecture in Peking by the Dutch Foreign Minister, and a factual outline of the organisation and development of the Non-Aligned Movement.

Of course, an account from one journal cannot be regarded as definitive. In fact, it excludes certain major areas of research such as world history, 'foreign' political philosophy, 'Western' political science and writings on the international Communist movement, Marxist–Leninist theories of international relations (principally Lenin's theory of imperialism and Soviet style international political economy), and the history of international relations (mainly descriptive accounts of conferences, treaties, wars, alliances, etc., occasionally incorporating Marxist–Leninist categories). Additionally, the proportional coverage of the subject matter is not necessarily indicative nor representative of Chinese writings as a whole. Two recent studies of Chinese publications on the United States and the Soviet Union referred to hundreds of articles many of which were *nei bu*, or for internal circulation only.[3] Nevertheless, the journal is typical of International Relations studies in China for the absence of discussion of what in the West would be regarded as methodological issues. However, as we shall see later, the general view of international politics is distinctive in that it characteristically emphasises multipolarity. That view notably pervades the journal as a whole, but it may be regarded as representative of the bulk of scholarly articles in the field.

Marxist–Leninist–Maoist views of international relations tend to be found either in those universities teaching international politics (and therefore also in the standard textbooks for students) or in Institutes specialising in aspects of the subject that were established in the 1950s and 1960s, such as world economics and politics, that are influenced by their more orthodox traditions. These have an old-fashioned air about them and their impact on the research institutes is neither extensive nor deep.

20.2 THE SIGNIFICANCE OF MULTIPOLARITY

Most of the articles that I have consulted in China's two principal International Relations journals (*International Studies* and *Contemporary International Relations*) in the 1980s characterise the world as essentially multipolar. Five centres (or poles) are usually identified as being the most important in shaping global developments: the United States, the Soviet Union, Japan, the European Community and the third world. Interestingly, China itself is usually mentioned as an independent (sixth?) centre in this context. After an initial reticence, its role is increasingly discussed in greater detail.[4] The Marxist theory of the 'third world' first enunciated in public by Deng Xiaoping in 1974 still receives some attention, but it is rarely used in analyses of specific problems and situations.

Multipolarity has proved a useful vantage point from which Chinese writers have been able to depict a more subtle and variegated view of the dynamics of international relations. Briefly, the emergence of multipolarity is depicted as a process involving changes in the relative military, economic and political centres of global influence since the Second World War. To this end,

Chinese writers have examined comparative military capabilities, relative economic growth rates, and quantitative changes in the proportions of the GNPs and total trade of the various centres relative to that of the world as a basis for explaining the changes in world politics. These changes are also regarded as a sufficient basis for projecting developments over several years ahead. For example, Chinese writers tend to explain many of the problems that the two superpowers have encountered with their respective allies as arising from the weakening of their positions of relative economic strength.[5] Chinese writings on both Western Europe and Japan display greater awareness of the complexities of their respective international positions, and of the constraints that limit their strategic and diplomatic options. Each centre is depicted as having its own characteristic strengths and weaknesses. Interestingly, some scholars argue that notwithstanding these developments the world is still essentially bipolar and look foward to China's emergence as a great independent centre which will bring a transformation to tripolarity.[6]

Although there is not much that is recognisably Marxist in these writings, Chinese authors increasingly pay attention to the socialist character of the Soviet Union and the East European countries. Within a context in which it is argued that capitalism has sufficient 'resilience' to last a long time yet and in which the socialist phase of development is also projected to continue long into the future, Chinese authors do not write about socialist internationalism, but they have debated whether a socialist international economy can coexist with a world (capitalist) economy. Chinese journals, as well as foreign policy spokesmen, pay considerable attention to North-South and South-South relations, but they do not accept the Western quasi-Marxist dependency arguments; instead the Chinese writers envisage that a conciliation of interests is possible despite the activities of the superpowers.

Chinese writers appear reluctant to give much weight to the significance of shared values, traditions and political cultures as factors binding the Western alliance. They do, however, pay much attention to the political capacity to marshal available resources to an effective strategy. The United States, for example, has been criticised for its lack of a co-ordinated diplomatic strategy and the increasing conflicts of bureaucratic interests among its foreign policy-related institutions.[7]

The writings on which the above analysis has drawn are primarily from the policy-oriented Research Institutes and government think-tanks. In so brief a survey, it is not possible to do justice to the variety and subtlety of the already voluminous Chinese writings on International Relations. However, there is still a long way to go toward developing an approach that is distinctively Chinese and Marxist.

NOTES AND REFERENCES

1. For further details on aspects of this see: Thomas P. Bernstein, 'Political Science', in Ann Thurston and J.H. Parker (eds), *Humanistic and Social Science Research in China* (New York: Social Science Research Council, 1980), pp. 130–9; Harry Harding, 'Political Science', in Leo Orleans (ed.), *Science in Contemporary China* (Stanford, CA: Stanford University Press, 1980); David Shambaugh and Wang Jisi, 'Research on International Studies in the People's Republic of China', *Political Science* (Vol. 7, No. 4, Fall 1984); David Shambaugh, 'China's National Security Research Community', *China Quarterly* (forthcoming); David Shambaugh, *Coverage of the United States in Key Chinese Periodicals During 1984*, (Washington, D.C.: USIA Office of Research, December 1985); Gilbert Roznan, 'China's Soviet Watchers in the 1980s: A New Era in Scholarship', *World Politics* (Vol. 37, No. 4, July 1985); and Michael Yahuda, 'New Directions: Chinese Scholarship on International Relations', in Michael Yahuda (ed.), *New Directions in the Social Sciences and Humanities in China* (London: Macmillan, 1987).
2. *Guo-Ji Wen-Ti Yan-Jin* (formerly known as the *Journal of International Studies*) published by the Institute of International Studies that was formally under the Ministry of Foreign Affairs. It was first published in 1959, only to be suspended in 1966. It resumed publication in 1981. Although it is thought to reflect the views of China's diplomatic community, contributors include scholars from a variety of institutes.
3. For extended discussion of this see Roznan, China's Soviet Watchers'.
4. Li Ning, 'A Year with Greater Tension and Tumult', *Journal of International Studies* (No. 1, 1983) and in *Beijing Review* (Nos. 1 and 2, 1983); Dung Yuanhong, 'Fluctuations in Euro–US Relations', *Journal of International Studies* (No. 1, 1983) and in *Beijing Review* (No. 12, 1983) as 'Crises in West European–US Relations'; Huang Suanjian, 'Economic Situation of the Western World in the 1980s and its Political Repercussions', *Journal of International Studies* (No. 4, 1982); Qian Dayong, 'Nixon and US Foreign Relations', *Journal of International Studies* (No. 3, 1983); Pei Monong, 'The Situation and Problems of the Asia Pacific Region', *Journal of International Studies* (No. 4, 1985); Wang Hexing, 'The Position and Role of the Third World in North–South Relations', *Journal of International Studies* (No. 4, 1986); Chen Zhongjing, 'Contemporary

International Strategic Posture', *Contemporary International Relations* (Xian Dai Guo Ji Guan Xi) (Nos. 1 and 2, 1986).

5. Xing Shugang, Li Hunhua and Lin Yingua, 'Changing Balance of Soviet–US Power', *Journal of International Studies* (No. 1, 1983) and in *Beijing Review* (No. 19, 1983); Bai Yulin, 'USSR–US Contest in Southeast Asia and Southwest Pacific', *Contemporary International Relations* (No. 1, 1986); Huan Xiang, 'Some Views on the International Situation', *Contemporary International Relations* (No. 1, 1986); Shen Qurong, 'Democratisation in International Relations and World Peace', *Contemporary International Relations* (No. 3, 1986).

6. See the discussion in *Liaowang* (Outlook), 21 July 1986 reporting a seminar on national defence strategy for the year 2000, as excerpted in *BBC Summary of World Broadcasts*, The Far East, FE/83/8/B11/1–2.

7. Jin Jinhui, 'Foreign Policy of the Reagan Administration', *Journal of International Studies* (No. 1, 1983).

21 *Im Osten Nichts Neues?* International Studies in the German Democratic Republic*
Leon Mangasarian

We begin this study with the seemingly banal point that foreign policy has been an instrument of vital importance in the development of the German Democratic Republic (GDR) as an independent state. The almost universal non-recognition of the GDR following its creation in 1949, which persisted until the signing of the Four Power Agreement on Berlin and the Basic Treaty between East and West Germany, meant that every form of foreign contact was a vital demonstration of the existence and purpose of 'the other German state'. Foreign contacts were so limited that they assumed a special level of importance.[1] Following the widespread international recognition of the GDR in the mid-1970s foreign policy became an even more important tool. Under the leadership of Erich Honecker the policy of *Abgrenzung* (demarcation), which ridicules the idea of German unity, has been marked by intensive efforts – both diplomatic and domestic – to construe the GDR as a completely separate and socialist German state.

The obsessive care with which the GDR cultivates its foreign relations is relevant to the study of International Relations (IR) in that authority has been centralised not only in the formulation of foreign policy but also in the selection of theoretical and practical areas of academic endeavour. Coupled with a highly centralised political system, a vigorous cult of the personality built around Honecker, and devotion to the works of Marx, Engels and Lenin, the study of IR in the GDR appears stifled. East German academic publications prefer to stick to tried and tested formulas. With a few exceptions, approved subjects or issues are investigated and slogans and official statements are inserted in all the correct places. Paradigm debates are not conducted in public in the GDR. A key problem with studying East Germany's 'IR literature' is that diversity is often found only in varying formulations of the officially approved position or policy. The researcher can observe trends but these are more with regard to the ruling Socialist Unity Party's (SED) thinking on foreign policy than developments in the academic field of International Relations. In addition, work on the numerous topics regarded as sensitive simply remains classified. From the outset the researcher is thus faced with a serious information deficit.

We recognise, of course, that East German society is based on a distinctive interpretation of socialism. The GDR's constitution does not grant East Germans an absolute right to express their views freely and publicly. An opinion may be expressed in accordance with the 'spirit and aims' of the consitution and it should not offend 'socialist morals'.[2] The role of the East German academic in the social sciences is to support the policy of the ruling SED, much in the same way that many of the so-called think-tanks in the West play only the tunes composed by those who fund them.

East German leaders boast – with considerable justification – of the GDR's social, scientific, literary, and sporting achievements. On IR they are considerably more reticent. As John Page has noted, 'there are many fields of research in East Germany [which] are regarded as state secrets. Once International Relations goes beyond the safe sphere of peace and understanding you can rapidly find yourself in a no-go area'.[3] Source material for even the most basic studies on the GDR's foreign policy is difficult to obtain. The GDR's restrictive information policy; the limited opportunities for Western academics and students to work in the GDR; the non-investigative role of the press and the lack of parliamentary opposition all contribute to the difficulties.[4] With regard to institutions devoted to the study of IR, even less material is generally available. This seems to stem in part from the overall concern with secrecy but more particularly from the unwillingness of the GDR authorities to publicise the methods and curricula used in the instruction of higher-ranking party cadres.

This chapter will survey the GDR's university system and then examine the universities and institutes involved in IR research and teaching, with special emphasis on the Institute for International Relations at Potsdam–Babelsberg, the Institute for International Politics and Economics in Berlin and the University of Leipzig. We will then turn to four broad approaches utilised in international studies in the GDR: general IR theory, peace research, public international law, and regional studies. (This chapter will not attempt to evaluate developments in Marxism–Leninism having a potential contribution to IR). This will be followed by a survey of the main IR periodicals in the GDR. We shall conclude with some thoughts on the future of IR in the German Democratic Republic.

In common with West Germany, the GDR has inherited some of Europe's older universities. Much has been made recently of the SED's emphasis on links with the old Prussian–German past. Clausewitz and Frederick the Great have been rehabilitated and Luther is now described as a proto-socialist. Less clear is the depth of the GDR's inheritance from the old system of Prussian state control over the universities.[5] In 1950 the Marxist study of social science was made a compulsory course for all students. In the following year a Ministry of Higher Education formally brought the universities under central control. At present there are 52 universities and other institutions of higher learning for a population of some 16.6 million. Total student numbers have declined from a peak of nearly 161,000 in 1972 to a figure just under 130,000 in 1985. Of this total only 2506 are listed as studying political science–sociology or regional studies. In comparison, some 83,000 students are listed as studying 'technical sciences' in the universities and technical schools.[6] The point to note is that GDR students do not always have the freedom to choose the subject they want to study. The state attempts to limit the availability of places in higher education according to projected manpower requirements. University applications are considered by commissions for the respective insititutions. The commissions have a broad composition including representatives from the university, the Free German Youth Movement or FDJ (which, despite its name is wholly dependent on the SED), the Free German Trade Union League, the SED, and the armed forces.[7] Active membership in the FDJ and, for men, completion of military service are unwritten prerequisites for admission to higher education.[8] Some 90 per cent of GDR students in higher education receive either a scholarship or a grant.[9]

IR as it is in taught in the Anglo-Saxon world has only limited recognition as a field of study in the GDR. IR is treated more as one aspect of the inter-disciplinary field of international studies. But even international studies is itself taught as a recognised field of endeavour only at one university: Leipzig. At other universities in the GDR international studies is approached as a sub-field through a host of other departments such as the faculties of Marxism–Leninism, Marxist-Leninist Philosophy, Law, History, Economics and Journalism. Regional studies, another favoured approach, will be discussed below. Apart from the Karl Marx University of Leipzig, five undergraduate institutions of higher learning can be said to house departments which treat international studies as a sub-field: the Humboldt University, Berlin; the Friedrich-Schiller University, Jena; the Wilhelm-Pieck University, Rostock, and the Greifswald University. The opportunities for GDR undergraduates are thus quite limited. It would appear that at the undergraduate level the above-listed academic fields are considered more appropriate areas of endeavour by university authorities. Nevertheless, as the teaching of Marxism–Leninism occupies a central position at all institutions of higher learning in the GDR, all students have at least this avenue from which to study some aspects of IR.

21.1   THE GDR's LEADING INSTITUTIONS FOR IR

The most important teaching and research in international studies in the GDR is clearly being done at the more specialised Institutes. The two leading organisations are the Institute for International Relations (*Institut für Internationale Beziehungen* – IIB) at Potsdam–Babelsberg and the Institute for International Politics and Economics (*Institut für Internationale Politik und Wirtschaft* – IPW), Berlin. The Potsdam-based IIB, founded in 1964 is a part of the Academy for State and Legal Sciences of the GDR[10] but is in reality run by the Foreign Ministry. As the Foreign Ministry's main research organ, the IIB is empowered to co-ordinate all foreign policy research in the GDR through the Council for Foreign Policy research of the GDR. The IIB is also formally instructed to support 'political instruction for the masses' (*massenpolitische Arbeit*) and propaganda for foreign policy questions.[11] The IIB is thus strongly policy-oriented and its director, Dr Gerhard Hahn (appointed by the foreign minister), also serves as the vice-president of the GDR's Committee for European Security.[12] According to the 1981–85 Central Research Plan of the GDR, the seven main themes covered by the IIB were: East-West relations, international economic relations; peaceful coexistence and class struggle; East German relations with the West; armaments politics; foreign relations within the Western community of states; foreign policy of the developing countries; expanded study of China. Areas of consistent special interest are European security, US foreign policy, international law and the role of international organisations. The IIB serves as the GDR's diplomatic academy and between 35 and 50 students graduate annually following a course of study lasting five years with the *Diplom Staatswissenschaft-Außenpolitik* (political science with a concentration in foreign policy) awarded by the *Akademie* itself. Interestingly, there appears to be no higher degree awarded for the study of IR in East Germany: doctorates are awarded only for Political Science.[13] The *Diplom* is a first degree, and is roughly equivalent to a combination of the Anglo-Saxon bachelor's and master's degrees. Diplomats and other GDR officials also attend special courses at the Institute which normally last for several months. Areas of study include foreign languages and the political, social, economic, and cultural affairs of the countries to which they are to be posted.[14] Students of IIB are clearly the elite of the GDR academic crop and the standards of the institution, as demonstrated by the calibre of the GDR's diplomats, appear high.

The IIB's younger rival is the Institute for International Politics and Economics (IPW), Berlin, founded in 1971 through the merger of the former German Institute for Contemporary History, the German Economics Institute, the State Secretariat for West German Questions of the Council of Ministers, and the Section for West Propaganda of the National Council for the National Front.[15] The Institute's main roles are in research and publishing although it was granted the right to confer academic degrees in 1976. The IPW houses some 400 researchers and is technically a part of the GDR's Council of Ministers (*Ministerrat*) but is said by some Western researchers actually to be integrated within the SED. Research interests of the IPW have broadened in recent years, but study of the Federal Republic of Germany remains a special area of concentration.

The Institute for International Studies (*Institut für Internationale Studien*) at the Karl-Marx University in Leipzig was founded in 1969 as the Institute for West German and International Questions. It continues to be a centre for the study of the Federal Republic of Germany but has broadened its areas of research to include: East–West cultural and scientific exchanges; problems related to the cross-border spillover of television and radio; human rights with an emphasis on the Helsinki Agreements; propaganda methods of the Western countries; the involvement of international organisations in human rights questions of East–West relations. In addition to the regional studies Institutes which will be discussed below, the University of Leipzig also houses a number of smaller institutes devoted to related areas of international studies. The *Sektion Marxismus–Leninismus*, is especially concerned with Western European issues such as expansion of the European Community, social democracy and social reform, and Western interpretations of Marx. The *Franz Mehring Institut* concentrates on the strategy and tactics of the 'worker movement' and trade unions in Western Europe. In the *Sektion Geschichte*, an inter-disciplinary centre for the comparative study of revolution was established in 1976. The centre concentrates on the study of 'anti-imperial' revolutions in developing countries.[16]

21.2 APPROACHES TO THE FIELD

International affairs are studied through a variety of approaches in the GDR. As stated above, IR has at least partial recognition as an academic field of endeavour in East Germany. Interestingly, according to Professor Dr Karl-Heinz Röder, president of the National Association of Political Science of the GDR, political science does not exist as an independent field of study in East Germany. Rather, political science themes are studied by academics working in a variety of other academic fields including IR.[17] Nevertheless, degrees are granted in *Staatswissenschaft* which can only be translated as 'political science'. We may note, however, that in what would be the literal translation, 'state science', there is a better sense of this German endeavour's close relationship to the state which predates the existence of the GDR.

We turn now to four of the broad conceptual approaches which are utilised in international studies in East Germany. For the purpose of this analysis we will label them: general IR theory, Peace Research, International Law (Völkerrecht), and Regional Studies.

In the general IR approach important, albeit limited, changes have been appearing in the East German IR literature since the early 1980s. (It should be stressed at this juncture that by 'IR literature' we mean a rather narrow body of work, produced under considerable state influence.) The depth of change remains unclear, however, as many of the old basic concepts continue to appear with great regularity in textbooks and academic articles. In a recent paper entitled '35 Years of GDR Foreign Policy for Peace and Socialism',[18] the authors set out the three basic principles of foreign policy which remain universally taught in East Germany: proletarian/socialist internationalism (party–party and socialist state–state relations respectively); anti-imperialist solidarity; and, peaceful co-existence. The distinguishing characteristics of socialist internationalism as it is traditionally taught are: solidarity among socialist countries; co-operation with equal rights (*gleichberechtige Zusammenarbeit*); communal defence of the socialist community; rapprochement of the socialist peoples and countries; and, the eventual creation of a socialist 'nation'. Regarding proletarian internationalism, the traditional central issue has been the political views of the Soviet Union. The oft repeated line in GDR literature is that 'Proletarian internationalism without solidarity to the USSR and the Communist Party of the Soviet Union is unthinkable'. This view remains. Nevertheless, the policies of Mikhail Gorbachev have caused some unease for a GDR leadership which prefers to maintain a regime of central control and dislikes *glasnost* (for among other reasons) because of the inevitable comparisons which would be drawn with West Germany. Following the comments of the SED's chief ideologist, Kurt Hager, regarding changes in the USSR – 'Should we feel obliged to change our wallpaper just because our neighbour does?'[19] – subtle shifts in the literature can be perceived which may indicate some modification of proletarian internationalism and a new manner of *Abgrenzung*, this time directed at the East.

The principle of anti-imperialist solidarity is used as a theoretical tool to define the GDR's relations with the developing countries. Anti-imperialist solidarity identifies three groups of developing countries: (1) those developing with a socialist orientation; (2) those developing with a capitalist orientation; (3) those countries for which the development path chosen is not yet clear. In theory, the GDR assists a range of national liberation movements and developing countries in building political and economic independence. In practice the GDR's limited means with which to assist the developing countries goes mainly to states with a socialist orientation.[20]

The concept of peaceful coexistence is perhaps the central theoretical principle of East German foreign policy and is accorded high stature in the literature. This doctrine is meant to apply to relations between the socialist and the capitalist community of states. (Relations between socialist states are meant to be governed by socialist internationalism.) As taught in the GDR, peaceful coexistence has two main components. The first stresses relations between the capitalist and socialist countries as insuring the equal rights, sovereignty, and the territorial integrity of all states. It also emphasises non-interference in the domestic affairs of states. The second calls for the development of international economic co-operation on the basis of mutual benefit and for the resolution of international questions through peaceful means. Until the mid-1980s there was an overt reverse side to this concept, namely the idea that peaceful coexistence was at the same time a special form of class struggle between the capitalist and socialist worlds. It was frequently stressed that peaceful coexistence did not mean acceptance of the status quo or ideological coexistence, nor did it mean peace between antagonistic classes.[21]

It is in this important concept of peaceful coexistence that a degree of theoretical modification is evident. In a recent article entitled 'Is There a New Theory of International Relations in the GDR?',[22] Wilhelm Bruns of West Germany's Friedrich-Ebert-Stiftung argues that while there is no new theory, there is increased discussion, greater willingness to re-define issues and to accept Western concepts and analytical methods. According to Bruns, the idea of peaceful coexistence as a form of class struggle has now fallen from favour and that during the period 1985–8 came to be replaced with the concept of a joint effort to prevent war through more constructive relations with the capitalist countries. The antithesis to peace among the academic and political leadership in the GDR is no longer merely war but rather the annihilation of humanity. Indeed, a recent East German study by Max Schmidt, Chairman of the Scientific Council for Peace Research at the the Academcy of Sciences of the GDR, argues that not only nuclear but also 'merely' conventional war in Europe is unthinkable in view of the widespread radioactive contamination following the accident at Chernobyl and the poisoning of the Rhine following the fire at the Sandoz chemical complex. Schmidt writes that given Europe's 200 odd nuclear power stations and the concentration of chemical production sites even conventional war could lead to an nuclear and chemical desert in Europe.[23] The key point of peaceful coexistence is therefore no longer class struggle but rather the search for common interests through which to prevent war and a far greater degree of international co-operation. According to Bruns, the new questions being posed by East German researchers are over the peace and reform capabilities of the 'imperialist countries'; 'rules' for the East–West *Streitkultur* (dispute-culture); economic co-operation with the West; the role of human rights in International Relations; and even the concept of interdependence, which as recently as the early 1980s was considered something of a 'dirty word'.

The climate for peace reseach has warmed in the GDR particularly in comparison with earlier deep suspicion over this approach. As a 'system-critical' endeavour, peace research was viewed as a symptom of internal crisis in Western society.[24] New security policy writings are drawing more on Western conceptions and East German academics now use the terms *gemeinsame Sicherheit* (common security) and *strukturelle Nichtangriffsfähigkeit* (structural non-offensive capability, which appears to be the term GDR researchers have chosen for a version of non-provocative defence). Since 1983–84 stress has been placed on developing new security policies for the 'nuclear age'. Among some of the concepts stressed in recent literature from the GDR are: the idea that security can no longer be achieved *against* a potential opponent but that it must be achieved *with* the opponent through an overlapping security programme; better measures for joint observation and verification of respective security interests; calls for discussion of all relevant questions not only in military areas but also in political, economic, and humanitarian spheres. We should note, though, that nothing resembling academic pluralism is developing in the GDR. The view that pluralism is a 'Trojan Horse' which would deliver over the GDR from socialism to the mercy of the special interest groups still seems to rest on solid foundations.[25]

Some concepts remain markedly unchanged. For example, the old formulation for socialism and peace, 'the stronger (including militarily) the socialism, the more secure the peace' continues to be widely used in IR literature in the GDR. Furthermore, while the academic community has accepted the new concepts and formulations, there exists considerable opposition in the military to the new ways in which the 'traditional enemy' is viewed.[26]

21.3 PUBLIC INTERNATIONAL LAW

A further approach to international studies in the GDR is through *Völkerrecht* or, as it can be translated, public international law or law of nations. The importance of *Völkerrecht* for the GDR rests partly in the insatiable quest of the country's leadership for full international recognition and partly in the historically troubled relationship with West Germany.

A good overview on academic thought in the GDR on *Völkerrecht* may be found in the *Völkerrecht Lehrbuch* (Public International Law Textbook)[27] published by the Institute for International Relations at Potsdam. The first point stressed by East German works on the subject is that *Völkerrecht* is always a product of the state and can function only through being exercised by states. In addition, it is emphasised that the content and function of *Völkerrecht* is 'the regulation of relations among fully independent and sovereign states'.[28] It is further stressed that under *Völkerrecht*, relations between individuals, between an individual and his/her country or some other country cannot be governed. Such approaches, as practised by some 'imperialist countries', which seek to influence a country's internal affairs, are criticised by East German writers as a direct attack on the *Völkerrecht* prohibition of such acts.[29] Through the above interpretation, GDR academics argue that *Völkerrecht* stands in full agreement with Marxist–Leninist legal theory.[30]

Völkerrecht, as it is studied in the GDR, receives much criticism from West German academics. The view of some is that *Völkerrecht*, more so than other areas of academic endeavour in East Germany, provides a selectively critical platform for the conduct of state policy and the dissemination of propaganda. Theodor Schweisfurth's concluding comments on this theme illustrate this view:

> As a Marxist–Leninist science, *Völkerrecht* is by definition Party-oriented. From the study of *Völkerrecht* in the GDR, no 'critical accompaniment' to its foreign policy should be expected but rather unreserved support for the positions taken by the state. . . It plays the role of legal champion of the East German foreign ministry.[31]

21.4 REGIONAL STUDIES

A favoured approach to international affairs since 1960 has been through regional studies. A number of Institutes were established in that year including the Africa Institute at the Karl-Marx University, Leipzig, and the Faculty of Latin American Sciences at the Wilhelm-Pieck University, Rostock. Other centres for regional studies since established include an institute for Asian studies at the Humboldt University, Berlin, a Centre for North African and Near East Studies, also at Leipzig,[32], and a Faculty for North European Studies with an attached Institute for Scandinavian and Finland Research at the Greifswald University. The centre for Near East Studies at the University of Halle has been closed and apparently consolidated with the Leipzig centre.

The regional institutes are involved in both research and teaching. They are highly inter-disciplinary, and draw on staff with expertise in economics, history, languages, literature, art, political studies, sociology, philosophy, and ideology. All of the regional Institutes come under the co-ordinating powers of the Central Council for Asian, African and Latin American Sciences of the GDR (ZENTRAL)[33], which has been based at the Institute for International Relations, Potsdam, since 1969. ZENTRAL thus co-ordinates *all* research and teaching in regional studies at the university level in East Germany, but is subordinate to both the Ministry of Education and the Institute for International Relations at Potsdam.[34]

It is extremely difficult to evaluate what influence these regional Institutes have on East German foreign policy. With regard to developing countries in Asia, Joachim Glaubitz has posited that given the centralised organisational structure of regional studies and the interweaving of scientific and field personnel throughout the system, it should be assumed that GDR decision-makers use the analysis provided by this Institute. He points out, however, that for the developing countries two other institutes – the Institute for International Relations at Potsdam and the Institute for Social Sciences, which is a part of of the Central Committee of the Party – exist far more exclusively to provide counsel on foreign policy.[35]

21.5 RESEARCH AND PUBLICATIONS: AREAS OF STUDY AND NON-STUDY

In his work, *Die Außenpolitik der DDR*,[36] Wilhelm Bruns provides a survey of current trends in East German literature regarding the GDR's foreign policy. By way of introduction, Bruns notes some common tendencies displayed by GDR researchers in their writing: (a) the foreign policy of the GDR tends to be described as 'successful' and while doing so researchers often omit certain circumstances or facts; (b) much work is merely the paraphrasing of Party and State declarations and of official foreign policy communiques; and, (c) problems are not often thematised. Bruns also makes the point that the very critical nature of East German work on the capitalist countries makes the non-critical approach to GDR foreign policy all the more striking.

Among Bruns's findings are that many important foreign policy areas are ignored by GDR writers. This is true, although we may speculate that a high proportion of such work is deemed sensitve and thus classified for official use only. As with some of the other social sciences in the GDR, the published work may not be indicative of many areas of concentration. The 'ignored areas' which Bruns highlights include German–German relations which are considered by the GDR to be a branch of foreign policy. Writing in 1985, he observes that there has not been a single book published in the GDR on this topic. Nor have the two major IR periodicals – *Horizont* and *IPW-Bericht* – published any significant analysis on German–German relations. Another area which is ignored is the question of the GDR's specific role in co-ordination of foreign policies for the socialist community of states. In other areas of foreign policy, Bruns finds that questions are being partially examined. For instance, while there are many works on relations between the GDR and the Soviet Union, they do not address topics such as the extent of East German freedom of manoeuvre in foreign affairs. (The Western literature often compensates for this deficiency through quite imaginative speculation.) Other areas which are incompletely addressed include the SED and Party–Party relations, and the Africa policies of the GDR, particularly with regard to the structure and extent of development assistance. Bruns does find certain foreign policy sub-fields to be well-researched. The literature on the GDR's relations with Austria, Finland and Japan is relatively rich. Especially extensive is the literature on the nature and principles of the East German foreign policy with regard to various regional and multilateral proposals, particularly regarding peace and disarmament. Bruns argues that although the literature in these latter areas is largely regarded as propaganda in the West, such works should nevertheless be taken more seriously; a view with which this author strongly concurs.

21.6 IR PUBLICATIONS: A PROBLEM OF SOURCES

The limitations imposed by both availabilty and content of source material is a recurring cause of frustration among students in the GDR. The GDR imposes strict controls on the import of printed materials, and while this is not such a problem in technical fields, the very nature of IR means that little or nothing of relevance to the field can be imported from the West by an individual.[37] Undergraduate admission to the reading rooms for Western publications appears to be strictly limited on a case by case basis. Nevertheless, university students in the GDR seem fairly enterprising in obtaining West German publications. The situation at the more specialised Institutes discussed above appears to be rather different. Here, access to the special libraries, which contain collections of Western newspapers and academic journals appears to be the rule rather than the exception. It is presumptuous to assume, however, that all students/academics in the GDR are engaged in a continuous struggle to achieve access to Western sources: In recent years it has been the writings of Mikhail Gorbachev and other Soviet reformers that are among the most sought after. Limitations with regard to the content of the GDR's IR literature have been discussed above. A further key reason for the importance of foreign publications is simply that the number of academic journals and newspapers published in the GDR with relevance to IR has always been extremely limited. The three main sources are *Horizont, Socialist Monthly Newspaper for International Politics and Economics*; *IPW-Berichte* (published by the Institute for International Politics and Economics of the GDR, Berlin), and the *Yearbook of International Politics and Economics* (published jointly by the Institute for International Relations, Potsdam and the Academy of Sciences, Moscow). The journal *Deutsche Außenpolitik*, ceased publication in 1983 for reasons which remain unclear. In this same year *Horizont* went from being a weekly to a monthly.[38]

The new *Horizont* is by far the most interesting and possibly most daring of the above troika of publications. Published in tabloid form, *Horizont* usually has three or four lengthy, theoretical articles accompanied by some twenty shorter, less weighty stories. Recent lead articles have covered SDI, socialist foreign policy, and the question of relations between divided Europe. In comparison with other GDR publications the writing style is free from rhetoric and sometimes refreshingly direct. The shorter articles tend toward journalism but have covered such diverse themes as Saudi Arabia's economic planning to 1990, an interview with the director of the US Environmental Protection Agency and, most recently, an article about life in the former German city of Königsberg (today Kaliningrad). Königsberg may not be an IR theme *per se*, but the topic is doubly delicate in that not only does Königsberg lie in the former German territories east of the Oder–Neisse Line (lost in the Second World War) but it is in the part of East Prussia which is now held by the Soviet Union. The tone of the article is excessively complimentary of contemporary life in the city. Nevertheless, this is precisely the type of subject that most GDR publications do not attempt to cover.[39]

The *IPW-Bericht* has been published since 1972. The format is more that of an academic journal. The *IPW-Bericht* covers economic and security questions in greater detail than does *Horizont*, and has recently followed aspects of Western European co-operation and US relations with the European members of NATO.

The joint GDR–USSR *Yearbook of International Politics and Economics* is comprised of a series of short chapters which can be divided into three sections. First, are a series of broader or more critical themes such as 'the capitalist world economy', 'East-West relations' and 'the Gulf War'. This is followed by a section devoted to regions and regional groupings. The third section is a collection of country studies. In comparison with the above two publications, the chapters tend be less creative and more dogmatic. Figures are frequently cited but often with no source. The contributions are written by different individuals but no credits other than names appear. In the 1986 edition, out of a total of 80 contributors, 43 have names which appear to be Russian or 'Soviet'.[40]

Further publications of use to the IR student or researcher in the GDR are *Asien Afrika Lateinamerika*, published by the Central Council for Asia, Africa and Latin America Studies, and *Einheit*, the academic organ of the Party. *Asien Afrika Lateinamerika* appears particularly useful through its consistently broad selection of foreign book reviews. *Einheit* provides access to the Party line on political economy, security issues, and history.

21.7 A FUTURE FOR IR IN THE GERMAN DEMOCRATIC REPUBLIC?

The state of international studies and many of the social sciences remains unfavourable in the GDR. The study of International Relations remains stifled by a number of factors:

1. Through the crucial importance which manipulation of all aspects of international affairs by the SED has played in the development of the GDR as an independent state.

2. Through a centralised academic system which receives its Five Year Plans from highly centralised bodies.

3. By the lack of public academic debate on possible competing paradigms.

4. Through the historically limited development of IR as a field of academic study (this is also evident in the other Germanic countries).

5. Through both qualitative and quantitative restrictions regarding the available literature.

Is there a future for IR in East Germany? We conclude this study by briefly noting two features of GDR society – one with potentially positive implications for the development of a modern socialist approach to the social sciences and the other which will certainly prove a major debilitating factor to any reforms whatsoever.

The positive point is the unintended impact of the highly critical nature of much East German work in the social sciences. As we indicated above, the very fact that writings on the 'imperialist countries' are so critical throws into sharp relief the limitation of themes and the self-congratulatory nature to be found in work on, say, the socialist community of nations and the GDR's foreign policy. This is not merely noticed by Westerners but also by a great number of East German students and ordinary people. The blatant deficiency of issues and approaches within the realm of the GDR's academic institutions and the media merely encourages students to struggle for access to unapproved philosophies and outside sources.[41] One of the results of this struggle seems to be the development of broad abilities for critical thought among many East German students. Although critical thinking which does not meet Party approval is submerged in a self-muzzling doublespeak to meet the requirements of 'official situations' (i.e., university seminars and written work), outside of such situations this doublespeak is largely discarded. This perhaps seems a minor point but it would appear to bode well for the study of the social sciences under a socialist regime more committed to reform.

The point against is that the state bureaucracy – an institution marked by continuity during a century when so much in Germany has been subject to radical change or dismemberment – would be a major opposition force to reform initiated from above[42]. This phenomenon has been well illustrated with regard to the Gorbachev reforms. In common with other countries in the socialist community, and Western countries such as the Federal Republic of Germany, the GDR has a pervasive bureaucratic structure which seems to have a vast number of sheet anchors to protect the state from winds of change.

Whether these winds will even blow in the GDR is another question entirely as it remains unclear whether there are any serious reformers in upper ranks of the SED. And without an initiative from the Party, IR in the GDR will remain in its current underdeveloped state.

NOTES AND REFERENCES

*   Thanks to Dirk Rumberg for comments on an earlier draft of this chapter.

1.   See: Heinz Rausch and Theo Stammen (eds.), *DDR, Das politische, wirtschaftliche und soziale System* 2.überarbeitete Auflage (München: C.H. Beck Verlag, 1974), pp. 249, 258–59.

2.   Inge Christopher, 'The Written Constitution – The Basic Law of a Socialist State?', in David Childs (ed.), *Honecker's Germany* (London: Allen & Unwin, 1985), p. 25.

3.   Personal correspondence with the author. See also: John Page, 'Education under the Honeckers', in Childs (ed.), *Honecker's Germany*.

4.   See: Wilhelm Bruns, *Die Außenpolitik der DDR* (Berlin [West]: Colloquium Verlag, 1985), p. 10.

5.   See: David Childs, *The GDR: Moscow's German Ally* (London: Allen & Unwin, 1983), p.167. Childs draws no comparison. He points out that regional or state governments of Germany prior to 1933 had far greater control over the universities than did pre-war British governments, namely with regard to finance and appointment to professorial chair. Professors appointed were required to take an oath of allegiance to the state. In addition, a Prussian law of 1899 stipulated that the deliberate promotion of social democratic aims was inconsistent with holding a position at a royal university.

6.   Staatlicher Zentralverlag für Statistik, *Statistisches Jahrbuch 1986, DDR* (Berlin (East): Staatsverlag der DDR, 1986), pp. 303–308.

7.   Childs, *The GDR: Moscow's German Ally*, p. 177.

8.   Although this is a point of some debate among West German academics. See Thomas Ammer's book review, 'Studenten in der DDR heute', *Deutschland Archiv* (August 1988, Vol. 19, No. 8), p. 887.

9.   Kurt Sontheimer and Wilhelm Bleek, *Die DDR, Politik, Gesellschaft, Wirtschaft* 5. erw., neubearb. Auflage (Hamburg: Hoffmann und Campe, 1979), p. 188.

10. Until the early 1970s, it was named the German Academy for State and Legal Science 'Walter Ulbricht'. The shift from 'German' to 'German Democratic Republic' and the dropping of the suffix 'Walter Ulbricht' neatly illustrate the GDR's shift in direction during this period.

11. *Gesetzblatt der Deutschen Demokratischen Republik* (Berlin (East): 27 February 1985, Teil 1, Nr 6), p. 75.

12. Bundesministerium für innerdeutsche Beziehungen, *DDR Handbuch*, 3.,üb. und erweit. Auflage (Köln: Verlag Wissenschaft und Politik, 1985), p. 900.

13. Theo Ammer, 'Zur West-Forschung in der DDR', in 'Ständiges Sekretariat für die Koordinierung der Bundesgeförderten Osteuropa-Forschung', *Westforschung in Osteuropa und in der DDR – Konferenzbericht und Materialien* (Köln: 1982), p. 70, and *Handbuch der Deutschen Demokratischen Republik* (Leipzig: 1984), p. 544.

14. *Handbuch der DDR*, (Leipzig), p. 70; and *DDR Handbuch*, (Köln), p. 900.

15. See: Anita M. Mallinckrodt, 'Propaganda als Instrument der Außenpolitik', in Hans-Adolf Jacobson, Gert Leptin, Ulrich Schneuner and Eberhard Schulz, *Drei Jahrzehnte Außenpolitik der DDR* (München/Wien: R. Oldenbourg, 1980). See also: Rausch und Stammen, (eds), *DDR*, p. 263.
16. Ammer, 'Zur West-Forschung', pp. 75–6.
17. Karl-Heinz Röder in personal correspondence to J. Bellers at the Institut für Politikwissenschaft, Westfälische Wilhelms-Universtät, 10 June 1987.
18. Werner Hänisch and Dieter Vogl, '35 Jahre Außenpolitik der DDR für Frieden und Sozialismus', *IPW-Bericht* (Vol. 13, No. 9, September 1984), p. 10.
19. Kurt Hager, in an interview with *Stern*, (9 April 1987), reprinted in *Neues Deutschland* on (10 April 1987). See also: Albrecht Hinze, 'Unter der Decke etwas Hoffnung', *Süddeutsche Zeitung* (15 April 1988).
20. Hager, *Stern interview*, pp. 42–3; and Hänisch and Vogl, '35 Jahre', p. 10.
21. See Bruns, *Die Außenpolitik der DDR*, pp. 48–51.
22. For this section I have drawn heavily on one of the few recent works which addresses the theory of international relations in the GDR. Wilhelm Bruns, 'Gibt es in der DDR eine neue Theorie der internationalen Beziehungen?', *DDR Report*, (Bonn: Vol. 21, No. 3, 1988), pp. 129–32.
23. Max Schmidt, Europa: Behütetes Haus oder Risikogemeinschaft, *Horizont* (Vol. 21, No. 3, 1988), p. 3.
24. See: Wilfried von Bredow, 'Rezeption und Kritik der Friedensforschung in der DDR', *Deutschland Archiv* (Vol. 8, No. 12, December 1975), pp. 1292–1304.
25. See: Karl-Heinz Baum, 'Theorie des Pluralismus ist ein trojanisches Pferd', *Frankfurter Rundschau* (22 September 1982).
26. Bruns, 'Gibt es in der DDR eine neue Theorie der internationalen Beziehungen?', pp. 130–31.
27. Arbeitsgemeinschaft für Völkerrecht beim Institut für Internationale Beziehungen an der Akademie für Staats- und Rechtswissenschaft der DDR, *Völkerrecht, Lehrbuch, Teil 1* (Berlin (East)): Staatsverlag der DDR, 1981), p. 20.
28. See for example: Völkerrecht Lehrbuch pp. 19–20.
29. Völkerrecht Lehrbuch pp. 21–22.
30. Völkerrecht Lehrbuch p. 22.
31. Original text: 'Als "marxistische–leninistische Wissenschaft" ist die Völkerrechtswissenschaft der DDR grundsätzlich "parteilich", d.h. ein "kritisches Begleiten" der Außenpolitik der DDR ist von ihrer Völkerrechtswissenschaft nicht zu erwarten, sondern nur die vorbehaltlose Unterstützung des Standpunktes der Staatführung . . . sie spielt die Rolle eines Advokaten des Außenministeriums der DDR'. From Theodor Schweisfurth, 'Völkerrecht als Instrument der Außenpolitik', in Hans–Adolf Jacobson, Gert Leptin. Ulrich Schneuner and Eberhard Schulz, *Drei Jahrzehnte Außenpolitik der DDR* (München/Wien: R. Oldenbourg Verlag, 1980), p. 292.

32. See: Zeitschrift des Zentralen Rates für Asien-, Afrika- und Lateinamerikawissenschaft in der DDR, *Asien, Afrika, Lateinamerika* (Vol 13, No. 2, March–April 1985), pp. 449–50; and Rektor der Karl-Marx-Universität, *Wissenschaftliche Zeitschrift Karl-Marx-Universitt Leipzig* (Vol. 34, No. 6, November–December 1985), pp.110–11.

33. *Zentraler Rat für Asien-, Afrika- und Latinamerikawissenschaften der DDR.*

34. Friedrich-Ebert Stiftung, *Universitäten, Hoch- und Fachschulen in der Deutschen Demokratischen Republik*, from the series: Die DDR – Realitten Argumente (Bonn: Verlag Neue Gesellschaft, 1980), pp. 39–40.

35. Joachim Glaubitz, 'Ost- und Südostasien sowie Ozeanien', in Hans-Adolf Jacobson, Gert Leptin, Ulrich Scheuner and Eberhard Schulz, *Drei Jahrzehnte Außenpolitik der DDR* (München/Wien: R. Oldenbourg verlag, 1980), p. 716.

36. Wilhelm Bruns, *Die Außenpolitik der DDR.* pp. 12–15.

37. Following the Honecker visit to West Germany in 1987 the restrictions on the import of non-political magazines were meant to be eased. Colleagues report that in taking West German newspapers to East Berlin the newspapers have been confiscated but not the magazine supplements.

38. *Deutschland Archiv* (Vol. 16, No. 7, July 1983), p. 702.

39. Gerhard Zazworka, 'Kaliningrad', *Horizont* (Vol. 21, No. 2), p. 15. Although we should also note that Soviet Press has, of late, begun to refer to Kant as the 'wise man from Königsberg'. See: 'Nasch Semljak Kant', (editorial) *Süddeutsche Zeitung*, 15 April 1988; and, 'Wo Russen in Kant ihren Landsmann sehen', *Frankfurter Allgemeine Zeitung* (14 April 88).

40. Institut für Weltwirtschaft und Internationale Beziehungen der Akademie der Wissenschaften der UdSSR und Institut für Internationale Beziehungen an der Akademie für Staats- und Rechtswissenschaft der DDR, *Jahrbuch der Internationalen Politik und Wirtschaft* (Berlin (East): Staatsverlag der DDR, 1986).

41. For some examples see: Peter A. Thüt, 'Studenten: Kleines Glück im verordneten Mittelmaß', in Werner Filmer and Heribert Schwan, *Das andere Deutschland, Alltag in der DDR* (Düsseldorf: Econ Verlag, 1985 (1987 paperback edn published by Goldmann Verlag)), pp. 187–88.

42. E.N. Williams argues that Brandenburg–Prussia became a European power in the seventeenth and eighteenth centuries through the very clamping of a bureaucratic absolutism on the Prussian people 'and by eliciting (or imprinting) traits of national character which have made Prussianism one of the shaping forces of modern world history'. E.N. Williams, *The Ancien Regime in Europe, Government and Society in the Major States 1648–1789* (Harmondsworth: Penguin Books, 1970), pp. 322–3.

22 The Study of International Relations in Italy

Fulvio Attina

The world community of students of international politics is divided along different lines, the most important of which concern paradigms or general views of the world: the Hobbesian or anarchy paradigm, the Grotian or community paradigm, the Marxian or market paradigm, and the Pluralist or Transnationalism paradigm which – in opposition to the first three – takes into account a world populated not only by states but also by individuals, social groups and various collective actors. Another important divide among the students of International Relations is the methodological approach they adopt: users of the state-centric approach (according to whom international politics can be interpreted on the basis of some attributes of states and of their foreign policies) differ from followers of the systemic approach (who maintain that international politics cannot be interpreted without reference to a structure that binds the behaviour of states as actors of a social interactions system). Today the controversy between the 'Classical' and 'Scientific' approaches has lost its importance (fortunately!): support of quantitative data and parsimonious use of game theory and related methods are welcomed, while tolerance is shown towards researchers devoted to testing hypotheses with an intensive manipulation of quantitative data. A plurality of approaches, of methodological strategies and of research techniques means that inside the limits of a single paradigmatic view scientists can produce several and very different theories because they use different approaches and methods to simplify reality and shape abstract models for its interpretation. It is also to be recognised that it is possible and useful to compare theories that share the same paradigm and to confront their resistance to hypothesis testing in order to choose among them. But it is rather difficult (or impossible, some think) to choose among theories that arise from different paradigms which are basic and autonomous sets of ideas and values. However, intersecting the four paradigms with the two methodological approaches (state-centric and systemic), we can arrange theoretical interpretations of international politics in eight groups. In this short presentation of what is happening in Italy attention will be paid only to the groups for which the Italian contribution is significant.

Contemporary Italian International Relations theory – in spite of the Machiavellian heritage – avoids the use of terms like realism, power politics and equilibrium. Inequalities among states are not denied at all, and are fundamental to the theoretical interpretation of the essence of political relations among states. Instead, the stress is put on terms like international order, structure, and system organisation. Morgenthau is considered with due respect, but the name of Kaplan as a proponent of the system approach has been reverently mentioned and today Waltz, as a symbol of the structural–systemic approach, seems to have gained predominance. This series of American scholars – to which others like Modelski, Keohane, Rosenau, and Singer could be added – shows that Italy, too, pays tribute to a traditional hegemony in the discipline, but European theorists like Aron and Bull are also given close attention. This, however, does not prevent us from saying that Italian specialists in International Relations have developed their own perspectives and concepts in the field. The following exposition of theories gives an account of what is being done, and has been done, in the stream of the Hobbesian, Grotian and pluralist paradigms; no Italian scholar is inspired today by the Marxian paradigm, although attention to world economic processes seems to be on the rise.

22.1 INEQUALITY AND ORDER

The Hobbesian paradigm may be defined as the view of the world centred on the mutual insecurity of states (because of their unequal resources and capabilities), and the hierarchy established by the more powerful states to resolve insecurity and the state of nature in interstate relations. Anarchy, or the Hobbesian state of nature, is just an original imaginary state and all theories of this paradigm – including the power politics theory – argue that major powers dominate international politics; therefore it is wrong to call it anarchical, and more suitable names for the Hobbesian paradigm are the hierarchy or inequality paradigm. To this general view of the international system belong the models of Luigi Bonanate and Carlo M. Santoro who proceed, however, with a different methodological approach. Bonanate developed a hierarchical order model through a structural–systemic methodology; he contends that international politics can be interpreted only through a conceptualisation in terms of system theory and chiefly with the systemic concept of structure. But the roots of his theory are more in the works of Hobbes and Clausewitz than in those of Berthalanffy or Kaplan.[1] His model does not merely describe the hierarchical structure of the international system as a concentration of resources and power (as Kaplan or Waltz do) but proposes an empirical explanation of the establishment of the hierarchical structure. The establishment is found in those wars which directly or indirectly affect a group of states, submitting them all to the rules decided by the victorious states. Consequently we can analyse a group of states as a system. But beyond this system-constitutive effect, in interstate relations such wars have the same constitutional effect that peaceful or violent revolutions have in a state: just as the winners of a domestic revolution decide norms and institutions for an orderly political life (for many states this happens through a pact among factions or parties with the writing of a constitution), the winners (or winner) of a systemic war decide rules by establishing order in an international system. In democratic states the differentiation of executive, legislative and juridical powers is the condition for the peaceful changes of order, while in an international system, the legislators and defenders of order are the same actors (the winning or constituent states) and the order is consequently static and conservative. The only way to change is the resort to arms: the verdict of a new systemic war will confirm old states or will put new states in the constituent role. Between two systemic wars major states may be involved in minor wars or serious crises threatening their role, and their involvement serves to strengthen order or to extend it to the periphery of the system. Bonanate applies his model to the historical systems after the Congress of Vienna, but he argues that the contemporary international system has a peculiarity that strengthens the conservative nature of order: nuclear weapons make a systemic war highly improbable because at the end there will be not one or more winners but only losers. The two constituent states (the United States and the Soviet Union) are bound to maintain the balance of terror and they make a virtue of this condition by limiting aims and developing abilities to jointly manage (with explicit or tacit behaviour) crises threatening their role and the existing order. An important consequence of this condominium and of the abandonment of its mechanism of change (systemic war) in international order, is that political terrorism is seen as the last resort by dissatisfied governments and political movements.

The system-constitutive function of general wars and the order-constituent role of the winner(s) of a war are important conceptualisations in the structural–systemic modelling of inter-state relations. But does Bonanate's model stop short, and cover just the territorial and political domain of international relations? How does an ordering role based on military power and coercive force extend to domains of international life of such great importance as economic affairs? On the basis of military coercive power, the winners of a systemic war are apparently entitled to establish rules for international conflicts of a political and territorial nature and even to fix rules assigning them freedom to control the domestic politics of some other states.[2] However the power of the winning states is not created in a vacuum but in a normative and institutional setting that extends from political security to economic relations, at least. One can argue that constituent power belongs properly to that winning state which can lead the reshaping of political security rules and institutions as well as of the main functional regimes that make the world market. In addition, I believe that attention to the various contents of order may mitigate statements on the static nature of international order.

A similar evaluation of the exclusive relevance of military–coercive power in the theory of international politics is found in the model of Carlo M. Santoro,[3] who is far from the systemic–structural approach. He acknowledges that after a general war international systems assume a static order with an equilibrium or an imperial pattern, but he maintains that this rule cannot be adapted to the present international system, which has no imperial authority, and where the two major powers cannot work out an equilibrium order because they hold nuclear arms that prevent the solution of interest conflicts by resort to violence, as in the past. The two nuclear superpowers have 'concentrated' capabilities to solve serious international conflicts all over the world but they refrain from using them because of the fear of the holocaust or – to put it differently – because neither of them has the certainty of overcoming the other and winning. It was not different ideologies or objective conflicts of interest but the 'nuclearity' of the two major winners of the Second World War that put the world in a state of war that has the nature of a duel. Equilibrium and imperial orders are stable systems because of the conservative power of major states, while the 'duel' system is not self-maintaining at all because the two contenders aim at victory. Prevented from striking the last (nuclear) blow, each nevertheless aims at extending control over the system by exploiting crises or tensions to its own advantage. However, the first aim of a superpower is to hold on to its own cards in the nuclear confrontation or deterrence. This is achieved through large and advanced nuclear capabilities that provide each superpower with bargaining counters in the systemic duel but not with the war-avoidance card, as is commonly believed. In fact, while the system hierarchy becomes less rigid because of the spread of power to medium and even small states (nuclear proliferation, local wars, disobedience by allies of the superpowers), strategists and statesmen of the duelling states continue to stockpile arms and to formulate doctrines aimed at prolonging the duel instead of favouring the joint management of the system. Indeed Santoro bases the duel model of the contemporary system on the study of American and Soviet strategic thinking. But to deny that the bipolar system has an order or a political organisation is not to say merely that military coercive power (or its virtual use in the present nuclear duel) is the only relevant variable in international politics; it is rather to suggest a methodological option: the promotion of the duel to the rank of interpretative model is a consequence of a state-centric approach which disregards the fact that even in a war-system (or a duel-system) the political behaviour of states conforms to a constraining or structural pattern.

22.2 ORGANISATION AND COMPETITION

The need to investigate both fundamentals of and changes in the structural pattern of the political behaviour of states is stressed by this author.[4] As Bull pointed out, political scientists must recognise the Grotian paradigm of International Relations which focuses on the community of states constituted by their governments who, notwithstanding inequalities and hierarchies, mutually accept equal sovereignty, observe social, juridical and political rules and create institutions favouring co-operation and common as well as individual interests. In fact, the Grotian and Hobbesian paradigms point out two basic traits of the state system: the equal sovereignty and the unequal capabilities of its actors. Equilibrium and power politics theorists, with their state-centric methodology, are inclined to forget parity and to think only in terms of inequality; not only they, but system theorists too, who consequently (I say automatically) deduce the hierarchical structure of inter-state relations. Concern for equal sovereignty and for unequal capabilities forces us instead to recognise that the structure of inter-state relations (or the co-active behaviour pattern of units because they are part of a system) is an organisation made up of all sovereign states, but with different roles, according to capabilities and explicit goals, to which they conform in their co-operative and conflictual relations in order to prevent uncertainty and reduce insecurity. The organisation is a set of conventions (or rules) and institutions that guide state governments; their international conduct is therefore not casual or absolutely free or anarchical because, however varied it may be, it 'conforms' to the (degree of) parity–inequality existing in the conventions and institutions of the system. Conventions have the form of social principles and moral values, of international law, and of political rules of the game; institutions have the form of inter-governmental organisations and of functional regimes for the management of economic interdependence. On a theoretical continuum the system organisation changes from a plain democratic or horizontal form, where conventions and institutions fully respect the parity of states, to an absolute imperial or vertical form where conventions and institutions further the submission of all states to the will of one.

To ascertain the form of systemic organisation in historical periods analysts must look at the parity–inequality held by conventions and institutions, particularly the major security rules and function- al regimes, to which the international conduct of governments conforms. Some of them (like moral principles and international law) change slowly and even persist through a system shift after a general war; indeed to dominate a system the winners of a war must chiefly play the role of the major makers of security rules and world-wide economic regimes. However, system organisation, though by nature conservative, is not static between two general wars; it may move along the horizontal–vertical continuum. Great powers aim at strengthening a hierarchical organisation or at removing those in command; resolutely pursued, such aims will throw the system into a general war which has shifting consequences on all system traits. Evolution in systemic organisation is rather the matter of compe- titions or complex conflicts engaged in by the vast majority of states on overarching political issues. In this regard the making of a system is very important because a system receives from the past social cleav- ages around which governments develop enmities and solidarities;

when a cleavage becomes the basis of explicit political behaviour, a competition follows that usually forces governments to form opposing associations of various forms (alliances, blocs, movements, etc.). The competitive policies in favour of changing the rules and practices of cleavage issues can affect the parallel or connected conventions and institutions of the systemic organisation. From its past the contemporary international system has received moralprinciples, juridical norms and diplomatic institutions, but also cleavages.

The most important legacies seem to be the world expansion of the capitalist market, the cultural-political domination of the European (now Euro-American) countries, and the controversy on the political and class form of domestic regimes. These cleavages overlap in reality but the analyst may separate three corresponding political competitions: that over the private or state property principle as the fundamental basis of domestic regimes (or East–West competition); that over the control of the world market and international division of labour (or North–South competition); and that over the complete end of the colonial past (or centre–periphery competition). Different associations of countries have grown (and sometimes died) in each competition: NATO, the Warsaw Pact, SEATO and other containment pacts in Asia and the Pacific on the East–West axis; the seven most industrialised countries and the Group of 77 on the North–South axis; the Movement of Non-Aligned Countries on the centre–periphery axis. In the history of contemporary international politics the competitive policies of individual states and government associations have apparently affected the evolution of conventions and institutions of systemic organisation which has experienced a lessening degree of hierarchy (and a growing regional fragmentation). This is in spite of domination by the United States and the Soviet Union – the former as a global power with arms predominance (nuclear technological superiority, a world net of military bases and worldwide rapid deployment military capabilities) and control of functional regimes (commerce, finance, energy, etc.), the latter as the rival power whose nuclear force binds the United States to some political rules of the game.

22.3 INTERNATIONAL DEMOCRACY

The transnational or pluralist paradigm, which focuses on relations among a plurality of social actors as important as the states, is represented in Italy by Antonio Papisca. He began to apply transnationalism to the European Community, arguing that bureaucracies and governments, allied with a handful of business interests, monopolise the supranational process while political and social groups lack channels to express their interests. Community institutions and official actors still deny the legitimacy of processing social demands of a sort at the Community level and the direct election of the European Parliament has not yet reversed the pattern. Similarly, at the global level diplomatic institutions forged by state governments repress development and expression of transnational social forces. Like other writers of the pluralist paradigm, Papisca refrains from a clear definition of the system he analyses. He has, however, recently formalised the interplay of diplomatic institutions, inter-governmental organisations and organised transnationalism.[5] States have for so long established a world order and are able to perpetuate it through diplomatic (peaceful and violent) institutions. They also create inter-governmental organisations to better manage the system, but these institutions show some disadvantages. The principle of 'one state one vote' engenders confusion or immobility and where it is not practised (as in the IMF and the UN Security Council) resentments arise. Today inter-governmental organisations also face an overload of inputs which apparently cannot be processed in the context of the existing diplomatic order. The present crisis or 'dysfunction' of many international organisations goes with a diplomatic counter-offensive distinctly shown by summit and personal diplomacy on the part of political leaders, and by individual state actions like the United States boycott of UNESCO and the UN budget. Tensions at the 'public inter-state' level (shaped by diplomatic institutions and inter-governmental organisations) are the product of the growing pressure from the 'public international' or non-intergovernmental level of world affairs.

Present transnationalism is not just a matter of business, religious or cultural elites, it is also a matter of individuals and masses who feel conscious of being primary international subjects as they are entitled to civil, political, economic, social and cultural rights by positive international law. In the world system these subjects form the international social layer which claims primacy over the diplomatic layer (the nation states and their order). Today the chances of social transnationalism reside in international non-governmental organisations (INGOs) whose members cross states and assert 'pan-human' interests such as the promotion of human rights, environmental ecology, international development co-operation, and positive peace. Papisca maintains that the challenge of organised transnationalism to inter-state order performs a peaceful constituent role in opposition to war-induced order reshaping. The world system faces demands for international democracy (or political participation) from third world governments (who claim universal adoption of the 'one state one vote' clause and full implementation of equal sovereignty in inter-governmental organisation procedures) as well as from INGOs and transnational movements (who claim procedures of mass political participation in the decision processes of international politics). Papisca acknowledges difficulties in making certain statements on the future success of these demands, however he points to some 'interstices' in the inter-governmental system such as the consultative status of INGOs in relation to inter-governmental organisations, the Universal Declaration of Human Rights, the UN resolutions on the New Economic Order, some supranational authorities (like the High Commission for Refugees, the European Court of Human Rights, etc.), and some international parliamentary bodies (like the European Parliament or the Consultative Assembly of the Council of Europe): the demands of international democracy, Papisca says, can spring from these 'interstices'. Like other pluralist analyses, his model urges us to care about neglected human and social dimensions in world affairs and to acknowledge their relevance in a shrinking world. Still, however much one considers harmful to the world-village the exclusive steering role played by state governments (and they have been successful but sinful in the past) doubts cannot be removed about the very coming into existence of a democratic order among so many different actors. If ever established, anxiety may arise about the yield of such an international democracy. The state looks in good health and must still perform its developmental functions, especially in the third world, and research is needed on the way governments listen to the civil, political, cultural and economic claims coming from the non-governmental layer, open 'interstices', and even accept them in the conventions and institutions of systemic organisation.

22.4 SUBSTANTIVE RESEARCH

In opposition to the rather lively debate on the theoretical interpretation of the international system outlined above, substantive analysis looks restrained in Italy, and this is certainly because of restricted institutional and human resources. Empirical conflict analysis has received scant attention. A substantial amount of research is on foreign policy and European integration alone. A narrow decision-making or bureaucratic approach has received small credit in the study of Italian foreign policy, but Gori[6] has pointed out the usefulness of operation research and cost–benefit analysis. Bonanate[7] has applied his hierarchical order model to the explanation of Italy's alliance politics following the Second World War, while Gori[8] has examined Italian cultural diplomacy. Empirical research has focused on some traits of Italy's foreign policy system: findings exist on attitudes of opinion leaders[9] and of Parliament and government members, and on parliamentary debates on governmental foreign policy programmes.[10] In European integration analysis the functionalist and Neofunctionalist approaches have received little credit and more attention has been paid to the European Community as a development political system following the Easton systemic approach. Efforts have been concentrated on the analysis of political and social demands: the initiatives and roles of Europarties in the first direct elections have been analysed by Papisca[11] and the role of the European Parliament has been tested with a content analysis of its resolutions[12].

22.5 INSTITUTIONAL SETTING

Resources and people involved in research on international politics are small in Italian universities: since 1968–69, when three chairs of International Relations were established in the universities of Catania, Florence and Turin, only four others have been added (in Bologna, Padua, Milan and Salerno). In the 1970s the Italian university system passed through a huge explosion of teaching posts and student enrolment. The *Facoltà* of Political Science[13] established a lot of new chairs in the fields of Law, Sociology, History, Economics and Politics, but very few in international studies. International Law and Diplomatic History have a good and strong tradition in Italy and this establishment looked at International Relations as a strange and unknown branch of Political Science, the academic discipline from the United States with some resemblance to Sociology and an aspiration to overcome the tradition (well established in the Italian academy) of Political Philosophy. This prevented International Relations from becoming the name of courses taught by scholars with a background and interest in International Law or Diplomatic History, but it also determined that a Chair of International Relations could be established only in those *Facoltà* with a strong group of political scientists. About twenty *Facoltà* of Political Science offer two-year courses of specialisation in international studies.[14] History of International Relations (with some regional history) and International Law (including Private International Law, International Organisation, Law of the European Communities, etc.) share the field together with other disciplines[15] while International Relations is taught only in a quarter of the existing 'specialisation' courses. However, when in 1983 an advanced university degree (the *dottorato* or PhD) was introduced in Italy, a three-year course leading to the *dottorato* in International Relations started at the University of Padua. It is expected to contribute to the development and quantitative growth of the discipline and to feed the young generation of International Relations researchers.

Italian students learn the subject mainly from texts written by their professors; their various tastes on theory may account for this, but it is also true that publishing houses consider the market for International Relations textbooks too small to encourage the translation of foreign works. Indeed, one can count only four translated books strictly pertinent to the discipline: Deutsch's *The Analysis of International Relations* (Italian edn published in 1970); Aron's *Paix et Guerre Entre les Nations* (in 1972); Dougherty and Pfaltzgraff's *Contending Theories of International Relations* (in 1979); and Waltz's *Theory of International Politics* (in 1987).[16] Besides theory, lessons usually deal with substantive themes such as European integration, human rights, strategy and deterrence, conflict and war, and foreign policy-making. Quantitative methods for the analysis of international political behaviour has also been a topic of interest (especially in Florence). Important subjects like Italian foreign policy, East–West relations, regional sub-systems, international organisations, regimes and military alliances are all but neglected.

Outside universities a couple of Institutes are concerned with the analysis of international problems. The International Affairs Institute (IAI) and the Institute for the relations between Italy and the countries of Africa, Latin America and the Middle East (IPALMO) are based in Rome; both publish a journal and pursue various studies and current analyses on their own behalf or sponsored by private and public institutions. The Milan based Institute of International Political Studies (ISPI) has a glorious past and after a twenty-years crisis is now planning a recovery. The Italian Society for International Organisation (SIOS) is a big Institute which disseminates knowledge about the United Nations and related agencies, offers courses and assists research. To define the Italian culture of international affairs one has to look also at a number of centres of area studies (on Africa, the Near East, etc.) which, however, restrict themselves to the study of local languages and cultures. Economic affairs are the main interest of the Italo–Latin American Institute, which is based in Rome and directly sponsored by the Italian Ministry of Foreign Affairs. All the above Institutes receive assistance from the government in coping with continuous financial problems. European Community affairs are the focus of a number of Institutes based in various parts of Italy; these are devoted more to short courses and conferences than to research. Peace research and disarmament problems have recently attracted the attention of scholars, politicians and campaigners; in the last few years centres and archives for these subjects, with eventual relations with universities, have proliferated around the country.

Twenty years from its inception in Italian universities, International Relations shows a good performance, but important steps remain to be taken. Scholars have majored in the theoretical aspects of the discipline and have shaped their own perspectives. They are now expected to confront the rest of the world in this field. The time spent on examining the theoretical bases of International Relations helped to strengthen the self-consciousness of the discipline in the face of cold attitudes and distrust by scholars of other disciplines. The state of substantive research should be consistently improved to augment the discipline's stance in the academic world and also give International Relations a higher profile outside the classroom. To open the way for the professionalisation of International Relations in Italy, scholars should produce analyses on such substantive themes and crucial dimensions of Italian foreign policy as, for example, the future of the European Community policies and institutions, the problems of European security and *détente*, and relations in the Mediterranean. This work is necessary to promote the role of International Relations in public administration and to encourage its consumption in a society which still views international politics as something distant, to be left in the hands of the few.

NOTES AND REFERENCES

1. L. Bonanate, 'Sistema internazionale', in L. Bonanate (a cura), *Politica internazionale* (Firenze: La Nuova Italia, 1979), pp. 352–397.
2. L. Bonanate, 'Politica internazionale e politica interna', in L. Bonanate and C.M. Santoro (a cura di), *Teoria e analisi nelle relazioni internazionali* (Bologna: Il Mulino, 1986), pp. 85–106.
3. C.M. Santoro, 'Il sistema di guerra. Teoria e strategia del bipolarismo', *Il Mulino* (294/5, 1984), pp. 220–260.
4. F. Attina, *La politica internazionale contemporanea* (Milano: Angeli, 1983), and 'Elementi constitivi ed evolutivi dell'organizzazione del sistema globale, *Teoria politica* (No. 2, 1987).
5. A. Papisca, *Democrazia internazionale, via di pace. Per un nuovo ordine internazionale democratico* (Milano: Angeli, 1986).
6. U. Gori, 'Processi decisionali e scienze sociali: per una cultura della previsione', in U. Gori and O. Onori (eds), *Tecniche di analisi per le decisionali politiche ed economiche* (Milano: Angeli, 1980).
7. L. Bonanate, 'L'Italia nel nuovo sistema internazionale', *Comunita* (No. 170, 1973), pp. 13–75.
8. U. Gori, *La diplomazia culturale multilaterale dell'Italia* (Roma: Bizzarri, 1970).
9. C. Mongardini *et al.*, *Realtà e immagini della politica estera italiana* (Milano: Giuffré, 1980).
10. F. Attina *et al.*, *Governi e parlamenti nella formazione della politica estera italiana* (Catania: Culc, 1982).
11. A. Papisca, *Verso il nuovo Parlamento Europeo* (Milano: Giuffré, 1979).
12. F. Attina, *Parlamento Europeo e interessi comunitari* (Milano: Angeli, 1986).
13. The *Facoltà* is the main structure in the Italian university system. Each university is divided in a number of *Facoltà* which assemble the research structures (Departments and Institutes), organise teaching and courses, and award the *laurea* (a degree equivalent to MA). Each professor holds a Chair in a *Facoltà* (where he/she gives one course of lessons a year) and is affiliated with a Department (or Institute) where she/he conducts research.
14. The *laurea* in Political Science is granted after four years of study. In the first biennium all students follow the same courses; in the second biennium they choose a specialisation among five fields of study: History, Sociology and Politics, Economics, Administration, and International Studies. The two biennia consist altogether of 24 courses of lessons with oral examinations. The *laurea* is awarded after a final examination consisting of a discussion on a written dissertation.
15. International Economy is taught in almost all the *Facoltà* of Political Science, usually as theory and practice of international commerce. International Political Economy exists only in the *Facoltà* of Economics in some universities. Italian scholars of these subjects perceive themselves to be members of the economists community and do not express any interest in formal contacts with other fields of international studies.

16. Translated essays and articles have appeared also in scientific journals and in two readers: *Il sistema delle relazioni internazionali* (Torino: Einaudi, 1976) and *Teoria e analisi delle relazioni internazionali* (Bologna: Il Mulino, 1986). All students of the *Facoltà* of Political Science are able (at least) to read English and a second foreign language (usually French) and they make use of this ability in researching and drafting their International Relations dissertations; indeed, university libraries in Catania, Florence, Padua and Turin are well equipped with English and French books and journals of International Relations.

Part III
Subject Areas

23 Strategic Studies
Hugh Macdonald

Almost by definition, Strategic Studies has a continuously shifting focus. This makes its study and teaching stimulating, and its pertinent literature one of the widest among university subjects. At the same time, this attribute of changeability, looked at in another way, constitutes its most besetting problems.

Under the march of technologies, shifting patterns of inter-state relations, and frequently changing domestic regimes, novelty must be pursued, yet it easily induces superficiality. Hence comparatively little of this voluminous literature has a relevance with a half-life of more than a few months: quite long contrasted with weekend colour supplements, but a constant frustration in the search for what is enduring.

The pursuit of novelty tends to induce 'sub-specialisation' in the method and conduct of debate. A single conference topic might be discussed from several angles, or even a dozen. This in itself may be good, and is certainly the consequence of educational, social and organisational forces not intrinsic to Strategic Studies. The problem for the subject is that in so many meetings of experts discussing, for instance, recent arms control developments, SDI, or the narrowly shifting parameters of the Iran–Iraq war, the association between novelty and sub-specialisation pushes what is central to the subject – the nature of warfare, of states' interests, and of the pursuit of security, all under the impact of transformatory social phenomena – out to the margin or compresses it between the lines.

Insufficient attention is paid in the dominating 'literature and discourses of novelty' to assumptions being made about these central features of the subject. This helps to explain another besetting problem: a sense of agreement among groups which frequently identify one another as 'allies', but which may actually be speaking different evaluative languages about 'the issues of the moment'. This can be deeply misleading and, when uncovered, highly divisive. The history of attempts to implement deterrence strategies in NATO is replete with examples.

This touches upon another perennial problem, which deserves

more systematic thought than it receives: the nature of the relationship between academic and 'official' studies. If the subject has as its core the restlessly shifting interests of states in matters of military power, and yet states have themselves become the direct or indirect patrons of much of the work in the subject, then how can it avoid contradicting its own interests?

So, in the light of these difficulties, what have been the themes of recent times? Has the work carrying these forth added significantly to an understanding of the central concerns of the subject? In order to answer the first of these two questions a sub-classification of 'mainstream' and 'non-mainstream' work will be useful, though I shall show later how this returns to the core of the subject.

'Mainstream' work assumes the persistence of the Cold War and the centrality of the East–West divide to the rest of global politics. The Western agenda of debate will be familiar to most people: whether or not there is a Soviet grand strategy for domination of the world; emphasis by mainstream Marxist scholars on the changing composition (but unchanging nature) of (American) imperialism; the stability or otherwise of the strategic balance; the status of arms control; the autonomy or otherwise of Europe's security system; sustaining domestic support for alliance policies; the nexus of economics and politics in strategies for East–West relations.

In the East parallel work is being done, though not widely disseminated and almost exclusively directed by Parties. This is most obvious at present in the realm of arms control. A distinctive preoccupation of the Eastern countries has become what the different decision-making processes of Western governments betoken for the unity or diversity of the Western alliance. That alliance was previously (and still is, formally speaking) taken to be pinned down by American-dominated international capitalism. Yet there is now growing theoretical and practical acceptance of its durability, national diversity, and interdependence. Hence there is a need for Soviet-type socialism to do more than coexist as a separate social order. Without dissipating its identity (or collective security), it must form a new international order with that of the West. Eastern analysts have come to view the kaleidoscope of Federal German interests and their impact upon Western Europe as deserving of special attention. Unfortunately, language and other barriers mean that only a handful of Western scholars, not working for their governments, have access to such work, and can evaluate its intellectual merits. For the rest it is still largely a matter of making 'backward linkages' from observable decisions made by governments in the East, though *glasnost* is creating important new attributes of the way Soviet scholars and other representatives talk about their work and views.

'Non-mainstream' work in Strategic Studies I would define as sharing the assumption that the superpower nuclear balance is not, or should not be taken as, the pivotal point of world politics. Such studies are making measurable advances, stemming partly from the dissentient pluralist or actively radical work of individuals and Institutes in the 'allied' countries, chiefly in the West, and partly from work being fostered in (comparatively) newly influential centres in Scandinavia, India, Latin America and elsewhere. However, it is difficult to describe an agenda, still less an identity, for such work, for two reasons. Abandoning the main alliance systems as a preferred focus of conceptual work has meant a diffuse descriptive-analytical language in much that is being produced on a range of themes: global security through United Nations led disarmament; security as the product of equitable redistribution between 'North' and 'South'; European neutralisation; Europe as a third superpower; a new pattern of order driven by Sino–Japanese demography and productivity. More interesting but difficult still, to the extent that 'non-mainstream' work constitutes a search for a different security order, or at least more satisfactory and tractable explanations of that which obtains, is that there is considerable ambivalence about where the 'pole of preference' lies. Everybody writes as though new orders or perceptual frameworks would be better for all. But careful scrutiny of the alternative agendas suggests that not everybody believes that this would actually lead to a better outcome.

This leads to the second question posed earlier, and toward a reconsideration of the core of the subject in the light of the recent literature.

Regarding the 'mainstream', a small corpus of high quality works composed in the first two decades of the post-war world by Aron, Brodie, Osgood, Huntington, Bull, Schelling, Shulman and a few others, continues to command attention because of its penetrating insights into the impact of nuclear weapons, the continuing political instrumentality of force, the logic of deterrence, the distinctiveness and limitations of arms control, and the nature of the Western alliance. The best of subsequent work has elaborated and adapted these early theories. However, three areas whose significance emerged later have demanded new intellectual advances: the political economy of East–West and intra-alliance relations; the 'post-MAD logic' of deterrence, including ethics and new technologies; and the role of civil society – as distinct from the state but perhaps complementary to it – in providing coherence to strategic policies. From the Soviet Union the work of Sakharov and Medvedev has shown that freedom and originality of thought about world issues and the Soviet system continues despite enormous (past?) obstacles.

The greatest disappointment in 'mainstream' strategic thought has been the prevalent, but not universal, failure to distinguish between the active persistence of the Cold War structures of alliance, and the possibilities for developing more sophisticated models of the motives, objectives and political conduct of the opposing side. To be sure, for Western scholars this failure is mitigated by the secretiveness of the socialist systems, and complicated by ideologies and the wilful intrusion of 'alliance shibboleths'. Yet, in the end there has also been wilful failure of the disciplines of International Relations and Political Science, and most notably their protégés Strategic Studies and Soviet Studies, adequately to bridge their differences and combine their insights.

The maturation of the Soviet political system, its economic needs, the greater confidence acquired through strategic parity, and the loosening of control over Eastern Europe all seem to be driving toward a revolutionary reappraisal of the West. However this has only recently become apparent, and there remain legitimate doubts about the depth and strength of its roots. My judgement is that they go back much further in time and possess a span that has yet to become fully apparent. If so just as well, for, historically, central reform of Russian society has been exhaustingly difficult and expensive. For the new Soviet leadership today, donning Lenin's mantle will be hard to reconcile with the requirement of fundamentally re-examining his political thought.

The maddeningly slow (so it seems) cumulation of understanding in a strategic context which has exhibited qualities of both great stability and horrifying danger inspires much 'non-mainstream' work, within the West, in Eastern Europe, and from many quarters beyond. In itself this is a fascinating and portentous achievement, considering the heterodoxy and particularism found in the world's societies. From out of this, recent 'mainstream' work has been subjected to a persistent barrage of criticism, especially on the morality of deterrence, the nuclear emphasis of the superpowers' confrontation, and the preoccupation with military-technological refinements at the expense of political trust and alternative resource claims. There have also come voices insisting upon the wholeness of the international system, and hence the indivisibility of North from South or of societal well-being from the narrower conspectus of military security, implying that 'defence of the realm' should no longer be the first duty of societies.

For all its courage and combativeness, no work – 'non-mainstream' or otherwise – has yet successfully explained how the Cold War and its corollary nuclear dilemmas can be transcended, without acceptable risk of losing that sanctuarisation from war in its conventional and traditional forms which appears to be the special quality of stable East-West confrontation. In saying that, I by no means concur with the 'mainstream' argument that it has been nuclear weapons which have kept the peace for over forty years. Nevertheless, the complexities involved here go far to explain why the early 'mainstream' theorists have proved so durable. They in turn, more or less adequately, acknowledge their intellectual debt to the long dead Prussian General, Carl von Clausewitz, whose *On War* remains unsurpassed in its fluid exposition of what is unchanging about the nature of war and politics among civilised states, whose relations are shaped by considerations of power and the possibility of deliberate resort to force. Indeed that work still provides today a secular framework of understanding for Strategic Studies which, whether ultimately adopted, adapted, rejected or painfully lived with, constitutes the initial point of departure for 'mainstream', 'non-mainstream', and East, West, North and South alike.

24 Bucking the System:
A Peace Researcher's
Perspective on the Study
of International
Relations
Michael Banks

Fortunately for those of us who collectively study International
Relations, academic disciplines do not have the same lifespan as
people. If they had, the grim reaper's deadline of three score years
and ten would now be looming, and it would be prudent of us to
look back and ask: what have we achieved? This is because 1988, the
seventieth anniversary of the armistice that brought the Great War
to an end, will be our anniversary as well. The academic subject
of International Relations in British (and other) universities was
begun in a mood of horrified reaction to the monstrous fact of
that war. If we had need to respond in sterling fashion to the
interrogation of St. Peter in order to pass freely through the
pearly gates, there would have to be something worthwhile to say.

But do we have something worthwhile to say? No, or at least
not enough, in the view of this writer. And certainly not things
of the sort that St Peter might be interested in hearing. Consider
the probable dialogue.

Initially, we might offer a sophisticated explanation, far superior
to anything available in 1918, of the nature of the state and the
characteristic processes of the states system. We could describe
the origins of that system and trace its development, say from
Westphalia all the way to the collapse of the North–South debate,
or to the flummoxed mid-1987 response of the NATO powers
to Mr Gorbachev's initiative on European security. We could
explain in detail the theory of power politics and its apparent
penetration into every crevice of world affairs. We could report that

'force', 'competition', 'order' and 'profit' are the tools we find most valuable in accounting for international happenings, whether these happenings take the form of hegemonial stability or revolutionary change, intervention or positive sanctions, terrorist disruption or what the multinational companies might or might not be up to.

But this is St Peter we are talking to; the guardian of the last set of gates we are to confront. As academics, our entire careers have been punctuated by the need to get past gatekeepers of various kinds. We, of all people, should recognise under-performance – even our own. So far, all we have achieved by way of heavenly response is a delicately raised eyebrow.

Flustered, we shift our ground. The talk now is of peace plans. Kant, we remark, saw it all, but there are sound reasons why his prescriptions, forecasts even, have not come about; or at least not yet. We know all about those reasons, whether they operate in the field of disarmament or institution-building or the rule of law. Basically, we explain, they all have to do with the nature of human community. This has developed quite well at the level of the family, the voluntary group, even the nation. But when we look at global organisations or at the world economy it is simply not there. Some of us would say, 'not there yet'; but most of us would say, 'and cannot be there because the evolution of community has stopped at the boundaries of states. We have integration within states precisely because we have competition and insecurity among states; solidarity internally is a function of threats externally'.

At this stage St Peter is looking sceptical, but interested. We decide to raise the level of our game, and reach for the more technical of our heaps of lecture notes. There is all this difficulty, we say, with the theory of rationality in the domain of public policy. In foreign affairs, we have to worry about administrative logic, psycho-logic (so-called logic, we add with a smirk), and a fearsome thing called bureaucratic politics. As Rousseau showed long ago with his parable of the stag hunt, and as the economists now demonstrate with their models of the supply of public goods, sectional interests and the common interest are often not the same. Similar problems occur in each of our intellectual domains: in conflict theory, escalatory tendencies vie with dampening processes, and sometimes win; in political economy, the positive-sum benefits of perfect competition and comparative advantage are often swamped by the zero-sum effects of mercantilism and partisan chauvinism; and in strategic analysis, collective security, which must rank as our best-ever formula for world order maintenance, is doomed by sovereign responsibilities to fail every time it is tested. Everywhere, there is politics; or maybe it's human nature?

We feel that now that we are launched, we could entertain our listener like this all day. But it becomes uncomfortably clear that he's not interested. He glances at his watch, and speaks for the first time. Up here, he observes, we know about original sin. You who specialise in International Relations are not supposed merely to narrate the events as they happen, nor yet to comment on them; that is what we created historians and journalists for. Nor is it your job to give unending lists of reasons why well-meaning efforts can and do go wrong. You are there to identify the prospects for progress, not only the problems which obstruct it; and to devise positive ideas as well as negative ones. Social science exists to affect the climate of opinion, so that when policy-makers consider their options, they have both a genuinely full array to choose from, and also an unconscious tendency to choose the ones we want. Well?

It is evident that we have one last chance. Nervously, we begin with an objection, having been trained to comment that way in a lifetime of seminars. It's not that simple, we say (at which St. Peter frowns). We do ttry, but there are problems on every hand. Method offers one set of problems, theory another. Methodologically, there are lots of variables, but no effective way to set about measuring and comparing them. We even have conflicting views on what constitutes evidence, let alone proof. Most of us were brought up in a philosophical era dominated by scientific relativism (St. Peter shudders). So we try to be good positivists, and take things one step at a time. Grand theory is a false god; if we have icons, they are flexibility, empiricism and pragmatism. We respect facts, and we assign fail marks to our students if they confuse them with values. We use words like 'realistic' and 'practicable' as scholarly compliments, and we find that decision-makers listen to us when we do that.

Conceptually, we have similar commitments. It would be arrogant of us to claim truth; we commit ourselves merely to searching for it. So what happens is that we engage in debate; we have no paradigmatic consensus of the kind that Kuhn has specified as the basis of scientific progress, but we do hope for it. In our seventy years we have produced Realists locked in argument with Idealists, Traditionalists contending with Scientists, dependency theorists sparring with geopolitical analysts; our debates may seem to be endless, but they are the best we can do. The situation is not our fault. That's the way the world is, and we did not make it. . . . But the pearly gates have slammed shut.

Lucky us. The facts are that the International Relations discipline is not restricted to a mortal span, and if it is to be called to account for its intellectual record at all, the hearing is more likely to take place between the covers of *Millennium* than at the gates of heaven. So it is not too late to think again.

There is value, nevertheless, in the metaphor of a biblical lifespan. It suggests for example that we need to abandon our habit, beloved especially of textbook authors, of explaining away the shortcomings of the field by reference to its 'youth'. That argument is turning grey these days; our institutional paraphernalia – the menu of taught courses, external examiners, doctoral theses, learned journals with anonymous peer referees, professional associations – are now proceeding into their fourth generation. It suggests too that on the day of judgement, it is not good enough to protest that we are faced with problems of great complexity. Even as great a scientist as Albert Einstein is said to have fallen victim to the seductive trap of quietism. Asked why mankind could at once be so clever as to invent the atomic bomb and so stupid as to build and use it, he replied that politics is harder than physics. A better question to him might have been: how was it that minds of his calibre were working on the comparatively simple issues of weapon development in the first place rather than trying to solve what he himself regarded as the harder problems of International Relations theory? More generally, then, the biblical metaphor suggests that the time has come for us to re-examine what we have been trying to do for most of our seventy years, and especially in the most recent of those years. Rather than struggling to arrive at better answers to our old questions, perhaps we should now set about finding answers to quite different questions.

We did, of course, begin work as a discipline with a set of questions which would today fit a peace research agenda, though they would occupy only a small proportion of it. International Relations was established as a consciously idealistic exercise, with much attention given in the 1920s and 1930s to such topics as international institution-building, disarmament, national self-determination, intellectual co-operation across borders, peaceful change and the rule of law. In that first generation of scholarship there was a fairly clear vision of the study of world affairs as a progressive field, analogous perhaps to the more recent emergence of 'development studies' as an area of interest to scholars since the 1960s. The generally shared objective was to analyse existing conditions and to judge them against the standard of theoretically and morally superior alternatives, in the hope that real-world decision-making would be guided towards a better sequence of decisions.

In the second and third generations, that approach was abandoned. The socioeconomic disruption of the 1930s, the rise of the extreme political right in several major states, the collapse of the League of Nations, the events of the Second World War and the subsequent Cold War dealt a twenty year series of blows to optimistic thought about International Relations. At the London School of Economics, in Britain generally, and internationally, the subject fell into a mood of fatalistic empiricism. Scholars came to see their job as one of keeping in close touch with the realities of every-day and past international events, rather than one of speculating about progress. Peace Research as an approach to International Relations was, therefore, not quite stillborn. It flourished briefly, then suffered from infant mortality: a baby thrown out after 1945 along with the bathwater of inter-war false hopes.

Today, most of us in the field have been so conditioned in the post-1945 art of destructive criticism that our net input to the public debate on world affairs in Britain, Europe, the West and indeed the world has been negligible. Our contribution consists almost entirely of commentary on current events cast within a tacit acceptance of whatever the existing policies happen to be. It is painfully noticeable that all the major efforts of global statecraft to take major initiatives that might improve the conduct of international politics have been inspired either by the international relations theory of an earlier age, or by sources – academic or political – outside the mainstream of Western International Relations thinking. The United Nations was an amalgam of collective security theory with balance of power and a limited degree of functionalism; the Bretton Woods plan was devised by economists; the Marshall Plan and the later modernisation efforts at economic aid and technical co-operation to close the North–South development gap came from outside our field; the human rights conventions were inspired by lawyers; the growth of the European Communities was partially underpinned by David Mitrany's work of fifty years ago; the various summit conferences have been modelled on the theory and practice of the nineteenth century Concert.

Meanwhile, the great issues of our age do form talking points within International Relations, but the mainstream contribution to them seems always to be reactive and backward looking. The new ideas come from outside. On the North–South gap, the running has been made by Third World theorists, moderate in the UNCTAD forum and radical in the dependency literature, while the principal disciplinary response has been one of critique. On nuclear war and the problem of devising some basis for security other than the (grudgingly acknowledged) madness of deterrence, the pace of debate has been forced not by scholars but by the amateurs of the Campaign for Nuclear Disarmament. On the profound questions of distributive justice, order and progress, the field has left the question-raising to neo-Marxists and humanist philosophers outside its accepted membership, leaving itself unable to offer a conceptual framework that can account for the upsurge of demands for revolutionary change in the third world. And on what may well turn out to be the most serious world problem of all, the 'global village' problematic of pollution, population expansion, resource shortages and the limits to growth generally, the Club of Rome has inspired Green political parties while the International Relations discipline has for the most part wished that the issue-area would go away.

When and where did we go astray? We can see now that the answer is 'from the very beginning'. In the 1920s, when the disciplinary agenda seemed on the surface to be so attractive to a Peace Research oriented scholar, we put our discipline into a mental cage from which it has so far been unable to escape (although the prospects now are far better than ever before). Within that cage, our arguments about the most fundamental issues – security, reform, peace, development – were doomed either to revolve in circles (if you wish for peace, prepare for war) or, as we run from side to side in search of an exit, the arguments were doomed to oscillate, from the assertion of power politics (Realism) to the denial of power politics (Idealism) – and back again.

The walls of the cage are formed by the definition of our subject: inter-state relations. We might have known, back in the 1920s, that to circumscribe our sphere of attention in this way would cripple both our imaginative and our critical faculties, because the evidence was already there, in centuries of speculation about the unoccupied space between states. But we were caught up in a combination of moral impetus and historical circumstance. The moral impetus was provided by the 1914-18 war; the circumstance by the need to find a niche within existing university structures, and to claim it as our territory. From the Great War we derived our abiding preoccupation: war and peace, interpreted with particular reference to current events. In the historical circumstance of the need of universities to organise themselves, we had to define our subject, and we had to do that in ways which did not trespass upon ground already occupied by our academic neighbours – in sociology, law, political science and elsewhere.

Our subject therefore became established as a study of the external relations of states, with a particular stress upon the role of force and war. That is the theoretical focus which has so damaged the discipline. It need not have been done that way; we could have defined our subject as world society, with the individual person and the whole global system serving both as boundaries of study and as the two points of reference. Or we might have followed the Marxist prescription which had proved so vigorous in the period prior to 1918 in its discussion of imperialism, the state and warfare and constructed our mental world in terms of classes and economies rather than sovereigns. We might even, had the foresight been available, have developed systemic and ecological frameworks for our subject matter, and then developed as a branch of evolutionary biology. Most productively of all, we might have defined our field as Peace Researchers now define it: as the study of conflict and violence at all levels in human society, with special attention to those factors which make for constructive as opposed to destructive outcomes.

But what we did was to adopt a self-defeating formula: the legalistic, institutionalist and static framework which identifies sovereign states as operating without an overarching government, and then struggles to find patterns among the relatively anarchical interactions of foreign policies. In this way, the passage of time has endowed inter-state relations with a status somewhat greater than that of our 'primary dependent variable'. – that which the discipline exists to explain. It has become also the token of our right to exist as a subject, a kind of administrative sacred cow.

We allow, and indeed encourage, differences of opinion about the various explanations of how foreign policy is made or how wars begin or whether intervention is justified or how far protectionist measures will ensure domestic prosperity. But the idea that we should properly be discussing something else is ruled out of order. We have become the victims of a bureaucratic impulse to demarcate our territory, which means that we analyse the differences, and not the similarities, between war and revolution, between arms races and industrial strikes, between nationalism and the ideological basis of a political party, between domestic law backed by sovereign coercion and international law which lacks that sanction. By doing this, our every act of orthodox scholarship tends to rationalise, reinforce and extend the self-fulfilling nature of the system which we have so arbitrarily excised from the far more elaborate web of real world events and relationships.

The 'core' of our discipline, international politics as distinct from the wider field of International Relations or international studies, has therefore become a stale and repetitive account. It has the appearance of 'new' knowledge with each edition of a standard textbook, but that is because the examples and narratives are new; not the underlying ideas. Over and over again, we ask the same basic questions: What are the primary features of the international political system, and how did they come about? What choices are open to a state within the system, and what factors condition them? Which outcomes of international interactions are more likely, and which less? How far does the system provide for justice, in any of its forms, and what systemic features set limits on that provision?

There is a procedural logic that follows from these questions. Once posed, they steer us towards historical evidence in order to find the answers to them. We become delvers into the data: historians of a kind, although our constant search for generalisations is not always regarded with approval by those for whom the term 'historian' should properly be reserved. Our questions take us right down to the detail of our subject-matter, in such a decisive fashion that we are constantly struggling to preserve our detachment from it, and cannot always succeed in doing so. In the corridors of LSE's International Relations Department the talk is as much of Harrier jet deployment or of the chances of the Sandinistas against President Reagan's imperial surrogates as it is of the level-of-analysis problem or the development of better mediation techniques. Most of us have become experts in the identification of trees on the global landscape; but what about the wood of which each tree forms only a part? We do pay lip service to the saving scholarly graces which might lift us above the wood so that we can see its profile: long-term as distinct from immediate historical perspective, humanistic compassion, inter-disciplinary insights, and above all a philosophical awareness that our 'discipline' is ultimately an ideology. But our 'Realism' ensures that it is indeed lip service, and little more.

None of this would matter if we could safely regard the real world of international events as a fully developed system with its own logic and an existence wholly independent of our study of it. But most of us, especially when pressed, do not take that view. We regard the international system as being rather primitive. We are aware of the need of politicians for new ideas. We accept that statesman-like leadership can and does shape events, and that such leadership, in turn, can be inspired only by ideas, insights, visions of alternative paths which it is our responsibility to produce.

Yet we have allowed the study of International Relations to produce a literature of partisan empiricism. Things happen, and we put them in our books and syllabuses; because they are on the record, they become the overriding 'truth'. Other things do not happen; they become 'unrealistic' possibilities, counter-factuals which must either be downgraded, or left out altogether. It is a commonplace among us to observe that the peculiarities of our study have caused the discipline to become the slave of international events and not their master, a kind of epiphenomenon of the real world. But it is less of a commonplace to observe that we are rigidly selective in our choice of the events to which most weight is given. We should be far more conscious that many of the international events are themselves caused in part by our own past theories, and furthermore that our theories of today are already helping to promote the repetition of those events tomorrow. If the world is to change, we must change, or the next seventy years will repeat the mistakes of the last seventy in the discipline. Is that really what we want?

25 Foreign Policy Analysis and International Relations

Steve Smith

Broadly speaking, the history of the development of foreign policy analysis (FPA) can be characterised as having three main phases: an initial period of development from the mid-1950s to the mid-1960s when it arose out of a deep dissatisfaction with the simplistic nature of realist accounts of foreign policy; an explosion of FPA in the United States in the late 1960s and early 1970s, as a tightly bound group of scholars gravitated towards a specific methodology (the Comparative Foreign Policy – CFP – approach); and the period since the early 1970s, which has seen the decline of the CFP approach and the emergence of a much more eclectic and diffuse set of methodologies and approaches. Of course, FPA's development was never quite so simple and straightforward; there have always been many competing accounts of foreign policy, and these have had differing impacts in different academic communities at different times. Nevertheless, to examine where we are now in the study of foreign policy it is useful to have this broad sketch of where we have been.

This threefold development of FPA in the United States was mirrored in Britain, albeit with a lag of a few years in each case; paradoxically, the strong and relatively united school of FPA in Britain at the present stands in marked contrast to its counterpart in the United States, where there is every indication that the subject has lost its way. This is because the quest for a general theory of foreign policy behaviour was never as popular in Britain as it was in the United States; this, combined with a lag of five years or so between developments in the United States and their adoption in Britain, meant that just as FPA was gaining adherents in Britain, its bubble had all too obviously burst in the United States. Foreign policy analysis is therefore in a very different situation in the United States than it is in Britain, for when positivist paradigms crumble there is little left; the British school of FPA was always rather sceptical of these paradigms. Instead, attention was focused on less ambitious approaches, for example, those integrating the study of foreign policy with explicit historical methods, or those taking a much more middle-range view of the job of constructing theory. Today in the United States there is still an evident desire to create a general theory of foreign policy, and positivistic, inductive assumptions still characterise most of the self-consciously FPA literature; in contrast, FPA in Britain coheres around middle-range theory or specific case studies – there is simply not the sympathy for the quest for general theory.

If this characterises the relative situations of FPA in Britain and in the United States, it must be immediately noted that the vast bulk of literature dealing with foreign policy is not within the FPA approach at all. This fact has crucial consequences, since it obscures the very different assumptions underlying the rather distinct approaches that dominate the specialist, and self-conscious, activity of FPA in each country. Nevertheless, it is clear that if we wish to study foreign policy at present then our choice of how to do so is by no means restricted to the specialist work of FPA scholars. Currently, there are five main ways of studying foreign policy: through a domestic politics perspective; International Relations theory; comparative foreign policy theory; case studies; and middle-range theory.

25.1 DOMESTIC POLITICS PERSPECTIVE

Much of the analysis of foreign policy sees it as the external activity of a political system. While no analyst would claim that states are closed entities, the assumption of much of this work on foreign policy treats the state as a self-contained unit (at least in decision-making terms) and sees foreign policy behaviour as determined by processes within the decision-making structures of the formal state apparatus. Such a perspective encourages notions of choice and decision, and implies that decision-makers either act with a certain rationality (even if it is bounded) or represent formally a set of national or societal perceptions and predispositions. The problem with such approaches, which are of considerable importance in the study of foreign policy, is simply that they over-exaggerate choice and freedom, and underestimate both systemic influences on state behaviour and situational impact on decision-making. Furthermore, by stressing choice and decision, they ignore or play down constraints and non-decisional influences on behaviour; as such they hinder the task of explaining the dynamism of international relations.

25.2 INTERNATIONAL RELATIONS THEORY

Just as foreign policy may be the unwanted stepchild of domestic politics and comparative politics, so domestic politics is largely ignored by those who seek to explain foreign policy by the major theories of International Relations. Although many writers attempt to include domestic factors in more systemic accounts, the explanatory strength of international relations theory comes from its consideration of systemic causes of state behaviour. Thus, although Realism has much to say about the relative domestic merits of certain kinds of political systems, the work of the Realist theory is done by a systemic mechanism, *regardless* of the domestic values and structure. The popularity of its main concept for analysing foreign policy – national interest – should not obscure the fact that this has only theoretical structure in a systemic, not a sub-systemic context. The same goes for the work of the Neorealists. The problem, of course, as Singer discussed over a quarter of a century ago in his famous article on the level-of-analysis problem, is that systemic theories lose explanatory power as one moves away from very broad generalisations. Thus, while systemic theory may well be indispensable to a full account of foreign policy, its necessarily narrow definition of the content of the term 'foreign policy' means that other accounts are required to explain the different content of foreign policy in specific situations. International Relations theory is simply too general to stand as *the* theory of foreign policy, given the very different empirical content foreign policy has in the contemporary international system.

25.3 COMPARATIVE FOREIGN POLICY THEORY

It was, of course, exactly this problem with both state-level and systems-level accounts of foreign policy that FPA was intended to overcome. This was not only the motivation of the pioneering works of Snyder, Modelski and Rosenau: their work can be seen as an attempt to combine external and internal causes into a generally applicable theory of foreign policy. Nevertheless, as noted above, the CFP approach has declined greatly since its heyday in the

United States in the early 1970s. Yet it is equally evident that a very large number of those who work in the area of FPA in the United States still cling to the epistemological assumptions of CFP: it is still a search for *a* theory, via data analysis, with the current task being to get the search back on the rails again. The problems of the approach are not so great that it is now discredited after twenty years of promise, but that its epistemology is so firmly rooted in positivism that there is no real question of amending the approach so as to utilise other accounts of foreign policy; positivism, after all, is not only a methodology but also a clear guide to constructing theory. Added to these problems is the generic difficulty of general theory, namely a lack of empirical content or referents. Just as the state, CFP's independent variable, can be called into question by developments in International Relations in the last decade, so can the commonality of the dependent variable, foreign policy. Together these call into question the possibility of constructing a general theory of foreign policy, given the variety of types of state involved, the very different situational contexts, and the varying salience for these actors and contexts of the components of foreign policy.

25.4 CASE STUDIES

Despite the rather dismissive attitude of many FPA writers to the dominance of case studies as accounts of foreign policy, they remain overwhelmingly the dominant way of writing about the subject. This is not a problem as long as it is clear that case studies *per se* cannot lead to the construction of theories of foreign policy. To understand empirical events may well require in-depth case studies, and these are certainly likely to be far more illuminating than the products of general theory, but historical case studies do not FPA make. Further, the crucial issue is the extent of implicit theoretical assumptions within these case studies. Historians have well-developed ways of attempting to assess the impact of theoretical assumptions on their work, but it is absolutely vital to point out that the examination of human behaviour requires an *a priori* model of motivation and psychology. All too often this remains unstated, thereby not only preventing the cumulative build-up of findings but also having a critical effect on the findings. For these reasons most case studies remain idiosyncratic, both with regard to the subject and in terms of the view of the analyst.

25.5 MIDDLE-RANGE THEORY

The final method of analysis of foreign policy is the use of various middle-range theories that have been developed over the last twenty years. These concentrate on specific aspects of a generalised foreign policy system, such as decision-making structures, belief systems, or implementation. The great advantage of such approaches is that they allow the content of foreign policy and also its causal mechanism to vary between types of state and their situational context. Middle-range theories also provide an alternative to the stark choice between general theory (whether inductively generated or deductively given) and historical analysis. They therefore offer a meeting ground for historian and social scientist, and there are many examples of historians writing about foreign policy with explicit reference to these middle-range theories. There remain a number of problems, among which the more commonly noted are that the theories are almost exclusively US in origin, and that there remains a tremendous task in combining the middle-range theories to provide a theory of foreign policy. Finally, it must be noted that the cumulative findings from these middle-range theories are not that extensive: the academic community remains unwilling to test the theories of others.

If this is the range of approaches to foreign policy analysis and if the subject is approached in rather different ways within the United States and British FPA communities, it remains the case that most of the work on foreign policy is not within the FPA approach. This is for the rather obvious reason that virtually every attempt to explain International Relations involves an explanation of foreign policy. This should indicate the problems of developing *a* general theory of foreign policy, since all of International Relations seems to be about foreign policy. For this reason, perhaps, the British FPA community has a more realistic view of the way to develop accounts of foreign policy behaviour than do those FPA scholars in the United States who continue the search along the road to general theory.

26 International Political Economy and International Relations: From *'Enfant Terrible'* to Child Prodigy, or Just a Cuckoo in the Nest?

Roger Tooze

As it has become more accepted as a legitimate and important field of study (bearing in mind that what is legitimate is not necessarily important, and vice versa) the version of 'international political economy' (IPE) with its origins in International Relations has grown into a major academic endeavour – if growth is measured by the number of academics and students now engaged in IPE research and teaching, and by the volume of literature produced. The outpouring of words, the vast majority of which have been American, has been such that it is difficult for the IPE 'specialist' to keep up to date, let alone the 'general' International Relations scholar. Yet, when we survey the field of IPE in the late 1980s we should, I suggest, view its achievements with some circumspection: quantity, of course, is no necessary indication of quality. In the confines of a short study, what follows is a somewhat sceptical selective overview of the present condition of IPE and International Relations.

The present structure of IPE as a field of inquiry is principally the result of two forces and the responses engendered by these forces. The first is the hegemony of the United States which has largely provided the agenda of IPE by defining the central issues and, in a process of intellectual hegemony within the academic study of International Relations, the methodology and core concepts for 'solving' the problems so defined. The recent debates over the notion of 'regime' and the claimed loss of US hegemony in the world political economy illustrate the point. The second is the academic hegemony of economics which, in a different but supportive fashion, has also tended to define the issues of IPE – i.e., as 'economic' problems, capable of rational solution by economic analysis but unfortunately dependent upon (irrational) 'political will' for the implementation of these solutions. Moreover, because of its dominance in academic and policy arenas, economics has provided an ideal type, a model social science, which furnishes the appropriate epistemology and legitimated the form and content of research, against which 'progress' in IPE (and for that matter International Relations) can be, and has been, measured. The combination of these forces produces (with notably exceptions) an IPE which claims to be a value-free, social scientific, theoretically based endeavour.

Critical responses, from within and from without the United States, identify both these hegemonies as promulgating implicit values for the achievement of particular purposes. They are therefore not value-free and are social scientific only to the extent of adopting an anachronous model of science and an inappropriate conception of social science, and they are theoretical in a limited, self-serving way. Hence, critical responses offer not only a different agenda and research programme for IPE but, significantly, a different epistemology.

Now, within this tension between hegemonic form and critical response we can briefly assess the development of IPE from its origins within International Relations. IPE originated in the concern that conventional (largely Realist) International Relations was not capable of identifying and analysing evident problems in the 'real' world that lay within the interstices of International Relations, International Economics, Politics and Economics. As such, the academic purpose of IPE was both to express dissatisfaction with the problematic of International Relations and to broaden that problematic to include the interaction of politics and economics at the international level. Coupled with this came the questioning of boundaries previously established by existing disciplines; leaving aside the vexed and essentially irrelevant question of whether International Relations is itself a 'discipline'. Most important, the distinction between foreign and domestic, and between politics and economics became increasingly challenged with the apparent breakdown of the post-war international economic order and the increasing inter-penetration of national economies. The net effect of these and a whole range of technological, political and economic factors, particularly the creation of a world market and the internationalisation of production and services, is to change the locus of study to 'world' rather than 'international' (making IPE rather a misnomer!), while at the same time re-emphasising the centrality of the state in understanding any form of world political economy.

For an IPE constituted in this way, one measure of progress is the success of the IPE problematic in displacing or modifying those it emerged as a criticism of. Clearly, IPE has not displaced any of the established disciplines, nor perhaps should we expect it to in the space of under twenty years, but it is 'established' in some senses as a field of inquiry in its own right. Given the events of the 1970s and 1980s in the world economy, it would be rather surprising if this were not the case. IPE has, however, succeeded in the respect of broadening the problematic of International Relations by helping to challenge some of its core assumptions and findings. Notably, it has pushed International Relations analysis away from a sole focus on 'actor' and 'interaction' models towards a consideration of 'structural' and economic power, which provides the context for action. Structural analyses, however defined, necessarily lead to a reconsideration of the operation of an anarchic international order, with interesting conclusions about the form and content of authority in this order. Moreover, the breakdown of the distinction between international and intranational domains, with the integration of national economies into a world economy, not only brings a reappraisal of what constitutes foreign policy, but also raises fundamental questions about the nature of international relations and the nature of power. And, in relation to economics, IPE has reaffirmed the inseparability of the domains of politics and economics, returning to the origins of economics in Ricardo, Mill and Marx, for whom economy was defined socially and politically. The development of IPE in the 1970s is in this respect the re-politicisation of economics and international economic relations after the ideological success of liberal hegemony in constituting these relationships in a non-political, technical way.

Yet, IPE can only propose, it cannot dispose, and the hold of (hegemonic) convention is strong. Much analysis of the international economy still takes place within what Susan Strange has called 'the bondage of liberal economics' and much of International Relations resolutely defends its traditional domain. Part of the reason for this is that the dominant form of IPE still aspires to a value freedom that others perceive as a cloak for particularistic interests. This aspiration produces research seemingly determined to ape the empirical excesses of mainstream economics in the haste to establish legitimacy and policy relevance. But we should not rush in a direction that may not take us where we want to go, at least, not before we have an adequate map. In the case of IPE, 'adequate' must include values and purpose grounded in a reassessment of what constitutes an appropriate 'scientific' epistemology. The danger of not pausing at this stage is that IPE as 'child prodigy' could become a cuckoo in the nest of International Relations without the benefit of a warning cry.

27 The Relationship between International Relations and International Law

Ingrid Detter de Lupis

What is International Relations? One way of finding out what the study of such a subject entails is to look at the *à la carte* menu in the London School of Economics calender, provided, of course, that the LSE view is a representative one. Assuming that the LSE knows (roughly) what it is doing, the subject seems to include scrutiny of the most diverse questions, from strategic studies to the study of the role of money, from what is ethical to do on the battlefield to the role of the Nordic Council. In other words, it is a subject which comprises a host of multifaceted questions bearing on virtually any type of relationship between states or other transnational actors. Some of these questions imply study from within a state, such as foreign policy matters, while others, such as the structure of international society, can be perceived only from without. But where does international law fit in with all this? Is it, as even some teachers think, only yet another option which can be taken or disregarded according to the whim or taste of the student?

Any international lawyer who is asked to write a short note about the relationship between international law and International Relations is bound to throw in a short commercial for the law, emphasising its importance in international society. So am I tempted to say something to that effect. But I would like to disassociate myself from a number of traditional views adopted by my lawyer friends and colleagues. Apart from one or two international lawyers, few of those who teach international law have had the experience of working together with International Relations scholars. Shielded from the exposure to constant discussion of the behaviour of states and other entities in their strategic, political, economic or cultural relations, many international lawyers hang on to antiquated notions about their own subject and insist on unrealistic doctrines which have no contemporary justification. International lawyers of this type have done much to discredit the reputation of their subject among International Relations scholars, who increasingly ask whether international law exists at all, or who often say that if international law does exist, it is surely not of much consequence since states and others seem determined to violate it at every opportunity.

Naturally, if international law is studied as a subject detached from political realities, it does become artificial and unconvincing as a system. It is almost as if many international lawyers had not noticed this, being left one step behind: International Relations scholars may abandon the state paradigm, but when international lawyers catch up and admit the existence of other actors, they find International Relations specialists have largely reverted to emphasising the importance of the state as a unit.

Teaching international law in a department of International Relations has exposed me to constant impressions, from colleagues and students alike, in considering the application of my subject to virtually any field of International Relations. International law, if presented in a viable form, pervades every corner of International Relations and forms a coherent superstructure, or an intrinsic one, if you wish. I see the function of international law in International Relations as that of the skeleton of a fish: the consequences of removing it are obvious, especially if the fish is still alive when you start your operation.

It is a challenge to consider the emergence, growth, change and abolition of legal rules in the international society. It is indeed international law which provides the very structure of International Relations and which explains the intricate jigsaw of its component parts. In the view of C.A.W. Manning (and myself), International Relations cannot be studied without a good knowledge of rule-making coupled with the study of the application of rules; and it is that which international law entails.

I have always found it refreshing to teach international law to International Relations students. They have some basic knowledge of the behaviour of states in political, economic and other fields to begin with, and seem to work on the assumption that states obey certain rules, and excuse themselves when they break them. So, in a course on the International Legal Order, they simply say 'Please tell us what those rules are', and we can get straight down to work. When I teach in Law faculties I always have to waste a term (or more) to rid the students of the Austinian handicap from which they already suffer. Austin had said that 'law is the command of the Sovereign', and caused a lot of trouble to us international lawyers who have no Sovereign in our field. It often seems a dreadful waste of time to cure students of this indoctrination. Yet, however much I enjoy teaching in a department of International Relations, I now face another question: How was it that my students so readily accepted what I said? How could all those clever law students so readily accept what their other teachers had said to them about Austin? The answer, as far as I understand, is that in neither case were the students really thinking much for themselves.

This raises very basic questions about why students go on to University. Most do so to 'learn more', that is to amass detailed knowledge in some specific subject in order to be in a good position for some career and, in terms of promotion, to be one step ahead of their competitors. But is this really the right attitude? Is this really the function of universities? In my view universities are places where students should learn about method, analysis and synthesis so that they can think for themselves, and apply those skills to anything to which they put their hand. My father often jokingly suggested that anyone good at Latin, Mathematics or chess could make a career out of anything. Why? Because those subject all involve order, logic and method. It is not only the English 'inspired amateur' idiosyncrasy that produced Lord Denning, who after the study of mathematics became one of the most influential English judges, or Lord Scarman, who after a stint at Greats wrote more succinct judgements than many other judges. Yet, even if they had not read those particularly tidy and logical subjects at University, the study of law would soon have sorted them out, since law itself is based on the use of method and concepts and applied analytical skills. But what if the subjects themselves do not involve the cardinal elements of logic and order? Who teaches method? Well, if the subject does not itself contain the elements of method *per se*, the study of method must be furnished as a supplementary study aid. Who can study history without guidance on method? And, nearer at heart, who can study International Relations without a knowledge of concepts and methodology? Fortunately, some departments of International Relations now offer courses which will enable students to view their field of study more clearly. Inevitably, some attention in such a course will focus on different 'schools' and on who says what in International Relations. But more importantly, the students will be encouraged to think for themselves and question even established notions. These primary virtues and skills are also encouraged in the study of the International Legal Order, for here, too, we are concerned with the application of concepts in our analysis of state behaviour and, especially, in our study of certain contemporary disorders in the international society. We encourage students to present their own view when the time comes for them to write essays or to give presentations. My own rebellious nature recently led me to question one of the most fundamental notions in my field, that of customary law. Such a concept may work well for specific business communities, tribes or small societies. But can it work for states of a few hundred million people? Is it true, as the textbooks allege, that Mrs Thatcher, Mr Reagan or Mr Gorbachev, look around the world and say, 'Aha! Venezuela does that and Gambia too', and when they count the states doing the same thing and arrive at some impressive number they exclaim 'Eureka! A legal norm! Here is a legal rule reflecting the usage of numerous nations'? My impression, for some considerable time, had been that this is not how states behave and that what the textbooks said was not politically realistic. When I finally burst out into print[1] on this issue a German student exclaimed 'How can you say this? It is against all the textbooks!'. I had to remind him that at one stage all the textbooks had said the world was flat and for a very long time indeed no one had thought of challenging this proposition. The root of our problem is not ignorance, or lack of time to look things up, but the basic complacency of accepting a number of propositions only because everyone else is accepting those propositions. The issue is not that no one devoted themself to the problem but that no one even considered it to be a problem.

What we all have to do, teachers and students alike, is to adopt an open mind to established notions in our fields, and this includes an open mind as to how one related field of study may clarify another. It may be that a stringently presented system of international law has the potential of clarifying much of the substantive content of International Relations.

NOTES AND REFERENCES

1.   The Concept of International Law (Stockhom: Norstadt, 1987).

Index